# THE IMAGINATION OF REALITY

Essays in Southeast Asian Coherence Systems

*Two Witches Dancing,* by Anak Agoeng Gde Sobrat, Bali, 1937
Colored inks on paper. From the collection of the Rijksuniversiteit of Leiden,
donated by Rudolf Bonnet

This early drawing by one of the finest contemporary Balinese artists portrays
two *leyak,* people who can transform themselves through rituals performed in the Death
Temple into animals and other grotesque beings with the power to bring disaster and
illness to their fellow villagers. In the Balinese "Witch and Dragon" ritual drama,
sometimes there appears a pair of beautiful young girls who first dance gracefully and
then change into leyaks when they put on masks and dance in a different style. They are
now followers, or minor forms, of the great witch Rangda, who is herself a manifestation of the goddess Durga, who is in turn an aspect of Siva. For the Balinese the leyak is
an image of terror—a specific reality charged with horror and anxiety—and also a
visual embodiment of the conception—no less real for being more abstract—of cosmic
energy in one of its manifold transformations.                    HILDRED GEERTZ

# THE IMAGINATION OF REALITY

Essays in Southeast Asian

Coherence Systems

A. L. Becker
Aram A. Yengoyan
*editors*

ABLEX Publishing Corporation
Norwood, New Jersey 07648

Printed in the United States of America.

*Library of Congress Cataloging in Publication Data*
Main entry under title:

The Imagination of reality.

    Papers presented at a conference held at the
University of Michigan, Ann Arbor, in 1974.
    Includes bibliographies and index.
    1. Philosophy, Southeast Asian—Congresses.
2. Religion, Primitive—Asia, Southeastern—
Congresses.   3. Asia, Southeastern—Religion—
Congresses.   4. Language and culture—Congresses.
5. Symbolism—Congresses.   I. Becker, Alton L.
II. Yengoyan, Aram A.   III. Title: Coherence
systems.   IV. Series.
GN635.S58I45        301.2′1        79-15675
ISBN   0-89391-021-X

ABLEX Publishing Corporation
355 Chestnut Street
Norwood, New Jersey 07648

# preamble to the series

Our purpose in these books is to bring together as wide a variety of thinkers on language as we can. We feel a certain urgency in this task, for we perceive the field of linguistics to be deeply divided already, with no end in sight to current factionalism. Indeed, the prospects are for more, not fewer, theoretical splits.

And our perception has been that as theories and controversies have multiplied, the issues between groups of researchers have grown to seem bigger than they are. We see the present isolationism leading to a limiting introversion.

We believe, however, that many people may be working together *without knowing it*, because of the theoretical walls between them. Our hope is that juxtaposing their thoughts in this series may make an implicit consensus more apparent.

And what could the features of such an unperceived consensus be? Here we do not feel ourselves on sure ground, but the following broad-brush styles of thinking may unite many workers.

1. A rejection of constraints on data, a widening of the field of view to include phenomena that have sometimes been held to be "outside" linguistics. Some may wish to reject entirely any inside/outside dichotomy with regard to the study of language, in particular any distinction between the structure of a language and its use.

2. An attempt to integrate any study of language into the wide set of disciplines which relate human beings to reality: not only the traditionally more or less tightly connected fields of psychology, cognitive science, philosophy, anthropology, sociology and poetics, but also areas like law, therapy, music, education, politics, religion, and probably many more.

3. A conviction that knowledge can emerge not only through the success of some formal mode of description. Each formal theory provides both a way of seeing and a set of blinders. The value of a formal theory may lie as much or more in its 'failures' as in its 'successes.' And the purpose of clarity will often be best served by a refusal to impose a criterion of formal description upon the presentation of research results.

4. A change from the widespread research strategy of seeking the truth by generalizing over a number of cases to a strategy of studying the single case in all its richness, to find a general truth in the principles of organization that the individual displays. This reverence for the unique may focus on a single text, or on an idiolect, or on a particular history of acquisition, etc.

5. A sense of the futility of polemics, of wrangling. A willingness to listen. In George Miller's words,

> In order to understand what another person is saying, you must assume it is true and try to imagine what it could be true of.

We are groping as we write these words, as we launch this series. We are searching for a richer, more deeply connected, ultimately more *human*, linguistics. We invite you to join with us in this search.

GEORGE LAKOFF                    JOHN ROBERT ROSS

# contents

# IV INNOVATION IN TRADITIONAL COHERENCE SYSTEMS

# acknowledgments

Over the past ten years, the editors of this volume have had countless discussions on the questions of the nature of symbolic systems and coherence in Southeast Asian cultures, especially the insular areas where we have done the majority of our anthropological and linguistic work. We recognized that different ideas were being discussed concerning such problems, but there had been little effort to bring various scholars together as a means of exchanging ideas and experiences. In 1973 we planned a conference titled "Symbolic Systems in Southeast Asia" to discuss problems of mutual interest among a wide variety of scholars. The conference was held in May of 1974 at The University of Michigan (Ann Arbor). During the planning stage we attempted to work out a cross-section of thoughts and ideas as they related to questions of symbolic action and coherence. We realized that work was being done through many disciplinary views, such as Art History, Political Science, Geography, Anthropology, Ethnomusicology and Linguistics, and we invited scholars from all these disciplines.

We wish to express our appreciation to the Ford Foundation (grant number 340093) and the Office of Education (grant number 012795) for providing the financial assistance to bring the various participants together, both from within this country as well as from abroad. Special thanks are also extended to the Center for South and Southeast Asian Studies (The University of Michigan) for further financial assistance as well as other forms of assistance in the production of this volume. Over the years L.A. Peter Gosling, current Director of the Center, has always been supportive and we wish to thank him for his years of encouragement. The Horace H. Rackham School of Graduate Studies at The University of Michigan provided us with financial support for the final editing and typing of the manuscript. Our special thanks are extended to Dean Alfred S. Sussman for his interest in this project.

A great number of individuals assisted us either directly or indirectly. Mischa Cain's talents for editing and re-editing must be acknowledged and we thank him for his patience and concern. Jan Opdyke was responsible for the final typing of the manuscript and we are grateful to her and her sense for perfection. A number of our colleagues assisted in different ways, of whom Robbins Burling and Vern Carroll must be singled out for their constructive comments through various phases of the project. Robert McKinley was instrumental in assisting us during the planning stage and we thank him for his continuous interest in this venture.

# foreword

# Communication across Diversity

A.L. Becker

University of Michigan

> The whole of nature is a metaphor of the human mind.
>
> —Ralph Waldo Emerson

Moral imperatives lie behind most scholarship. For those working to understand conceptual systems of various sorts, particularly systems in other cultures, there is an undercurrent of uneasiness about the uses to which our understanding may be put, and probably we all have nightmares about forms of ideological oppression based upon some insight in our scholarship. The assumption has been, since the first intimations of colonialism, that communication across cultures is necessary and proper, and that it necessarily requires that people become more alike—that they learn our languages, our terms, our conceptual system—and abandon their own cultures to museums, where they will be properly looked after. The approach to other conceptual systems has often been that they lack some essential ingredient of our own, however great their exotic charm. American scholars may describe non-Western conceptual systems, in our terms or theirs, but seldom have we used them as models of the way the world really is, as versions of wisdom. Or as correctives of pathologies in our own systems.

At the same time, the possibility of communication across diversity, communication which preserves cultural diversity, like the possibility of good translation, has been thought attainable, if not yet attained. As we are learning that the language of those judged insane within our culture is not nonsense, so we are learning that conceptual systems outside our culture are not elaborated fantasy, but other ways of making sense of things. With our own insane and with other cultures, we are beginning to learn to communicate across diversity.

One familiar model for doing this is the model of translation, making a foreign text accessible and significant outside the language in which it was written. It is one of the impossible and utopian things we meet almost daily; and

1

it is somewhat paradoxical, at once exuberant, saying more than the original, and deficient, saying less than the original.[1]

Translation, as every translator learns quickly, is not just a matter of imitation, of finding our words to imitate their words, but it is also the recreation of the context of the foreign text. A culture, to one outside it, is very much like a text, or better, an assemblage of texts, to be translated. No one has seen this so clearly as Clifford Geertz, to whom this collection of sixteen essays is dedicated. In his words, "cultural forms can be treated as texts, as imaginative works built out of social materials. . . ."[2] There is something very ancient about this view, something which suddenly re-legitimizes and brings into serious current relevance a great deal of human learning—the Buddhist sutras, Spinoza, Emerson—in which Nature is conceived of as a symbolic text, an imagined reality.

To use the word *text* in this way is in form metaphoric, but perhaps the idea goes beyond the metaphoric, in that a linguistic text, written or oral, may be the same sort of thing as a meal, a ritual dance, or a temple, to mention some of the nonlinguistic texts described in these essays. And we can apply our ways of knowing about linguistic texts to these other sorts of symbolic constructions, in that all are ways that somebody says something to somebody about something for some reason; all texts, in order to be translated, require that we know a good deal about who said what to whom about what and why. The meaning of a text is its relation to its context.

A basic error—maybe *the* basic error—in the study of symbolic systems as texts is to see them, as many have since Aristotle and surely before, too, as imitations. Imitation presupposes something more real, more true, more fundamental that is being imitated. Philip McKean, in the fifteenth essay in this book, quotes Ernst Cassirer on this point: "Symbolic forms are not imitations, but *organs of reality,* since it is solely by their agency that anything real becomes an object for intellectual apprehension, and as such is made visible to us. For the mind, only that can be visible which has some definite form, but every form of existence has its source in some peculiar way of seeing, some intellectual formulation and intuition of meaning." Here is another powerful metaphor, conceiving of symbolic systems as "organs" of perception, not what we know and believe, but the means of knowing and believing.

We are left with a mixed metaphor, a text-organ. Said another way, we are thinking via the coincidence of metaphors, which is clearly the way that communication across diversity works.

Each author in this collection of essays is the translator of a text or series of texts (written or oral, said or enacted) produced by Southeast Asians, if we define Southeast Asia to include Papua, which seems reasonable. Most of these South-

---

[1] These terms are thematic in one of José Ortega y Gasset's final works on language, The difficulty of reading, *Diogenes, 28,* 1959, 1–17.

[2] Clifford Geertz, Notes on the Balinese cockfight, *The interpretation of cultures.* New York: Basic Books, 1973.

east Asians are Austronesian (or Malayopolynesian) people, to give them the name of the family of languages most of them speak, and all of them live in or surrounded by or adjacent to the Austronesian world, in which linguistic similarity implies at least some cultural similarity. Each of the authors seeks insight into something more general than the particular phenomenon he examines: the images behind them, the sources of power, or error, and above all or below all, of coherence.

The sixteen essays are a major part of what happened at a conference on symbolic systems in Southeast Asia held at Ann Arbor, under the sponsorship of the Center for South and Southeast Asian Studies of the University of Michigan, April 26 and 27, 1974. But they are not the whole of what happened. Some of the participants have published their ideas elsewhere, or not at all, and some of the authors included here talked about something different than they wrote about. As a way of providing context for these essays, and by way of gratitude to the others for their contributions, let me list some of the other things which happened: Benedict Anderson guided us through a profound and moving story by the great Indonesian writer, Pramudya Ananta Tur; Hildred Geertz showed and discussed slides of Balinese paintings from her and Clare Holt's collections, building an important bridge between the interpretation of texts and aesthetic understanding; and Edward Bruner drew detailed comparisons between the systems described in these essays and the assemblage of texts he has deeply studied in Batak culture. Some drew comparisons from further afield: S. J. Tambiah spoke of the Thai, Robbins Burling of the Garo and Burmese, Fred Eggan and Aram Yengoyan of the Philippines, Ray Kelly of New Guinea, and Vern Carroll of Polynesian analogies—and lack of analogies—for the texts we were deciphering. Paul Wheatley made a closing comment which was at center a gentle warning not to take perception itself for granted in the process of textual translation. At the end, the Michigan gamelan played. None of this appears in the book.

The essays that do appear have been put into four sections, depending upon what aspect of the process of textual translation they emphasize, though there are a few essays which might have been put in all of the four sections. The first section, "The Separation of Things," includes essays which describe the basic semantic dimensions or polarities on which imaginative works are constructed, dimensions of space and time, of self and other, of health and sickness. In "Indigenous Religious Systems of the Malay Peninsula," Geoffrey Benjamin describes the semantic field in which three Malaysian cultures—Malay, Semang, and Temiar—conceive of their worlds. Benjamin describes structural likenesses and differences between these cosmologies and relates them to a polarity from egocentrality to sociocentrality, and finally discusses why Islam fits the Malay world so well, and the others, less well. In "The Batek Negrito Thunder God: The Personification of a Natural Force," Kirk Endicott examines the process of personification—the way that characteristics are attributed to nonhuman beings. The core of the essay is a psychoanalysis of thunder, a detailed study of a single symbolic network. The third essay in this section, Ronald Provencher's "Orality as a Pattern of Symbolism in Malay Psychiatry," examines food and eating as a natural metaphor in the semantics of mental and physical health. Robert Harrison's essay, "Where Have All the Rituals Gone?: Ritual Presence Among the Ranau Dusun of Sabah, Malaysia," looks at the question of the sparsity of symbolic expression in some cultures, and suggests that those closest to the actual labor of production may be furthest from a concern with ritual activity and symbolic expression in general. In the final essay in this section, "In the World of the Sea Urchin: The Application of Husserlian Phenomenology to Cultural Systems," J. S. Lansing clarifies some basic notions of phenomenology and then employs them to explain the Balinese polarity of *kaja-kelod*—mountain-sea, north-south, head-body—and the importance of preserving their separation.

The second section, "Some Motifs in Tellantry," includes two essays which examine recurrent motifs in imaginative linguistic text-building and the values associated with these motifs. The term *tellantry* is introduced in Marie Adams' essay, "The Crocodile Couple and the Snake Encounter in the Tellantry of East Sumba, Indonesia," where it refers to imaginative linguistic discourse—myths, legends, tales, poetry, songs, chants, prayers, puns, name jokes, swearing, riddles, etc.—which is oral rather than written, and this contrasts minimally with the term *literature*. (Using two terms, *tellantry* and *literature*, emphasizes the importance of separating oral and written noetics.) Adams describes in detail two important motifs in the tellantry of Sumba. Vinson Sutlive, in "Iban Folk Literature and Socialization: The Fertility of Symbolism," describes the genres of Iban tellantry and the grammar of values that the most common motifs seem to presuppose and to preserve.

The third section, "The Coherence of Things," includes six essays on the ways texts and rituals are built. In "Mediators as Metaphors: Moving Men to Tears in Papua New Guinea," Edward Schieffelin describes how specific place-names from previous village sites are woven into oral texts in order to intensify the emotional response of specific members of the audience, who then, in a climax of emotion, seize brands from the fire and burn the dancer-singer. A similar kind of climatic but nonoratorical text is the cockfight in Savu described in James Fox's essay, "The Ceremonial System of Savu." Fox closely examines the difference between symbolic systems on the island of Roti which are built by oratory, and those on Savu built by ostension. Each medium—each channel of the imagination—appears to involve different presuppositions about the social context of ritual. Mary Foster's essay, "Synthesis and Antithesis in Balinese Ritual," examines the semantics of what may be called the *plot* of Balinese games and rituals, the way symbolic texts are given coherence in relation to temporal sequence. Foster's notion of plot draws in part on ideas of schismogenesis first developed in the Balinese essays of Gregory Bateson, ideas which are also important in A. L. Becker's essay, "Text-Building, Epistemology, and Aesthetics in Javanese Shadow Theatre," an examination of the constraints on the process of constructing and performing a Javanese shadow play. Judith Becker's "Time and Tune in Java" is a detailed structural study of gamelan music, based on a comparison of musical temporality and the Javanese calendrical tradition. The section closes with James Peacock's close examination of the textual strategies of Sumatran Muslim biographies, entitled "Dahlan and Rasul: Indonesian Muslim Reformers." Each essay in this section gives us a version of history, a model of temporal coherence in the plots of ritual dances in Papua, cockfights in Savu, games and rituals in Bali, musical compositions and *wayang* performances in Java, and the life stories of Islamic heroes in Sumatra.

Almost all the essays in the book are concerned to some extent with change in symbol systems and with the continuing relevance of traditional systems in changing societies. The three final essays, two about Bali, and one about Malay culture, are extended explorations of the question of change, the continuing adjustments of enchantment and rationality, to use James Boon's terms. This section, called "Innovation in Traditional Coherence Systems," begins with Boon's essay, "Balinese Temple Politics and the Religious Revitalization of Caste Ideas." Boon describes the current political relevance of temple building in Bali, demonstrating that modern change is very much like traditional innovation, preserving the cultural text by the continuous reenchantment—reimagination—of the rational order. Philip McKean's essay, "From Purity to Pollution? The Balinese Ketjak (Monkey Dance) as Symbolic Form in Transition," gives an answer to the often asked question, what is going to happen to Bali? His answer is like Boon's, that the text will be preserved by giving it new interpretations for new contexts, in order to preserve both separation and coherence in the important *organs of reality*. Finally, Robert McKinley's essay, "*Zaman dan masa*, eras and periods," is about the ways that Malays preserve the coherence of their texts and contexts through the interaction of different conceptions of time.

Learning some of the ways we all—American or Southeast Asian—imagine our worlds and constantly reaffirm their coherence in every act of telling about them, makes us aware that each essay in this book is itself an imagined text-world, and that, hence, each is a slightly different solution—more or less successful—to the problem of communication across diversity. We, the writers, are imagining new realities in our own texts. For readers at that level the book might better be called, "The Imagination of the Imagination of Reality."

# Part One
# THE SEPARATION
# OF THINGS

chapter one

# Indigenous Religious Systems of the Malay Peninsula

Geoffrey Benjamin

University of Singapore

and

The Australian National University

## INTRODUCTION

*Indigenous* here refers to those cultures which have evolved within the Malay Peninsula, viz., all the Orang Asli (aborigine) groups except the recently in-migrated Orang Kuala and Orang Kanaq of Johor, and all the Malays except such immigrant groups as the Minangkabau and the unassimilated Javanese, etc.

The problem discussed in this paper is rather far removed from the usual interactional concerns of social anthropology. Basically, it is a problem in ethnology: Malayan aboriginal religion and Malay folk religion ("Malay magic") are obviously ethnologically cognate in the sense that they derive, in large part, from a common cultural matrix. But these various religious systems differ in the organization and uses made of their otherwise very similar underlying ideas, and the best way to solve the problem of this variation is to discover the independent variables that have somehow acted to "transform" these underlying structures.

## ANIMISM

Evans-Pritchard's discussion of the term *animism* (1965:24–26) is enlightening. He points out that it has been employed ambiguously in anthropological writings, sometimes to refer to the belief in a pervasive life-force or personality that attaches to creatures and inanimate objects, i.e., belief in ghosts and spirits; and sometimes, more simply, to refer to the belief that creatures and inanimate objects have souls. As Evans-Pritchard reminds us, many writers have put forward the theory that belief in spirit somehow derived from belief in soul, and that ultimately spirit-belief evolved into the belief in supernatural beings that Tylor took to be criterial of religion proper. Now it is easy to agree with Evans-Pritchard when he dismisses these evolutionary guesses as "just-so" stories, totally without support. What is not so easy to agree with is his contention that these theories must be false because "the two conceptions [spirit and soul] are not only different but opposed, spirit being regarded as incorporeal, extraneous to man" (1965:26).

The mention of corporeality brings to mind some of the most interesting recent work on the sources of ritual power, namely Mary Douglas' insights into the importance of categorial boundaries and their transgression (1966; 1970). Even more to the point, Douglas' ideas have recently been applied to the Malay animistic system by Endicott (1970) in a study that makes it clear, for Malay beliefs at least, that souls are indeed manifestations of the same thing as spirits and ghosts. In Endicott's analysis, "essence" may be either incorporeal, in which case it manifests itself as spirit, or corporeal, in which case it forms the "soul" of the body that houses it. Analysis of my own data on Temiar beliefs (1967, forthcoming) and careful examination of the rather sparse literature on the other Orang Asli groups suggest that the same holds true for all the indigenous religious systems of the Malay Peninsula, for which we may set up the following identities as of general applicability:

spirit  =  free soul

soul  =  bounded spirit

But what is the nature of the "essence" of which both soul and spirit are manifestations? The animistic world view posits the division of the cosmos into two dialectically conjoined planes of existence: the plane of things, matter, categories; and the plane of essence, spirit, soul. Entities on the two planes are readily conceivable as independent autonomous manifestations; but the normal "resting" state of the cosmos is one in which for each entity on the plane of matter there is an equivalent entity on the plane of essence, and vice versa, in a one-to-one relationship. Any disturbance of this relationship, whereby essence escapes the bounds of matter, will introduce a dynamic imbalance into the system which may come to be regarded as the source of such things as power, danger, pollution, *mana,* and so on.

This fundamentally dynamic view of the cosmos would fit well into a more general dialectical theory, and it is not surprising that such a skilled dialectician as Simmel should, in a remarkable passage, best express the kind of relationship we are talking about here.

> Life is more-life—it is a process which pushes on, seeking to follow its own development laws. But life is also more-than-life; it is formative and produces objects that are independent of it. For life as a process to continue, it requires the

aid of form, which in its stability is the antithesis of process. Hence, life as process stands the risk of being shattered on the surface of the very object it has produced. (Murphy, 1972:134)

If for Simmel's *process* we read *essence* and for his *form* we read *matter*, we have here in a nutshell the fundamental premise of Malayan animism.

In Malayan animism this dialectic works itself out in the following manner: matter (or better, categories) tends to anchor essence progressively such that each category has its corresponding soul; on the other hand, essence tends to break through the categorial boundaries to coalesce and form free spirit (or soul). Tightly bound soul implies health, neutrality, safety, profaneness; free spirit implies un-health, activity, danger, sacredness.

## THE MALAYAN SYSTEMS COMPARED

The major dimension of difference between the various forms of animism in Malaya lies in the different categorial systems that partition spirit into souls. For the purposes of exposition I will outline below only those systems that have been subjected to detailed study—Malay, Temiar, and Semang—and hang the rest of the argument upon the contrasts that appear among them.

### Malay Animism

In the Malay system almost everything in the environment that note is taken of has the power to concentrate essence in itself, and hence to come to possess a soul. (In older Malay usage the word *semangat* referred both to "essence" or "spirit" in the general sense and to "soul" in the specific sense; in modern Malay *semangat* has restricted its range of application to the "spirit" of the nation and to the "soul" of a young baby.) But the degree of differentiation and fixity of the soul depends upon the degree of specificity with which the category that houses it is known. Hence a continuum exists from the bare differentiation of the vital principle *(Semangat)* by attachment to nothing more concrete than the experiences that frighten the Malays, to its almost complete differentiation by incorporation within an identifiable human frame. The less differentiated forms of spirit fall into the category labeled *hantu* (ghosts) in Malay, whereas the more highly differentiated forms are treated as the souls *(semangat)* of the various entities containing them. Notice that in this system shamans' spirit-guide familiars occupy an intermediate position between souls and ghosts.

The full schema of spirit differentiation within Malay culture is illustrated in Figure 1. The details will interest only specialists in Malayan ethnology, but the general pattern is significant for my argument. As one moves out from the human end of the continuum there is a progressive change in the character of spirit manifestations from bounded to unbounded, from safe to unsafe, from soul

Figure 1. The Malay animistic system (After Endicott and McHugh)

| | Defining Category | Manifestation | |
|---|---|---|---|
| Individuals | Man (i) individuality<br>(ii) life/death<br>(iii) humanity/animality<br>Negritos (i) individuality<br>(ii) life/death<br>Weretigers<br>Familiar spirits<br>Outstanding members of class | (i) semangat<br>(ii) nyawa<br>(iii) roh<br>(i) semangat<br>(ii) nyawa<br>belian<br>pelesit, polong, etc.<br>keramat, daulat, etc. | Souls (semangat) |
| Classes | Childbirth dangers<br>Species: trees, animals, etc.<br>Roughly bounded realms: mines, fishing grounds, etc.<br>Major realms: earth, water, etc. | pontianak, langsuir, penanggalan, bajang<br>hantu tinggi, hantu berok, etc.<br>hantu pemburu, hantu rimba, etc.<br>jembalang, jin tanah, hantu raya, etc. | Birth demons<br><br>Free spirits, ghosts |
| Unbounded entities | God | Tuhan, 'Allah | Deities |

Bounded, safe ⟶ Unbounded, dangerous

to ghost, and from well-defined to vague. In the Malay system, then, the degree of differentiation varies with the distance from man of the defining categories. This, it seems to me, implies a degree of differentiation in the conception of man's place in the cosmos: according to the Malay world view, man can, as it were, stand back and look at the rest of the cosmos as distinct from himself. In other words, the Malay cosmos is in no sense a projection of ego-centered conceptions; rather it has a quality of givenness which, for reasons that will become clear later, I shall refer to as *sociocentric*.

### Temiar Animism

In principle, every "thing" that the Temiar recognizes in the world may become imbued with soul. In the case of plants, animals (including men), and mountains this is accepted as being so without further question. But in the case of other things, such as large boulders, natural phenomena, or less material entities, such as diseases, dragons, or modes of cooking (sic), the presence of a soul has first to be revealed to a shaman or proven dreamer before other people become aware of the fact.

According to Temiar ideas, souls are not simply unitary entities. Through the operation of a cosmically based oppositional principle, all soul manifestations are split into two dialectically opposed parts. Depending on the context, this opposition appears morally as good/evil, cosmologically as culture/nature, and locationally as above/below. To take the latter first, the differentiation of soul is normally expressed as a distinction between the upper- and lower-body souls of the object so animated: respectively, the leaf- and root-souls in plants, the head- and heart-souls in man and animals, and the summit- and underground-souls of mountains. Though the various souls of each of these classes of objects are called by distinct names (see Figure 2), their underlying homology is clearly demon-

Figure 2. The Temiar animistic system

|  | Upper-body | Lower-body |
| --- | --- | --- |
| Man, animal | rǝwāy (common Austroasiatic for soul) | hup (? Temiar breath, heart, liver) |
| Plant | kahyɛ̄k (watery substance) | kǝnoruk (Malay *kurung*, enclosed space) |
| Mountain | pǝtǝri (cf. Malay *peteri*, princess) | sarak (Malay *sarang*, nest, lair) |
| Spirit-guide | cenǝy (Semang, elf) gonig | gonig (Malay, *gundik* concubine, spirit-guide) |
| Appearance to dreamer or shaman | mannikin, variously male or female | tiger (or occasionally *naga*, dragon) |

strated since they are always reported to appear in the same guise to dreamers and shamans, regardless of their derivation: upper-body souls manifest themselves as humanoid mannikins, and lower-body souls as tigers. These dream- and trance-based soul manifestations constitute the spirit guides among the Temiar.

In this respect Temiar animistic beliefs are different from those of the Malays, in that "things" do not differ in the degree to which they can fix and differentiate soul. Man's soul is neither more nor less labile, nor better known than, for example, the souls of mountains. In other words, in contrast to the Malay system, Temiar cosmic distinctions are established within man in the same way and to the same extent as in anything else.

There is no room here for any discussion of how this apparently neutral oppositional principle becomes imbued with moral and cosmologic content (see Benjamin, 1967, forthcoming). Here let us stress that this is not a merely dichotomous binary oppositional principle—it is a *dialectical* one. To paraphrase Murphy (1972:175), the opposed entities generate each other, cut against each other, clash, and pass into each other in the process of being transformed into something else. For example, Temiar informants state quite explicitly that, though their head-souls and heart-souls are regarded as different at one level of discourse, they become identical at another level (just *soul,* using the words for *heart-soul* or *head-soul* to stand for both). The theological message carried by this dialectic is good and evil are immanent in everything; good implies evil, evil implies good.

### Semang Animism

Semang religion has been little investigated in terms of modern anthropological approaches, but there is a large body of descriptive material by Evans (1937) and Schebesta (1957). Recent fieldwork on the topic by Endicott and me, however, does allow some conclusions to be drawn.

Just as in Malay and Temiar animism, almost everything that the Semang recognize in their environment may come to anchor spirit and possess a soul. Unlike the Temiar case, however, souls in Semang ideology are never regarded as partible: souls exist in one form only (*Kelaŋes*), which in man and animals is associated with the liver and heart (also *kelaŋes*) and in plants with the pith (*taʔaʔ*). Unlike the Malay case, on the other hand, Semang soul-conceptions do not imply any differences between the soul-embodying properties of men as opposed to those of plants or animals; in this respect Semang beliefs run parallel to those of the Temiar.

It is with regard to their conception of the spirit-guide, however, that the Semang appear quite distinct from both the Malays and the Temiar. The Semang cosmos has three well-ordered levels of hierarchy: the *mundane* level of the soul-possessing entities (man, animals, plants, etc.); the *celestial* level of the many Nature-gods and -godlings that fill the Semang pantheon; and the *intermediate* level of the *chenoi* (properly, *cenōy*). These *chenoi*, which are functionally equivalent to the spirit-guides of Malay and Temiar shamanism, are elflike creatures associated with various natural (especially plant) species, but conceived of as having an objective existence in their own right: they do not seem to be regarded as the manifestations of spirit set free from natural or imagined objects, as among the Malays and Temiar. Exactly what is the relationship between essence and category in the case of these *chenoi* creatures, is not yet clear. It seems likely, however, that they represent a distinct class of beings, possessing both body and soul on the mundane pattern, that can be cajoled by men into releasing their souls in the form of powerful free spirits which can then be used in a typically shamanistic manner.

To summarize this comparison of Malay, Temiar, and Semang animism: all three cultures exhibit animistic beliefs that fit into the general model of animism expounded earlier in this paper, but there are significant differences in the ways in which they structure the cosmos and the spirit domain.

(a) The *Malay* cosmos is structured upon an in/out (or man-world) axis, differentiation along which is in the nature of a continuum.

(b) The *Semang* cosmic axis is up/down (or God-man) differentiated into three discrete levels.

(c) The *Temiar* cosmos is structured upon a complex in/out: up/down matrix (as Temiar ritual makes clear), which is established within man to the same degree as it is in the rest of nature. Man, accordingly, is not differentiated to any significant degree from the rest of the cosmos.

### The Nature of the Spirit-Guide

The nature of the spirit-guide in these three animistic systems also exhibits significant differences.

(a) The Malay spirit-guides (for which there is a large number of names) are drawn from the released souls of entities intermediate between man and ghosts on the in/out axis of differentiation. The spirit-guides are thus formed of the souls of species remote enough from man to be relatively easily set free as spirit, but not so remote as to be dangerously uncontrollable.

(b) The Semang spirit-guides are derived from the souls of beings intermediate between man and God on the up/down axis, and their major function seems to be to act as a means whereby God may be approached. On this argument the Semang shaman functions as a priest. (I see no reason to reject Schebesta's analysis of Semang religion as God-oriented.)

(c) The Temiar spirit-guides may derive from the souls of any category whatsoever, real or imagined, animate or inanimate, human or nonhuman. Furthermore, shamanistic powers are ascribed not only to man but to any entity believed to possess the power of setting souls free from other entities and manipulating the resulting spirit for a specified end.

## THE PRACTICE OF ANIMISM IN MALAYA

Whatever the structural position of the source of spiritual power within these Malayan animistic systems, use of, or operation on, the spirits must involve the freeing of essence (soul) from the restraints of material or categorial boundaries. So long as the quiescent, one-to-one relationship between soul and things remains undisturbed, no religious action is possible. It is necessary first for some imbalance to have occurred in the system (usually spontaneously, but sometimes by deliberate human intervention) so that quiescent soul is set free as potent spirit, which may then be put to use to achieve specific ends. The deliberate use of free spirit forms the basis of shamanism, which exhibits a superficial similarity in form in the three cultures discussed here.

But such a system of beliefs carries with it a darker, negative side; if with skill man can control spirits and make them his allies, with carelessness he may well find himself controlled *by* the spirits in turn. This control may be exerted in two ways: just as soul may be lost, spirit may invade. Any thing in the environment which has somehow lost soul thereby becomes powerful, through the valency of its own soul deficiency, to abstract soul *from* man (or, in the Temiar case at least, from any other species) in an attempt to regain equilibrium. Conversely, soul which has been set free as invasive spirit may attack man (or any other species) and cause serious disturbance of his individual body-soul balance. In man, soul-loss and spirit-attack both result in sickness, against which therapeutic action takes the form of soul-recall and spirit-abstraction rituals, respectively.

In Malayan animistic practice, then, there are two cross-cutting dimensions:

(a) soul-*loss* vs. spirit-*invasion*

(b) soul-*fixing* vs. spirit *manipulation* (as the basis of ritual action).

### Soul-Loss

Soul-loss is an important cause of illness in all three systems, and the ordinary healer (Malay: *bomoh;* Temiar and Semang: *halā?,* which also means shaman) spends much time in finding and returning souls. If he does this by means of power gained from some aiding spirit he is employing shamanistic methods; but the methods employed are frequently nonshamanistic, involving magical procedures only. (The Temiar must also watch that their actions do not cause nonhumans, such as fruit trees, to lose soul.)

### Spirit-Invasion

Spirit-invasion is regarded as a more serious cause of disease in all three systems, and the healer must exert much effort to identify and "fix" the invading spirit. In the Temiar case, however, the aetiology of such diseases is immensely complex, as the number of possible combinations of invading spirits and attacked souls is very high: an invading spirit may derive from disembodied upper-body souls, lower-body souls, or plain undifferentiated soul, acting variously upon man's head-soul, heart-soul, or undifferentiated soul; the same applies, but in reverse, to cases of soul-loss or -abstraction. To complicate matters further, simultaneous spirit-invasion and soul-abstraction may occur, to generate monstrous composite soul-manifestations whose the material embodiments the Temiar regard as particularly dangerous. The majority of the recognized soul-hazards and transactions involve man, as one might expect, but there are a considerable number that involve nonhumans only. So far as I know, Malay and Semang animism are spared this extreme florescence of spirit-based conceptions, probably for two reasons: they do not regard the soul as partible; and they focus all their attention on man as the object of spiritual attack.

### Soul-Fixing

Soul-fixing is the major element in Malay magical practices, involving the use of spells and magical substances. The former are uttered to specify, make known, and hence to place bounds around, the disturbing spirit; the latter are used to harden boundaries in order to prevent soul-escape, or sometimes to soften boundaries across which a spirit straddles ambiguously, and hence dangerously. These practices, however, play little part in Temiar religion, and not very much more in Semang religion. (It is interesting to note, though, that members of all three groups hold the shamans of the other two groups in especially high regard when it becomes necessary to undertake soul-fixing magic.)

### Soul-Manipulation

Soul-manipulation is the basis of shamanism in all three groups, and there is a great deal of similarity in the surface form that this shamanism exhibits. But the *details* diverge considerably; and this is even more true of the *aims* of shamanism in the three groups.

(a) *Malay shamanism* is rarely employed for any other function than relief of individual suffering, usually sickness. The Malay shaman is a professional whose identity is public knowledge and whose patients come to him as clients. Only very rarely (as in the *bela kampong* ceremony) does the Malay shaman undertake ritual action to ensure the well-being of the whole community. It seems to be well authenticated that Malay shamans are also employed as sorcerers to put their powers to nefarious use (Gimlette, 1929).

(b) *Semang shamanism* seems primarily to have a priestly function, in which the shaman serves as the intermediary with God for the whole community. Though the Semang shaman also acts as a healer in cases of individual sickness, his main function seems to be to use his power over the *chenoi* spirits so that they will intercede with the deity in ensuring continuity of the seasonal cycle of thunder, flood, and (plant) fertility. The Semang deity either *is*, or is closely associated with, thunder; it is believed that men's sins against him can be expiated by a human blood offering, which the deity then stores up and transforms in due course into the blossoms of the seasonal fruit trees. Blood in Senoi and Semang symbolism very clearly stands for soul. Hence Semang religion seems to be concerned with maintaining a proper circulation of the vital essence between the celestial and mundane levels of the cosmos, through the joint mediation of the *chenoi* and their earthly representative, the shaman. Failure to carry out these observances would lead, they fear, to a failure of the natural seasonal cycle upon which Semang life so closely depends. Schebesta makes a very strong case (1957:134) for the interpretation of Semang shamanistic ceremonies as a form of prayer, in the true sense of the term.

(c) *Temiar shamanism* is neither primarily concerned with therapeutic action nor at all with the deity. Rather, the Temiar cultivate the spirit-guide relationship as a self-sufficient religious activity in which they enter into highly personal mystical relationships with the disembodied souls of various natural species and of other entities. These relationships range in degree from mere receptivity toward the advances made by spirits in dreams, to full-scale intense public shamanism. There is, then, a gradation from the private and slight degree of "adeptness" (*hala?*) that all Temiar are believed to be capable of, to the public declaration by an acknowledged full shaman that he is prepared to make the power-for-good of his many spirit-guides available to the whole community. The Temiar shaman's duty is neither toward a clientele nor a deity, but to his own personally revealed spirit-guide (*gonig, cenōy*). What this intense cultivation of the spirit-guide achieves, in Temiar belief, is the maximization of the influence of good over that of evil within a cosmos in which, as we have seen, the one is part of the other. (The full development of this argument must await the publication of my book *Temiar Religion: the Dialectical Animism of a Malayan Hill-tribe.*) It is striking that among the Temiar, but not among the Semang and Malays, shamanistic seances are held just as frequently when circumstances are perfectly healthy and untroubled as when there is disease or misfortune.

If we now take an overall view of the pattern of variation revealed by the preceding analysis, some interesting paradoxes emerge.

(a) The Temiar and Semang religions share a greater superficial similarity of form than does either alone with Malay spirit-religion. Nevertheless, when their theologies are compared it becomes apparent that the Temiar and Semang religions are fundamentally different in structure. One could argue, following Schmidt, that the Semang have a primitive monotheistic religion (though admittedly overlain with a surface polytheism) which is, in Malayan terms, *sui generis* and remarkably resistant to change—just like the rest of Semang culture (Benjamin, 1974b). If so, it seems likely that many of the constituent elements of Temiar religion—but not its underlying structure—have diffused from the Semang.

(b) Even though Temiar religion appears superficially to have much less in common with Malay spirit-religion than with Semang religion, I believe it is possible to show that Temiar and Malay spirit-religions are nevertheless "transforms" of the same basic religious system, and that they represent two poles of the same continuum. To demonstrate this, let us now turn our attention to the sociopolitical context of these cultures, to see how far it will serve as the independent variable we initially set out to look for.

## THE SOCIETAL DIMENSION

The most obvious contrast between the Malay and Temiar patterns of animism lies in the differing characters of their religious representations: Malay animism is sociocentric in structure; Temiar animism is egocentric. This contrast may be tabulated as follows:

(a) Malay animism is based on a fixed number of nationally known spirits (McHugh, 1955); Temiar animism is based on the infinitude of personally revealed spirits.

(b) Malay cosmology sets man apart from the rest of the cosmos; Temiar cosmology establishes exactly the same distinctions within man as in the rest of the cosmos.

(c) The Malay shaman manipulates "society"-given spirits for the benefit of a private client; the Temiar shaman uses his own personally revealed spirits for the benefit of the community.

(d) In Malay cosmology, the major axis of spirit differentiation is divided into discrete categorial units; in Temiar cosmology, the major spirit-differentiating oppositions are dialectically part of each other.

These marked differences in character imply a difference in the degree of *differentiation* acknowledged by the two cosmologies. Malay cosmology views the individual as differentiated from, and acted upon by, the rest of society, and it views man as sharply differentiated from the rest of creation. Temiar cosmology, although acknowledging that the individual has a degree of personal autonomy from society, and man from the rest of creation, makes it clear that that autonomy represents no more than a muddled, dialectical pattern of differentiation between the major elements of the cosmos. (Various theories of religious evolution make much of this notion of differentiation, but I shall not discuss the point here.)

Translated to a political mode of expression, these differences imply that whereas Malay cosmology sees man as *acted upon* by society and nature, Temiar cosmology sees man as freely *participating in* society and nature. This contrast provides us with a clue to the independent transforming variable we set out to look for. The most obvious contrast between Temiar and Malay sociopolitical organization is that the former are segmentary and egalitarian in structure (Benjamin, 1966); the latter, centralized and hierarchical. Now from the point of view of the local (village) community, centralization implies that power will be perceived as extrinsic in character, deriving from a locus outside of the villagers' control. Segmentary organization, on the other hand, implies that power will be perceived as *intrinsic* in character, being in the hands of the villagers themselves. This is precisely paralleled in the two cultures by their differing perceptions of the nature and source of spiritual power: in Temiar animism, spiritual power is intrinsic, deriving from personal revelation and used at the individual's own discretion; in Malay animism, spiritual power is extrinsic, deriving from socially maintained spirit knowledge and used at the behest of others.

What, then, of my claim that Temiar and Malay animism form the two poles of a chain of cultural transformations? To clinch this argument it will be necessary to show that as the degree of centralization and hierarchy increases in the sociopolitical domain, so also does the degree of "sociocentricity" in the religious domain. Full documentation of this possibility must await the results of ethnographic research now being undertaken by several workers among a variety of Malayan aboriginal groups. Nevertheless, I believe that it is possible to provide some evidence for this argument from the meager data so far available from some of the more southerly aboriginal groups.

Two aboriginal groups, the Mah Meri and the Jah Hut, have become famous in recent years for the high quality of their wood carvings. (A fine permanent display may be seen at the National Museum, Kuala Lumpur.) Although the techniques of Mah Meri and Jah Hut woodcarving are the result of their deliberate introduction to foreign art styles in the past few decades, the *subjects* of their carvings derive from wholly indigenous symbolism and ritual practice. All the carvings represent spirits of disease or misfortune, and all are characterized by visual attributes that immediately identify the spirit for anyone versed in the relevant culture; this holds true whoever was the artist who produced the carving. In other words, the Mah Meri and the Jah Hut possess a developed, "sociocentric" *iconography* (see Werner; 1973, in press). In this respect they contrast strongly with the Temiar, whose spirits' attributes are a matter of great mystery, but align themselves with the Malays (and Negritos, for that matter), whose spirits' attributes are a matter of public knowledge (McHugh,

1955). In sociopolitical organization, the Mah Meri and Jah Hut (along with most other central and southerly aboriginal groups) have long been reported to possess an institutionalized system of political ranking (which, despite earlier doubts, does seem to be more genuinely indigenous in character than similar structures farther north) (cf. Benjamin, 1968); and it is a matter of simple observation that their economies are much more closely tied to the outside world than that of the Temiar. They are not Muslims, however, and therefore bear a much less central relationship to the traditional state than the Malays. They appear, therefore, to occupy an intermediate position on both the religious and sociopolitical continua between the Malay and Temiar poles.

We have yet to fit the Semang into this picture. In fact, as I suggested earlier, the Semang do not really fit at all onto the Temiar-Malay continuum we have just been discussing, but sit disjunctly apart from it. Yet a few relevant points can be made. Semang deities and *chenoi*-spirits have a considerable degree of objectivity about them, as Evans' and Schebesta's accounts make clear: their identities and attributes are well formulated (though very complex), and are known to all. In that sense, Semang religion qualifies as sociocentric in structure. In terms of their experience of power, however, the Semang diverge significantly from both the Temiar and the Malays, in that their conditions of life (Benjamin, 1974b) lead them to perceive power as not deriving from any human agency at all, whether within or outside the community. Since their relationship to the human societies around them is wholly opportunistic in character, they have never (until recent military influence, that is) felt constrained by *human* agencies. Rather, the Semang have always seen the constraints on their behavior as deriving from the forces of nature, especially as manifested in the deity. Hence one can maintain that the Semang, too, illustrate the correlation between sociocentric religious representations and the experience of power as extrinsic; the difference here is that it is God they fear, not man.

A few ethnological points may be made here. It makes sense in terms of the foregoing analysis that the main cosmic axis should be vertical (man-God) among the Semang and horizontal (man-world) among the Malays. The point of interest here is provided by the Temiar, whose ritual organization makes a very rich usage of a combined vertical/horizontal matrix. I suggest that we have here two source traditions (the ''Austric'' and the ''Negrito''?), the Temiar and Malay systems deriving from the one and the Semang system from the other. The Temiar, however (as in other domains of culture, such as language and kinship) have been in a position to borrow a large number of cultural elements from their Semang neighbors, but putting them to different uses. To some extent the Malays, too, have borrowed elements of religious culture from the Semang, including many features of their tiger-shamanism (*belian*), and the blood-thunder-mockery complex (*chelau*). This pattern of cultural relations—two source cultures, one highly conservative and the other undergoing continuous differentiation in step with social evolution—seems to hold for the ethnology of indigenous Malaya in general. As my papers on the prehistory, linguistics, and kinship patterns show (Benjamin, 1972; 1973; 1974a), there is an essential homology between the patterns of differentiation in all these domains.

## MALAYAN ANIMISM AND WORLD RELIGIONS

Several universalizing or world religions have been present historically in the Malay Peninsula: in chronological order, Brahmanism, Islam, Christianity, and recently Baha'i have all had some influence on one or another of the indigenous cultures. Of these, only Islam requires any detailed discussion, as it is the only one of the religions just named to have maintained a close syncretism with animistic religion in Malay for any length of time.

Brahmanism was associated with the advent of Indian people and Indian patterns of political organization to the Malay Peninsula. How far these influences spread among the indigenous populations is still a matter for debate. It seems probable, however, the Brahmanism as a functioning religious system did not spread far beyond the boundaries of Indian settlements or beyond the courts of the simple states that later developed in the region. (This is not to say, however, that component elements derived from the Brahmanic complex did not diffuse out and form part of the practices of non-metropolitan populations. Plenty of evidence suggests that this happened to early Malay culture, and surprisingly [according to Schebesta, 1957:116–19] to Semang culture also; but neither the Malays nor the Semang could be said to have been Brahmanists in any overall sense.) If it is true that Brahmanism in the Malay Peninsula was closely associated with the development of the state, then it would hardly be surprising that it remained closely associated only with the political center. Heine-Geldern in a germinal paper (1956) has pointed out that Brahmanic religion implies that the here-and-now is a microcosm of the cosmos (as is evidenced by the cosmological underpinnings of such architectural complexes as Borobudur and Angkor Wat). In terms of the argument presented in this paper, the Brahmanic world-view would therefore imply a geographically "intrinsic" model of the source of power, which would be very unlikely to be taken up by people dwelling beyond the pale of the court and its immediate environs, whose experience of power would be "extrinsic" in character.

This last point provides the major clue to Islam's being so much more widely adopted than Brahmanism had been. Like Christianity (which in the Southeast Asian context is relevant to a discussion of the Philippine situation), Islam is centered organizationally quite away from the local scene, and thereby, in terms of the present argument, it may serve as a further analogue to the "extrinsic" model of power that I earlier claimed was embedded in Malay culture. Yet matters are not so straightforward as they might seem. Whereas the ancient spirit-religion provided (and presumably continues to provide) a perfectly good analogue of "extrinsically" experienced power at the level of the local village community, Islam's adoption by both the rulers and the ruled (replacing the Brahmanism of the former, but syncretizing with the animism of the latter) suggests that a further level of analysis must be pursued if we are to understand why the Malays (and one or two other groups) adopted Islam and why most other indigenous Malayan groups rejected it. Obviously, there is more to this question than the mere presence or absence of the centralized state.

Viewed historically, the most significant change that Malay society has undergone parallel to its adoption of Islam, is its progressive *peasantization*. By this I refer to the socioeconomic situation whereby the ordinary Malay feels himself not only under the political sway of the rulers of his own state, but also under the sway of indirect and only vaguely understood economic forces emanating from the world at large. If we accept the standard version of Malayan history, this would have started with the establishment of Melaka as an international trading post. I am suggesting, therefore, that through historical accident, Islam was the first religion to arrive on the Malayan scene that could provide an adequate cosmological analogue to the socioeconomic circumstances that were developing at the "real world" level. (That Catholic Christianity, centered as it is in Rome, could equally well have served the same purpose is indicated by the closely similar historical and ethnological situation of the Philippines, where Islam and Christianity now survive each in those areas where it was the first such religion to arrive on the scene—except for a band of disputed ground along their border.) A closely similar argument has also been put forward by Geertz (1956:90–91) and Wheatley (1964:185).

In order to clinch this argument we must (1) demonstrate that the spread of Islam went hand in hand with the spread of the economic system that defines the "peasant" social type and (2) explain why many Malayan societies have never accepted Islam. The first is a problem for historians to work on. The second problem is the subject of the next section.

I shall deal only briefly with the reasons for the Temiar and Semang to reject Islam, despite many continuing attempts to convert them to that religion.

(a) The socioeconomic situation of the Temiar and the Semang does not bring them so fully into the wider world system that they would be predisposed to seek a world religion. They remain even now substantially in control of their own day-to-day economic undertakings, through the ease with which they can fall back on traditional, noncash, subsistence methods of livelihood. They do not, in other words, feel more swayed by extrinsic than by intrinsic forces.

(b) Those aboriginal groups that *have* become peasants do indeed show a tendency to seek membership in a world religion—which is precisely what the foregoing argument would lead us to expect. But *which* world religion they choose is the result of a variety of factors, some historical and some structural. In the north, where there is a long history of animosity between aborigines and

Malays (resulting mainly from the callous slaveraiding which went on until well into the 1930s in some areas) such peasantized aborigines as the lowland Semai have almost completely rejected Islam, even though in almost every respect they are now barely distinguishable in lifestyle from their Malay neighbors. Instead, they have taken readily to the Baha'i religion and to various forms of Christianity: some evidence suggests that, in addition to the reasons just expounded they have done this as a deliberate attempt to protect themselves against pressures to convert to Islam. Furthermore, they are strongly resistant to circumcision and to giving up pork, a major item in their diet. In the south, however, where there is a far higher degree of cultural and social-structural continuity between the aborigines and the Malays, the former seem much more ready to accept Islam and even to seek conversion without being pressured into it. (A European ethnographer working among aborigines in the south has reported [personal communication] that his [non-Malay] informants spend as much time in urging him to become a Muslim as they do in answering his ethnological enquiries.)

(c) The Semang still have an essentially unitary world view although they have long had relations with the outside world, and although this contact has expressed itself in the details of their social organization (Benjamin, 1974a; 1974b). Unlike the problem that peasants have of finding a balance between the pulls of the Great and the Little traditions (see below), the Semang have an essentially opportunistic "foraging" approach to *all* their contexts of activity. On settling down, then, they are unlikely *freely* to take up a world religion. Those Semang who *have* nevertheless adopted a world religion have become Muslims, which suggests (correctly, I believe, for most cases I have examined) that they have done so as a result of forced enculturation rather than through the choice implicit in the Christianity and Baha'i of the lowland Semai.

### Malay Religious Syncretism

One problem still remains: as in the rest of Southeast Asia, almost all the communities that claim allegiance to Islam, Christianity, or Buddhism also have recourse to animistic beliefs and practices. Why is it, in Malaya, that Islam did not oust the spirit-cults?

Here we may follow a clue provided by studies in Burma and Thailand and look for internal contradictions in the area of theodicy kind of the theology of the world religion. Buddhism, of course, has its own peculiar theological contradictions, and the specific details of the arguments that have been developed to explain syncretism farther north in Southeast Asia will not help us in looking at the Malay case. Nevertheless, I believe that Islam contains at least three internal contradictions on the issue of divine justice (theodicy) that might have relevance to the retention of animistic religion among the Malays.

(a) How are the declared omnipotence, omniscience, and all-benevolence of Allah to be maintained in the face of the ordinary peasant's experience of daily suffering?

(b) How is the conflict to be resolved between the doctrine that every Muslim has direct, unmediated access to Allah (there is no priesthood) and the doctrine that it is the duty of the state to organize the Islamic church (cf. Gellner, 1969)?

(c) Islam imposes organizational responsibilities (such as the forty adult men needed for the Friday mosque service and the obedience to rational bureaucratically maintained laws) that are only fully to be satisfied in an urban sophisticated milieu (cf. Hassan, 1972). Malay culture is still essentially rural in its orientation; hence the maintenance of Islamic practice there is likely to be strained.

In a manner parallel to what has been observed in the Buddhist countries of Southeast Asia, these theodicies can be resolved, or at least made less apparent, by recourse to the animistic system. For example, a Malay has only to declare that suffering derives from the action of the spirits for the all-benevolence of Allah to remain unchallenged; if then he still has qualms about having thereby challenged the omnipotence of Allah, he can ease the situation somewhat by declaring (as Malays nowadays frequently do) that spirit beliefs have nothing whatever to do with "religion" *(agama)*, but are simply "beliefs" *(kepercayaan)* deriving from the domain of "Malay culture" *(adat)*. The way in which the second of the two theodicies is resolved by appeal to the spirit-cults requires a far closer examination of the sociology of Malay life than it is possible to undertake here: the close relationship between Islam and Malay ethnic identity in modern Malaysia would play a large part in such an explanation.

As to the *mechanism* of syncretism between Islam and animism, two points are relevant. First, the power of the Word in Islam is much the same as the power of the word in *semangat*-based spells, which would allow easier syncretism between the two in practice. Second, the use of the Arabic language in spells and in talking about religion prevents the explicit use of the *semangat* soul-concept, but this does not mean that rituals (especially those surrounding life-cycle transitions and crises) are not structured as if the *semangat* beliefs held true.

Lastly, a parenthetic point. A further reason that the Temiar and the hill Semai resist Islam even when they are drawn into the world of cash economy, may well be that their religion obviates the need for theodicy-resolution because it makes the *dialectical* confrontation of Good and Evil the very centerpiece of the theology.

## ACKNOWLEDGMENTS

Earlier versions of this paper have been presented for discussion at seminars in the Anthropology Department, London School of Economics; the Sociology Department, University of Singapore; the Faculty of Social Sciences, University of Penang; the Anthropology Department, Research School of Pacific Studies,

Australian National University; and the Anthropology Department, Monash University. I would like to thank the participants for their helpful comments. I would also like to thank Kirk Endicott, Robert McKinley, and Vivienne Wee for their discussion of many of the problems raised in this paper. The faults that remain, however, are solely the author's responsibility.

My fieldwork among the Temiar has been financed at various times by the University of Cambridge, the Royal Anthropological Institute, and the Ministry of Education and Science (London); fieldwork among the Semang has been financed by the Wenner-Gren Foundation. To all these bodies I would like to express my gratitude, and my regret that it has taken so long for the results to appear.

I would also like to express my gratitude to Professor Derek Freeman and the Research School of Pacific Studies, Australian National University, for their offer of a Visiting Fellowship at the Anthropology Department, October–November 1973, which gave me the opportunity to prepare this paper.

## REFERENCES

Benjamin, G. Temiar social groupings. *Federation Museums Journal,* 1966, *11*, 1–25.
Benjamin, G. *Temiar religion.* Unpublished doctoral dissertation, University of Cambridge, 1967.
Benjamin, G. Headmanship and leadership in Temiar society. *Federation Museums Journal,* 1968, *13*, 1–43.
Benjamin, G. Austroasiatic subgroupings and prehistory in the Malay Peninsula. *Working Paper* 8, Department of Sociology, University of Singapore, 1972. (To appear, revised, in *Austroasiatic studies,* Philip Jenner, Ed., University of Hawaii Press, 1974.)
Benjamin, G. Indigenous kinship systems of the Malay Peninsula, 1973. (Ms., to appear as a *Working Paper,* Department of Sociology, University of Singapore.)
Benjamin, G. Prehistory and ethnology in Southeast Asia: some new ideas. *Working Paper* 25, Department of Sociology, University of Singapore, 1974a.
Benjamin, G. Introduction. In Paul Schebesta, *Among the forest dwarfs of Malaya* (pp. v–xii, 2nd impression). Kuala Lumpur: Oxford University Press, 1974b.
Benjamin, G. *Temiar religion: the dialectical animism of a Malayan hill tribe.* London: Academic Press, forthcoming.
Douglas, M. *Purity and danger.* London: Routledge, 1966.
Douglas, M. *Natural symbols.* London: Routledge, 1970.
Endicott, K. *An analysis of Malay magic.* London: Cambridge University Press, 1970.
Evans, I. H. N. *The Negritos of Malaya.* London: Cambridge University Press, 1937.
Evans-Pritchard, E. E. *Theories of primitive religion.* London: Oxford University Press, 1965.
Geertz, C. *The development of the Javanese economy.* Cambridge, Mass.: Harvard University Press, 1956.
Gellner, E. A pendulum swing theory of Islam. In R. Robertson (Ed.), *Sociology of Religion,* pp. 127–140. Harmondsworth: Penguin Books, 1969.
Gimlette, J. P. *Malay poisons and charm cures.* London: J. and A. Churchill, 1929.
Hassan, R. Islam and urbanization in the Medieval Middle-East. *Eastern Anthropologist,* 1972, *25*, 107–122.
Heine-Geldern, R. Conceptions of state and kingship in Southeast Asia. Cornell University, Department of Far Eastern Studies, Southeast Asia Program, *Data Paper, 18,* 1956.

McHugh, J. N. *Hantu hantu: an account of ghost belief in modern Malay*. Singapore: Donald Moore, 1955.

Murphy, R. *The dialectics of social life*. London: Allen and Unwin, 1972.

Schebesta, P. *Die Negrito Asiens: Religion and Mythologie*. Modling: St. Gabriel-Verlag, 1957.

Werner, R. *Mah-Meri art and culture*. Kuala Lumpur: Muzium Negara, 1973.

Werner, R. *Jah-Hut art and culture*. Kuala Lumpur: University of Malaya Press, in press.

Wheatley, P. *Impressions of the Malay Peninsula in ancient times*. Singapore: Donald Moore, 1964.

chapter two

# The Batek Negrito
# Thunder God:
# The Personification of a
# Natural Force

Kirk Endicott

The Australian National University

## INTRODUCTION

Among the most difficult problems in the anthropological study of religion is the explanation of the images and characteristics attributed to supernatural beings. The mental process by which form is applied to otherwise unfathomable experiences are difficult to observe and study, in part because the anthropologist is presented with a finished cultural product which is already believed in in the same way as are the phenomena of the natural world (as defined and explained in that particular society). Yet in some cases certain characteristics of the beliefs themselves—especially inconsistencies and variations from group to group—reveal something of their inner nature as mental constructions. I believe this to be so in the case of the thunder god belief of the Negritos of the Malay Peninsula. In spite of the demise of the nature-myth theory as a general explanation for supernatural beings, the concept of personification of a natural force is appropriate, I think, in cases like this, in which the association of the being and a specific phenomenon is close and clear. But of course to call this *personification* is only to state the problem; one must investigate to determine the nature of that personification. This paper intends to make such an investigation of the thunder god beliefs of the Malayan Negritos, especially those of the Batek groups of the northeastern part of the Peninsula.

The Negritos of Malaya number only about 2,000 persons today. They live in dialect groups of a few hundred persons each scattered about the foothills in the northern half of the Peninsula. Those living on the western side of the mountain range dividing the Peninsula longitudinally are called *Semang* in the older literature, and those to the east, which include the Batek, are called *Pangan*. They are generally believed to be the remnants of a once more numerous and widespread race which also survives in the Andaman Islands and in isolated pockets in the Philippines. Traditionally they were nomadic hunter-gatherers, and most groups continue to forage for wild foods even where they now carry on small-scale trade, wage labor, and planting as well. In addition they retain many of the values, habits, and the fluid social organization usually associated with a foraging economy (Endicott, 1974). The cultures of the Malayan Negritos might be characterized as conservative but opportunistic. They have borrowed many words, ideas, and techniques from other ethnic groups in the area, but have assimilated them in such a way as to perpetuate rather than break down their traditional way of life.

The Negrito religion, like the economy, is eclectic but well integrated. Some of the elements are ancient enough to be shared with the Andamanese and Philippine Negritos (Cooper, 1940); others have been borrowed from the Malays since the adoption of Islam. Many aspects of the Negrito cosmology, such as the belief in a watery underworld ruled by a dragon, are clearly recognizable as belonging to the pre-Moslem Indonesian complex which persists, for example, in a number of variations among the "pagan tribes" of Borneo.[1] Yet other basic features of that complex, such as the belief in spirits *(antu),* are firmly rejected by the Negritos. The belief in a thunder god and even his name are apparently very ancient among the Negritos. The chief of the spirits of the Negritos of the northern Camarines in the Philippines is called *Kayai,* and he is said to indicate his displeasure with human beings "by speaking through the thunder" (Garvan, 1964:227), as does Karei, the thunder god of the Semang. But the total complex of belief and ritual to be examined here contains elements from many different sources, not just the ancient Negrito tradition.

The basic features of the Semang (western Negrito) belief and ritual concerning thunder have been well described in the literature, especially by Evans and Schebesta (Evans, 1968:139–158; Schebesta, 1929:47, 67, 87–88, 96–97, 184–194, 198–199, 217–223, 250, 252; Schebesta, 1962:10–23, 26–35, 71–75, 87–102; Skeat and Blagden, 1966:177–178). In brief, it is believed that thunderstorms are caused by an immortal being (Karei) and that they are punishment for man's transgression of certain rules. These rules concern social behavior (e.g., a prohibition on incest) and behavior in relation to the non-human environment (e.g., prohibitions on mocking certain animals and on mixing certain foods). A thunderstorm may be accompanied by a devastating flood which is thought to be caused by another immortal being who dwells in an underground sea and is related in some way to the thunder god. In order to cause the storm and flood to abate, the Negritos believe they must offer their blood, which they extract from the calf by lightly scratching it with a knife, to the heavens and the

---

[1]See Needham (1964) for a detailed account of the similarities in the thunder-related beliefs and rituals of the Semang and the Penan of Borneo.

earth. The offering is sometimes accompanied by an invocation denying the breaking of a rule or declaring that compensation has been made or simply telling the storm to go away.

On the face of it this appears to be a straightforward belief in a powerful supernatural being who enforces proper human behavior through the means of violent storms but can be appeased by a sacrifice of blood. This interpretation is the standard one in the literature, and most of the further published discussion centers on such questions as whether Karei can properly be termed a deity and whether the blood throwing is a true sacrifice or act of worship (Skeat and Blagden, 1966:178; Evans, 1968:140; Schebesta, 1962:10, 71, 90–94). Although great attention has been paid to this complex of ideas,[2] there are a number of unresolved ambiguities and contradictions in the beliefs and unexplained differences among the beliefs of different dialect groups. One basic problem is that the Negritos do not firmly distinguish the thunder causer from the thunder itself. As Schebesta says, "amongst almost all the Semang tribes the thunder is called Karei. The thunder itself is feared, but even more feared is the being who stands in the background and wields the thunder, the being whom Jahai, Sabubn and Menri all call by the same name, Karei" (Schebesta, 1929:184–185). Most statements made by Negritos about thunder can be interpreted as referring to either a personified or unpersonified phenomenon. The Negrito languages do not distinguish persons from things in the pronoun system, so to say "it is thundering" is the same as saying "he is thundering." The expression *karey ʔo-gerger* could mean "Karei, he is thundering" or "thunder, it is rumbling." The usual answer to the question "what is that?"—referring to a clap of thunder—is "Karei" ("Gobar" or "Ketok" among the Batek), which could be the name of a natural phenomenon or of a deity thought to be making the noise. The ambiguity is not merely linguistic; the Negritos talk about Karei in both personified and naturalistic ways in a single conversation. For example, while talking with one informant about the characteristics of Karei and getting a description which obviously indicated an anthropomorphic being, I asked who the friends of Karei were and received the answers "wind" and "rain," which are not personified in any context. A similar problem exists concerning certain other entities which are personified by some informants but not by others. Schebesta eliminates one erstwhile deity from the Semang pantheon for this reason. This is Karpeg'n, which means "above" (Schebesta, 1962:11, footnote; Skeat and Blagden, 1966:509). One informant said that "Karpeg'n was not a person, but the firmament," and Schebesta (1962:11) comments: "One cannot help asking how Bejuan and Ramog'n could describe Karpeg'n as a celestial person!"

Another difficulty is that Karei, as a supernatural being, is described by the Semang as being related to a number of other supernaturals, but the identities and relationships among the members of this pantheon are defined differently by the

[2]See Freeman (1968) for a thoroughgoing Freudian analysis of the image of the thunder god and the earth goddess and the emotions felt toward them.

different dialect groups and sometimes even by different informants in a single group (Schebesta, 1962:10–34). Schebesta had to organize a meeting of his Jahai and Lanoh informants in order to get them to produce a consistent classification of supernatural beings (Schebesta, 1962:12; 1929:187). The greatest difficulty encountered by Schebesta in this connection was in sorting out the relationship between Karei and Ta Ped'n, a somewhat more benevolent being who is generally regarded as the creator deity though acting under orders from Karei. Ta Ped'n is described by different dialect groups as the younger brother of Karei, the son of Karei, or identical with Karei (Schebesta, 1962:31). Even though Karei is nearly everywhere regarded as superior to, and more important than, Ta Ped'n (1962:12, 14, 18, 21), Schebesta concludes that Ta Ped'n is the true ruler of the firmament, identified with the sun, and Karei is not a deity at all but a mere personification of thunder, the natural phenomenon, which has pushed Ta Ped'n into the background in the popular imagination (1962:30–33). He terms Ta Ped'n the "supreme and peerless lord of heaven" and calls Karei an "interloper in the circle of the celestial *orang hidop* [immortals]" (1962:32). I can only surmise that Schebesta, who was schooled in the theories of Wilhelm Schmidt and in particular in the expectation that hunting-gathering peoples would have a benevolent "high god," must have recoiled from accepting Karei, whom the Semang sometimes describe as evil (1962:12, 31), as the supreme deity of the Malayan Negritos. This attempt to explain away the importance of Karei is unconvincing and, as I shall show, unnecessary.

Further problems exist regarding the relation between the thunder and man. It is tempting to see Karei as a deity with moral significance and to interpret belief in him as a means by which a people who lack the political institutions to regulate social behavior can enforce a set of moral laws. Indeed the rules against incest and improper behavior between relatives would seem to promote social harmony, but those against such acts as mixing certain foods and mocking certain animals (though it is permissible to mock humans) have no obvious social value. Also the nature of guilt itself is unclear; it is normally said that the offender must make the blood sacrifice, but in fact it is considered sufficient for anyone to do it, and usually it is the older women who perform the rite first (Schebesta, 1962:80, 81, 83, 90). Furthermore, there is some mystery as to why Karei demands the blood and why he is appeased when it is given. Schebesta claims that Karei does nothing with the blood but is simply pleased to see it offered; Ta Ped'n, however, is supposed to put the blood into the "fruit umbels so that there will be much fruit" (1962:88). This leads to the curious result, as Schebesta points out (1962:103), that the more the people break the rules, and atone with a blood offering, the better will be the fruit harvest. This would seem to put moral behavior and economic well-being in opposition. Such problems as these suggest that reconsideration of the conventional interpretation of the thunder god belief is warranted. The beliefs of the Batek, which I shall describe here, point toward a new interpretation which I believe can clarify many of these problems for the Malayan Negritos as a whole.

My hypothesis is that the Negritos think about thunder in terms of two systems of ideas: a naturalistic system and a mythological system. Each of these is reasonably consistent in itself, but they are not completely consistent with each other. The problems arise when there is shifting back and forth between the two frames of reference. The personification of thunder can be seen, however, as a relatively stable, though not fully consistent, conjunction of a notion of thunder as a natural phenomenon (in terms of the Negrito world view) with certain myths of ancient Negrito culture heroes.

## THUNDER AS A NATURAL PHENOMENON

Thunderstorms are common occurrences in the Malayan jungle, and it is not unexpected that they should have a place in the Negritos' conception of the natural world. Their own world view, and their folk meteorology in particular, does not correspond exactly to that of the Western naturalist, but it does make sense of what the Negritos know about nature and is an adequate guide for dealing with the practical problems of survival in that environment.

The Batek ordinarily speak of thunder in terms which suggest an essentially naturalistic conception of it. The Batek Dek, who live on the Aring River in Kelantan, say that their equivalent to the Semang term *Karei* is *Gobar*. They say, for example, *"gobar ?o-keŋluŋ,"* "Gobar is making noise," when they hear thunder. But the term *Gobar* is apparently derived from Malay *gobar*, "gloomy (of sky)" (Winstedt, 1965:114). In other words, the Batek Dek expression could be rendered: "the gloomy sky is making noise." The Batek Nong on the Cheka River in Pahang say *"keto? ?o-gerger,"* "Ketok is thundering," and Ketok was reported by Schebesta to be the "supreme being" of that group, an enormous personage who is identified with light and "whose eyes are the sun and moon" (Schebesta, 1929:276). Yet the Batek Nong told me that *keto?* merely means "sky" (Malay *langit*), and they were amused at my suggestion that it was a being with the sun and moon for eyes. I think Schebesta, influenced by the western Negritos who seem habitually to personify the thunder-maker, was misled into placing Ketok in the same category. The Batek Nong attribute all weather to Ketok in much the same way as they do thunder. For example, they say *"keto? ?o-mah hǫc,"* "it is going to rain."

The Batek Dek and Batek Teh of the Lebir River in Kelantan consider thunder to be a normal part of the seasonal cycle unless it occurs in a particularly violent thunderstorm which happens to pass directly over their camp. The incidence of thunder varies considerably during the year in that area. During February and March, which are relatively dry months, it is often heard rumbling in the distance, but it seldom takes the form of a storm. Gradually a pattern develops, which is well established by July, of a thunderstorm blowing up every afternoon but lasting only about an hour. In November, December, and January the rain becomes less concentrated but the total amount of precipitation is greater, frequently resulting in flooding. Thunder, however, is seldom heard during these months. The Batek say that the rumbling thunder in February and March causes flowers to form in the heavens and fall to the fruit trees on earth. The storms of spring and summer are supposed to help the fruit to ripen, and the dying away of the thunder in the fall corresponds to the end of the fruiting season. The rumbling of thunder in the distance and thunderstorms which do not pass directly overhead are not normally regarded as a result of human misbehavior, and making a blood sacrifice is not even considered. Only when I pressed them to account for a particular storm in the distance would the Batek sometimes speculate that someone somewhere else must have broken a rule. On the whole, however, the occurrence of thunder beyond one's own camp seems to be regarded as part of a natural cycle, which includes the all-important fruit season, and the cause of any particular storm is seldom sought.

Unusually severe thunderstorms occurring directly overhead, especially at night, may be interpreted as unnatural, however, and be attributed to a breach of some prohibition. But the prohibitions themselves are normally explained in terms of the natural order rather than in moral terms. The Batek believe that it is dangerous to mix or confuse certain things which ordinarily are distinct, and the rules against storm-causing acts (called *lawac* by the Batek Dek and *tala ɲ* and *cəmam* by the Batek Nong) are meant to preserve the distinctions among certain natural and social categories (which are also natural by Batek reckoning). The prohibitions on mixing foods and on incest and too close contact among some relatives of opposite sex are all explained as existing to prevent the mixing of incompatible smells. The prohibition on mocking certain animals seems intended, at least in part, to prevent confusion between men and animals. The prototype of the prohibited behavior, given in a Batek Dek story, is dressing a monkey like a man and making it dance or otherwise act as if it were human.

The disaster that results from breaking these rules can also be seen as the collapse of certain important natural divisions. The destruction is believed to come not only from the storm overhead but also from a flood which wells up from an underground sea and dissolves the earth under the offenders' camp. The catastrophic mixing of earth and water, from above and below the ground, seems to reverse the process described in the Batek Dek creation story in which a magical bird created the land by feeding on the bottom of the primordial sea and building up an island of dry land from its excrement. Gobar and the *naga* (dragon or snake) which lives in the underground sea are described as if they were holding back the waters of the sky and the underworld which constantly strain to recombine with the land. They are said to be unable to "hold out" (Malay *tahan*) when men violate the prohibitions, i.e., when they confuse the categories of the natural world. Thus the punishment of a *lawac* act is a disastrous mingling of water and earth which is also a breakdown of the division between sky and earth and earth and the underworld.

The blood sacrifice may be seen as helping to repair such a breakdown in the natural order, quite aside from its status as an offering to the anthropomorphic deity. Blood is regarded by the Batek as the physical embodiment of ɲawaʔ, the life-soul. The ɲawaʔ of the first humans were supposedly borrowed from the banana plant, which has sap that turns to the color of blood when it dries, and this is why men, like banana plants, are not immortal but die and are replaced by their children. The continuity of life is maintained by the orderly flow of ɲawaʔ. The controlled transmission of blood by man can also be life-giving. The Batek give their blood to one another for use as medicine, to be rubbed on the skin or drunk, depending on the ailment. One Batek Dek story describes how an ancient Batek culture hero once killed a giant bearcat and the drops of blood which he scattered about became all the useful plants and animals. I think the throwing of blood in a thunderstorm can also be seen as a creative, life-giving act which helps to restore order by contributing ɲawaʔ to the natural cycle of the fruit seasons and by bringing man, who had disrupted the order, back into harmony with the processes of nature. The belief that the blood (or the shadow of the blood, as the Batek say) enters the ripening fruit illustrates both the life-giving potency that is attributed to the transmission of blood and the interdependency that is believed to exist between man and nature and which can be disrupted by acts which are contrary to the natural order. A belief that the throwing of blood contributes directly to the fruit cycle may explain why the Negritos seldom trouble themselves about what the deity does with the blood once he receives it. Since all blood has the same power to restore order, persons other than the actual offender may make the blood sacrifice when a thunderstorm strikes.

   Thus the naturalistic conception of thunder is that it is a normal meteorological phenomenon which is an integral part of the seasonal fruit cycle, but one which can get out of hand if man disrupts the orderly processes of nature by confusing the categories of the natural world. This system of explanation is complete in itself, without any necessary reference to anthropomorphic deities.

## THUNDER AND MYTHICAL HEROES

The Malayan Negritos have a reasonably rich oral tradition (Evans, 1968:144, 159–189, 230–244; 1923:185–195; 1927:26–28; Schebesta, 1929:216–221, 237–239, 251–252; 1962:10–77; Skeat and Blagden, 1966:211–215, 221–223). Many of the stories are borrowed or influenced by outside sources—even, in one case, the Ramayana (Skeat and Blagden, 1966:219–220; Evans, 1968:147–148)—but they are normally given a characteristic Negrito cast. The heroes of the stories are usually halaʔ, superhuman personages who can travel easily between the earth and the sky-world. (The term halaʔ is also used for the most accomplished shamans who are thought also to be able to journey to the heavens while in a trance.) Typically the heroes are described as coming to the earth and living on it for a period of time during which they create certain landmarks and creatures which continue to exist in the present-day world, but they themselves eventually withdraw to the sky-world or the underworld where they remain today. Frequently the heroes occur in pairs, usually a pair of brothers or sisters, but sometimes a brother and a sister or parent and child. Among the Batek Dek even Allah, the Moslem deity, is given a younger brother—Tak Allah.

Among the western Negritos, one such pair of mythical characters is Karei and Ta Ped'n. They are regarded as father and son, respectively, by the Jahai and as older and younger brother by the Lanoh and Kenta Bog'n (Schebesta, 1962:12, 13, 18). They are variously described as looking like a large person, usually a Malay *raja*, or like a gibbon or *siamang* (a close relative to the gibbon) colored either dazzling white or black (Schebesta, 1962:11, 13, 14, 24, 31; Evans, 1968:144, 145; Skeat and Blagden, 1966:210). The image of the heroes as apes or monkeys may be derived from a widespread set of stories (probably influenced by the Ramayana tale of Hanuman, the monkey-king) in which two "tribes" of monkeys or apes engage in a war. In some versions of the story, this war is said to be the cause of a great fire which separated early man into Negritos and Malays, the Negritos being those who had their hair and skin singed by the heat. The human beings are considered in some of the versions to be descended from these apes or monkeys and in others to be innocent bystanders (Schebesta, 1962:57–59). It would be natural enough to identify the ancient mythical heroes with the mythical monkey tribes to some extent as both are prior to modern man in a sense.

A typical example of the Karei and Ta Ped'n stories is the following one which was recorded by Evans at Grik, apparently from Lanoh Negritos. Kari (Karei) and his younger brother Tapern (Ta Ped'n) once went on a fishing expedition up the Perak River. When they stopped to have a smoke and a meal, they stuck their fishing rods in the ground, and when they looked up, the fishing rods had become mountains, the present Gunong Kenderong and Gunong Kerunai. The next night they made a circular hut in which they performed a magical ceremony and then ascended to the sky (Evans, 1968:144). Nowadays both characters are believed to reside in the sky, and one or the other of them is thought to cause the thunderstorms which enforce the *lawac* prohibitions. The thunder deity is supposed to make thunder by roaring, spinning a top, rolling a stone along a plank, or beating a rope upon it, and the lightning is the flashing of the deity's eyelids, the jerking or swinging of a flowing rope, or the flashing of a crystal which he throws down to earth (Schebesta, 1962:15, 16–17, 21, 24, 71–72). There is a hint in the literature, which is made explicit by the Batek Dek, that these mythological characters were the ones who established the rules of proper human behavior before they ascended to the heavens to enforce them. According to Schebesta, just before Ta Ped'n rose to heaven (apparently for the final time), he became very angry with men for marrying their close relatives (Schebesta, 1929:251).

The underground being who causes floods in conjunction with the thunderstorms is conceived of as a *naga,* a dragon or huge snake, by all the Malayan Negritos. In the myths of the western Negritos, this being is identified with one or more female mythological characters (Schebesta, 1962:28). Usually there are two earth-women, Manoij and Takel, who are "almost merged into one person" (Schebesta, 1962:14). Among the Lanoh, Manoij is regarded as the wife of Karei and Takel, at least by some informants, as the wife of Ta Ped'n (Schebesta, 1962:14). But the Kenta Bog'n say that Karei and Ta Ped'n have celestial wives, Jalan and Jamoi, and that Manoij and Takel are the grandmothers of the celestial husbands and wives, respectively (Schebesta, 1962:18). A number of other mythological figures occur occasionally in the stories in various relationships to the beings just mentioned, but the basic principles seem to be that there is a complementary opposition between the sky-world and underworld and that the mythical beings proliferate in sets of two.

The Batek Dek says that Gobar is really two Batek *hala,* an older brother called *Mawas* and a younger brother called *Nawas.* In most stories they are pictured as looking like Batek youths, but there is a small set of comical stories in which Mawas looks and acts like a gibbon, which is one meaning of the term *mawas* in Malay. After Mawas and Nawas ascended to the sky, they became Gobar who is pictured as being old above the waist, with a long beard, and young below the waist. I do not know whether this combined image is meant to express the conjunction of the older Mawas and the younger Nawas or to express a relationship, which is otherwise undeveloped, between Gobar and the moon in its waxing and waning phases (or the sun as it rises and falls). A Mendriq informant told Schebesta that Karei does not die, but "grows old and becomes young again, like the moon" (Schebesta, 1962:24).

According to Batek Dek tradition, Mawas and Nawas once lived on earth with their aunt *(ba?).* They led a Negrito-like existence, the men hunting with their blowpipes and the aunt digging wild tubers. Mawas and Nawas were the *hala?* who taught the ordinary people that they should no longer commit incest after the first few generations of human beings had reproduced in this way. One day the aunt dug up some earth and the two brothers packed it around their blowpipes. Then they climbed to the top of a tall tree and made balls of dirt which they shot into the air with their blowpipes. The earth formed a rock in the upper part of the heavens. The tree then grew until they reached the rock where they now stay. The aunt went into the ground and became the earth-snake *(naga)* who is called *grandmother* (Yak) by men. Mawas now sits in the eastern sky and Nawas in the west. They both make thunder by spinning tops (like the stone tops of the Kelantan Malays) which they made from some of the dirt they shot into the sky. The lightning is either the flashing of the breechcloth they use as the top string or the flash of the knives they wear in their belts. The thunder of the younger brother, in the west, is said to be slightly stronger than that of the older brother, and the former is said to be more refined and clever than the latter. Otherwise Mawas and Nawas are undifferentiated by the Batek Dek. The Yak-

*naga* is a single being in the Batek Dek scheme of things. She has an agreement with her two nephews that she will cause floods, by pushing water up from the underground sea, to help punish *lawac* transgressions.

The Batek Nong recognize two main celestial beings: Jawac and his younger brother Jawec. Although I did not get an explicit description of Jawec, Jawac is said to be covered with long hair, including a long mustache, and to look like a coconut monkey (*bawac;* Malay *berok*). This rhyming of the name of the being and that of the animal he resembles, like the Batek Dek use of a single name for both in the case of Mawas, seems intended to ensure that the name automatically evokes the proper mental image. Jawac is regarded as living among the clouds, and although meteorological phenomena are attributed to Ketok (the sky), in everyday usage, it is said that Jawac causes the rain and wind, by opening the clouds, and the thunder and lightning, by pulling a cord with a stone on the end (probably a top). Jawec, on the other hand, is said to live above the clouds on a large island in the sky which is covered with fruit and flowers, and it is his job to guard these and to drop flowers to the fruit trees on earth at the proper time. This island is also inhabited by man *cemroy,* fairylike beings which are also found in the cosmology of the western Negritos (called *Chinoi*) but not in that of the Batek or Mendriq of Kelantan. In addition to these celestial beings, the Batek Nong also believe that there is a *naga* under the earth who can cause a flood from below. The *naga* is regarded as female and is called *Yak,* grandmother, as is that of the Batek Dek. But the Batek Nong *naga* is considered to be the wife of Jawec, who is sometimes called Tak Jawec (Grandfather Jawec), or, by other informants, the wife of Jawac. Although the relationship between the earth and sky beings is different for the Batek Nong and the Batek Dek, the *naga* being the wife of the sky-beings instead of the aunt, the asymmetry of two sky-beings and one earth-being is the same. As with the Batek Dek, these three beings cooperate to punish the breaking of certain rules, but in the case of the Batek Nong, Jawec only reports transgressions to the *naga* and does not take an active part in causing the storm or flood.

Although I was able to collect several long stories from the Batek Nong, they explicitly denied that any of the characters in the stories should be identified with Jawac and Jawec. It was said that the heroes in the tales—Teng, Tak Ogn, Kelmay, and Bongsu or Mun—were like Malay (Moslem) *nabi,* prophets, and they have now withdrawn to distinct places and no longer play a part in everyday events. An earlier report, however, relates that Teng and Bonsu (Bongsu), two brothers, live above the seven layers of the sky and look after the fruits and flowers which eventually drop to earth; another being—Jawait (Jawac)—lives below the clouds and makes thunder (Evans, 1968:146). It may be that the infusion of the mythology with Moslem elements, which are very evident in the stories I collected, has led at least some of the Batek Nong to think of the stories in a different way, perhaps as analogous to the sacred texts of the Malays, and thus to separate those characters from the ones which are thought to operate in the ordinary world of the present. The replacement of two brothers, Teng and Bongsu, by a single personage, Jawec, obviously changes the structure of the pantheon, but it preserves the tendency for mythical beings to occur as pairs of siblings by making Jawec the brother of Jawac.

The blood sacrifice can be seen as having a moral connotation when it is considered in relation to the heroes who in a mythical frame of reference are described as causing the thunderstorms. At least in the Batek Dek case it is clear that the beings who laid down the proper rules of conduct are the same ones who are later identified with the storm. In all cases the principal supernatural beings have an agreement to watch for violations and inform each other of them and act together in punishing them. There is a feeling among the Batek that even though some innocent bystanders may be harmed by the storm and nonguilty persons may make the blood offering, it is the guilty person above all who will be punished and who should perform the rite. The Batek Nong say that when the *naga* dissolves the earth beneath a camp, the innocent persons will be able to run and save themselves, but the guilty one will not. The invocations made with the blood offering often disclaim guilt or proclaim that the debt is paid (Schebesta, 1962:78–86) as well as command the storm to stop or go away. While throwing the blood, the Batek Dek shout: "There; there is no offense because of me!" And alongside the naturalistic belief that the blood offered is put into the ripening fruit is a conviction among all the Negritos, that the blood is also a sign of the peoples' contrition and as such makes the deities happy and well disposed toward them. The Batek Nong emphasize and elaborate this side of the meaning exclusively. They no longer make the blood sacrifice at all, though they remember that they once did. Instead they sing for the deities when they have broken a dietary or mocking prohibition *(tala ɲ )* and offer a small colored mat (which the shaman holds up and blows, presumably to propel the shadow of the mat aloft) for incest or improper behavior among relatives *(cɔmam)*. The blood (when it was still used) and the mats are thought to be received by Jawac and passed on to Jawec who in turn sends them to the Yak-*naga*. They are taken as signs (Malay *tanda*) of the peoples' sacrifice, and they make the deities happy even though they do nothing with them.

## CONCLUSIONS

The evidence seems to support the hypothesis that the thunder god belief of the Malayan Negritos is formed of the conjunction of certain naturalistic and mythological ideas. The image or images of the supernatural beings are drawn from mythology, sometimes more than one set of myths, and their supposed powers and general patterns of behavior in the present-day world are derived from the properties of storms and floods as seen by the Negritos. Many of the apparent contradictions in the thunder god belief seem to result from the peoples' thinking of the deity partly in a naturalistic frame of reference and partly in a mythological one, sometimes switching back and forth even in a single conversation. For example, the Batek Dek say that Gobar is just the sky when it thunders and also that it (or he) looks like a gibbon, but this does not mean that they see a threatening sky as having the form of a gibbon. It is just that the gibbon character from the myths has become associated with that particular natural phenomenon, perhaps through an imagined resemblance between the cry of the gibbon and the roar of the thunder. Similarly, the conclusion drawn by Schebesta that the more people break the rules, the better will be the fruit harvest would not make sense to the Negritos because the two premises—that breaking rules calls for the offering of blood and that the transmission of blood contributes to the fruit crop—are derived from two logically distinct domains of thought. The moral connotation of the blood sacrifice is meaningful only in the mythological framework, whereas the abundance of fruit is normally thought about in terms of natural forces and cycles with which men merely realign themselves by throwing blood.

Even though all the Negrito groups seem to have well-developed sets of naturalistic and mythological conceptions, the various dialect groups differ as to which of the two contexts they normally use in thinking and talking about thunderstorms. The Batek Dek usually think of thunder as Gobar or as caused by Gobar, and they mention the mythical heroes Mawas and Nawas only in the context of storytelling sessions. The Batek Nong mention Ketok, the sky, and the mythical hero Jawac about equally when discussing thunder and its causation. But the western Negritos (Semang) apparently think and talk about thunder mainly in terms of the mythical hero or heroes which are thought to cause it. Because the Batek Nong have both types of conception in mind almost simultaneously, it is easy to lose sight of the broader pattern in which they are separate. Apparently this led Schebesta to believe that Ketok was a mythical being like Jawac and to arrive at the extraordinary conclusion that he was a being so vast that the sun and moon formed his eyes.

The basic mode of conjunction between the naturalistic and mythological conceptions of thunder is that the male celestial heroes are identified with the sky and the female heroes are identified with the underground sea. This produces some anomalies, however, because the sky and underground sea are seen as unitary whereas the mythical figures, especially the celestial ones, tend to proliferate in sets of two. Thus Mawas and Nawas together make Gobar; Jawac and Jawec are Ketok; and I suggest, Karei and Ta Ped'n also form a unit which is equivalent to the sky though this is not stressed by the Semang as much as by the eastern Negritos. Perhaps the less personified sky being of the Semang is the elusive Karpeg'n, ''the above,'' whom Schebesta eliminates from the pantheon for being insufficiently manlike. The unity of the pairs of sky heroes is emphasized, however, by all the Negrito groups. For the Semang this takes the form of an assertion, made by most groups, that Karei and Ta Ped'n are already the same being even though they are spoken of as separate in ordinary discourse.

Schebesta takes this as a justification for pushing Karei into the background, as a mere personification of thunder which has usurped the place of the thunder-making god Ta Ped'n, but ironically the unitary high god he seeks can be discerned, without downgrading either Karei or Ta Ped'n, in the sky itself, as the unification of the two mythical figures. The unity of the Mawas-Nawas and Jawac-Jawec pairs is clearly expressed by the rhyming of the names. This has the effect of calling to mind both halves of the pair whenever one of the members is mentioned.[3] The Batek Dek often try to find a name for a child which rhymes with that of the proper sex parent, probably for a similar reason.

The identification of the female myth heroes with the underground sea is not quite so complex because, except for the Semang earth-mothers, they have not proliferated into pairs or large sets. This does produce some complication of the relationship between the singular earth figure and the dual celestial ones. The Batek Nong informants disagree over whether the Yak-*naga* is the wife of Jawac or Jawec and sometimes will even speculate that she is the wife of both, even though this would be a serious breach of morals in their society. The Batek Dek resolve the problem by making the *naga* the aunt of the two brothers above, a proper if less symmetrical relationship.

Although in each case the celestial figures are identified with the sky, the division of labor in the performance of the activities attributed to the sky varies from group to group. Among the Batek Nong, one deity, Jawac, is supposed to be in charge of the weather, and the other, Jawec, is responsible for causing flowers and fruit to appear. Among the western Negritos it is usually Karei who causes thunderstorms and, at least among the Jahai, Ta Ped'n who causes the fruit to grow (Schebesta, 1962:15). Among the Batek Dek, however, both Mawas and Nawas cause thunder, though from different parts of the sky, and the fruit is said to be caused by *tahun,* the fruit season, which is not personified at all. The arbitrariness of the distribution of the supposed functions of the sky to the mythical figures of the various groups reaffirms the basic independence of the naturalistic and mythological sets of conceptions which are combined to produce the personification of natural forces among the Malayan Negritos.

## ACKNOWLEDGMENTS

I spent twelve months living with various Batek dialect groups between January 1971 and April 1973. I wish to thank the National Institute of Mental Health (U.S.A.) which supported this fieldwork with a predoctoral fellowship (No. 7 F01 MH 33054-01A2) and the Department of Aborigines of Malaysia *(Jabatan Hal Ehwal Orang Asli)* for their kind assistance and cooperation.

[3] I thank Jim Boon for first pointing this out to me.

# REFERENCES

Cooper, J. M. Andamanese-Semang-Eta cultural relations. *Primitive Man: Quarterly Bulletin of the Catholic Anthropological Conference,* 1940, *13,* 29–47.

Endicott, Kirk. *Batek Negrito economic and social organization.* Unpublished doctoral dissertation, Harvard University, 1974.

Evans, I. H. N. *Studies in religion, folk-lore and custom in British North Borneo and the Malay Peninsula.* Cambridge: Cambridge University Press, 1923.

Evans, I. H. N. *Papers on the ethnology and archaeology of the Malay Peninsula.* Cambridge: Cambridge University Press, 1927.

Evans, I. H. N. *The Negritos of Malaya.* London: Frank Cass and Co., 1968. (Originally published, 1937.)

Freeman, Derek. Thunder, blood, and the nicknaming of God's creatures. *Psychoanalytic Quarterly,* 1968, *37,* 353–359

Garvan, J. M. *The Negritos of the Philippines.* (Hermann Huchegger, Ed.) Vienna: Verlag Ferdinand Berger, 1964.

Needham, Rodney. Blood, thunder, and mockery of animals. *Sociologus,* 1964, *14,* 136–149.

Schebesta, Paul. *Among the forest dwarfs of Malaya.* (Arthur Chambers, trans.) London: Hutchinson and Co., 1929.

Schebesta, Paul. *Die Negrito Asiens: Religion und Mythologie.* (Frieda Schütze, trans.) New Haven: Human Relations Area Files, 1962. (Originally published, Studia Instituti Anthropos, *13,* 1957.)

Skeat, W. W., and Charles O. Blagden. *Pagan races of the Malay Peninsula,* 11. New York: Barnes and Noble, Inc., 1966. (Originally published, 1906.)

Winstedt, Sir Richard. *An unabridged Malay-English dictionary* (6th ed.). Kuala Lumpur: Merican and Sons, 1965.

# chapter three

# Orality as a Pattern of Symbolism in Malay Psychiatry

Ronald Provencher

Northern Illinois University

## INTRODUCTION

A quarter of a century ago, Claude Lévi-Strauss noted that " . . . the world of symbolism is infinitely varied in content, but always limited in its laws" (1963:203). As examples of his meaning, he cited many languages but few laws of structural linguistics, many myths but few types of myths. And in a brilliant display of his intuitive talent for structural analysis, he showed that psychoanalytic therapy is but a modern European instance of a broader type of phenomenon that includes shamanistic curing. The basis of this type of therapy is that certain kinds of psychopathological disturbances are accessible only through the language of symbols. Ordinary speech, no matter how symbolic it may be, cannot penetrate beyond the conscious level. The effectiveness of psychoanalytic and shamanistic symbols consists of stimulating an organic transformation or reorganization by inducing the patient intensively to live out a myth whose structure analogizes organic and psychological functioning. Abreaction, or insights, whereby unstructured traumatic experience is organized formally and symbolically, is the key to this process. Lévi-Strauss explains that the difference between psychoanalysis and other forms of shamanistic curing is that in psychoanalysis the patient rather than the physician presents the symbolic myth and the physician rather than the patient relates the myth to the traumatic experience of the patient (1963:198–204).

The folk psychiatry of Malays does not rest easily at either pole of this dichotomy. As in nonpsychoanalytic instances of shamanistic curing, the curer presents and manipulates a system of signs and symbols. But the patient, members of the patient's family, the curer's helper, and other witnesses of the curing ritual often participate in interpreting signs and in selecting an appropriate organizing myth. Moreover, any or all of them may participate in relating the myth to the traumatic experience of the patient (Firth, 1967). This minor cavil not only points out that it is unnecessary to oppose psychoanalysis to all other systems of shamanistic curing, but it also suggests the need for more caution in positing broad structural similarities between symbolic systems than is implied by the notion of a limited number of laws.

The "limited laws of symbolism" are themselves myths that organize the chaotic experience of ethnographic detail which is the total of the contents of the many different systems of symbolism. Laws derived from psychotherapeutic systems of symbols may be the most myth-like of all because their formulation and confirmation present anthropologists with opportunities for personal therapy. For example, I would feel more at ease about describing orality as a pattern of symbolism in Malay psychiatry if my own personality were more anal-compulsive and less orally fixated. Also, I am very much aware of the Western bias of social scientific theories of personality disorders. My use of the term *orality* is not intended to convey an image of arrested personality development. Rather, I view orality as a pattern of symbolism that is part of interrelated sets of customs, perceptions, and attitudes of many members of Malay society. Orality in this sense is a normal aspect of many mature Malay personalities and as such differs from orality in Western personalities.

## LIBIDO AND FOOD

During abreaction or while acquiring insight, a patient in psychoanalysis learns to recognize and accept his primary desires, desires that cause symptoms if repressed from conscious awareness. Malay patients and curers do not openly acknowledge repressed libido as a cause of illness. Yet behavioral routines of Malay patients, such as *latah, lupa,* and *mulut kasar,* possibly are structurally parallel to recognizing and accepting repressed libido. A spirit, usually directed by a sorcerer employed by an envious acquaintance or relative, possesses the body of its victim and initiates one of several stereotyped performances which includes rude statements, obscene gestures, and occasionally requests for a favorite food. Forced by a curer *(bomoh)* to confess the identity of its master, allowed to behave improperly, and given food, it leaves the body of its victim.

Malays seem to recognize the possibilities of genital libido through their interest in love magic and in their recognition of frustrated love as a common motive for sorcery. *Playboy* magazine sells well. Evidence of repressed sexual impulses is mixed. Although Murphy (1959) reports that psychological examinations of young adults revealed very little evidence that their sexual impulses were repressed, cultural restraints on sexual behavior are fairly strong. A woman ought to be a virgin at the timé of her first marriage. An unrelated man and woman who remain in the same room together without witnesses are guilty of the sin of *khalwat* ("close proximity"). And heterosexual handholding in public was frowned upon until very recently. But prostitution flourishes, and married women are expected to have affairs.

Repression of nongenital libido may be very important in Malay society. Malays disapprove of persons who do not control their everyday aggressive impulses. Moreover, they shun victims and aggressors alike. They rarely have open arguments or quarrels. Usually, they do not spank children. Good parents ignore recalcitrant children, heaping favors and attention on the more obedient. Children learn to conceal aggression. Secretly, they may pinch their younger siblings but they pretend great affection. Aggressiveness between strangers takes abstruse forms, such as claiming a higher status than one is entitled to. The rare displays of physical aggression usually become insanely intense. A spanking becomes a thorough beating, a quarrel becomes manslaughter, and a riot, a massacre. Malays do not consider persons who lose their tempers in very thorough fashion to be entirely accountable for their actions. Perhaps it is bare recognition that psychical energy, however repressed, finds release.

Something like an oral fixation of libido may be represented in Malay preoccupation with food. Their cuisine includes a wide variety of foods. They eat often—breakfast, a large dinner, supper, and hearty snacks between meals. Prepared food can be bought in most Malay settlements. Even rural villages have eating shops, and vendors sell snacks in urban communities. Prepared food of some sort is more or less continuously available for snacks in private kitchens. At least that is the ideal. One must offer something to any visitor who enters the house and the visitor must consume some of it. A proper host joins his guest. Regular exchange of prepared food between households signifies close friendship and allows good cooks opportunities to display their skills. Malays traveling by automobile stop frequently at roadside eating shops. And finally, of course, almost all major ceremonies *(khenduri)* require the consumption of large quantities of food. It is the intensity, the thoroughness, of Malay interest in food that attracts notice, just as Malays notice the intensity of Western interest in sex.

The joys of eating are not without restraint. As Muslims, Malays eat neither pork nor meat from animals that have been improperly slaughtered. Very few of them drink alcoholic liquor. Many of them fear that packaged foods are not *halal* ("kosher") and prefer packaged foods that have halal labels. In 1965, for example, a rumor spread throughout West Malaysia that *Aji-no-moto* brand monosodium glutamate, a common ingredient of Malay cooking, was made from the skin and bones of animal carcasses. The company applied for and (after inspection of its manufacturing procedure) received a "halal certificate" from the Religious Department of the State of Selangor, much to the relief of many Malay housewives. Also, many Malays who live in town and own refrigerators do not buy frozen food available at fairly reasonable prices, because they fear it has been stored with foods that are not halal. This concern over the pollution of food is especially great among Malays who have recently moved to urban areas, because of the closer proximity of other ethnic groups who prepare and consume impure food and drink.

Other restrictions on diet are not specifically Islamic. Some curers and some holy men *(wa.i)* are vegetarians and themselves prepare all food they consume. It is said that such diets confer special health, magical, and spiritual benefits. Some of their restrictions appear to be derived from Hindu and Buddhist attitudes that were current in Malay culture during pre-Islamic times. Also, many women follow a very restrictive *post partum* diet which appears to be a very ancient part of Malay culture, and small children are kept from eating too much "cool" *(sejuk)* food. Like people of Latin America, the Mediterranean lands, the Middle East, and India, Malays believe that some foods are cool and others are "hot" *(panas)*. Small children are especially susceptible to illnesses caused by eating too much cool food, but everyone must eat hot and cool foods in balanced proportions to avoid illness.

Behavior during Ramadan *(bulan puasa),* the fasting month, further illustrates Malay attitudes about food. Breaking the fast during the day is permissible as long as it is not broken in public. Malays who break the fast in public may be arrested. The fast and other rules about food are important symbols of Malay social identity. Another important point about the fast is that it provokes very deep emotional cravings for food and drink. *Maghrib,* the prayer at sundown, marks the end of the daily fast during Ramadan and it is celebrated intensely with cold drinks, ices, and special sweets. Malays stay up at night during Ramadan, eating the most exotic foods they can afford.

## ANXIETY AND SOCIAL RANK

Malays begin developing anxieties about food at an early age. Commonly, an infant nurses in supine position, with its mother leaning over its body. An infant spends many hours in its very comfortably padded miniature hammock *(ayunan)* swayed rythmically back and forth by attentive adult relatives and neighbors. As it grows older, the infant is held and amused by these same adults who literally adore it. The mother gradually teaches the infant to eat solid foods, often in the same supine position in which it nurses, sometimes causing it to choke. Although introduced early, solid food does not gradually replace the mother's milk. It is in addition to breast feeding. Weaning is usually delayed as long as possible; often it is begun several times before it is finally accomplished. The trauma of it is drawn out painfully. When weaned, a younger sibling is likely to replace the child at its mother's breast. The great affection of adult relatives and neighbors that once was his as the youngest child is preempted, too.

At this time, when his diet has just changed entirely to solid food and he has been deprived of affection, an older sibling, perhaps only five or six years older, may be responsible for feeding him at least part of the time.[1] To a large extent, he is cast into the care of his older siblings, who may resent the brief period when he replaced them in the affection of adults and who may resent the work he now causes them. When adults are not nearby, the older children ignore his cries and even tease him, by withholding food or by pinching.

As the child learns to feed himself, he is taught that his right hand is for eating and his left is for cleaning his anus. Deceptively, his toilet training appears to be extremely casual. As he becomes three or four years old, he imitates his siblings relieving themselves at a ditch or in the toilet. Older children tease him when he has accidents and when he goes naked, saying "don't you know shame?" *(tak tahu malu)*. He learns the disadvantages of junior rank as he receives his lessons in toilet training and shame.

Girls, from the age of five years, begin gradually to enter the adult world through service to their households. They learn to cook and they participate more and more in preparations for feasts. But formally they participate much less than males in feasts. Female pubescence is marked by no particular rite. A girl may demonstrate her ability to read the Koran at this time, but usually it is delayed until just before her marriage, and the rite is overwhelmed and made almost insignificant by the great feasts of marriage. Menstruation relates to food through restriction of cooking and food handling on days of menstrual flow and through the custom of not fasting on days of menstrual flow during Ramadan. The days of fast lost by a menstruating woman must be made up subsequently during a specially designated time.

Often, boys become increasingly alienated from their households after having lost position as the youngest child. For a brief period in early adolescence, just after they have been circumcised, they may receive and give great affection to other members of their households. They look forward to circumcision and the attention they receive at that time. Afterwards they begin to participate formally in ritual feasts *(khenduri)* where food and social rank are elaborately displayed.

In sum, toilet training and pubescence are dealt with in a context of deep interest in the symbolic relationships between food and social courtesy. Aspects of socialization and physical maturation that could focus on anal and genital gratification or trauma are modified to fit within the dominant pattern of oral symbolism. Some individuals are more deeply affected than others. If the oldest sibling is a male, for example, he may be required for a time to fulfill some of the service obligations to the household usually fulfilled by girls, in addition to his formal ritual obligations as a male. If the youngest sibling is a female, she may never become involved in service to the household and as a female she will have very few formal ritual obligations. Incidentally, these social types—eldest sib-

---

[1]Professor Charlotte Otten pointed out to me that sudden weaning can cause severe digestive disturbances. This would add to the psychological trauma of weaning suddenly several times.

ling who is male and youngest sibling who is female, those who participate most and least in this pattern of symbolism—are most often affected by psychological and psychosomatic disorders.[2]

Feasts are the arenas in which symbolic relationships between food and society are acted out most explicitly. Food is elaborately displayed. So is social rank. Clothing, titles, pronouns, greeting gestures, seating hierarchies, and sitting postures signify a wide variety of differences in social rank that are much less noticeable in other settings and entirely absent from the kitchen where the family eats simpler meals. As one junior in rank, the adolescent must perform the most complex and uncomfortable acts of courtesy. He sees the old men, the objects of courtesy, actually relax and enjoy the feast.

The feasts, by their richness and their frequency, establish and validate the social rank of the household that sponsors them. Poor households borrow in order to give the minimal variety of feasts commemorating birth, adolescence, marriage, and the dead. They invite only their closest relatives and neighbors. Rich households give the basic feasts and more—to celebrate success, recovery from illness, or the beginning or end of a journey. They serve a more expensive variety of food and invite more guests. To do less would undermine their social rank, invite criticism, and perhaps make them more subject to a charge of sorcery. Giving too many rich feasts can have the same effects. One must give feasts and attend feasts, balancing give and take, advancing slowly.

Feasts are more richly furnished and more frequent in urban communities than in rural villages. The fear of sorcery is greater, too. To accept food or drink prepared by another is truly an act of faith. Most urban Malays who become ill suspect that they have been poisoned. Having avoided food and drink from the households of known sorcerers, they rarely suspect a particular person at first.

Sorcerers poison food with actual substances *(racun)* and through word charms *(santau)*. At a stranger's house one can test food or drink that is offered in hospitality. If common sense suggests that it ought to be warm to touch, but is cool, or vice versa, the food or drink may be poisoned. One says a word charm silently to combat the effects of the suspected poison, then one eats and drinks as a guest should. When vomiting *(muntah)*, diarrhoea *(cirit)*, hemorrhage *(cucor)*, stomachache *(sakit perut)*, hoarseness *(parau)*, headache *(sakit kepala)*, fever *(sakit panas* or *demam)*, dizziness *(pusing kepala)*, or insanity of some sort *(gila)* strikes, the victim or one of his relatives seeks a cure. If sorcery is not suspected, the hot-cool balance of the diet may be shifted slightly, a traditional herbal remedy may be taken, a patent medicine may be bought and consumed, or the patient may be taken to a clinic and treated by a nurse or physician trained in Western medicine. Many visits to the clinics are provoked because the government and most firms require their employees to show evidence of going to a modern clinic or hospital in order to get sick leave. Some attendants at clinics do

---

[2]The overrepresentation of eldest male siblings and youngest female siblings in psychiatric wards is pointed out in Hartog (1972a). My field studies of morbidity in 1971–72 confirm this.

a brisk business selling signed appointment slips to Malays who need sick leave but who are unwilling to be treated by Western methods. In any case, illnesses that do not respond quickly to other forms of treatment are known to be caused by sorcery, and a traditional curer will be sought. If the first one fails, another will be sought, and so on. Illnesses that do not respond to treatment at a clinic or hospital are very likely psychosomatic or related in some way to anxiety, depression, or some other mental condition. Western-trained psychiatrists are in short supply, and their methods of treatment do not appear to help Malays very effectively.[3]

## THE CURE

Many successful curers *(bomoh)* work in pairs with one acting as an assistant. This is particularly the case if trance is part of the curing ritual, but it is often true even when trance is not used.

During the first visit, the helper takes a personal history statement from the patient or from a relative or friend in one area while the curer prepares for the ritual. It is simple—incense, chants, and a cursory physical examination of the patient, followed by a divining ritual to determine whether the case can be cured. Sometimes divination is delayed until the second visit. Usually, common limes *(limau nipis)* are blessed and then the rind at each end is sliced off and allowed to fall to the floor or into a bowl of water. The number of limes varies. Three, five, seven, and nine are common numbers. Pieces that are sliced off land fruit-side or peel-side down, and the proportion of such casts as well as their sequence and the pattern in which they land determine whether or not the case can be cured, whether it will be easy or difficult, and what the possible causes may be. The limes themselves are blessed and given to the patient so that they may be added to his bath water. He is given instructions for bathing, praying, and eating. Other rites of divination may be employed. An egg, for example, is made to spin by the touch of a knife point at its midline and the direction of the spin determines answers to questions put to the egg.

Once a case is accepted, other kinds of rituals ensue. They appear to be diagnoses as well as cures. Several of the more common types are mentioned here.

A peeled lime is placed in the patient's mouth. The curer rubs the patient's body, stroking towards the lime. After twenty minutes or so of rubbing, the lime is removed from the patient's mouth. The surface of the lime appears to be covered with rust *(tahi besi)* and small splinters. All the witnesses to this miracle speculate about the manner in which the substances entered the patient's body and they wonder who could be responsible.

In another kind of seance, the *bomoh* paints the patient with a paste of rice

---

[3]The short supply of Western-trained psychiatrists is reported by Hartog (1972b). Hartog, however, fails utterly to comprehend the importance of Western psychiatry and the importance of native practitioners as a source of mental health care for Malays.

flour and then rubs it off with a fresh egg. The rubbing is toward the abdomen from the limbs and then toward the throat of the patient. Finally, the uncooked egg is cracked open and its contents emptied into a bowl so that everyone can examine the bits of dirt, rust, and the rusty needles that appear within the white and yolk of the egg.

The *bomoh* may substitute a ball of dough for the egg and similarly extract bits of dirt from the body of the patient. The ball of dough, made of rice flour and egg whites, is rolled over the surface of the skin of the patient and periodically broken apart and examined. Small red hairs, not bits of rust or needles, are extracted in this fashion and are thought to be as deadly.

The immature seed pod of the betel nut tree *(pinang)* is used in similar fashion for extracting bits of dirt from the bodies of patients. The pod is swept across the body of the patient repeatedly. Then the pod is opened and the contents examined by all witnesses.

The bits of dirt are not only seen as causes of illness, they are carefully examined and their characteristics discussed in an effort to understand their meaning and thus further diagnosis of the case. Imaginations are given free rein. The *bomoh,* patient, and witnesses together construct a suitable diagnostic myth that arranges the traumatic experiences of the patient so that they may be comprehended and overcome.

None of the foregoing kinds of seances requires the *bomoh* to enter a state of trance. Others do. The *bomoh*'s preparations for a trance usually include a formal rehearsal of Islamic prayers, complete with prayer rug and appropriate attire. Immediately after prayer, the *bomoh* begins to rock back and forth or to turn the head from side to side rhythmically until there is a sudden series of muscle spasms and loss of consciousness. After the muscle spasms begin but before losing consciousness, the *bomoh* vomits a large volume of mud, blood, pieces of bone, and odd artifacts into a bowl held by the helper. As the *bomoh* loses consciousness, a live white rooster is placed under the right arm as a gift to the tiger spirit that has briefly possessed the body of the *bomoh* in order to explore the spirit realm of paths frequented by the patient and there to devour all the magical objects that were harming the patient. Slowly the *bomoh* regains consciousness and everybody present begins to inspect the vomit.

In other trance seances the possessed *bomoh* sucks dirty blood from the body of the patient or travels through the spirit world and reports seeing the patient's food being poisoned.

In each seance, the *bomoh* chants a sequence of names of powerful beings, beginning with Allah and ending with an ordinary household spirit. Also, the patient must pay cash at the end of some performances. Amounts vary quite a bit, but they are heavy with magical numbers and can be paid only in particular combinations of different denominations of money. Each denomination is wrapped in a different-color cloth. The colors symbolize different ranks. After that the patient may be instructed to drink the glass of *ayer tawar* (fresh water) that was poured at the beginning of the performance.

# INTERPRETATIONS

These are thrilling performances. After witnessing them, patients tend to "open up" in their talks with the *bomohs* and their assistants, gossiping about their friends and relatives, confiding their worst suspicions, recounting some of their most traumatic social experiences. The symbolism that seems most effective in forcing remembrances of traumatic social experiences to the surface of consciousness is that which refers to contaminated food. Contaminated food may symbolize social trauma in general because large ritual feasts are the occasions when the possibilities of consuming contaminated food are greatest and the large ritual feasts are the most important occasions for playing out the elaborate games of social rank which comprise Malay courtesy. This is all the more significant because systems of courtesy rather than group structures are the basic means by which Malay society is organized. Also, the evidences of contaminated food are very generalized signs which can be easily matched with the meanings of specific experiences. A more specific system of coordinating signs and meanings would impede the process of abreaction. Perhaps this helps explain Malay use of common foods (rice, eggs, limes, water, coconut oil) in their psychotherapeutic rites. Otherwise they have a fairly exotic pharmacology.

Problems of social rank are symbolized in many other ways during curing rituals. The spirits who possess the *bomoh* are always royal in rank. This fact forces patients and witnesses to pay strict attention to matters of courtesy, and it allows the *bomoh* the privilege of being direct and rude. When I questioned patients, they seemed to have some conventional understanding of the symbolism in the performances. The color of the payment cloths signifies social ranks (the colors of Indian castes), as do the chanted hierarchies of greater and lesser spirits. The *ayer tawar* (fresh water) has a connotation that plays on two expansions of the root word *tawar* ("tasteless"): (1) *tawar menawar* ("to bargain back and forth"), and (2) *penawaran* ("neutralizer of poison"). These relate to the reciprocity of feast giving and the fear of contaminated food.

The dirtied lime and egg, the defiled rich dough and seed pod, and the vomit and dirty blood were all recognized as signs of polluted food. *Bomohs* and patients identified the dirt on the lime and in the egg and seed pod as *tahi besi* ("excrement of iron" or rust). *Tahi* means "excrement," but seemingly with little emotional connotation since drifting clouds are "excrement of the wind," meteorites are "excrement of the stars," freckles are "excrement of flies," earwax is "excrement of the ear," and sawdust is "excrement of the saw." Probably it is *besi* ("iron") that bears the heaviest symbolic load. Perhaps *iron* refers to aggression so that *tahi besi* symbolizes the "leavings of aggression." At any rate, patients felt that the dirtied lime and egg might indicate the mixing of feces with food. But when asked directly if they suspected someone of putting feces in their food, the answer was, "no, it is just a sign of something bad." It may symbolize inhibitions concerning food and social relations in general, the trauma of learning the difference between one's right (eating) and left (wiping) hands. The latter trauma may be further symbolized in the fact that tiger spirits and weretigers have right forelegs that are exceptionally small.

Other symbolizations that we as Westerners may see include: (1) the peeled lime (which is ''cool'') in the patient's mouth suggests sucking at the breast; (2) the egg (which is ''hot'') suggests childhood or sex. Cool probably symbolizes giving and hot probably symbolizes taking.[4] I do not know whether Malays recognize these symbolizations, but if they do, even subconsciously, repressed and disorganized memories might flow more easily into consciousness and yield to organizing myth that is developed by participants in the diagnostic curing ritual.

Even the spirit entities that carry out the evil of sorcerers have what appear to be oral attributes. *Pelesit, polong,* and *pontianak* are blood suckers. The pelesit, a sort of helper of the *polong,* is conceived of as a locust/mantis vampire. Its description fits that of a rather chubby kind of mantis that sucks the life fluids from various sorts of insects and butterflies. The polong is a mannequin child. It and the pelesit are sometimes said to be *manufactured* by sorcerers from the tongues of dead infants who were the first children of first children—ones whose stored trauma of weaning and whose stored interest in matters of social rank would be greatest. I think it may be important that Malays sometimes equate blood with soul substance *(semangat)* and that the natural counterpart of the pelesit preys on butterflies which are symbolically equated with the conception of individual souls.

Finally, of course, Malay concerns with particles and substances intruding into their bodies appear to resemble classic Western instances of introjection, in which orally oriented persons are concerned with the distinction between their own person and the external world that they are busy consuming. Perhaps this is related to Malay cosmological concerns about distinctions between in and out and humanity and nature.

The original title of this paper was ''Eating symbols and having them, too.'' It would have been a misleading title. Malays do not really eat symbols. But if they could they would and they would have them, too.

## ACKNOWLEDGMENTS

I wish to acknowledge support from the Foreign Area Fellowship Program for research in Malaysia during 1964–65; and from the George Williams Hooper Foundation for Tropical Medicine of San Francisco, and the Institute for Medical Research in Kuala Lumpur for their support of research in Malaysia and Indonesia during 1971–72.

[4]Ingham (1970) presents an excellent discussion of similar symbolic relations among cool, giving, and female, on the one hand, and hot, taking, and male, on the other, in Mexican culture.

# REFERENCES

Firth, Raymond. Ritual and drama in Malay spirit mediumship. *Comparative Studies in Society and History,* 1967, *10*, 190–207.

Hartog, Joseph. Sibling rank of Malay psychiatric patients and juvenile delinquents. *Southeast Asian Journal of Tropical Medicine and Public Health, 1972a, 3*, 124–137.

Hartog, Joseph. The intervention system for mental and social deviants in Malaysia. *Social Science and Medicine,* 1972b, *6*, 211–220.

Ingham, J. M. On Mexican folk medicine. *American Anthropologist,* 1970, *72*, 176–187.

Lévi-Strauss, Claude. The effectiveness of symbols. *Structural anthropology.* (C. Jacobson and B. Schoepf, trans.) New York: Basic Books, 1963.

Murphy, H. B. M. Culture and mental disorder in Singapore. In M. K. Opler (Ed.). *Culture and mental health: cross-cultural studies.* New York: Macmillan, 1959.

chapter four

# Where Have All
# the Rituals Gone ?
# Ritual Presence among
# the Ranau Dusun
# of Sabah, Malaysia

Robert Harrison

University of Wisconsin at Milwaukee

## INTRODUCTION

All societies turn some events, rather than other events, into symbols, create
ritual dramas and develop mannered behaviors which act as markers of social
meaning. As Mary Douglas states: "There is no person whose life does not need
to unfold in a coherent symbolic system. . . . Symbolic boundaries are necessary
even for the private organizing of experience" (1973:72–73). These symbols,
rituals, and manners provide for the unfolding person an important means of
experiencing the groups of which he is a part in more than mundane terms. Taken
together they constitute an expressive system—almost another language—of the
culture. The repetitive and often cyclical nature of these social events also provides the investigator with the means of coming to understanding something of the
culture of a group whose experience is, or was, foreign to his own unfolding.

As with all tools of social investigation, such symbols and rituals are as
likely to mislead as to clarify when they are viewed apart from the context in
which they were presented and when their place in the society's cultural realm
has not been properly ascertained. Rituals reported out of context often appear to
involve more high drama than the participants themselves may perceive in the
situation. It is clear, too, that there has been a great deal of variation in the degree
to which societies have symbolically used and ritually incorporated their group
experiences.

This variation in the intensity of ritual incorporation and performance has
often been used as a measure of a society's concern for the sacred, as against the

55

profane. Such a measure, however, is tautological, in that the presence of ritual is thought to explain the degree of sacredness as well as vice versa. It is likely, as Douglas points out (1973:34–39), that there are a number of societies today whose concern for the sacred, though intense, may find little evidence in the creation and performance of dramatic ritual. Equally likely are societies in which rituals are relatively pervasive, though few of the rituals find dramatic expression. A society without high ritual is not necessarily a more secular society than one with high ritual.

Part of the reason for the association of ritual with religiosity and its lack with secularity is that much of the work on the symbolic organization of society and its relation to ritual has concentrated on those societies in which the relation between ritual and religiosity is most evident. The literature of the field is therefore skewed in favor of such assumptions. For instance, with respect to Southeast Asia much of the literature consists of studies of Balinese, Javanese, Malay, and Thai material. There is much less material on those societies which have a more muted ritual presence. Yet, Southeast Asia is occupied by hundreds of social groups of all degrees of complexity.

This concentration on systems which exhibit the most dramatic panoply of ritual symbols is natural; there is a tendency in all fields of social investigation to mine the richest ores first. And, perhaps it is fortunate that this has been true because many of these societies may undergo such rapid transformations within the next few decades that much of this rich material might be lost to us forever.

Yet this procedure does create some anomalies of method and interpretation. It permits the expectation, for instance, that all societies are as rich in such behavior as those emphasized in the studies. This is analogous to the assumption, common among anthropologists not too many years ago, that the basic structure of all societies would prove to be unilineal. This belief arose, largely because most of the societies then studied were societies which exhibited one form or another of the expected unilineal structure. Aberrant cases were interpreted to fit the norm by claiming that either they had experienced unilineal structure in the past and had undergone radical change or that in their present condition they were somewhat pathological.

Societies in which the ritual presence is below expectation may lead to the interpretation that the society has suffered heavy acculturative influences. This, of course, does not constitute an explanation. Alternatively, one might conclude that the reporter simply was not astute enough, nor with the group long enough, to ferret out the rituals that our expectations lead us to demand as present. Fortunately we have the reports of such sensitive investigators as Fredrik Barth expressing his concern for the evidenced lack of ritual among the Basseri of Persia:

> The Basseri show a poverty of ritual activities which is quite striking in the field situation; what they have of ceremonies, avoidance customs and beliefs seem to influence or be expressed in very few of their actions. What is more, the different

elements of ritual do not seem closely connected or interrelated in a wider system of meanings; they give the impression of occurring without reference to each other or to important features of the social structure. . . . (Douglas, 1973:37–38)

There is a tendency to assume that those societies whose religious demeanor is more muted lack something that their more dramatic neighbors possess. Whether this is true must be a matter of demonstration, rather than the product of superficial comparison. Indeed, it may be possible to interpret the situation in quite the reverse manner and equally superficially. If we remember that high religious symbolism and ritual, manners, and controlled behavior are, among other things, an investment in social order, it may well be possible to ask why some societies must make a higher symbolic investment in maintaining social order than others do. What, in this case, do the less ritually oriented societies possess that these others do not? What allows the societies with a more muted ritual presence to maintain order and continuity at a lower cost than seems to be the case for such groups as the popularly described Balinese and Javanese?

It is in part the purpose of this paper to examine this question in the context of the ritual behavior of the Ranau Dusun of Sabah, Malaysia.

## THE RANAU DUSUN

The Ranau Dusun of the northern interior of Sabah, Malaysia, are an example of a social group that has maintained a low investment in overt ritual display, yet it is a group of people who are far from secular in their attitudes. As of 1964, the Ranau Dusun constituted a population of about 21,500 persons, out of a total of 22,000 persons, living within the Ranau District. Generally the administrative district encompasses an area of some 1,500 square miles of territory whose physical, geographic, and cultural center is located in the Ranau Valley, an area of some 12 square miles whose major indigenous occupation is wet rice cultivation. It is this valley which gives the district its name and gives some identity to the Dusun who live within the district boundaries; hence the Ranau Dusun.

From this valley center the Dusun occupy the entire district engaging in swidden rice cultivation in those areas removed from the wet rice plain and apart from the areas close upon the major trail junctions leading to the west coast. On and near these junctions the major activity is cash crop production of tobacco, cabbage, and sometimes tomatoes. It is possible to grow these products as Ranau is generally high country. The lowest point in the district is the wet rice valley which is 1,500 feet above sea level. Toward this central valley the hill systems, such as the Crocker Range, the Trus Madi Range, and the Labuk Highlands, converge from all directions. As an indication of just how rugged the area is, 79 percent of all land, planimetrically, is over 25 degrees of slope. These hills have the effect of reducing communication and interaction and have isolated segments of the population. Equally, they have buffered the interior Dusun peoples from incursions of peoples from the coast, namely, the Bajau and Illanun. Though the district is sparsely populated, it is more or less evenly occupied. Except for the area in, and immediately adjacent to, the Ranau Valley and at the junction of trails leading to the west coast, Ranau District has a density of about eight persons per square mile.

The highest point near the district is Mount Kinabalu, 17 miles northwest of the Ranau Valley, which stands some 14,450 feet above sea level. It is the highest peak in the entire Malay Archipelago. As might be expected, Mount Kinabalu is of special significance to almost every group living in sight of the peak. For the Ranau Dusun it is the final resting place of the spirit of the person.

## ETHNIC DIFFERENTIATION

Ethnic differences within the area of the Ranau Dusun are gradual and indistinct. Those living in the interior who would be in regular contact with the Dusun are for the most part themselves Dusun. There are no linguistic and cultural differences so great that most of the peoples cannot be seen as one general *bangsa* ("class"), although there are some divisions largely the result of time and place. All the peoples beyond the district administration's immediate boundaries are Dusun peoples as well. Generally, there is close affiliation and tolerance for those recognized as members of the largest possible social aggregation: Dusun. Within the district the Dusun peoples consider the term *Ranau Dusun* an accurate assessment of their ethnic affiliation and use the term to describe themselves categorically to outsiders.

The two major incursions into Ranau Dusun life were the coming of the British Chartered Company, which after the Second World War became the Crown Colony, and the Japanese occupation during the Second World War. The Chartered Company made the wet rice valley the center of trade, exchange, and administrative control. The Japanese occupation effectively continued this practice, calling upon even further reserves of subsistence goods from the widely scattered swidden communities. The later British colonialism, after the Second World War, continued the practice of centralizing the administration in the Ranau Valley, adding to the list of government services available in the area a school, an aid station, postal service, an airport, and increased responsibilities within the district office itself. The valley became more intensely the center of economic and social exchange.

Undoubtedly, had it not been for the period of European and Japanese occupation and the provision of an alien though highly rational system of administration, the drift of Ranau Dusun culture would have been much more centrifugal then centripetal. The administration and the centrality of the wet rice valley and the inducements offered in the form of external economic goods must have counterbalanced the tendency toward drift which could so easily have taken place in such rough terrain.

Though the Ranau Dusun live in isolated groups and practice several different forms of cultivation—swidden rice, wet rice, and cash cropping—which might lead to a certain social and economic differentiation, the major fact is that, from their point of view, the cultural landscape is filled more with persons like themselves than persons who are different. For any Ranau Dusun, most of the world is filled with persons very much like himself in any direction for about as far as any one of them might care to or need to travel. And though there is awareness of the presence of Europeans, Bajaus, Illanun, Ibans, etc., these others do not occur in sufficient numbers nor do they have sufficient effect radically to alter the ethnic landscape on which the Ranau Dusun conduct their lives.

## RITUAL PRESENCE AND RELIGION

As the purpose of this paper is to examine the low profile the Ranau Dusun maintain in relation to ritual drama, it would probably be well, at this point, to offer evidence of low ritual profile. And before doing this, it is essential to give an indication of the sacredness of the world which the Ranau Dusun inhabit.

Generally, as mentioned before, the analysis of societies with respect to ritual events is in terms of a two-valued logic. Either societies are secular or they are religious. If they are religious, they show a profusion of religious symbolism and dramaturgic events, and perhaps, the equivalent of a high mass which acts as a central, unifying, and often explanatory ritual for the society as a whole. If there is little evidence of this, such a society is by definition secular.

Unfortunately the Ranau Dusun do not fit neatly into this two-valued logic. With respect to ritual, Barth's statement concerning the Basseri accurately reflects the situation of the Ranau Dusun. The Ranau Dusun appear to have few rituals. Yet they are by no means a secular society.

Perhaps a more crucial test than the presence of ritual to ascertain the degree to which a society accepts the presence of the sacred is the mode in which explanations of events are couched and the determination of what ultimately initiates action in the world. Among the Ranau Dusun all events, even those recognized as mundane, ultimately have sacred causes.

For example, the Ranau Dusun, at least those in the wet rice valley, know through the medical aid station about the notion of disease, germs, and even vitamins. Yet disease and health are but outward evidence of one's spiritual state, and are at best efficient causes. If a person dies of malaria, and the diagnosis is certifiable, malaria is only the way he died, not the ultimate cause. The reason for such a death may have been that the person committed some sacred or social delict. Equally quite by chance some spirit may just have taken his final soul or souls. No birth, death, movement of the stars, change of days or seasons, act of beast or man falls outside the sphere of sacred explanation.

This creates a religious milieu, or medium, within which each person lives and acts. This milieu is capped by a cosmology which explains the origins of the universe and with it the general order of events, days, and seasons. There is an explanation, too, for the presence of humans and the various animals in the world as well as the formation of the landscape on which both reside. There is also an explanation for the presence of the Ranau Dusun and for the recognized social divisions within which they live at the present time. From these also flow a series of prescriptions of how Dusun must live in the world and how they must behave while here, and where they will go when they are not here.

Besides this, the Dusun world is filled with spirits with whom people are continuously in interaction, even when they themselves are unaware of what that interaction is about. The presence of these spirits, or the creation of a situation which might place a person in jeopardy, is often signaled by one of a host of possible omens. There are omen birds, omen events such as rainbows, and snakes which cut across paths, similar to our feelings about black cats. Each of these signals a particular state of the world which requires interpretation then action or inaction.

### Spirits

Perhaps the major cause of action in the Ranau Dusun world is the hierarchy of spirits with which the Dusun cohabit. This pantheon consists of a series of levels of spirits many of whom are capable of quite malevolent behavior toward persons. This pantheon is capped by a high god, *Kinarohingan,* who differs from most Dusun spirits, and is most likely a syncretic addition from Christianity.

Below *Kinarohingan* is a major category of spirits called *Rogon.* Most of these are malevolent and often terrifying in demeanor. For the Ranau Dusun the most terrifying and feared is *Rogon tagahyah. Rogan tagahyah* is depicted as huge in stature and covered with red hair, including a beard, something not present among Dusun generally. *Rogons* usually are responsible for epidemics, disease, destruction, and starvation. Their presence in a human community may be the product of human behavior or they may be present independent of human acts which act as cause. Human behavior is often the cause of trouble for a community, especially with respect to the passions of which humans are heir. Yet trouble can be visited upon a community quite independently of human activity and even after people have done all they can, ritually and generally, to prevent it. That is, spirits and events generally can move independently of human action.

Next in the hierarchy is a series of malevolent spirits inhabiting the forest who can bring harm usually to individuals who do not remain wary. These spirits often change into animal forms or into ideal human form to entice their human prey farther into the forest where they are captured, eaten, or turned to stone. Often the failure to remain wary in the forest is the result of a person being greedy and therefore not cautious, being passionate and therefore reckless, being prideful and therefore heedless. The products of such passions are present for all to see in the form of stones or unusually shaped land forms into which such people have been turned.

Closest to humans in most respects is a class of mischievous or prankster spirits called *Miyons*. These spirits resemble humans in most respects though they remain invisible. *Miyons* live close to human habitations, normally in a tree of the *Ficus* species which is located close upon a natural spring. *Miyons*, as is true of most prankster spirits, are capable of bringing good fortune as well as illness. The behavior of *Miyons* is not always subject to the ritual influence of men. It is most prudent to keep a safe distance from *Miyons* when one is aware of their presence.

At the same level as *Miyons* is a series of spirits which are the result of man's own activities. Most prominent among them is *tung-anak-anak* which is often heard crying in the forest at night. *Tung-anak-anak* is the spirit of bastard children who have been put out in the forest to die so as not to contaminate the community with their presence. Essentially, the spirits of bastard children cannot be received on Mount Kinabalu any more than their corporeal presence can be maintained as part of the community into which they were born. Present-day Ranau Dusun no longer abandon such children, but they must suffer the consequences of such children's being placed in the forest in the past. Another spirit of this order is *katam waig*, or the water crab. This spirit attacks, by entering the body through the ear, those who do not accept hospitality when offered, or do not offer it when appropriate.

Apart from these spirits who can bring harm is the warm and nurturing spirit, *bomborian*. *Bomborian*, the spirit of rice, is often delicate, often shy, easily frightened, and quick to flee those who call her or startle her. For the Ranau Dusun, she is the most important spirit in the entire pantheon and she is most often conceptualized as a beautiful woman. Every person, too, has a guardian spirit who can act on his behalf in the spirit world and ward off the possible evil effects of other spirits. Theoretically, any person could contact his guardian spirit, but normally this is left to a spirit medium or *babulian* who is trained, in the presence of an older spirit medium, in the ritual responses which aid in contacting and communicating with the guardian spirit.

Lastly there is the spirit of the person, *mogaluh* or *godoh*. Being alive is being inhabited by one's spirit. This spirit is unlike the rest of the pantheon in that its normal place is inside the human body. When a person dies this spirit goes off to Mount Kinabalu. Generally the spirit is conceived of as being only loosely attached; a good scare or other sudden activity could remove it from the body. Once gone the human body becomes like a log and it is no longer really human.

### Rituals

It is in relation to these spirits that most of the ritual activity of Ranau Dusun life takes place. The most common ritual performed in relation to the major categories of spirits is the offering of food. Whenever an animal is slaughtered, some small bits of each part of the body—skin, hair, ear, intestines, etc.—are collected and left on a tall bamboo pole outside the house for the spirits present in the area to satisfy their hunger. The rice spirit too is given a small portion of the seed rice after each harvest as her source of food. These offerings are usually made automatically and with no prior preparation or fuss of any kind.

There is also a series of rituals connected with the major activities of the cultivation cycle. With the exception of the harvest ceremony, any set of members of a community may perform them for the community as a whole. Thus, one can say that the community is a religiously corporate social entity. It is a social entity, along with the family, against which spirits may act, and whose actions affect all members, young or old. Also a person, usually a *babulian,* can perform a ritual ceremony for the community, the benefits of which would fall equally on all the members of the social unit. Such rites and ceremonies need not necessarily be attended by all members for them to receive the benefits.

Therefore, the Ranau Dusun could be described as a society with a strong religious orientation. They have a ritual inventory with which to meet the vagaries of living in a cosmologically contingent world. And furthermore, the main social units, the community and the family, are corporate units in the world of the sacred, as the blessings and effects of living in a sacred world fall equally on all members, though it is not the rituals alone which are determinate. And for the Ranau Dusun the dramaturgy of ritual is relatively low key and includes few dramatic moments.

### Funerals

An example of a low-key ritual that includes little or no drama is the funeral. For the Ranau Dusun, death is a dramatic and often frightening event. All deaths have some supernatural final cause however well known the natural situation which produced it. Yet the ritual of burial involves almost no drama at all. What ritual they have is for the living not the dead. This ritual is to keep the spirits of the attendants from joining the spirit of the dead man or woman out of sympathy for his condition.

Burials are undertaken by the available kinsmen of the deceased, and when they are not available, by any four or five men of the same community as the deceased. The corpse is wrapped in a white sheet, a late concession to mission work, then encased in a bamboo sheath. The body is taken only by those involved in the burial to a prepared gravesite and interred. The corpse is buried facing Mount Kinabalu so that when the spirit rises it will be facing the correct way and there will be little chance of getting lost. As the grave is being filled, the workers, through a short ritual, ensure the presence within them of their own souls or spirits. No permanent markings are placed on the gravesite and after depositing the final effects, hat, clothes, etc., on top of the grave, the site is abandoned. The workers are given a meal at the house of the widow or nearest responsible kin and seven days later a party is held at the house in which the decedent died, thus completing the rites involved in a funeral.

Further to the south, among the Murut, burials involve the entire community. Usually at the gravesite an elaborate house is erected and painted in vivid colors. Often animals which are part of the spirit pantheon are painted on the sides of the house as is the name of the deceased, the known cause of death, and the hour and day on which it occurred. Burials involve all adult males, who accompany the corpse to the gravesite. A funeral feast is held after the gravesite ceremony. The Kayahs, Iban, Kenyahs, and Land Kyak also have relatively elaborate funerals when compared with the Ranau Dusun service.

One possible hypothesis for the diminished ritual aspect of burials is that the ceremony is a residual or what is left over after severe acculturation. This explanation sees the presence of the British and the Japanese as a force which has overwhelmed the ritual structure of the society. This explanation is unsatisfactory on many grounds. One, it tends to view the existing ritual negatively; an explanation is offered for the perceived lack of expected ceremony rather than for the ceremony that exists.

The acculturation hypothesis, however, can be put to rest relatively simply. Early travelers, especially Whitehead (1893), commented on the lack of ceremony surrounding the funerals they had the opportunity to observe in this area. Missionaries, too, for whom reverence for the dead is an important theological foundation, have from time to time indicated that they have not been very successful in raising much of a religious edifice on the Ranau Dusun attitude toward funerals and graves. This suggests that if acculturation had taken place, it might have gone, quite to the opposite of our expectations, toward an elaboration of ceremony rather than away from it. Informants also indicate that, to their knowledge, this situation has been the case for as long as they can ascertain. Apparently, the ceremony, as it now exists, is relatively closer to the aboriginal situation than our expectations or the acculturation hypothesis demands.

### Other Rites of Passage: Birth, Infancy, Adulthood, and Marriage

As with funerals, so with other rites of passage: there are few rituals and they are almost without drama. This is not to say that such occasions cannot be joyous, for the Ranau Dusun do celebrate. But these are not events which seemingly capture the entire community within the scope of ritual.

At birth a woman is attended only by a few women, who are involved in the process of labor. After the birth, when it appears that the child will live, neighbors drop in, rice beer is served, and the infant is displayed. After a ritual "lying in," the mother may leave the house, wash, and bathe the baby. Here, too, the presence of others and public ritual play little part in the actual process. After a month, when it is assured that the child will live, a name is given and neighbors are again invited over for some rice beer and food. This hardly constitutes an elaborate ritual procedure.

The passage from adolescence to adulthood, both for boys and girls, is hardly marked at all. Adulthood is not a status that is achievable through a ceremonial act. Actually it occurs quietly after a person has married and has had children. Marriage and children are the markers of adult status rather than the abrupt change that is often part of initiation ceremonies as practiced elsewhere.

Marriage, too, need not involve the entire community within the scope of the activities; the extent of community involvement in each case depends upon the wealth available to the uniting families, the age and status of each uniting partner, whether this constitutes a first marriage for each of them, and the familial desire or lack of it to hold a celebration. The distance between the bride's and groom's communities has some effect upon the intensity of nuptial celebrations and the length of time the revelry will continue in each area. If they are far apart, it is likely that few people will attend a fete outside their own area and it is likely to be short-lived.

### Harvests

Harvests, which occasion colorful rituals among many groups, are not exceptionally visible events in Ranau Dusun society, regardless of the mode or goal of cultivation. Usually each family in the community holds a party in turn. Often, and especially in communities cultivating swidden rice, all the member families of a hamlet or neighborhood will conduct the celebration. The few rituals associated with a harvest are conducted by each family separately within the confines of its own domain. The point at issue for such activities is the relation of the particular family to the spirit of the rice. Such rituals have little implication for the community as a whole.

### Manners

With respect to manners, the thrust of ritual in relationships is toward relatively egalitarian demeanor. With regard to the pronominal system, for instance, Ranau Dusun exhibit none of the differentiation relative to gradations of status that is quite common in other Southeast Asian languages. Unless status is specifically indicated, persons are addressed by the collateral term perceived to be appropriate for the addressee's age. This is true for kin, acquaintances, and strangers. Older men are addressed as "uncle," older women as "aunt," persons of one's own generation as "cousin," and younger persons as "child," "nephew," or "niece." When it is appropriate to address a person of especially high status, the common practice is to resort to Malay and use the terminology deemed appropriate within the context of their knowledge of that language.

### Art

One last example, art, should suffice to show the low ritual and dramatic profile of the Ranau Dusun. The Iban often turn almost everything they possess, even the most mundane objects and implements of subsistence, such as dibble sticks, into elaborate carvings and artistic creations; the Ranau Dusun exhibit no such tendency. There is essentially no carving. What weaving is done bears little if any design. Pottery and other crafted artifacts are usually left unadorned. The only figured artifacts are the field hats which people wear to work. These are usually plaited in geometric designs with each particular design being specific to a community. Such hats are a means of identifying the origin of the wearer when away from home. But the hats of the Tambunan and Keningau Dusun farther to the south, the latter being close upon Murut territory, tend to be much more ornate.

## ASPECTS OF EXPLANATION

### Grid and Group

Little further evidence is required to demonstrate that Ranau Dusun society, though religious in character, is not exceptionally dramatic in its ritual. Furthermore, the rituals that do exist provide no superstructure for the society and often appear as isolated events. Why should this be so? One could answer by demonstrating that Ranau Dusun life lacked what more elaborate ritually oriented cultures possess. More consistent with the methodology of this paper, however, would be an attempt to determine what Ranau Dusun society has that allows it to maintain such a low ritual profile yet maintain adequate social order.

The first concepts that come to mind are Douglas' concepts of "grid" and "group" (Douglas, 1973:77–92), which she related to the degree of ritual in a social system. As she states: "My considered view now is that magical rites are not the same the world over and that interest in magical efficacy varies with the strength of social ties" (1973:36). The stronger the need to maintain group solidarity by indicating that there is a "we" in contrast to a "they," the more strongly adhered to will be the rituals which are seized upon to mark these boundaries.

From the standpoint of "group," it is quite clear that "Ranau Dusun" and even "Dusun," as opposed to "Iban," etc., are only weakly demarcated notions. Groupness at the level of ethnic affiliation tends, throughout the Ranau area, to shade off and be relatively continuous from one section of Ranau to another, and the administrative boundary is only marginally a source of identification.

Much of the reason for this is that the Ranau Dusun are the most northern and most interior group of Dusun. On almost all sides are groups who are very much like themselves. Existing as they do in a rugged terrain, the Ranau Dusun have been spared incursions of people whose presence would more readily have promoted a stronger notion of "we," "they," "inside," and "outside." The

Japanese occupation may be largely responsible for the degree of ethnic identification which presently exists, as it was against this threat that the Ranau Dusun joined their efforts.

The effect of colonialization has been increased centralization and coordination but even this is weakly expressed. It is not a force which most people in the area feel threatened by, nor is it a force which most feel necessary to resist. In general the effect has been to make the interior more continuously "Ranau Dusun" and to negate the sharper, more discrete social entities inherent in such mountainous terrain. The social boundaries remain relatively amorphous.

The inherent contradiction which Robert McKinley found between the Iban cosmological order and the presence of others who present a "contradiction to the presumed universal validity of one's society's way of life . . ." (McKinley, n.d.), although as true for the Dusun as for all social groups, is not as pressing in Ranau as it appears to be in Iban territory. One should note that the Iban were continually encroaching upon the territory of others. As a consequence, the presence of others in the world who possessed territory the Iban felt was vital to their needs may have made the contradiction, which is always there, more stark.

For the Ranau Dusun no such situation existed. The presence of Bajau traders in small numbers could easily be incorporated and the contradiction laid aside. Except for the Japanese, other persons were never present in sufficient numbers to pose any real threat. For the Ranau Dusun, the persons who are still important are other Ranau Dusun and they exist, as it were, almost as a sea around them.

If the notion of "ethnic group" is not elaborately demarcated neither is the next order of group, the community. Interestingly enough, this is true for swidden cultivators, wet rice cultivators, and cash crop producers though for entirely different reasons.

### Community Social Boundaries

Among swidden cultivators the reasons for community boundaries being only weakly expressed are quite complex. In summary, one can say that the situation is aided and abetted by the community being a corporate entity in which all land within the geographically bounded areas is possessed communally. Furthermore, swidden communities are normally split up within this domain into smaller hamlets or neighborhoods. The social composition of these hamlet groups are relatively unstable since persons and families may change from one to the other with little social cost.

Since land is held corporately by the community and use is conferred through residence, a person or family can move from one community to another without incurring any more cost than the move between hamlets of a community. There is, in fact, relatively great migration of persons and families between one community and another. This situation is similar to that Freeman (1955) reported for the Iban swidden rice cultivators. Other groups producing swidden rice seem to exhibit similar patterns as well. This relatively high migration between communities has two effects which are important here.

First, though the community remains intact as a corporate entity controlling land, its social boundaries remain rather diffuse and weakly expressed. Second, kinship is not the basis of recruitment for community membership; any person has throughout the entire social space of Ranau Dusun domain a widely distributed social field of kinsmen. Normally, small unit mobility and consanguinity are inversely related when many kinsmen are present in one community, but the effect of mobility has been to distribute kinsmen throughout the entire available social space. Though no Ranau Dusun is, of course, related to every other Ranau Dusun, there is probably no sector or area in which a kinsman cannot be contacted. In such a situation, there would be little need for the community to stand out as an effective social barrier. Indeed there are substantial ecological reasons against it.

This distribution of kinsmen throughout the entire territory means that there is also a much higher effective threshold for social control through familial ties. Everywhere a Ranau Dusun goes he can presume the presence of relatives, though actual demonstration of such relations would be quite difficult. Under such circumstances one need not erect elaborate social barriers against the presence of the stranger whose behavior is always at least possibly unpredictable. Nor does a Ranau Dusun have to mount any dramatic display of the ''we'' of our group against the ''they'' of theirs as he is embedded within the context of the entire social matrix.

Within the wet rice and cash crop communities, the sense of community is equally weak. For those people, too, kin are equally distributed throughout the Ranau Dusun world. Land, however, within these systems is private, familially owned and considered a valued good. As such, persons from other communities on the fringes of the wet rice area are likely to keep in contact with relatives who reside within the area and attempt to reduce social distance by the best means possible.

Community social boundaries are, however, weakly expressed for another set of equally complex reasons. First, the possession of agricultural land as private domain has split the community into a residential unit wholly apart from agricultural land. Residential land is still the corporate property of the community, tilled land, the property of the family. Second, in both the wet rice and cash crop areas the communities exist crowded in close upon each other. Unlike swidden farming communities, the community itself is no longer the sole source of labor. Persons at the boundaries of the community have available to them neighbors who may actually reside in another community. In such situations, propinquity rules. Within the wet rice area, the further need for persons to engage in stream clearance and silt removal from water channels, and generally to maintain the irrigation system has created conditions for a great deal of cross-community cooperation. Predictably, the rituals expressing community solidarity—one against the other—are equally weak.

### Family and Stratification

*Grid* can be taken to indicate two types of social situation. It might indicate the presence of a strongly etched familial system in which there is an unambiguous assignment of persons to positions within the known network. Or, *grid* could equally refer to a system of stratification which tends to allocate persons to particular strata or class relative to the resources of the society. *Grid* in Douglas' terms relates to the sense of position persons have within a social group. The stronger the sense of position, Douglas reports (1973:77–92), the more heightened the sense of ritual. It is, of course, possible to have both a strong sense of familial position in a society and a strong sense of social place through class assignment.

With respect to the Ranau Dusun, neither is exceptionally strong. With respect to familial ties, as mentioned earlier, relations tend to be located throughout the entire space of the Ranau area. With respect to the system of stratification there is an increasing difference between the "haves" of the wet rice area and the swidden rice farming communities which see themselves as disadvantaged relative to the availability of industrial goods, schooling, and medical aid. Economically, they are disadvantaged, for they bear a much higher cost in bringing their goods to market. The only advantage which they experience is that they have less impeded access to the goods of the forest which are in high demand.

But the economic disadvantage is not as great as the perceived cultural one. That is, the wet rice valley being the seat of government administration is also the center of news and important events. That is where the action is, and not everyone can be there. In order to catch up, some swidden communities have begun to open their own wet rice schemes under the assumption that some of the advantages which have accrued to those on the Ranau plain will become more available to them when they are more stably located.

There is less difference in wealth between individual families in the swidden areas than in the wet rice areas but in no case is it highly pronounced nor have the differences been codified into a system of class behavior. Within the swidden areas, the means of moving fields and planting tend to randomize the risk of economic loss between hamlets and between member families of a hamlet. With respect to the wet rice areas, the differences exist and undoubtedly they will become more important over time. The system is still quite young, however, and there has been too little time for great differences to solidify into distinct strata.

### Authority Structure

The authority of Ranau Dusun life is vested largely in the headman of each community. In the past it is probably true that this was as high as formal authority extended. Each community was in essence a duplicate of the other and a relatively independent unit. Coalitions between communities could and undoubtedly did occur where one headman would then become ascendant over the others. Within Ranau, protected as it was from wholesale incursions upon its territory, it is doubtful if this ever happened to any great extent or with great frequency.

On the borders of the territory, especially in the area leading to the west coast, the main area of trade, undoubtedly coalitions occurred more frequently. In those areas there was warfare as well, though it never penetrated deeply, with one exception. This was the Mat Salleh rebellion. Mat Salleh, in rebellion against the Chartered Company, fled inland and built a fort in Ranau. The people of the area did aid and abet this movement, though not wholeheartedly. So weakly expressed was this support that Mat Salleh was forced to leave for Tambunan where he built another fort.

Today authority extends beyond the village downward from a series of native chiefs who act as judges and supervise the administration of native law, *adat*. These judges sit in concert, with the judge from the area of the case presiding as chief judge.

Although the presence of native chiefs tends to diminish the importance of the headman, villages still operate as largely autonomous units. Hence, there is no high authority structure that directs the lives of community members. There is no indigenous superstructure and consequently no creation of a drama of social order related to any high position.

Ranau Dusun life remains largely egalitarian though there are differences in individual wealth. With respect to the symbolism of social order this has two consequences. First, there is no superordinate structure, such as princes and a nobility, for whom it is necessary to erect a validating mythology and concordant rituals. A noble caste or class would be very active creators of a mythology and a cosmology which would tend to justify their use of power. They would, of course, be active participants in creating rituals and social dramas which would for most occasions maintain, and tend to emphasize the social distance between themselves and others which would be essential to keep the mythology alive.

Second, with no superordinate structure to maintain in the form of a noble class, there is little need to erect a ritual structure that would aid the "haves" in the control of the "have nots." The notion of social control carries with it, generally, the assumption that if the controls were not there, people would behave differently than they usually do. This may be untrue; our notion of social control as a scientific concept may well be a projection of our own condition of living in a highly stratified society in which people would behave differenly if controls were removed. To accept this assumption as a universal condition is quietly to accept Hobbes' notion of the "war of all against all." Ranau Dusun, living in a more egalitarian society, do not need to invest economic or social capital in maintaining a system of stratification, through myth and ritual. Rather than living with a system of control, they live within a system that allows them to deal with the consequences of behavior positively or negatively.

### Sense of Person

If there is no strong sense of "we" against "they," of the inside world against the outside world, which permits a strong sense of group, there is within Ranau a strong sense of person. This should not be confused with the notion of individualism as it is applied to our industrial society. The Ranau Dusun live in a diffused social world and there is an accompanying loss of coherence in publicly maintained symbolic structures, but that does not mean that there is no collective conscience, or that personal behavior is motivated by a kind of rational, amoral pragmatism (Douglas, 1973:153–188). Rather, there is a notion that the affairs and behavior of a person have an overriding importance in maintaining the health and prosperity of the entire community. Not only will the person suffer the consequences of his own acts but if those acts are of social importance they could bring disease and pestilence upon the entire community. What a person does causes heat, and heat can cause illness or crop failure. The analogy here is to the all too well-known effect of sunlight and fire on a swidden plot.

If there is an outer world against which the Ranau Dusun must guard themselves, it is not other persons as much as it is the natural world itself. This natural world is filled with entities and forces inimical to man. The forest, mud, rain, rivers, rainbows, animals, and darkness all contain agents and forces which only wait to be released upon the hapless community. The mechanism, or one of the more important mechanisms, of release is the asocial behavior of the individual. There is a tragic sense to this for the Ranau Dusun, as they are all too aware of men's inherent and very natural passions which operate quite to their own and the community's undoing.

The natural world is not only filled with natural forces which prey upon man, but it is also filled with the products of man's own negative behavior. The bad things or negative things men do ultimately are exported to, and reside in, the forest. The forest is seen as an almost cosmic entity. This is part of the meaning of the spirit *tung-anak-anak* who cries woefully in the night begging to be joined by the spirits of living men. An illicit sexual union results in an unwanted pregnancy and the product of that pregnancy is put out to the forest there forever to haunt men in the communities in which they dwell. The killing of a community member may release the deceased's spirit to the forest, there to await the coming of other men to join him in his lonely vigil.

No wonder, then, that forests are unpleasant places for the Ranau Dusun. This causes a good deal of conflict, for the forest is also filled with a bountiful supply of absolutely essential goods. Beeswax, damar, gutta-percha, rattan, tropical fruits, pigs, monkeys, all of these and more are there for man to use. But getting them requires going there and coming back and that requires good behavior.

With respect to the person and the weight that is placed upon him to maintain the balance between his needs and passions and the community's need for order, the concept of a personal spirit operates to maintain the balance in favor of the community. This spirit which others have called a *soul* is very loosely attached to the body. Loss of life can occur quickly and almost unwittingly by the spirit's leaving the body. So loosely attached to the body is this spirit and so important is it to the maintenance of life that it is the responsibility of every person to see that he does not act in such a way as to place in jeopardy the life of another simply through untoward behavior. A shout might remove the spirit, expelling air as in sneezing could also do it, and being severely frightened could have the same effect. Also the spirit can be captured by the presence of other spirits without the person being immediately aware that this is taking place. So spirits of the deceased before and upon burial are especially inimical, as are the many spirits of the forest.

If there is a segment of Ranau Dusun life in which ritual is intense, it is around this notion of the spirit's ability to leave the body. Such rituals reinforce the notion of the person's effect upon the world and bring behavior into line with communal demands. Social control of this order, as with the concept of community, is quite diffused, but it is nonetheless effective.

### Productivity and Ritual

There is another means by which social control is maintained within the community, which I would hypothesize relates to the diffused presence of ritual and ritualized behavior. That is social control partially maintained through the rigors of subsistence productivity and the perceived consequences of individual acts to subsistence crops. The Dusun are not equally busy; those engaged in wet rice cultivation are more intensively occupied than their neighbors in the swidden communities, but everywhere there is a good deal of concentration upon the demands of productivity.

The major focus of Dusun life for both wet rice/cash crop producers and swidden rice farmers is the fields from which they wrest their main sources of subsistence. Whatever activities are to take place within the community are programed in relation to the amount of time available after subsistence activities have been carried out. Even though productivity does not absorb all their available time, it does absorb a good deal of it.

To live in a world where private events can have major public consequences is to live in a contingent world. And during the period when crops are in the process of growing, a person does not want to commit an act which could severely limit the yield from his labor or the yield from the labor of others. The Ranau Dusun, as is the case with many other groups, will not speak of even the possible size of a harvest least such words seal a contract with fate. Untoward behavior, as well as words, might commit one to the same contract. As the size of harvest is for the Ranau Dusun a measure of one's being right with the world, one would not want the yields from one's fields to give public evidence of private behavior. The focus then on productivity and productive activities, aside from the notion of the loss of soul, puts an effective brake on the impulsiveness of a person's possible actions.

Furthermore, I contend that the closer the attachment to productive endeavors, the less likely will be involvement with expressive end dramatic symbolism. This means playing a vital and central role in the maintenance of any ongoing productive system. Rulers, for instance, who are no longer vital to the maintenance of the state will evolve a more elaborate symbolic architecture than those upon whom the health and wealth of a state actually depend. This relation to productivity, or perhaps a better term might be *functional role,* cuts across the concepts of "grid and group." Concerning stratification, often those who occupy continuously higher strata may be less and less related to actual productive activities and substitute ritual in their stead.

Evidence for this relation occurs at many levels and for many different periods. For instance, increase in ritual behavior is positively correlated with the move of aboriginal populations to reservation status. Among the Australian aborigines, the extent of ritual has increased with increasing confinement. The Sun Dance and Ghost Dance of the Great Plains Indians spread fastest among the various groups confined to reservations. In both situations, the very means of subsistence had been cut out from under the society. Undoubtedly, the sense of group must have played an important part as well, for I can hardly imagine a situation in which it would be more severely threatened.

The development of the classic mode of courtly behavior in Japan reached its peak in the emperor's court during the Tokugawa regime when the military ruled in the emperor's stead. The later Meiji restoration and much of the social movements of that period saw a reduction in the spheres of courtly ritual behavior. The development of the code of chivalry in European history occurred under similar conditions. It developed at the court of Eleanor of Aquitaine, wife of Henry II of England, while she was kept from acting as monarch in her own realm. The code of chivalry signaled the shift of power away from the armored knight who was now partially freed to pursue more honorific ends. Again from French history, the period from the reign of Louis XIV through that of Louis XVI was one in which courtly behavior was very much in evidence. However dazzling the Sun King may have appeared, the realities of power were shifting to the newly emerging urban middle class and the industrializing urban centers which were their domain.

One further example will suffice. A study of modern American corporations done in the early 1950s devised a scale in which the distance between the management hierarchy and the production floor was measured. Corporations which were "shirt sleeve" operations were those whose officers were well known to the employees and where there was a myth that the boss could actually come down himself and accomplish any of the tasks workers on the line were asked to perform. These corporations maintained a more egalitarian ethos, and a great deal more interaction took place between all levels of the operation. Basically the rituals to be performed were often those of eschewing ritual "Don't call me sir."

These corporations were contrasted with those in which there was a great distance between production and management. Here relations between managers and workers were often highly formalized and contained within specific areas for interaction. Further, executive specialization, subject to Parkinson's Law, created a situation in which it was difficult to measure the actual output of any executive employee. As most executives are highly involved with abstract symbol manipulation, one could take few measures to ascertain their level of productivity.

Under these conditions, such corporations turned to the manipulation of ritual as the means of adequately assessing a person's deserved position in the management hierarchy. Proper behavior and a proper background became the criteria against which one was given a "Bigelow on the floor" or "a key to the executive washroom." Rituals of activity—the business lunch, and the status of one's home life—rather than one's relation to productive labor became the indices for upward mobility. I would hypothesize that in this situation, executives closest to the actual production facilities would exhibit the slowest rate of upward mobility.

Although this may seem to be exceptionally far removed from the world of the Ranau Dusun, I would suggest that it is not. Part of the reason for their low ritual profile is their relation to productive activities and their concern with subsistence generally. No doubt this is only a partial explanation and the sense of group and positions within it are more powerful explanatory tools. Our concern, however, has been to delineate that constellation of social, economic, and ecological circumstances which would allow the Ranau Dusun to accomplish, at a lower social cost, the same ends in terms of social order as other, more dramatic societies. As such, it must be considered in relation to all the other factors which produce this end.

### Ritual Friendships

In the Ranau Dusun social system, the sense of group is weak and diffused and the egalitarian thrust has made ambigous the sense of place within groups. The Ranau Dusun exist in a social field of ever-increasing ambiguity from the nuclear family outward. In such a system, the sense of person is more strongly etched. Social control is effective without a highly structured and visible panoply of ritual because the person is made to see the immediacy of the relation between his behavior and the state of the universe.

In such a system of kinsmen diffused throughout the social field, it is not unexpected that the notion of friendship should play an important role, so much that friendship itself almost approaches the high ritual asserted to be usually absent. The institution of formalized friendship is called in Ranau Dusun terms *sangkoluangan* (*sang,* "to be one," "a unit or set"; *koluangan,* "friend").

This relationship comes into being when two persons of the same sex, and often though not essentially of the same age, choose to perform a ceremony establishing their friendship as a formal one. That is to give public recognition to their shared feelings. For men, the ceremony is often performed in the privacy of the forest and is often associated with a hunt. The relation comes into being when one or both of the partners-to-be gives a gift and acknowledges its purpose. The gift given or exchanged is usually edible foodstuff, and most often, an animal killed while hunting.

After exchanging gifts, the partners adopt a new name. For the duration of the relationship, they will address each other and refer to each other in terms of a reciprocal name they now share. The name is derived from the material of the gift exchanged. For instance, if two men, or women, were to exchange chickens, the reciprocal name would be *sangmanok;* if they were to exchange a wild pig it would be *sangbaka.* Other persons in the community are constrained to address the partners by their regularly known names.

Such relationships are considered to be quite close. The partners are always seen together and they are supposed to lend each other freely any of their material possessions as well as to exchange work without demanding recompense. Further, a partner would be sworn to avenge the other, ritually or actually, should the situation demand it.

The relation is so close that during the term of the partnership it is considered bad form for the children of the partners to marry. This is by no means an extension of the incest taboo, as partners need not be related. It is simply noted that marriage between the children of friends often produces conflict which should be avoided where possible. *Sangkoluangan* are intense, highly visible social relationships. The people of Ranau claim that such relationships were more evident in the past than they are now. Even today, however, their notions about friendship are couched in the most romantic terms. In the social sea in which Ranau Dusun swim, friendships seem an important counterbalance to the diffused and indistinct social networks of most relations. Aside from marriage and family, friendship is the most strongly etched social relation throughout the area.

## REFERENCES

Douglas, Mary. *Natural symbols.* New York: Random House, 1973.
Freeman, J. D. *Iban agriculture.* London: Her Majesty's Stationery Office, 1955.
McKinley, Robert. *Human and proud of it!* (Mimeograph.) Department of Anthropology, Michigan State University, East Lansing, Michigan, n.d.
Whitehead, J. *Explorations of Mt. Kina Balu, North Borneo.* London: Gurney and Jackson, 1893.

# chapter five

# In the World of the Sea Urchin: The Application of Husserlian Phenomenology to Cultural Symbols

J.S. Lansing

University of Southern California

The study of symbolic systems has led anthropologists to invade the domain of philosophers, seeking answers to questions like "What are symbols? How are they constituted, and what is their role in thought and action?" But it is often difficult to bridge the gap between philosophical theory and anthropological data.

Phenomenology is an abstruse branch of philosophy, but its successful application in the fields of linguistics and hermeneutics suggests attractive possibilities for anthropology. Phenomenological ideas have been incorporated into the theories of several sociologists (Schutz, 1967; Berger and Luckmann, 1966; Schutz and Luckmann, 1973; Natanson, 1970; Natanson, 1973), and it is to these theories that anthropologists interested in phenomenology usually turn. There are, however, major problems in the sociological interpretations of phenomenology, which can be avoided by closer attention to the methods of the founder of German phenomenology, Edmund Husserl. This essay begins with a very brief survey of Husserl and the phenomenological method; then a variety of phenomenological models is considered in light of their application to understanding Balinese ethnography.

Husserl was concerned with investigating the relations among man, culture, mind, and nature on an abstract level. Trained as a mathematician, his original *Logical investigations* (1970) led him to consider the foundation of logic and mathematics in thought. According to Paul Ricoeur, Husserl's research was

> . . . linked to a dual movement of ideas: in the first place, it is related to the studies of pure logic which Trendelenberg (from 1840) and Erdman (1892) had been led after the collapse of the Hegelian dialectic; and in the second place, mainly, it is linked to a movement issuing from the mathematical sciences. This movement sought to re-establish in opposition to Kant the Leibnitzian thesis according to

**75**

which mathematics is an "extension of general logic." Mathematical judgments are not synthetic, as Kant believed, but rather analytic. Thereafter a rigor in demonstration was sought which had not been attained by the great mathematicians of the Eighteenth Century. All of the indemonstrable postulates introducing immediate intrusions without logical value were hunted down. Mathematical notions were analyzed to their simplest elements, and the general goal was to introduce nothing into deduction other than these elements and the relations by which they are combined. This same movement concluded in Germany with the works of Hilbert and Cantor, in England with those of Russell, and in Italy and France with logistics (1967:5).

Husserl was thus led to investigate the status of logic within a more general theory of knowledge. Phenomenology developed as a method for investigating the nature of knowledge by setting aside all questions pertaining to existence, whether of the knower or the known. For Husserl, the phenomenological method disentangled the theory of knowledge from ontology.

## THE PHENOMENOLOGICAL METHOD OF HUSSERL

Husserl took as his task the creation of a philosophy without presuppositions. His first method for the achievement of this goal was inspired by the Cartesian method of doubt and cogito (Husserl, 1960). But Descartes' radical doubt was transformed into a more sophisticated tool, the *epoche* or phenomenological reduction. This is a method for suspending the "natural thesis of the world," which is a naive or unconsidered belief in the real existence of the world. By suspending this belief, the encounter of the self with the world is transformed into the constitution of the world for the self. This is done by "bracketing" the question of the objective existence of the world; this is not a denial of the real existence of the world, but a turning of attention away from that question, toward the question of what is "in" the world. The world is lost only that it may be regained at a new level, the world of phenomena or appearances which is the "prior" world. This reduction provides access to this world by liberating us from what Ricoeur aptly termed the *mundane illusion*. Having performed the reduction, one is aware of oneself as a transcendental subject constituting "the" world for oneself, in the "essential positive movement of consciousness."

What did Husserl mean by "constitution"? In the course of the development of phenomenology, Husserl created a great many models of consciousness. The model of "constitution" is, however, basic to his phenomenology and thus bears some elaboration. The model begins with the premise that consciousness is always directed towards something; consciousness "intends" an object. Before the phenomenological reduction, this is an encounter, afterwards it is a constitution. The difference lies in the subject's awareness.

Husserl focused on the act of constitution, which has a dual component. The object intended Husserl termed *noema;* the act of intending, *noesis.* Whether the brown object on the table before you is merely a brown object, or a book, or the Bible, or a ritual object, or what you owe a fine for at the library depends in part on its physical reality, but also on what you intend when you see it. You are not likely to mistake the Bible for a rabbit, but whether you see it as a book or a Bible depends not on it but on you. Thus consciousness prescribes the mode of givenness or presentation of the object. As Ricoeur said, "Every unity of sense announced in consciousness is the index of interconnections of consciousness," which follows from the premise that it is consciousness which prescribes the mode of givenness.

How does consciousness prescribe the mode of givenness? There is no simple answer, but a few general remarks may be made. First, it is necessary to draw a distinction between the reflective and nonreflective states of consciousness. In the nonreflective state, one thinks without being aware of doing so, whereas in the reflective, the "I" appears, one becomes aware of oneself thinking. Human beings tend to switch from one to the other very quickly; animals remain forever in the nonreflective state (or so we suppose!).

The biologist von Uexküll (1909) created some very interesting models of animal consciousness based on this distinction. As von Uexküll put it, "in the world of the sea urchin, we find only sea urchin things." Every individual consciousness lives in a unique world, a world bounded not only spatially but temporally. For sea urchins and similar creatures, von Uexküll defined a simple "species model" consisting of three parts: the world as sensed, the *innenwelt* or "inner world" (which may be considered as the correlate of the world as sensed), and the world of action.

Thus, vastly more complicated models are required as we move from the lifeworld of a sea urchin to that of human beings. Husserl's most basic model for the investigation of one's own mind is the "transcendental reduction," an extension of the phenomenological reduction.

My consciousness is at times nonreflective, as when I am engrossed in a problem or sensation, but at other moments I am aware of myself as a being. Over and above my awareness of myself as a person, with fingers and toes, I am aware of myself as a more or less pure consciousness which Husserl calls the *transcendental subject.*

> Posited as real *(wirklich),* I am now no longer a human Ego in the universal, existentially posited world, but exclusively a subject for which this world has being, and purely, indeed, as that which appears to me, is presented to me, and of which I am conscious in some way or other, so that the real being of the world thereby remains unconsidered, unquestioned, and its validity left out of account (1962:8).

In order to discover this transcendental subjectivity we can "bracket" literally everything, so that all that remains is that-which-does-the-bracketing, the pure ego. The bracketing operation is called the *transcendental reduction.* Having performed it, we are free to investigate the region of "pure consciousness,'' phenomenologically defined. For Husserl, its essence is temporality; the subject constitutes itself, and the matrix within which the transcendental ego develops is temporality.

Within this framework, Husserl went on to develop models of the relationships between subjects and objects of different orders. It is these models which are potentially of greatest interest for anthropologists. But they must be understood in the context from which they developed.

Phenomenological sociology, such as that of Alfred Schutz, generally begins at the level of the lifeworld. This is a serious mistake, for the lifeworld is for Husserl a limiting concept, the end rather than the beginning of analysis, the final setting of man-in culture-in-nature with all attendant complexities. A complete exposition of a lifeworld as it actually exists (not in terms of its formal components, which was Husserl's interest) would involve analysis of the almost limitless minutiae experienced in the lifeworld, and is thus neither feasible nor interesting.

But it is possible to make use of phenomenological techniques to understand events occurring in the lifeworld. We must build up to the lifeworld, as Husserl did, establishing each step on a secure footing. For this purpose we may make use of other, simpler models. In so doing we are not lifting Husserl's models out of context, but simply applying his abstract models to particular cases. Relevant models might include:

1. *Realität:* a structure or space which can be formally or mathematically defined (i.e., described completely).
2. Scientific nature: the ''idea'' of nature in general. The first step in delimiting ''scientific nature'' phenomenologically is to circumscribe (a priori) the field of nature intended by the type of interest or attitude that is correlative to it. (Lest this appear to be mere ''idealistic hocus-pocus,'' consider how the realms investigated by physics, chemistry, biology, and astronomy are to be differentiated from each other.) This is ''objectified nature,'' which is ''experienced'' selectively. By *experienced,* Husserl means that the aspect of value is removed, the subject becomes a pure spectator of the realm, in particular an observer of an object whose ''real existence'' is either conceded, or ignored (Ricoeur, 1967:40–41).
3. The natural attitude: a key element in the phenomenological reduction (from which it proceeds); this is the naive or unconsidered belief in the reality of my experiential world. In this realm, man is constituted as *animalia.*
4. The *Umwelt:* (the environing world) here ''the person is at the center of a surrounding world *(Umwelt);* qualified by its perceived, affective, and practical properties; enriched by culture, science and art; and, consequently, always in a state of becoming insofar as its sense is remodeled consequently by the history of man . . .'' (Ricoeur, 1967:70). Thus, the ''reality of physics, atoms, etc., which was taken just now (in the natural attitude) as an absolute, plays a part in my *Umwelt* only if I 'know' it, only if science as cultural activity has modified the look and conception of the world wherein I live. For the historian and sociologist, nature is the countryside of a civilization at a certain epoch . . .'' (Ricoeur, 1967:70). Marx made a similar observation when he said that nature as such exists now only on a few Australian coral islands. The world is this way for the scientist himself outside the laboratory.

5. The *kommunikative Umwelt:* "No ego can become a person in the normal sense for itself and the other, a person banded together with other persons, unless understanding should institute a relation to a common surrounding world" (Husserl, 1962:191). Hence, what is implicit in this communal elaboration of a surrounding world is the formation of a "whole in which each person is a member and in which the network of exchange constitutes a surrounding world of communication *(kommunikative Umwelt)* (Ricoeur, 1967:71).

6. The *Lebenswelt:* (lifeworld) man-in culture-in-nature, the foundation for the idealizations of science, whose formal description is the goal for the later Husserl. As Ricoeur notes, the "Lifeworld does not appear until the end of the Fifth (Cartesian) Meditation, since it represents the concrete fullness towards which the constitution of the Other and of the intersubjective communities points." The *Lebenswelt* forms the counterpole of constitution, not the reduced terminus from which it is oriented" (Ricoeur, 1967:138–139).

7. Multiple lifeworlds: the possibility of a general theory to account for the constitution of many lifeworlds is intriguing, and has been the starting place of phenomenological Marxism, such as that of the Frankfurt School.

As has previously been noted, phenomenological sociology generally begins with the lifeworld. The results have tended to be speculative, and problems of verification have been awkward. A different approach, more in keeping with Husserlian logic, would begin with simpler models and build up to structures and events in the lifeworld. This can be illustrated with an example from Balinese ethnography.

## THE APPLICATION OF A PHENOMENOLOGY TO A BALINESE EXAMPLE

We begin with a Balinese notion about space, which may be considered as a *Realität* consisting of a linear continuum on which any object may be assigned a value corresponding to its position on the line. Objects toward one end are *kaja,* higher, closer to the divine world, possessing greater positive or beneficent spiritual power. Objects located at the other end are *kelod,* lower, closer to the demonic, possessed of chthonic or malevolent power, the opposite of *kaja.* Thus we have a continuum of "spiritual force" from divine to demonic.

Whether a Balinese applies this *Realität* in his understanding (actually constitution) of a given object, viz., a temple, a person, a mountain, a house yard, can be determined directly by asking, or indirectly by inference. When my Balinese informant and I visit the beach, I may swim past the reef, but he will invariably wade in the shallows, if he ventures to bathe at all. In terms of "scientific nature," the sea is the same for both of us, we may freely agree on its physical properties. But the sea in his *Umwelt* is not the same as it is in mine. In his "environing world," the sea is *kelod,* intrinsically dangerous and malevolent, a place to avoid.

The same *Realität* is also applied to people's bodies. The head is *kaja;* the lower body, *kelod*. Balinese are thus acutely conscious of body positions, because they carry this meaning, "symbolic" meaning if you will, but nevertheless part of the intrinsic constitution of the human body for a Balinese.

How does an anthropologist discover that Balinese "see" the human body in terms of a *kaja-kelod Realität*? Is this not in principle undiscoverable, a thought process which may or may not be going on in someone else's head, but which is acessible only to the thinker himself?

One day I attended a ceremony for a friend's son in a Balinese village. At age 105 days, infants undergo the 105-day-old ceremony, a brief ritual involving only close relatives and guests.

> According to the father of the child, this was a "purification" ceremony. I was puzzled by this description, for it is a tenet of the religion that infants are the most pure and innocent humans by virtue of the fact that they have only recently come from the world of the gods. Why, then, must they be purified? When I questioned my informants, they explained as follows:
>
> The passage of the infant through the mother's body sullies the child. If he were born from her head, perhaps no ceremony would be needed, but the passage through her lower regions makes purification necessary. The analogy was drawn to rolling in the dirt: one's body gets dirty and must be washed or harm will come, but one's soul remains pure (Lansing, 1974:86–87).

This explanation makes perfect sense, given the unstated presupposition that the human body is constituted in terms of the *kaja-kelod Realität*. The reluctance to touch other people's heads, the fact that gods are carried on platforms held above people's heads, that persons of lower caste must keep their heads lower than those of persons of higher caste when they pass before them, all strengthen the hypothesis that this *Realität* is applied to the human body. As Clifford Geertz observes, ". . . accounts of other people's subjectivities can be built up without recourse to pretensions to more-than-normal capacities for ego-effacement and fellow-feelings" (Geertz, 1975:53).

In the Balinese *Umwelt* (environing world), the *kaja-kelod Realität* provides a basic symbolic framework for the arrangement of objects in space. Thus, the model is useful in interpreting not only rituals, such as the purification ceremony, or native beliefs, such as my friend's reluctance to swim, but more mundane topics. The social organization of some traditional Balinese villages *(Bali Aga)* follows the *kaja-kelod* orientation closely, and would be hard to understand without it.

The village of Sembiran, on the north coast, is a case in point. Sembiran is laid out on hilly ground a few kilometers from the sea. Clans *(dadia)* own house land, and at the *kaja* end of each clan's territory is the clan temple. At the *kaja* end of the clan temples are the most important shrines. The complete village organization is symbolized in the *Balai Agung* (see Figure 1), a ritual meeting place and temple.

In a large open courtyard are arranged a number of roofed platforms *(balai)*. At the *kaja* end of the courtyard are the *balai* for village elders in their

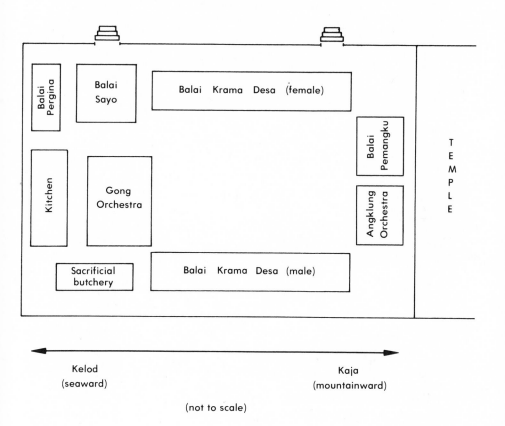

Balai Agung Sembiran

Balai Pergina

Balai Sayo

Balai Krama Desa (female)

Kitchen

Gong Orchestra

Balai Pemangku

Angklung Orchestra

TEMPLE

Sacrificial butchery

Balai Krama Desa (male)

Kelod
(seaward)

Kaja
(mountainward)

(not to scale)

capacity as priests and heads of the village, and the *balai* for the ceremonial *angklung* orchestra. At the *kelod* end are the kitchen and place of animal sacrifice. On either side of the courtyard on the *kaja-kelod* axis are two *balai,* on which the villagers are seated, males on one side and females on the other. The seats at the *kaja* end of both *balai* are reserved for the village leaders. The entire village is seated in a generational hierarchy, with the most recently married couple seated at the *kelod* end and the oldest married couple, who are the ritual heads of the village, at the *kaja* end.

This order symbolizes the organization of the village. Upon marriage, a couple is given a seat in this *balai,* at the *kelod* end. They take a new name, which is the same for both of them, and become full members of the village. In some villages, such as Jullah, communal land owned by the village was allotted to them at this point. The land would be worked by the couple for a period of years, after which the village lands would be redistributed and the couple would be given a new plot. As new couples became village members and took their places behind our couple, it would gradually ascend the village hierarchy. Each seating area has its special duties and rank. Thus at a certain point men join the village dancing group and sit in the *Balai Pergina*. At another period they are members of the gamelan orchestra, and are seated in the *Balai Sekehe Gong*. If husband and wife live long enough, they will become heads of the village *(kabayan)*, and take their seats at the very head of the *balai*.

So if we wish to interpret village organization, birthday rituals or why the seaside is unpopular, we can make use of our knowledge of this spatial model. But if we are to be good phenomenologists we cannot pretend that the Balinese see *everything* in terms of this structure. We are still at the level of the *Umwelt*, the "environing world," defining one of the symbolic structures used in the construction of objects in it. To get to the level of the lifeworld, it is necessary to look at other structures, other aspects of the *Umwelt*. A Balinese temple festival occurs in the lifeworld of those who participate in it. Clearly it is not possible, given our understanding of what is meant by "lifeworld" *(lebenswelt)*, to give a complete description of this lifeworld. But the more we know about the constitution of the *Umwelt*, or the "symbolic prestructuring of reality," the more we will understand of what occurs in the temple festival. We know why, when women bring offerings to the temple, they carry them on their heads: because heads are *kaja*, so to carry things on one's head is the most honoring position. Once in the temple, we will find many examples of the *kaja-kelod* structure in everything from the spatial layout (with the most important shrines in the *kaja* area and offerings to demons at the *kelod* end); to social behavior, as lower caste people duck their heads in the presence of Brahmins and Satriyas.

What we are after is not a complete analysis of the lifeworld, which, given Husserl's analysis, is impossible anyway, but an understanding of the symbolic prestructuring of reality. Phenomenology provides a methodology for investigating the constitution of symbolic systems, not only as systems, but as systems actually deployed by people immersed in particular cultures. This emphasis distinguishes phenomenological research from structuralism, where the constitution of symbolic objects is left in limbo. Lévi-Strauss, for example, deals with symbols in terms of a hypothetical *pensée sauvage*, without considering their roles in the constitution of particular social worlds. From a phenomenological perspective, his analyses are left unfinished.

The style of phenomenological investigation proposed here retains the general framework of the lifeworld developed by Husserl and elaborated as a social theory by Schutz *et al.*, but suggests a different emphasis: systematic analysis of the symbolic prestructuring of the social world. Such investigation proceeds from the *Umwelt* (environing world) to the lifeworld by way of circumscribed symbolic systems *(Realität)* abstracted from the *Umwelt*, tested for their role in the constitution of objects in the *Umwelt*, and finally fitted into the lifeworld.

# REFERENCES

Berger, P. L., and Luckmann, Thomas. *The social construction of reality.* Garden City, N.Y.: Doubleday, 1966.

Geertz, Clifford. On the nature of anthropological understanding. *American Scientist,* 1975, *63,* 1.

Husserl, Edmund. *Cartesian meditations, an introduction to phenomenology.* Tr. by D. Cairna. The Hague: M. Nijhoff, 1960.

Husserl, Edmund. *Ideas: A general introduction to pure phenomenology.* Tr. by W. R. Boyce Gibson. New York: Collier Books, 1962.

Husserl, Edmund. *Logical investigations.* Tr. by J. N. Findlay. New York: Humanities Press, 1970.

Lansing, J. S. *Evil in the morning of the world: Phenomenological approaches to a Balinese community.* Ann Arbor: Michigan Papers on South and Southeast Asia #6, 1974.

Natanson, Maurice (Ed.). *Phenomenology and the social reality: Essays in memory of Alfred Schutz.* The Hague: M. Nijhoff, 1970.

Natanson, Maurice (Ed.). *Phenomenology and the social sciences* (2 vols.). Evanston, Ill.: Northwestern University Press, 1973.

Ricoeur, Paul. *Husserl: An analysis of his phenomenology.* Evanston, Ill.: Northwestern University Press, 1967.

Schutz, Alfred. *The phenomenology of the social world.* (G. Walsh and F. Lehnert, trans.) Evanston, Ill.: Northwestern University Press, 1967.

Schutz, Alfred, and Luckmann, Thomas. *The structures of the life-world.* Evanston, Ill.: Northwestern University Press, 1973.

von Uexküll, Baron J. J. *Umwelt und Innenwelt der Tiere.* Berlin: J. Springer, 1909.

# Part Two
# SOME MOTIFS
# IN TELLANTRY

chapter six

# The Crocodile Couple
# and the Snake Encounter
# in the Tellantry
# of East Sumba, Indonesia

Marie Jeanne Adams

Harvard University

The crocodile is the major predator on the coastal plains of Sumba, a small island in eastern Indonesia, and the people believe that large snakes, such as the python, prey on man. One might think that these feared creatures would be shunned in popular or sacred stories. On the contrary, these reptiles are widely used images in the oral tradition, or tellantry, of Sumba and in many other island cultures of Indonesia. ("Tellantry" is a new word being introduced here, referring to the language arts which develop to be spoken and listened to, that is, utterances embellished beyond the minimal needs of ordinary discourse, such as myths, legends, tales, poetry, songs, chants, prayers, puns, name jokes, swearing riddles, and any other special forms.)[1]

Without losing their essential character as especially powerful creatures, these reptiles play many different roles. The humorous friendly crocodile in a short animal tale is strikingly different from the implacable avenger of serious stories. Each role, of course, must be considered according to the kind of tale and in relation to its local context. Using particular cases, I should like to illustrate the subtleties of the symbolic use of these reptiles: the crocodile image in one form of tellantry, the clan-owned myth, and the snake figure in a commonly known story that incorporates traditional wisdom. Based on my year's stay in the Kapunduk district, I intend to provide the contextual references that turn these reptile figures into appropriate symbols for the Sumbanese and into intelligible

---

[1]With this new term, *tellantry*, we may properly limit the use of the word "literature" to written material. This paper is part of a longer study in progress on animal figures in Sumba tellantry.

ones for us. Because of the importance of context, I offer a good deal of information on the general setting and elaborate on certain features of the culture, such as the common use of symbolic speech and the importance of place and of explicit social rules, that will contribute to understanding the several uses of the reptiles as symbols.

## THE SETTING

The Sumbanese use as political regions sections of coastal land divided by rivers running to the sea. Near the river mouth they establish a capital village, which serves as a royal residence and ceremonial center. East Sumbanese will first identify themselves as members of one of these named districts or traditional kingdoms. Inhabitants of each capital believe that they are following a rule of life credited to a founder priest-deity (Marapu Ratu) who, replicating on Sumba the heavenly community from which he originated, fathered the royal leadership and instituted the *kabihu,* the Sumbanese equivalent for patricians and their responsibilities.

According to the most sacred priestly chant, which recounts these great deeds, the founder-ancestors of the various clans (*kabihu* or "houses," *uma* or clan-sections) were companions of the priest-deity's voyage from the upperworld to the local capital. The objects and animals these founder-ancestors brought with them define the roles and duties of the various clans (Adams, 1974). Following the ancestor priest-deity's rules, that is, the affirmation and preservation of the inherited way of life, is the explicitly avowed and reiterated purpose of the clan leaders.[2] In the phrases of the priestly chant, the performance of the oncoming generation should be as similar to the forefathers' way as are leaves of trees in successive seasons and as colts repeating the form of their sires.

In the capital each important clan possesses a large house in which members store their surpluses and hold assemblies and rites of worship. Formerly such a capital was situated on a hilltop near a major river (Figure 1).[3] For the entire community the hilltop capital, situated between the Upperworld of the distant heavens and the Underworld beneath the surface of the earth and sea, was the pinnacle of the human sphere. The way of life in the capital village was the standard, the measure of all things, the focus of Sumbanese life interests.

---

[2]When asked the "why" of any custom, a Sumbanese is likely to answer, "Because we always do it that way," or "Because our ancestors did it that way," or "Because the customary rules (inherited from the ancestors) say it must be done that way." This reply should not be dismissed as meaningless. This is the most important statement about the conscious culture of the Sumbanese. The people explicitly want to maintain the inherited way of life. They do in fact initiate and gradually effect changes for various reasons, but the conscious aim is to repeat a certain set of patterns. There are some far-reaching implications for this position.

[3]The figures and the explanatory notes appear at the end of the article in Appendix 1.

Today the capital of Kapunduk dominates a region of about 15 square miles comprising several smaller villages. After two generations of government pressure, the last clan has moved down (1963) from the "big capital" on a high spur overlooking the Kapunduk River valley; and the core of the capital population, numbering about 1,500, now occupies hamlets along the river. Culturally the most conservative community of East Sumba, the Kapunduku maintain their hereditary organizations and their loyalty to their royal leader, entitled Tamu Umbu, who is regarded as supernaturally powerful (sacred king) and the owner of the land and all other wealth (livestock, objects of value). Faithful to the traditional structure of the community, they retain the distinction between the ritual capital and the surrounding world by holding major ceremonies in a hamlet, Maru, at the foot of the former capital (Figure 2).

In conducting all rites and ceremonies and in negotiating all exchanges, whether of food, services, or women, among social groups, the Kapunduku employ a special poetic diction delivered in a cadenced style. This ceremonial language consists of a series of figurative images set rigidly in paired phrases of parallel meaning. The imagery, drawn from many aspects of life, from the birds chattering in the trees to the baby lolling in its mother's skirt, characterizes the purposes and positions of the interacting parties. Because this language is required for so many occasions, negotiators or speakers, called *wunangu,* can be found in almost every hamlet (Adams, 1971a). There is a conscious savoring and lively appreciation of the various speakers' performances in terms of style and aptness of phrasing. Frequent use of this rich ritual language shows that the Sumbanese are skillful both in creating and in interpreting metaphoric imagery.

To understand metaphoric and symbolic usage on Sumba, we should first recognize the importance of place in Sumbanese thought. References to place provide a consistent and meaningful grid for ordering and expressing Sumbanese thoughts, much as do time units for European thought. Ready evidence of this habit of mind appears in the frequent association, in ceremonial language and in other forms of tellantry, of creatures with their habitat, in phrases such as bird-of-heavens, shrimp-of-sea, horses-on-hills, buffaloes-in-mudholes. Places also define social beings. Royalty may not be referred to in discourse by personal or dynastic names but as lord of this village or lord of that (clan) house. In harvest myths, which are recounted at all-night rituals, the stock characters are Lady Kahu, Person-of-the-Heavens, and Lord Ndelu, Person-of-the-Earth. The deep interest in places and their names is evident on many levels of expression from the most complex and sacred priestly chant at the Marapu Ratu feast to the conventional daily greeting, which inquires not about being but about place. "Where are you going?" the people unfailingly ask, and one must not fail to reply giving one's destination, even if it is simply "Upriver" or "Downstream." The sacred chant rendered by the Big Speaker at the Marapu Ratu (priest-deity) feast offers the cosmological "history" of Kapunduku in the form of a long enumeration of places visited or named (meaning *laid claim to*) by the founding ancestors before reaching the present capital site.

The importance of place relates to Sumbanese belief in a structured cosmos, comprising the sensible world (including the visible portion of the firmament, the earth, and the sea), other places known about, and forces thought to affect daily affairs or immediate surroundings. A large part of what goes on in this cultural cosmos falls within human control. To solve their problems the Sumbanese give much more attention to interhuman techniques than to manipulation of the material world around them. Tangible and intangible elements in this cosmos are believed susceptible to manipulation by the same means that one human being applies to other human beings. Thus for a whole range of problems that arise in their cultural cosmos, the Sumbanese apply the procedures that they find effective in interhuman relations. For example, to obtain abundant crops they perform welcoming ceremonies and offer fine flattering speeches, reciprocal compensation, and abundant food and entertainment to the "spirits" of good crops.

As a whole, the rules governing all activities, including efforts to solve major problems, stem from the priest-deity (Marapu Ratu). If the community follows along the path of effort projected by these rules, it may normally expect not only to survive but also to reach the goals thought desirable by this cultural community. Mishaps and failures indicate that the sufferer is at fault (Adams, 1971b). Although according to local legends many communities have failed, the formulaic solutions of the Marapu Ratu are sufficiently effective in relation to human problems that a number of communities survive in East Sumba, continuing to cultivate the land, reproduce, and organize various group undertakings.

Some living creatures, such as large wild animals, respond less well than others to Sumbanese techniques of manipulation and escape Sumbanese control. From this point of view, these animals become useful as symbols for dangerous and exceptional qualities. The three nonhuman characters which play leading roles in Kapunduku myth (crocodile, great snake, and monster forest-cat) are of this nature. The crocodile is a known threat to human life. The Sumbanese believe that large snakes, such as the python, are inimical to man. (In fact, a small deer is the largest creature a snake could overpower.) Dangerous character is also attributed to forests, even the rather small forests that occur here and there on the coastal plains, but especially the thick forest of the interior highlands where coastal men must travel on trading visits. In fact, forests are places where people get lost and travelers are killed by stealthy attack. In stories the predatory character of "forest" is projected in vital form as a monster forest-cat who swallows things whole. In terms of actual power we might distinguish these three figures along a line of "reality": the predatory crocodile does exist; the large snake is only believed to be a danger; and the monster-cat is an entirely imaginary creature. As mental images, however, these three creatures enjoy the same kind of reality in Sumbanese stories.

For the Sumbanese, these animals share certain features. Their natural *place* is outside the capital community. All three possess an intrinsic quality of threat, being considered larger and in some way or other more powerful than man. Toward all three in nature the Sumbanese adopt a policy of noninterference. There is a pronounced reluctance to kill crocodiles or large snakes, and forests are avoided. One or two persons would not enter a small forest to cut down trees (firewood is gathered by women in the savannahs). If a large trunk is needed for a rare ritual purpose, such as a clan-house pillar, a foray is conducted with great ceremony by many more men than are needed.

Nevertheless, the imaginary creature, the monster-cat, requires a different kind of analysis from that of the real reptiles. The cat symbol incorporates several layers of meanings, but its basic identification as a forest creature remains constant through different types of tellantry. The reptiles, however, appear in stories in quite different roles, much as in life one might meet them under different circumstances. Because I am stressing the importance of context in interpreting symbolic figures, I confine the following discussion to various forms of crocodile and snake appearance, dealing first with the crocodile as it appears in clan myths.

## THE CROCODILE

Clan myths are a special type of tellantry that can be narrated in the vernacular but only at certain times and places (Adams, 1970).[4] In the various districts of East Sumba, one encounters a plot which represents the ancestor of a "house" (clan) arriving on the scene as a crocodile. By magical transformation into a handsome youth, the crocodile wins a local girl and thus fathers the family represented by the house. For this frequently encountered story I suggest a general interpretation that accords with Sumbanese attitudes. Because of the underlying assumption that the capital community is the focal point of human culture, its inhabitants bear the responsibility of being the human beings. Therefore logically someone outside this community is by definition not human. The crocodile-lover can then be understood to represent a person who is a stranger, not a member of the recognized circle of social groups acceptable for marriage or one belonging to any group with which it is not customary to have marriage ties (for discussion of marriage links between groups, see Adams, 1969, Ch. 3). This nonhuman being is pictured as a powerful crocodile (or python) because he possesses extraordinary powers; he is a being capable of resisting the constraints of human marriage rules and withal succeeding in achieving his aims. He is able to make such a strong impression on the community, through forcefulness of personality, wealth, or other exceptional qualities, that he succeeds in winning a "human" partner in marriage, which is *the* sign of communal acceptance. The

---

[4]In Adams (1970) I distinguish three types of Kapunduk myths according to where and when they are told: the myths chanted in ceremonial language only at the sacred pillar inside the clan house; the clan myths in the vernacular told on the porches of clan houses in the dry season; and harvest myths told in the fields.

people will regard his children born in the community as ''human.'' Members of clans claiming such origins recount their story with great assurance and pride, showing how firmly they identify themselves with the powerful character and success of their putative progenitor.[5]

Although I assign a general framework of meaning to this common plot, I would like to emphasize that, in my experience on Sumba, small differences in the narrations are significant in relation to local contexts (Adams, 1971c). It is important to recognize further that in other clan myths, very different meanings can attach to the crocodile figure. I shall illustrate this point by analyzing the crocodile heroes of a specific clan myth of Kapunduk. In order to grasp the symbolic meanings, this myth requires detailed consideration of its local references.

## THE CROCODILE COUPLE

The story concerns the clan Pupunderi, whose temple-house from its beginnings stood in the Kapunduk River valley, but *outside* the hilltop capital. A crocodile story, the founding myth of this clan as told by its elders differs from the general crocodile-lover type cited, and it is just these differences that make the story fit the Pupunderi clan in Kapunduk. It is a convention of this kind of storytelling that the opening states the condition for which the rest of the story provides a background. Briefly and simply, the myth is a precisely drawn image of the clan's role in Kapunduku society:[6]

> The Marapu (deities) of clan Pupunderi are human beings who became crocodiles. The man, Umbu (lord) Mbora Pupunderi, and the woman, Rambu (lady) Wandal Pahoka—she was from clan Pahoka at Mboro Mbaku, the sacred origin village of the founder priest-deity—became crocodiles. Rambu Wandal had no husband, Umbu Mbora had not yet married. She attracted him, well, they attracted each other. Actually her rightful marriage partner-to-be lived in Melolo (a district on the east coast). He came to the village Mboro Mbaku to take her for his bride. But Rambu Wandal, drawn in her heart to Umbu Mbora, did not want to go to Melolo.
>
> One day she said, "I'm going to go bathing in the river," but that was not the simple truth. Umbu Mbora did the same. He said, "I'm going to Mboro Mbaku to bathe." They both arrived at the river at the same time and dived in together. When they reached the deep waters of the sea, they both turned into crocodiles and they married in the water. They continued in crocodile form as Marapu. Umbu Mbora did not want to take a wife from another place. Let me become a crocodile, he said.

[5]Although not a specific focus of my research, I encountered several cases in which the clan myth claimed crocodile origin, but families recounted the adventures of a progenitor who was one of several kinds of ''outsider.''

[6]This account follows my notes on the clan leader's narration: a similar version recounted by a Big Speaker (Wunangu Bokulu) of Kapunduk appears at the end of this article in Appendix 2.

The situation of clan Pupunderi in Kapunduk is typical of a clan with an outpost function. Its temple-house is situated outside the hilltop capital, and services for its deity may never be held in that ceremonial center. Pupunderi is not considered a traditional founder-clan of Kapunduk (for discussion of Kapunduk clan organization, see Adams, 1974); the name belongs to a large clan well known in the neighboring Lewa district, and in ordinary conversation members claim to come from Lewa. Probably, as usually is the case, the founder broke away from a Lewa prince or king because of a quarral and entered the service of the king in Kapunduk. In Kapunduk, however, the Lewa group did not obtain a place in the capital village, but accepted an outpost station with both aggressive and defensive tasks. In such a case the king in turn provides brides to the house at little or no brideprice. These brides must be of sufficiently high quality to be able to manage the heavy responsibilities of such an isolated community, which may contain 70 or more people.

In earlier times of internecine strife, such outposts situated in exposed locations outside the walled, hilltop village required a leader of exceptional courage and boldness. The outpost is characterized by the presence of a very large imposing house-temple and by the possession of a special kind of deity (Marapu Pawerungu), that is, a deity who can irresistibly attract its desired object. If the outpost is situated near a river, as is Pupunderi, this kind of deity is in the form of a crocodile (if near a forest, it will be a snake).

One of the most widespread and deep-seated beliefs about the crocodile is that it can seize, as a victim, a guilty person crossing a river. The firmness of this belief suggests that it represents the other side of the coin of faith in the normative rules which assure proper fulfillment of life, so that failures are attributed to breaking the rules, that is, to guilt caused by an unacknowledged infraction. The apparently arbitrary is made to fit conceptually into the order believed to characterize the cultural cosmos.

Thus located near a river, the crocodile deity with his irresistible drawing power can capture thieves who, in order to flee the Kapunduku capital area with livestock or gold treasures, will cross that river to get out of the district. In sum, the crocodile nature of the deity, Umbu Mbora, corresponds to the essential powers or function of the clan house. Every feature of the story corresponds to Pupunderi's situation.

The drawing power of the deity is paralleled in the attracting power of Umbu Mbora in the love affair. His attraction is such that Ramba Wandal is brave enough to run away with him in the presence of her prospective proper marriage partner. She and her lover flee from Mboro Mbaku, an ancient capital considered in Kapunduk to be the fount of traditional law, which means, in this case, that they leave behind them traditional marriage procedures. Further, the runaway character of Umbu Mbora's marriage signifies marriage without payment of brideprice, which as just mentioned is a prerogative of clan Pupunderi. That Rambu Wandal was slated to be given to a distant land indicates that she was of high class standing, thus according with the high quality of brides required for clan Pupunderi. Their marriage is not fixed by ties of mutual obligation consequent on an arranged marriage, but rests on personal relations and the fact that they both, upon reaching the deep sea, share a common identity just as upon reaching their outpost residence, they will share a common responsibility.

That the wife becomes a crocodile is significant in another sense. She not only shares her husband's function but she also becomes a crocodile "outsider," that is, although native to the capital she and her descendants are henceforth committed to residence outside the hilltop center, the difference between the capital village and the outside being represented in the story as the difference between inhabiting the land and residing in the sea. The closing remark reaffirms Umbu Mbora's loyalty to Kapunduk. He wants a bride only from there, and he willingly performs his outpost function.

In the following chart I list features of the story with the frames of reference and inferences which are based on common attitudes expressed by the Sumbanese in Kapunduk. We see that techniques of social control are embedded in a complex orchestration of elements in an artistic and memorable form.

| While They Are Human | Reference | Inference |
|---|---|---|
| She is from Mboro Mbaku. | Mboro Mbaku is believed to be the site of an ancient settlement near Kapunduk where the founder priest-deity and his companions establish the formal rules of Sumba society. | She is from the center of legality. |
| He is a member of the Pupunderi clan. | Pupunderi is well known as the name of a clan in the capital of the Lewa kingdom southeast of Kapunduku. | Member of a strong clan, he is an outsider. |
| She is attracted to him. | In love affairs (as distinct from marriage) women may take the initiative. | She, that is, Kapunduk, wants him. |
| They are both attracted to each other. | Under the strict circumstances of village life, a love affair requires cooperation of both parties. | Their relationship rests on mutual need. |
| She is slated to marry in Melolo district. | Only women of high standing (royalty or their servants) marry to distant districts such as Melolo. | She must be of high quality. |
| Although present, her proper marriage partner is rejected. | In exceptional cases, young people try to avoid the arranged marriage rules, but it is unheard of daring to do this at such an advanced stage. | For her to reject a traditional alliance, the lover must have had compelling powers of attraction. |

| While They Are Human | Reference | Inference |
| --- | --- | --- |
| They both intend to bathe in the river. | In ritual, bathing marks the end of a certain state. | For both of them this indicates a preliminary to entry into a different state. |
| They deceive their companions in order to go bathing. | Normally elopement is a deceptive device agreed upon in advance by both parties in order to reduce brideprice obligations. | The brideprice is low. The union rests on obligations other than brideprice. |
| Staying underwater, they continue toward the sea. | Human beings cannot do this. | They are going beyond human performance. |

| As Crocodiles | Reference | Inference |
| --- | --- | --- |
| In the deep sea . . . | In relation to the land occupied by human beings, the deep sea is a different kind of world. | They are becoming creatures different from human beings. |
| . . . they become crocodiles. | Such change shows superhuman powers. | They possess superhuman powers. |
| Crocodiles | Crocodiles can live in the deep sea. | They will continue to inhabit a place different from a customary human dwelling place. |
| As clan deities (Marapu of Pupunderi) they remain crocodiles. | The character of clan deities determines the duties of clan, here Pupunderi; as deity he retains his special powers. | Together they will carry out the clan duties of seizing the guilty. |
| He rejects the idea of a bride from elsewhere. | He foregoes ties to earlier alliances. | He prefers his tie with her (Kapunduk) over all others. |
| He affirms his acceptance of a crocodile nature. | He affirms his acceptance of his place in Kapunduk. | He is loyal to Kapunduk. |

## THE SNAKE ENCOUNTER

I have already mentioned the symbolic appearances of a great snake as a powerful outsider-lover and as a forest-outpost guardian figure. Drawing on the snake's ability to shift from a formless lump into undulating form, moving without arms and legs (as compared with human beings, this is a measure of exceptional power), another clan myth of Kapunduk uses the snake as a symbol of the creator-lord of the land, a deity credited with the power to create hills and valleys, thus giving form and shape to the landscape. Outside of clan myths, there is another powerful image of the snake in a widely known story for which I know of no restrictions on time or place of telling, which seems to be left to personal predilection, a story that I refer to as the *snake encounter*.

The snake encounter refers to a private meeting between a person and a snake at which, upon demand, that person obtains the right to wealth, talent, and success; but if that person is tempted into eventual marriage with the snake, the encounter results in early death. It is thus a personal experience which is desirable but which if pursued to extremes proves dangerous, even fatal. The specific features of accounts of the snake encounter in Kapunduk are given in the form of a numbered list, for ease in matching subsequent commentary.

1. There is a common belief in Kapunduk that an individual while he or she is alone may meet a creature, identified as a snake in the temporary form of a human being,[7] outside the capital village under a tree, beside a big boulder, or in the open fields, but not in the gardens near the house. Instances of this encounter recounted to me concerned only men. Not only must the subject be alone, the Sumbanese stress, but also he must be "attuned," that is, he must feel that it is his fate *(talanga ndewa a nda)*. He may have this experience also vividly in a sleeping or walking dream. It is essentially what we would call a *psychological experience*.
2. If the person becomes frightened, the creature runs or does not speak with him. It is important not to be afraid; it is essential to be bold enough to face the creature, even to the point of grabbing its mane or body hair.
3. The next step is to demand straight off wealth, talent, lively spirits, or knowledge of how to succeed in one's endeavors.
4. Following this encounter, the individual returns to that spot and sacrifices in a prayer ceremony. He may then bring a gold or silver piece or some small object as a sign of this experience to his own sleeping room in the clan house. This sign is considered henceforth the "seat of his spirit" *(mandidungu ndewa)*.[8] When his clan house celebrates a feast for the founder priest-deity, a special prayer sacrifice is also made in the person's room for the benefit of his *mandidungu ndewa*.
5. After this, other people cannot refuse one's requests, they will feel constrained to yield.
6. One must be careful not to be so tempted by this creature as to yield to its aim, marriage, for later when the children are grown, the human partner will be called into the world of the wife or husband to help marry off their children, that is, this person will die young, before his or her own human children are married or before he or she has human grandchildren.
7. The antidote to being tempted into marriage is also given by the informed older men entitled *elders (Ama Bokulu:* "big fathers"):

[7]Personal accounts show that there are actually many shades or levels to this experience. In terms of creatures met, it could be a huge snake (most elaborately a snake crested with gold ornaments), a little snake, a goatlike figure, a crocodile, a lizard, or for women, a monkey. The man or woman may keep the experience more or less secret.

[8]An inherited piece may be used, or in some cases the sign is said to appear in one's room following the encounter.

When she demands you marry her, you ask her, What is your *kabihu* (clan)? She answers, *Kabihu* so-and-so. You answer, That's just my clan, too, so we are brother and sister and can't marry. Then repeat your demands. (Adams, n.d.)

## COMMENTARY

The snake encounter depicts the value assessment of personal drive toward success (whether wealth, outstanding performance, or an object desired) in Kapunduk society.

1. First of all, the Sumbanese make clear that the snake encounter arises in the private experience of an individual when he is alone in a place considered the antithesis of the capital community, or in the privacy of a dream. The circumstances are in strong contrast to the customary form of prayer request for benefits (wealth, outstanding performance, and knowledge). These prayers are public ceremonies, and requests are uttered in traditional phrases common to all by skilled speakers or elders in the company or at least their assistants and on occasions fixed by custom (*huru;* Indonesian, *adat*) (Figures 5–8). In contrast to the restrictive specifications on narrating myths, which relate essentially to group interests, the snake encounter may be recounted at any private conversation, that is, it functions within the personal sphere.
2. The basic requirement for success is boldness and conviction of manner. These qualities are essential for advancement in a strict class society in which from birth one's attitudes and activities are channeled into fixed paths, all of which maintain and benefit the class at the top and reinforce the distance among classes as a guarantee of stability. Advancement, gains, or acquisitions of skills must be made according to the rules, and all lower classes are trained not to make a demand on superiors within the system. Boldness is the necessary requirement for those with natural leadership, exceptional talent, or desire for powers not accorded by cultural rule.
3. This boldness expresses itself not only in seizing opportunities, as one seizes the mane of the magic snake, but also in verbalizing demands. We can realize the significance of this if we consider that requests, not money, are the medium of exchange. Like denominations of money, requests range in psychological coinage from the most self-denigrating pleas to outrageous demands in commanding tones. There are built-in limits for this system. Repeated personal requests (that is, ones outside of the customary codes of kinship or accepted lines of reciprocity) will be resented and gain one the reputation of a witch. On the other hand, repeated refusals to fulfill obligations make one subject to illness (this may in fact stem from psychological conflict or poisoning) and early death. The successful demand, which gains one's ends *without negative reciprocation,* is the ladder to achievement; and an outstandingly successful person is thus justified by his or her success.
4. To confirm the experience in the form of a prayer sacrifice and to bring a sign of it into one's room in the clan house is in effect to socialize the ambition and drive of the individual, to channel this drive into leadership within the clan, thus avoiding pursuit of a private, deviant ambition.
5. Furthermore, once the experience with successful outcome is made public, one gains the benefit of the ''bandwagon effect.'' As noted in the awed attitude evident toward

certain individuals in Kapunduk, if others believe that an individual is bound to succeed or possesses special powers, they are inclined to go along with him, they tend not to refuse his demands.

6. If, however, one becomes too zealous, too devoted to a goal of personal success, one may die young. To die before one's children are married, or before one has grandchildren, suggests that one does not fulfill the proper preoccupations of one's life. This might be due in this case to keeping up with the difficult tasks of becoming wealthy and seeking success in this harsh and demanding setting. On the negative side, success too personally confined leads to accusations of sorcery or condemnation even by one's own clan.

7. Finally, the most telling point is that the antidote to being tempted into this unusual bondage (marriage to the snake of success) is the mention of clan rules. This is a reminder to keep one's ambitions on the proper path of one's clan group, not to go too far in pursuit of private desires. Within one's clan, efforts and rewards are shared. Staying within these customary obligations is one way to be safe from overzealous, self-destroying drive.

The snake encounter may best be considered as a parable on the possibilities and hazards of personal drive and ambition within a stable social structure which stresses group effort and communal rewards. In spite of what seems to an outsider to be a rigid and unalterable social structure with numerous built-in guarantees of inherited class rights (such as hereditary personal servants), individuals in fact do rise through the classes or win personal eminence for various talents or qualities. The snake encounter parable offers a symbolic open door for individual achievement.

These all-too-brief comments are intended to convey some idea of the precision and succinct ordering of the many-layered images of Sumbanese tellantry. Whatever other kind of analysis one may wish to perform on this corpus, it is worthwhile and interesting to consider each figure in the rich particulars of its immediate setting.

# APPENDIX

## Text of Clan Myth Belonging to Clan Pupunderi, Haru Hamlet, Kapunduk District, East Sumba, Indonesia

Informant: Hina Malutaka, Spokesman *(Wunangu),* Kapunduk dialect

Tau mandjadi wuja, tau wenu, tau monu. Tau ja la Haru, Marapu la Haru. Nggara tau? Tau Pupunderi. I Mbora Pupunderi dangu Rambu Wandal Pahoka (Kabihu Pahoka) ndjadi wuja.

Njuna, ba tau ja. Umbu Mborq ndadu na lalei; Rambu Wandal, ndadu ningu tau olina. Na wukuja i Rambu i Umbu Mbora, karengga pawuku. Na tuba tau olina la Umalolu, la Rendi ja. Hemeingu ka ku paphanja wananja hu deta. Hemeinguneka la Mboru Mbaku. I Rambu kikunja i Umbu Mbora, nda na mbuhangu palaku la Umalolu.

Longgi paihi la loku wanai Rambu. Akalneka. Hama i Umbu Mbora. Akalneka ba halaku paihi wana. Marunggu taka la Mboru Mbaku hi tama la wai. Runu pangalangu la loku. Hama i Rambu taka la loku tama pangalangu la wai. Djadi bei wuja, pakanoma la wai da wuja.

Tama tjo da la libu muru na ma mandjalungu pandjadi wujangu. Marapu ha padaingu lai nu. Mbora nda na mbuhangu palalei hau pangia. Mata ka ta ndjadi wujangu, wana.

(Adams Field Journal, 1969. 37:29)

Figure 1. Hilltop capital of Rende district, East Sumba, Indonesia. Stone and cement monuments to leaders of the past mark the center of the village, between two rows of large, peaked clan houses.

Figure 2. Maru, ceremonial village at the foot of Kapunduk capital, formerly located on the hill at left. East Sumba.

Figure 3. Men gathered to hear the exchange of negotiations in ritual language by special speakers, *wunangu*, at right. Mara Wua, East Sumba.

Figure 4. Rites to open the planting season include display of vigorous dancing by men and women. Maru village, Kapunduk district, East Sumba. This dancing enlivens the community and, it is believed, entertains the invited spirits.

Figure 5. Rites always involve group participation, such as this outdoor ritual in honor of the great ancestor's arrival on the shores of Sumba island. Kapunduk district. Big Speaker (Wunangu Bokulu) Ndapungu Lalu Pingu of clan Ngieur, Natangu village, East Sumba.

Figure 6. Ritual, even if held on behalf of an individual, involves a number of men. Besides the sponsor of the rite, there is the main priest-speaker in the center; he is accompanied by a man who prays and one who responds. Here the speaker will pray to recall the spirit of an individual who disappeared and for whom proper burial rites could not be held. Melolo district, East Sumba.

Figure 7. Preparations for major indoor ritual before the planting season involves many men in a wide range of activities, such as this serious effort to organize the proper number and kind of chickens to sacrifice. Maru village, Kapunduk district, East Sumba.

Figure 8. At the preplanting ritual, the Maru temple-house is filled and surrounded with people who listen to the long chants about the deeds of the ancestors. The group nature of formal ritual is illustrated here also in the large number of offering baskets to the various clan ancestors. Kapunduk district, East Sumba.

*Field photographs by M. J. Adams, 1968–1969.*

103

# REFERENCES

Adams, M. J. *System and meaning in East Sumba textile design: A study in traditional Indonesian art.* Yale University Southeast Asia Studies *Cultural Report* No. 16. New Haven: Yale University Southeast Asia Studies, 1969.

Adams, M. J. Field journals, Kapunduk, n.d.

Adams, M. J. Myths and self-image among the Kapunduk people of Sumba, *Indonesia,* Ithaca (No. 10), 80–106, map, 1970.

Adams, M. J. Work patterns and symbolic structures, *Southeast Asia, an International Quarterly,* Carbondale, *1* (No. 4), 321–334, illus., 1971a.

Adams, M. J. History in a Sumba myth, *Asian Folklore Studies, 30* (No. 2), 133–139, illus., 1971b.

Adams, M. J. Themes and variations in eastern Indonesia, *Manusia Indonesia,* Jakarta (Nos. 4-5-6), 425–440, illus., 1971c.

Adams, M. J. Symbols of the organized community in East Sumba, Indonesia, *BIJD, 130* (Nos. 2-3), 324–347, 1974.

# chapter seven

# Iban Folk Literature

# and Socialization:

# The Fertility of Symbolism

Vinson H. Sutlive Jr.

College of William and Mary

The purpose of this study is to analyze the folk literature of the Iban and its significance for their socialization. Though less developed in other art forms than many societies in Borneo at approximately the same techno-economic level, the Iban have created a vast and comprehensive oral literature.[1] The central thesis of this study is that their oral literature is crucially important to our understanding of Iban culture and persons, "untrammelled individualists, aggressive and proud in demeanour" (Freeman, 1955:10).

Iban literature is by no means a perfect reflection (Lessa, 1966) of the culture, nor does it exhaust the possibilities of form and expression. The culture cannot be understood merely within the literature, but it is most doubtful that it can be understood without it. The literature is both reflective and refractive, created in the wider context of Iban culture. Some reflections are true, others distorted and difficult if not impossible to recognize. Nevertheless, the images and their structural relations must be examined for the insights they provide into the perceptions and projections of the Iban. The circumstances of the Iban composers have defined the limits within which they may juxtapose the universal themes of man and nature, individual and group, cause and effect, fellow and foreigner. In creating their expressions they have drawn on and recreated their world, whether faithfully or in fantasy, for setting, plot, characters, and the sanctions that give these meaning.

Iban literature has developed as a body of knowledge and dreams, in which

[1] A list of the major forms of Iban folk literature is found in Appendix 1. Appendix 2 lists some publications of folk literature in Iban.

are combined ethnoscience, traditions, and beliefs about the world, man, and society. It carries a message of values, affirmations, and contradictions, encoding both the adaptive responses and the abject regrets of the group. As well as embracing the core values, the literature includes treatments of such issues as intergenerational conflict, the oedipus complex, and deviance. "Collective ego-ideals" exist for both men and women in the figures of the god Keling and the goddess Kumang, but since some persons realize that they cannot play god, lesser figures also exist. *Antu* are patently projections of stresses with "teleological functions" (Spiro, 1952:497) before which most braves cower but whom the "shemen" engage in battle. Apodictic statements command conformity in statements to the effect that "Thou shalt!" and "Thou shalt not!" followed by mechanisms for compromise, such as, "If you must, do it this way. . . ."

The relationship between the Iban and their literature is reciprocal. On the one hand, the literature has been produced from the perceptions of the society. On the other hand, it has a constraining and constitutive effect on the perceptions of the members by the dual processes of eisegesis and exegesis. I am interested in this constitutive role, the development of the "culturally constituted behavioral environment" (Hallowell, 1955). For our perceptions are the only reality we know, and the purpose of our actions is to control the state of our perceived world (Powers, 1973).

Through his extensive literature, the individual is impressed with his ethnic identity vis-á-vis other groups. Fluency and self-expression are highly valued by the Iban. The lips of newborn babies are touched with chilis and salt that their speech may be powerful *(bisa)*. Chants are sung to nursing infants, and youngsters imbibe a surprising amount of the literature by age five. It is not unusual to hear children of five quoting long sections of narratives and verses.

A most important aspect of Iban socialization is that of learning to teach. Each Iban becomes a teacher of what he has learned. As Pettitt has written,

> We cannot read deeply in ethnological literature without being struck by the fact that primitive education was a community project in which all reputable elders participated at the instigation of individual families. The result was not merely to focus community attention on the child, but also to make the child's education a constant challenge to the elders to review, analyze, dramatize, and defend their cultural heritage. Their own beliefs, understanding, and faith, their personal integration in the culture, and their collective unity, all were prompted by the necessity of assuming the role of educators of their children (1946).

As he listens to the materials repeated on the longhouse *ruai* and now broadcast each evening at 6:30 and 8:00 over Radio Malaysia, Kuching, the individual is made aware of the great crowd of ancestral witnesses who surround him and to whom he owes his life. A part of the autonymic process of self-identification involves familiarity with and acceptance of these "global" symbols. Although the group of which he is immediately aware may be limited to his longhouse community or ceremonial fraternity *(sapengabang)*, the individual readily identifies with fellow Iban of other districts and divisions through the introjection of common symbols.

In the pluralistic state of Sarawak, the Iban have been the most aggressive of the indigenous peoples. This aggression has led to their supplanting some groups, and assimilating members of others, in their movement into and through the state. The observer cannot help being impressed by the self-confidence of the Iban and the security they feel in their world. Restating the thesis of this study, the confidence of the Iban derives in part from their comprehension of their environment and the symbols by which they have articulated their relations to their world, to one another, and to other groups.

There are few situations in which the Iban cannot find some appropriate expression in their literature. These expressions imply a high degree of familiarity with the circumstances of life and are powerful defenses permitting the individual to rationalize his behavior in most settings. Though the literature is almost "all-embracing" this study cannot be; we turn now to consider selected examples of the place of folk literature in Iban socialization.

## IBAN CULTURE: A PLACE FOR ALL THINGS

Iban culture is a product of a holistic approach to life, and has resulted from, and led to, a keen awareness of the natural, social, and metasocial environments. It involves an all-embracing causality, born of the conviction that "nothing happens without cause" *(nadai utai nyadi ngapa')*. This causality has been linked with the sensitizing of the Iban to every part of their world, in which everything has been invested with the potential for sensate thought and action. Thus, in Iban lore trees talk, crotons walk, macaques become incubi, jars moan for lack of attention, and the sex of the human fetus is determined by a cricket, the metamorphized form of the god, *Selampandai*.

### "The Earth is Pulang Gana's"

This sensitivity is clearly expressed by the Iban who perceive themselves as participants in widely ramifying ecosystems. The Iban live in a reciprocal relation with their land, from which they came as *Tanah Kempok* (Molded Earth). They receive life from the land and make offerings annually to its owner, Pulang Gana. Man-land-god relations are ritualized in the acts of smearing earth on the forehead and making libations to the soil upon moving into a new area. Bastards are prohibited from coming to the fields of other families lest they offend the earth.

The quality of soils has figured prominently in the migrations of the Iban, who have sought the humus-rich lands covered by stands of dipterocarp. Concern for soil quality has been incorporated into the invocation to Pulang Gana in the ritual, *Manggul*, in which the prayer is made on behalf of the soil, that

> If the land is worn and used,
> is acrid and foul-smelling,
> reeking of urine and offal,
> May it be changed to become
> land that is arable and light,
> land that is fat and rich,
> land that can become, that is clean,
> land that will bring us good fortune.
> May all that is planted on this land
> be luxuriant, multiplying,
> increasing, bearing,
> that our rice may hang heavy and full-headed.

### "The Hills Are Alive"

The hills have been charged with particular meaning and are considered the result of special creative acts of the gods. Recognizing that their strength comes from the hills, the Iban describe them as the places of divine residence, such as *Panggau Libau*, the home of Keling and the other gods (Gerijih, 1964). Vision quests take the Iban to the hills *(nampok ka bukit)* to meet benevolent spirits. The hills are cool *(chelap)* and healthy, in contrast to the lowlands which are hot *(angat)* and, by implication, unhealthy. On their return from successful trips, the Iban make thank-offerings on the nearest hill *(niat ka bukit)*.

### Insects, Animals, and Birds

Quite literally, no insect is too insignificant to be included in Iban lore. Cooperation is encouraged by reference to the ants, who, though small, in concert can achieve great tasks. The enmity between otter and fish can be traced through many intervening episodes to the termites who ate the bark of the *terentang* tree. Alung, who could not finish the last sliver of grub, was saved from that morsel's retaliation by the beetle and rat *(kerit chit, tebok bubok)*. At the meeting of all nonhuman animals, the chairperson was *Buntak Dayong*, the mantis, and the assembly deputed the mosquito to infect man and keep him from destroying their forest refuge.

All animals appear in the literature, but the favorite—on the basis of number of appearances—undoubtedly are the mousedeer and tortoise. When the animals fished with derris poison, only those two were crafty enough to trick the evil spirit who was consuming the daily catches. When their fellows cheated them in the division of the catch, the mousedeer and the tortoise were wily enough to deceive the rest, end up with the boat and all the fish, and give rise to the popular plea for equality, *mit kelikit, besai kelikai,*

To the large, much
To the small, little.

In a delightful bit of *double entendre* the mousedeer and tortoise attempt to "make out" with Dayang Ridu, but, in addition to her resistance, they also run into a stiff bit of competition from "Gourd's Sherd" *(Bujang Kerimpak Labu')*, the son of Keling and Kumang whom Dayang Ridu keeps hanging around on a peg in his metamorphized form.

Freeman (1958) has dealt with the seven omen birds and their father-in-law, Sengalang Burong.[2] One should note, albeit briefly, that other birds are included in Iban literature. Killing and eating the mynah *(tiong)* is prohibited because a flock of mynahs once came to the rescue of an Iban ancestor who was hard pressed by the legendary Kantu. To see an owl alight on a house or to hear an owl call during daylight is a portent of death, a belief that is shared by some North American groups.

## RICE IS LIFE: THE FERTILITY OF SYMBOLISM

Hill rice cultivation is considered the distinctive feature of Iban culture. It separates men from animals and Iban ("human") from Punan (read, "nonhuman").[3] In Iban mythology, rice is a gift from the gods. Sengalang Burong, the brahmany kite, gave the first seed to Seragunting with instructions for its cultivation. He directed that rice should supplant the tubers on which the Iban previously had subsisted.

In one account, rice was first given to a young girl, Dayang Petri, the seventh child of the gods. Unlike her older siblings who ate charcoal, Dayang Petri refused to eat anything but rice, which had been given to her by the grandmother of the Sparrow King *(Ini' Rajah Pipit)*. In this edenic situation, the rice was as large as a mango. Once planted, it lived for years. The reaping baskets walked to the farm, where the rice jumped into them until they were full, and then they walked home. Paradise was lost, however, when Dayang Petri in her impatience, slashed the grain to reap it herself and mischievously startled the baskets.[4] The wonderful properties of both basket and rice disappeared, and the Iban were reduced to cultivating rice.

In a mythological variant, rice is described as a treasure stolen. Two culture heroes observed a goddess (note the prototypical female cultivator) growing rice, at that time a crop unknown to them, and were determined to get some

[2]It it interesting to note the explicit reference in this myth to uxorilocal residence.
[3]Explicitly stated in the phrase, "In the beginning our ancestors did not plant rice but lived off roots in the jungle like the Punan."
[4]Hence, harvesting must proceed in cautious stages, to apprise the rice that it is going to be harvested. On the first day of harvest no fewer than three (see following myth) nor more than seven panicles may be cut.

of the seed. Their requests were repeatedly denied. Two attempts to steal the seed were unsuccessful when the goddess searched the men. On the third try, one of the men placed three seeds under his foreskin and they were not found. The two heroes returned, planted the seeds and introduced rice cultivation to the Iban.

As with numerous other peoples, rice cultivation is not merely a technique of acquiring food but a total way of life that is supported by and in turn supports Iban theology, cosmology, and eschatology. Rice farming has been highly symbolized and elaborated into a complex system of beliefs and rituals. The basic premise of the rituals observed in connection with rice cultivation is that rice, as well as other objects, has a soul *(samengat)* or is enlivened through the souls of the ancestors. For the Iban, life begins and ends with rice. To eat means implicitly to consume rice. The first food the infant tastes after his mother's milk is rice gruel. In adult life there is no more certain standard of success than always to have an abundance of rice.

In the cycle of existence, the soul of the dead person, having been ritually advised that it is dead,[5] crosses "The Bridge Whose Crossing Makes Anxious" *(Batang Titi Rawan)* to "The Opposite" *(Sebayan)*.[6] After a period of self-indulgence, doing all in *Sebayan* that is forbidden on earth—explicitly, gluttony, drinking, and reveling with members of the opposite sex—the soul then proceeds on a journey of several river networks. The journey is a complex one (Harrisson and Sandin, 1966), and as recounted on the memory boards used by Iban chanters, retraces the wanderings of the Iban. Although each name of river and site is mythically significant and varies according to chanter, the most important stages, having both particular and cosmic referents, are *Mandai Awai* ("Suffering"), *Mandai Mati* ("Death"), and finally, *Mandai Jenoh* ("Peace"). At the last stage the soul is changed into rice-nourishing dew to descend upon and enliven the grain, ensuring thereby the presence of the rice-soul.

Iban farming is thoroughly ritualized and although analysis requires dissection into natural and supernatural spheres, for the Iban, technology and ritual are complementary parts of a single living body of culture. Discussion of the rituals in any detail is impossible within the scope of this paper, and a listing of the principal liturgies must suffice.

1. The Festival of the Whetstone *(Gawai Batu)*
2. The First Augury *(Beburong)*
3. Confirming the Site *(Manggul)*
4. Visiting the Burned Site *(Ngabas Tegalan)*
5. Planting the Sacred Rice *(Nanam Padi Pun)*
6. Tabooing the Fields *(Ngemali Umai)*
7. Washing Off the Charcoal *(Masu' Arang)*
8. Breaking the New Rice *(Matah Padi)*

[5]In an extension of the man-plant simile, the dead soul is likened to a withered flower which must be ritually severed by the shaman from the remaining family stem.

[6]In *Sebayan* all is reversed exactly from this life.

9. Carrying the Harvest Mats *(Nganjong Penyedai)*
10. Harvesting *(Ngetau)*
11. Storing *(Besimpan)*
12. Discarding the Pollen *(Muai Miang)*

One should note the important role of women in the symbolism of fertility. We have noted the prototypical female cultivator. Iban males admit that Iban women know more about grains and strains than they. In hill rice cultivation, women handle the seed; on the plains, women alone may transplant.[7] The senior active female in the *bilik* is the "head" reaper, who sets the pace *(ngindu')*. It is significant that the terms for *pace-setting* and *female* have the same root *(indu')*, and the task of the pace-setter is literally to "fecundize" the seeds she handles.[8] In storing the grain, the same woman places it in the bark bins as the moon is waxing, and she should be the one to open the bins during a later waxing of the moon.

Parenthetically, there is a striking absence of transitional rites for Iban women, in contrast to the large number of rites for males.[9] Can it be that the fecundizing, fertilizing, reproducing role of women is so clearly recognized that it does not require ritualization, whereas ambiguities about the male role must be resolved?

### Padiculture and Structural Units

Discrete units are defined by references to rice and the hearth. The *bilik*-family is described as "those of one pot" *(saum periok)* and the ritual group as "food-sharers" *(sapemakai)*. The longhouse community persists as a viable form of organization in part because of the mythical charter, but more particularly because of the disparate abilities of families to produce rice. Upward mobility among the Iban is predicated on successful rice cultivation, and though a man speaks with the tongues of men and angels, and have trophies aplenty to his credit, without rice it profits him little.

### Rubber and Value Changes

The introduction of rubber *(Hevea)* at the beginning of this century led to shifts in the structure and value system of the Iban. Paradoxically, rubber contributed to the permanence of longhouse communities in some cases and to their fragmentation in others. Rubber planting further opened a new way to wealth and

[7]Men may aid in transporting the seedlings from the beds to the fields, but transplanting is the work of women.

[8]Pulang Gana's wife's name is "Fertile Land Who Caps the Bamboo," and his daughter is "Seed Dissolving in the Soil, Maid of the Pleiades Until Ready."

[9]One male Iban leader estimated that by the time he had achieved his status he had sponsored or had had sponsored on his behalf more than fifty different rituals.

economic security. The conflict between traditional planters and rubber gardening was soon expressed in the widespread story that rubber ate rice. According to one version,

> Aing of Telok Bulat, Binatang, put his rice out to dry on a mat and went off to his farm. When he returned, the rice was gone—not a kernel was left. The next day, the same thing happened again. As there was no strong wind on either day, Aing became suspicious. On the third day he put his rice on the mat and pretended to leave for the farm. He sneaked around the house and climbed up into the loft to keep an eye on the rice. Slowly, the branches of a rubber tree near the house bent, coming closer and closer to the rice, until the leaves—notice that they are shaped like a dragon *(naga)*—ate the rice.

The commitment of some conservative Iban to the cultivation of hill rice has assumed interesting expressions. The mother of Anyau Bakit commented that she could scarcely bring herself to eat lowland rice and that Chinese rice almost made her ill *(asai ka' mutah)*. An acquaintance of mine has extensive holdings in rubber and, fortunately, a fairly successful shophouse. He returns each year to his former area to farm hill rice. His harvest is unexceptionally meager. Asked why he went back each year only to suffer personal hardships and loss, his reply was, "It's our tradition—the way of our grandparents from the beginning of time."


## THE CORE VALUES

From observations of behavior and analysis of folk literature, it is possible to construct a "grammar of values" (Von Mering, 1961) which serve as clues to the symbol systems manipulated by the Iban in their psychobiological adjustments. Consideration of all such values is obviously beyond the scope of this study, and we shall consider five of the major cultural norms.

### Self-Sufficiency

As soon as an Iban child is old enough to be left by his mother, he will stay with other children in the longhouse while his mother goes to the fields. An older adult keeps charge of the children in case an accident occurs or a fight breaks out. The adult's supervision is necessarily casual and limited, for the children play over the veranda and porch, on the ground around the longhouse, and in the water if it is near the house and they know how to swim. Children quickly learn that they are "on their own," for adult threats of punishment are idle and meaningless and rarely is a threat followed up. Because parents are away during much of the daytime, children necessarily learn to fend for themselves at an early age. Parents are indulgent of their children, rationalizing their easy-going ways in terms of the affection and support they want to enjoy from their children.

The absence of physical restraint and the assurance of acceptance of his actions contribute to the confidence and self-reliance of the Iban child. Older brothers and sisters care for younger ones; by age seven or eight, children begin to assume responsibility for washing their own play clothes; and by age ten most children can at least boil rice. Young men learn to clear forests, build farmhouses, farm, fish, hunt, and distinguish the best types of trees for a variety of uses, ranging from fire-laying to boat-building. Young women help their mothers in cooking and serving food, sowing and weeding the farms, collecting palm fronds and reeds for weaving, and gathering edible ferns and palm cabbages.

Independence training is one facet of a larger value which we shall call *self-sufficiency,* or *adequacy* in the face of natural and cultural demands. A myriad of stimuli, impress the individual with the expectation that he be equal to the tasks confronting him.

The Iban value of self-sufficiency is encapsulated in the numerous and popular myths of Keling, the god of warfare and adventure. The accounts of Keling and his consort, Kumang, reflect the history of the Iban, as well as provide guides to personal behavior. Keling is the "collective representation" of what the Iban man should be. Keling is aggressive, proud, resourceful, brave, independent, and endowed with tremendous personal magic. His travels are almost as many as his storytellers. Always in quest of adventure, he makes his way through difficult jungles, flooded rivers, conquering human enemies and defeating the worst of evil spirits.

Keling is never in want, his farms never fail. His dress and equipment are the finest, his magic all powerful. Keling allows no obstacle to stand in his way. In one story, he dispatches a dozen different *antu,* then hosts of traditional enemies, before destroying the entire army of the Malay king. It is evident that the Keling stories recall much of the history of the Iban and their competition with other ethnic groups for land.

Kumang, like Keling, is also independent and resourceful. Alas, she appears in a slightly disadvantageous position by comparison with Keling, for male biases appear to have dominated the editing of these accounts. In one story, Kumang violates a ritual prohibition against bathing and, as a result, is spirited away to the top of a giant tree, requiring Keling to risk life and limb to rescue her. In another story, through her carelessness, their son, Bujang Kerimpak Labu', whom she had placed in a gourd, is washed away while she is bathing.

Generally, Kumang comes off much better in narratives, and she and Keling stand in opposition to poor Apai Salui, "Father of Stupidity," and his wife, Chelegit. If Keling and Kumang stand as examples to be followed, Apai Salui and Chelegit embody characteristics to be avoided. Apai Salui is greedy, indecisive, and utterly lacking in values. In one insightful episode, Apai Salui is wealthy, owning a concrete house, bins of rice, and trunks of money. He passes by the bamboo hut of poor Suma Umang (the Malay) who is penniless and does not know where his next meal is coming from. Hearing the wind whistle through a broken bamboo support of the hut, Apai Salui is so enraptured with the sound that he exchanges all that he has with Suma Umang for his hut. One day, the wind blows stronger, the hut collapses killing Apai Salui. The Iban interpretation of their relations with the Malays is obvious.

The strong emphasis on independence and self-sufficiency creates numerous interpersonal and intergenerational conflicts. These conflicts are expressed structurally in *bilik* partitions and longhouse divisions. Iban parents often despair privately over their willful children, forgetting that "the child is father to the man," and that Iban children are ordering their conduct according to the patterns of behavior which they have observed and learned from infancy.

Intergenerational conflict is clearly seen in the legend, "Kumang Lays Eggs" *(Kumang Betelu')*. Keling notices Kumang surreptitiously laying eggs in a rice bin. Angered and embarrassed over such an abnormal mode of conception, he takes his "spear" and pierces each of the seven eggs Kumang has laid. Instead of killing the children, all of whom are boys, he merely blinds them. Unable—or unwilling—to care for them, Keling takes them into the jungle to lose them. Ambivalence toward father is expressed as first one *Antu Gerasi Papa'* ("giant spirit") gives them a salve for the recovery of their sight, and another threatens them and they kill him. After many perilous adventures, the sons return to Keling and Kumang and are reconciled.

A strong orientation to achievement is implicit in the literature related to self-sufficiency. Pioneering continues to be a highly valued activity, and the names as well as the feats of earlier pioneers are still remembered. Head-hunting was an integral part of the grammar of values, certain proof of bravery. Currently, men who distinguish themselves in military service are permitted to occupy the places reserved formerly for headtakers. Finally, the trips of Keling, Telajan, and other culture heroes serve to maintain a high intensity of interest in traveling and in the acquisition of trophies.

### Egalitarianism

In inter-*bilik* affairs, the Iban soon learn that to intrude into the affairs of another family is to invite trouble. "He wants to be more than others," or "He wants to make himself big," are common criticisms of the person who offers advice or criticism.

Through example and lore, the Iban find that it is safest to do their own work and to let others do theirs, offering no suggestions lest they be cut down for impugning the abilities of others. "He knows more than others" is a stinging criticism which humbles and encourages the policy and practice of noninterference.

In a popular children's story, "The Macaque's Tail," a group of macaques descend onto a tree trunk that a man has been splitting before returning home for his lunch. One macaque is more mischievous than the others and shakes a wedge stuck in the trunk until the wedge pops out and the macaque's tail is caught in the crack. Hearing the cries of the macaque the man returns and kills it. "And such is the end of everyone who interferes with the business of others," concludes the story.

Equality and fair play are important elements in myth and ritual, and many proverbs underscore those norms.

> Let the law be equal for all,
> Just as a bushel measure is
> the same for everyone.
> Do not ask some to climb the
> thorn three and others to
> climb the smooth areca.
> Do not divide like the tapir,
> much to the large, little
> to the small.

The emphasis upon egalitarianism for the sake of the individual and the community is seen as stultifying by many Iban, especially young people who are more inclined to subscribe to the stress on achievement. In the longhouse, powerful leveling processes are operative prescribing the subservience of the individual to the group.

### Respect and Responsibility

Tensions between individualism and community, achievement and egalitarianism, are related to, and reinforced by, belief in the *antu*. In the absence of means of enforcing sanctions and judgments on dissident members, and in the potentially disruptive situation in which men might do what pleases them, belief in, and fear of, the *antu* is

> crucial to the psycho-biological functioning of the individual, and to the survival of (Iban) society and its culture (Spiro, 1952:102).

Belief in the *antu* serves the function of displacing the hostilities of the Iban. Living in a close community within sight and hearing of one another, at a relatively simple level of technology, and in a jungle where on occasion even such skillful jungle-people as the Iban get lost, the *antu* symbolize natural and social problems. The *Bunsu Kamba'* are the "Little Ones Who Make Men Lose Their Way." *Antu Kelansat* are "moochers," "hangers-on," "the dependent ones," who induce Iban to take them on their backs and then refuse to dismount. *Antu Gerasi Papa'* are the large, terrifying male figures. And the *Antu Kok-lir* is the vengeful spirit of the woman who has died in childbirth and returns to eat men's testicles.

Belief in the *antu* is purposely engendered in Iban enculturation. Techniques to develop such belief include stories about the *antu*, personal accounts about *other* persons who have seen them, and ritual dramatization. One midnight in Rumah Usan, Menyan, a group of Iban, and I were talking and some children were playing noisily nearby. Though they had been scolded several times, the children kept on with their play. Suddenly, one of the *bilik* doors burst open and out stepped an old woman wearing a long, tattered gown and a frightening mask. The children fled to the far end of the house. When I asked the meaning of it all, the people laughingly replied that the woman was playing *antu (Antu Muam)* in order to make the children respect the real *antu* and not violate the sanctions.

*Antu* are the enforcers of the numerous *pemali* (prohibitions). In the absence of more formal means of control, the *pemali* indicate parameters for appropriate behavior. They include references to situations that might be personally belittling and lead to fighting, such as,

> It is forbidden to point in another's face,[10] and
> It is forbidden to strike the floor with the fist,[11]

the breach of which is subject to a fine. *Pemali* also are related to life crisis events through appeal to "sympathetic magic." At the time of childbirth, for example,

> It is forbidden for a husband to kill any
> living thing lest the wife die.
> It is forbidden to cut any creeper lest
> the child die.

*Pemali* observed in connection with death ensure that respect will be shown for the deceased and his surviving kinsmen. Thus,

> It is forbidden to sing during the mourning
> period.
> It is forbidden to leave a corpse unattended
> lest a dog step over it and the corpse become
> a "spirit snake" (nabau).
> It is forbidden for a widow(er) to cut the
> hair or bathe with soap lest she/he be
> said not to have mourned the deceased.

Respect between members of Iban society is problematic in light of the high frequency of exchanges that occur. No greater offense can be committed against an Iban than shaming him, and members of the society learn means both of eschewing speech and actions which may shame another person and of rationalizing feelings of guilt or shame which they may have. Thus, belief in the *antu* who stand ready to enforce the *pemali* is one part of the symbol system through which the Iban attempt to regulate their behavior.

[10]The intense feelings about this taboo was related by a group of Iban who threatened to kill an education officer for pointing his finger in their faces, when he knew the taboo.

[11]The implication in such action is, "If you were a speck of dust, I would crush you," and in one instance when a young man pounded the floor before a shaman, the factions of the two men almost joined in battle.

Another facet of the theme of respect is found in the oft repeated concerns for consideration. Sympathy, understanding, and feelings for others are explicitly encouraged in proverbs, such as,

> You itch, so do others;
> You hurt, so do others;
> What you feel is what others
> also feel,

and in folktales, such as the story of the "Civet and the Crane." The crane invited the civet to feasts, but all the food was placed in long-necked jars. Unable to get at the food, which was easily reached by the crane, the civet invited the crane to dine with him, and put the food in shallow dishes. When the crane complained that he had been able only to wet his beak, the civet remonstrated with him, reminding the crane that what may be enjoyable to one may not necessarily be so to another, and that friendship must show itself in consideration.

### Community and Cooperation

Given the physical conditions to which the Iban have adopted, individualism has been essential to their growth and expansion, cooperation to their survival and solidarity. The "dialectics of social life" (Murphy, 1971) are readily apparent in the tensions that exist between these polar norms.

Concern for the community is more important than individual success. On some occasions, a member of a longhouse may set himself up against the group, arguing against a community decision or criticizing the results of some group action. Other members will politely but firmly reprove him, reminding him by some appropriate proverb that the group is more important than the individual, goodwill than personal gain. For example, after one community fiasco, the following proverb was cited:

> The chicken has died, don't criticize.
> The spur has broken, don't make a fuss.
> The bushknife has broken, don't say anything.
> The shortknife has broken, don't argue about it.

If the individual does not accept a gentle rebuff and remains contentious, other members may cite proverbs to the effect that he is more stupid than the group he is criticizing, for the community will endure though he may perish.

> You say that Malau is stupid, but it
> is you who are foolish and short-sighted.
> You say that I am silly, but it is you
> who are senseless.
> You call yourself the "Keling of heaven,"
> but in fact you are the "Keling of Sebayan."

The longhouse is a tangible symbol of the prized community. The mythical charter for the longhouse is given in tales relating to Sengalang Burong who, with his daughters and sons-in-law, lived in the first such structure. Although the origins of longhouse organization are forgotten, it has been rationalized by Iban for its defensive functions during times of headhunting. It is also important as a ritual-ecological unit, the various horticultural rites serving to achieve a roughly simultaneous development of the rice fields and, thereby a greater spread of the omnipresent birds.

Traditionally, individuals and families who refused to join longhouses were referred to as *Antu Uging*. They *must* have been weird, thought the Iban, for the longhouse is *the place* to live.

The Iban concept of community is by no means limited to immediate kinsmen or longhouses. The growth of the Iban who now are the most numerous of the indigenous groups in Sarawak may be attributed in part to their flexible bilateral organization by which non-Iban have been incorporated into and rationalized as members of kin groups. Iban locate their longhouses as nodal points from which ties radiate outward, articulating to nearby communities as members of a common food-sharing group, and to more distant communities through those members with whom they share connections through descent, marriage, and friendship. Through such rituals as "tying the fishnet" *(nyambong)* and genealogizing *(betusut)*, and the confidence of acceptance based on the universal Iban prescription for hospitality, individuals feel a part of other communities and of the larger social grouping of Iban.

### Luck

This category subsumes the "imponderabilia of life," fully felt but not so completely understood. In the vagaries of nature to which the Iban have adapted, *luck* has come to mean those events which sometimes are perceived as being good, sometimes bad, but over which the individual and the group have almost no control.

Good luck is the *summa bonum* among the values of the Iban. It is apparent in success and personal achievements, and blessed is the person on whom it falls. The man who has it harvests bountiful crops of rice year after year. Formerly, the man with good luck was in the right place at the right time, so that he was able to perform acts of bravery or to take human heads. He was invited to feasts and asked to bless the assembly, in the hope that his fortune might infect others. At present, parents are considered blessed with good luck if they have many children all of whom are obedient, pass school examinations, obtain salaried positions, and support them in their old age.

Despite the importance attached to luck, and the lack of scientific explanations for much that happens in their lives, the Iban are by no means passive about their fate. Rather, they have developed an elaborate complex of beliefs and rituals to ensure good luck. We have noted the rituals connected with farming. Similar rituals exist for life crises, traveling, building a new house, and taking on a new job. Medicines *(ubat)* and charms *(pengaroh)* are commonly used. Carved figures stand like sentries beside paths to house and farm. Offerings are made on the occasion of every event of moment.

The notion of luck serves not only to explain successes but also to rationalize failures. When the shaman Biga' left his farm after planting and went on a shamanic tour of the Oya River area, his crop failed and the failure was attributed to bad luck. Iban children in the first grade in rural schools are already two years behind their urban counterparts who enter kindergarten at age four. Their attendance is casual and few do any study at home. Yet recently when I asked a teacher in a rural school how his son had fared in the Common Entrance Examination, the father replied wearily that he had failed; "No luck" *(nadai nasit)*, was his reply.

Good luck is not seen as a substitute for industry, but rather as complementary to it. Keling and Kumang possess greater magic and are more fortunate than mere mortals, but these powers have a heuristic value in inspiring the gods to greater efforts through the success that they ensure. For the Iban, even if he has

> One rice bin, two rice bins,
> (even) a hornbill stone,
> If he does not attack the enemy,
> his manhood will never be proven.
> One fish basket, two baskets,
> (even) a magical whetstone.
> If he does not work his farm,
> he certainly will not get any rice.

The individual's luck is changeable, otherwise recourse to augury and other rituals would be utterly meaningless. So those who have failed may hope for better things, and those who have succeeded should enjoy their good fortune but beware lest ill times befall them. The Iban basically are optimistic opportunists, who on the average, are ready to maximize their chances as if they were heaven sent.

## CONCLUSION

Understanding the culture and socialization of the Iban is not only greatly enhanced by analysis of their folk literature, it is quite impossible without such analysis. Myths, folktales, proverbs, taboos, and rituals shape the cultural lenses through which the Iban perceive their world. When we discover that folk literature serves as a Platonic "vehicle of truth," we must agree with Hallowell that its

> significance for actual behavior becomes apparent. For people *act* on the basis of what they believe to be true, not what they think is mere fiction. Thus, one of the

generic functions of the "true" story in any society is to reinforce the existing system of beliefs about the nature of the universe, man and society (1947:549).

Analysis of Iban folk literature is not only enlightening, but is also a delightful experience. It is easy to understand how generations of Iban have taken pleasure in it, have been instructed through it, and to conclude that it will continue to be an important tool in the total socialization process.

### The Forms of Iban Folk Literature

*Ensera,* myths and legends relating to the birth of the gods, the creation of the earth, and exploits of culture heroes.

*Jerita,* folktales which are both etiological and moralizing, including human, superhuman, and animal characters.

*Entelah,* riddles, whose creation is a favorite pastime of adults as well as children.

*Sempama, jako' sema',* proverbs and aphorisms, culled usually from legends and folktales; shorthand expressions whose meanings are more than the statement itself.

*Pemali,* taboos, scores of which are adduced for the variety of social circumstances, from where to sit to how to sit; closely related to *pantang.*

*Penti,* prohibitions peculiar to a particular family.

*Sampi,* prayers and invocations.

*Sudi', belian, pagar api, tubu' ayu,* monologues performed by the shaman in the outward movement from *bilik* to *ruai* to *tanju'* to ground.

*Sabak, senggai,* laments by which the soul of the dead is led through *Sebayan* and its course.

*Timang,* praise songs; *pengap,* chants; *pantun,* "songs"; *pelandai,* love songs; *ramban* and *jara',* antiphonally performed chants.

*Geliga,* admonitions delivered at the outset of festivals.

## APPENDIX 2

Following is a partial list of publications of Iban folk literature by the Borneo Literature Bureau.

Alli Majang. *Sempama Jako Iban*, 1968.
Ambon, Felix. *Tupai Miai*, 1967.
Ballai, Tawi. *Tembawai Bejuah*, 1967.
Baughman, Burr. *Iban Kalia*, 1962.
Duncan, William. *Bujang Sugi*, 1965.
       *Anak Bujang Sugi*, 1965.
       *Menteri Adi*, 1965.
Ejau, Andria. *Dilah Tanah*, 1964.
       *Madu Midang*, 1967.
       *Batu Besundang*, 1968.
Enggu, Edward. *Limau Senaman*, 1962.
       *Pengap Gawai Tajau*, 1964.
Entingi, Dunstan. *Pelandok Seduai Tekura*, 1963.
       *Wat Lamba*, 1967.
Gerijih, Henry. *Satangkai*, 1963.
       *Raja Langit*, 1964.
       *Aur Kira*, 1965.
       *Raja Berani*, 1967.
Jaraw, Boniface. *Entelah Iban*, 1968.
Mawar, Frederick. *Engkeratong Ayam Raja*, 1967.
Moses Beti. *Telajan*, 1964.
Sandin, Benedict. *Tigabelas Bengkah Mimpi*, 1962.
       *Sengalang Burong*, 1962, 1967.
       *Raja Durong*, 1964.
       *Tusun Pendiau*, 1966.
       *Raja Simpulang Gana*, 1968.
       *Pengap Gawai Sakit*, 1969.
Sanoun Ijau. *Sungai Borneo*, 1962.
Sullang, Moscelyn. *Kerapa Nawai*, 1963.

# REFERENCES

Douglas, Mary. *Purity and danger*. New York: Praeger, 1966.

Freeman, J. D. *Iban agriculture*. London: Her Majesty's Stationery Office, 1955.

Freeman, J. H. *Iban augury*. (Mimeographed.) 1958.

Gerijih, Henry. *Raja Langit*. Kuching: Borneo Literature Bureau, 1964.

Hallowell, A. I. Myth, culture and personality, *American Anthropologist, 49*, 544–556, 1947.

Hallowell, A. I. *Culture and experience*. Philadelphia: University of Pennsylvania Press, 1955.

Harrisson, Tom, and Sandin, Benedict. Borneo writing boards. In *Borneo writing and related matters. Sarawak Museum Journal, Special Monograph* No. 2, Kuching, Sarawak, November 1966.

Lessa, William. Discoverer-of-the-sun, *Journal of American Folklore, 79*, 3–51, 1966.

Murphy, Robert. *Dialectics of social life*. New York: Basic Books, 1971.

Pettitt, G. A. Primitive education in North America. Berkeley: University of California Press, *Publications in American Archaeology and Ethnology, 43*, 1, 1946.

Powers, W. T. *Behavior: The control of perception*. Chicago: Aldine Publishing Company, 1973.

Spiro, M. E. Ghosts, Ifaluk, and teleological functionalism, *American Anthropologist, 54*, 497–503, 1952.

Von Mering, Otto. *A grammar of values*. Pittsburgh: University of Pittsburgh Press, 1961.

# Part Three
# THE COHERENCE
# OF THINGS

# chapter eight

# Mediators as Metaphors: Moving a Man to Tears in Papua, New Guinea

Edward L. Schieffelin

Institute for the Study

of Human Issues, Philadelphia

## INTRODUCTION

This paper is an essay in symbolic analysis. My underlying theoretical concern is to examine the means by which certain kinds of cultural symbols, which normally operate in mundane human contexts, may attain considerable emotional and expressive force through traditional art forms by coming to represent what they normally mediate. Specifically, I shall focus my analysis on the poetry, or lyrics, of ceremonial songs sung by the Kaluli people of Papua, New Guinea. I wish to examine how two sets of cultural symbols common in the discourse of everyday life, namely land and food, combine in the poetry of Kaluli songs to reconstitute Kaluli awareness and feeling about the past. To simplify matters, I will omit reference to the formal rhythmic structure of the songs and the poetic subtleties of the sound system[1] and deal only with the structure of metaphorical reference and the changes that occur within it.

## KALULI CEREMONIES

The Kaluli are swidden cultivators living in the tropical forest of the Papuan Plateau on the island of New Guinea. They live in isolated longhouses separated from each other by a walk of an hour or two over forest trails. Each longhouse holds a community of about sixty people, comprised of the male members of several lineages of two or more patrilineal clans, plus their wives and children.

[1]A guide to the pronunciation of Kaluli can be found in Appendix 1.

Like most people in New Guinea, the Kaluli are much concerned with social reciprocity and exchange, and their most important social occasions are those connected with reciprocity: weddings, pig-killing festivals and exchanges, or distributions of meat among relatives and affines. These occasions or important junctures in their preparation are nearly always celebrated by the performance of ceremonial dances and songs.

Kaluli ceremonies are staged at night in the central hall of a longhouse, and performed by the guests to an audience of their hosts. There are various types of dances, but all ceremonies are similar in structure and intent. We are concerned here with the one known as the *Heyalo* (sometimes called *Feyalo*) which is performed as follows:

As soon as it is dark, and the hosts have settled down expectantly in the longhouse, a group of up to twenty dancers, elaborately painted and decorated, approach out of the forest where they have secretly been preparing. They enter the longhouse which is lit by torchlight and dance around the central hall singing to the accompaniment of their drums and the sound of rattles affixed to their costumes. Their songs, which seem simple and nostalgic, refer to various landmarks and places in their hosts' clan territory. After a while, the audience (the hosts) become very deeply moved. Some of them burst into tears. Then, in reaction to the sorrow they have been made to feel, they jump up angrily and burn the dancers on the shoulders with the torches used to light the ceremony. The dancers continue their performance without showing any sign of pain. The dancing and singing and the concommitant weeping and burning continue all night with brief rest periods between songs. In the morning the dancers, who often carry second- or third-degree burns on their arms and shoulders, pay compensation to those people whom they made cry.

From the Kaluli point of view, the important aspect of the ceremony is not that the dancers must face the ordeal of being burned, but that the hosts are moved so deeply that they weep.[2] Their violent reaction is felt to be an understandable reaction to the pain they have experienced, and the dancers pay them compensation at the end of the dance as a gesture of reconciliation and friendship.

Now, for the purposes of this paper, I am not concerned with *why* the Kaluli perform the *Heyalo,* or whether it expresses rivalry and hostility or friendship and affection between host and guest. (For this, see E. Schieffelin, *The sorrow of the lonely and the burning of the dancers,* New York: St. Martin's Press, 1976.) I am concerned rather to determine simply why and how it is so moving.

[2]The sorrow the hosts feel is not one that is merely ritually expressed. Anyone who has observed a *Heyalo* performance can see clearly that it is genuinely and deeply felt. People wail quite uncontrollably, tears pouring down their faces. Often they cannot bear being present at the performance any longer, and run out of the longhouse to wail on the veranda. Occasionally, the ceremony is so moving that the guests weep too, though they are not supposed to cry at their own performance.

## THE PROBLEM OF THE SONGS

A *Heyalo* ceremony is considered to be a failure if the hosts do not weep, and the guests bend every effort to make their performance moving so that they will. The effectiveness of the *Heyalo* depends in part on the dramatic qualities of the performance: the brilliance of the costumes, the sonority of the drums, and the grace and stamina of the dancers. But the key element, according to the Kaluli, is the songs. Whatever else there is to a performance, they say, it is the songs which move a person to tears.

A *Heyalo* ceremony contains about twenty-seven songs, each of which is sung several times for a dancing period (about 20 minutes), after which there are a few minutes respite while dancers adjust their drums, pull on a smoking tube, or wet their lips before starting up again with a new song. The songs are generally short, about twelve lines, and are not traditional, in that they must be newly composed for each ceremonial occasion. They are composed, however, according to a traditional framework.

The basic stanza is simple: the first line, called the *mo:*, which means the base or foot of a tree, forms the base line for the song and is repeated every other line (and sometimes more often) until the end. The lines that alternate with the *mo:* line in the central portion of the song are called the *usa fo:k*, or middle trunk; the last line, which is similar to the *usa fo:k* in content, is called the *dun* or branches. The content of the songs refers to various places and landmarks of the surrounding locality in a mildly nostalgic way.

One song sung in the longhouse of clan Ga:sumisi goes:

|   |   |
|---|---|
| mo: | Mother ee mother ee mother ee |
|   | I am leaving my house, I am leaving Malosona, I am/ |
|   | leaving my house |
|   | Mother ee mother ee mother ee |
|   | I am leaving my river pool, I am leaving Kaifaili,/ |
|   | I am leaving my river pool |
|   | Mother ee mother ee mother ee |
| usa fo:k | I am leaving the weeds of my pandanus garden, I am/ |
|   | leaving Yasawell, I am leaving the weeds of my/ |
|   | pandanus garden |
|   | Mother ee mother ee mother ee |
|   | I am leaving the place of uncut forest, I am leaving/ |
|   | Sowansa, I am leaving the place of uncut forest |
|   | I am leaving my place of uncut forest, I am leaving/ |
|   | Sowansa, I am leaving the place of uncut forest |
|   | Mother ee mother ee mother ee |
| dun | I am leaving my high place, I am leaving Nagiba:da:n,/ |
|   | I am leaving the little pandanus there. |
|   | (Composed by Baseo of clan Bono: November 1968) |

All the places named, Yasawel, Kaifaili, Sowansa, etc., are real localities near the Ga:sumisi longhouse at a place called *Malosona*. People in the audience

129

from that longhouse knew and were familiar with them, and several were moved to tears. Baseo, composer of this song, composed it with a particular person in mind. It was a young woman who had recently married and moved away from her own community to live at her husband's longhouse some distance away. The song named areas associated with the community of her parents where she had grown up, and was intended to make her become homesick and weep.

The key elements in the song here are the place names, for as the Kaluli point out, it is upon hearing the names of familiar localities that people become nostalgic and sorrowful. Place names are moving, they say, because they remind one of the past, and of beloved friends and relatives now absent or dead who once lived there. The Kaluli can quite explicitly discuss those whom they mourn in terms of any particular place named in a song, though these persons and events are not in the least obvious from the composition of the song itself. Nor is it clear what it is about the song that should evoke such a response. Certainly, the Kaluli do not react with nostalgia and tears to place names spoken in everyday contexts. It is only when they are composed into songs that their tragic reference is released and the Kaluli find them moving. Nor is the tragic quality of *Heyalo* songs a question of subtle poetic composition. The song lines consist largely of conventional frames; all that is required to compose a song is to gather a number of place names (pertaining to one local area) and insert them into these formulae. Not even great knowledge of a locality or its inhabitants is required. Though composers may know an area well and sometimes make up songs with a particular person in mind (as in Baseo's song just given), it is not uncommon to find that several men have each contributed a few locality names to a song when no one of them knows the area well enough to compose a song alone. They may have no idea who is associated with these localities, but if there are people from these places present, the song will ferret them out at the ceremony and cause them to weep. It is as though the place names (when appropriately framed in the song formulae) are effective by themselves.

The song lines in the *Heyalo* in which locality names are expressed and given such emotional power, are usually quite simple. The Kaluli indicate, they evoke a mood of pathos and nostalgia:

> I am leaving my (hill, house, river pool, I am leaving/
> (place name)
> At (place name) the (tree, sago palm, landmark stone)/
> stands out against the sky.
> I am hungry at (place name) I am hungry at the (tree,/
> landmark) there.
> At (place name) the (species name) sago is waving in/
> the wind.
> I am leaving (place name) I am leaving the (food name)/
> garden there . . .

The song lines seem to rely for effect on images of hunger, departure, and solitude. Yet whenever I discuss the singing of place names in lines such as these with Kaluli friends, they usually began speaking of gardens planted in the area, or stands of sago palms nearby. If the subject was the singing of river pools, they spoke of fishing there. One quickly gets the impression that these remarks about sago and garden places are related to the kinds of images projected in the song frames. Both seem to have a hidden concern—or reference—and that reference is food.

*Heyalo* poetry, then, is constructed by framing the names of various localities in conventionalized song lines which project a mood of pathos in images pertaining in one way or another to food. To resolve the significance of this, the questions to which we must address ourselves become ethnographic rather than poetic: What is the relationship of the Kaluli to their lands that place names should be capable of evoking such emotion, and secondly, what is it about food, as the covert reference in the song formulae, that can release it?

## LAND, THE MEDIATOR OF IDENTITY

The plateau region that the Kaluli inhabit consists for the most part of gently rolling parallel ridges covered with dense tropical forest. To an outsider, the plateau forest has an immense anonymity, with its endless galleries of trees and hundreds of seemingly identical brooks and streams. But to the Kaluli on their own territory, the land is familiar: large trees, cliffs, river pools, sago swamps, and garden sites are all well-known places.

Every prominent landmark is given a name of its own—such as Wilip, a hill in the territory of clan Waliso:, or Sisande, a large pool in the Isawa River. Occasionally, a place is named after some event in the past, like Kusakini, where a large Kus tree was cut down by someone long ago. Apart from important landmarks, the Kaluli generally rely for sense of location and direction upon the many watercourses which flow northward through their country from the slopes of Mount Bosavi about ten miles to the south. Accordingly, most places in the forest are named after the stream or watercourse that gives the land its contours in that locality. A place is given the name of the local stream plus a suffix which indicates its character in that area. Thus, the area about the Kiden stream near its spring would be called Kidenelip; Kidensawel would be the place where there is a waterfall; Kidensadugu is the place where the stream levels out after a steep descent, and so on, down to Kidenso:k, the mouth of the stream at the Walu River (or Kidensagu if there is a waterfall there). The waters, as they turn and fall, generate new localities for every new configuration of the land. The name of a locality carries, in effect, its own geographical coordinates which place it in determinate relation to the brooks and streams that flow through the forest.

The Kaluli live primarily off the produce (mainly bananas and pandanus) of extensive swidden gardens cleared in the forest. Their staple starch is extracted from sago palms which grow wild in boggy places along the sides of streams.

Though gardens are productive, the soil becomes exhausted quickly, and the people must move to plant a new garden in another place about every two or three years. Old gardens return to forest, on a fallowing cycle of about twenty-five years. Each community builds its longhouses and plants its gardens within its own particular territory, an area of 2 to 4 square miles which is bordered by the lands of other longhouses or by uninhabited regions used for hunting.

The identity of each longhouse community is primarily associated with the region in which it is located rather than with the clan membership of the people who inhabit the longhouse. Thus, lineages of clans Ga:sumisi and Wabisi whose community's successive longhouses have been located in the vicinity of Ba:golo Ridge are called Ba:golo people. Less frequently, but more particularly, they may be referred to as Ga:sumisi, the predominant clan, or Malosono, the present site of the longhouse as of 1968. Similarly, a branch of clan Didesa, together with lineages of Wabisi and Ferisa are known as Kagabesi people, since they have lived for some generations in an area known for its large *kagab* trees. Kagabesi means "those who stay at the *kagab* trees."

In this way, a place name becomes a metaphor as soon as a longhouse is built in that locality, for then it comes to stand for the human community in the longhouse. At the same time, it becomes a mediating symbol of community identity as it differentiates that longhouse community from, and places it in (geographical) relation to, other communities located at (and named after) other places in the forest. Hence, to identify himself to others—or to refer to another's identity—a man usually refers to the locality name of the appropriate longhouse. In warfare, place names are used in the opposite manner—not to mediate, but to intensify the antagonism and throw the enemy into confusion.

A longhouse doubles as a fortress in troubled times, and the longhouse community is implicitly a defensive unit. Most of the members of a raiding party entering another longhouse territory for an attack are traveling in unfamiliar country whose shortcuts, ambush points, and other important features are not well known to them. Kaluli defenders are aware of this and turn the situation to psychological advantage by projecting themselves in battle yelling place names from their home territory as war cries. The places named in war cries are usually prominent landmarks—hills, ridges, and rivers—or important house sites with which people identify themselves, or after which the community is named. Gardens, sago places, and small house sites are never shouted in battle. War cry names are particularly potent if they are names of places where enemies have been killed or wounded in the past. War cries are yelled to confuse and frighten the attackers. The Kaluli explain: "They are afraid because they do not come to these places and don't belong here. . . ." Disoriented, it is thought, they scatter and retreat. Attackers, for their part, yell the names of their own localities to rally their courage and re-group in a dispersed battle in the forest.

The fact that the Kaluli use their own place names to project their fierceness in battle and, conversely, believe the enemy become disoriented and lose courage when forcefully reminded that they are in a strange country is bound up with the intimate familiarity an individual feels with his lands.

For any particular individual, the names of places on his home ground denote such areas as forested ridges, garden areas, sago places, and house sites where he has lived most of his life. He knows this land and its streams intimately, even to the quality and distribution of the vegetation and the location of individual kinds of trees. In part, this is because he knows the resources of the forest: where he might look for *bau* bark to floor a house, cane for tying bundles, nettles to rub on a stomach ache, or ferns for cooking with pork. More importantly, his awareness of the area is shaped by his awareness of his own, and others', participation in it through shifting cultivation and sago cutting.

Changes in the quality of the forest reflect the hand of man: one's own activities and those of one's relations. The Kaluli would sometimes point out an apparently undifferentiated spot along the path in the forest and tell me a house had been built there where so-and-so lived years before. "These are the weeds of my father's garden," Jubi told me one day as we descended to a part of the forest where the trees were somewhat lighter and thinner than on the ridge we had just left. "We lived at Sulusawel up there. I was small like Seyaka."

In effect, as one moves along tracks and pathways through successive areas of different kinds of forest, one passes sites representing a history of houses and gardens and the people who made them over the previous fifty years. These sites mark to people the various contexts of their own past experience.

The Kaluli identify themselves with their lands because they are reflected in them. And this, in turn, is in part the source of the nostalgia with which people react to place names in ceremonial songs.

## FOOD, THE MEDIATOR OF SOCIAL RELATIONSHIPS

One need not live very long among the Kaluli to see that food has a special importance for them. This is not because, after all, one needs food to live, or because the Kaluli do not get enough to eat. Rather, it is because Kaluli feelings about the treatment of food are basic to their sense of human relationships. A man once explained to me that one should give food to little children "so that they will know you and like you and not be afraid of you." This advice could apply to the whole range of Kaluli social relationships. The giving and sharing of food among people means affection, familiarity, goodwill; it is an opener of relationships, a communication of sentiment. A young man smitten by a girl may try to slip her a small packet of salt to let her know how he feels. Close kinsmen sometimes describe their relationship by saying, "We can pick from each other's gardens without asking." A man expressing his grief over a friend's death will say, "He gave me pork!" Two particularly close friends or kinsmen who share a meal of meat, say a bandicoot *(mahi)* for example, call each other "my bandicoot" *(ni mahi)* thereafter implying a brotherly identification between them.

Friendly relations between longhouses are predicated on hospitality. People automatically offer food to their relatives and friends when they come to visit and expect the same when they go to other longhouses. The failure to offer food to a visitor at the appropriate moment or to give meanly is bad manners, defaults on the relationship, and implies that the visitor is not welcome.

More formally, food is the subject of the elaborate and complicated ceremonial exchanges between affines and classificatory relatives that articulate and develop the formal social and political relationships existing between different longhouse communities. Presentations of pork or dried forest game are binding reciprocal statements of commitment and obligation made in the medium of food.

Through presentations and hospitality a person develops his own network of close associations with those kinsmen and affines in other longhouses upon whom he wishes to rely. This giving and sharing of food does not merely express the social relationship, but validates and develops it because food is not only a medium for the exercise of social obligations, but also for the expression of subtleties and nuances of personal feeling; it is through the treatment of food that friendships become realized.[3]

The way in which food is involved in Kaluli feelings about their relationships emerges poignantly in their behavior at the time of a beloved person's death. Kaluli people do not regard death primarily in terms of fear. Rather, their fear of death is the fear of losing someone, and of being left alone.

After a death, a series of formal mourning taboos on certain foods must be observed by the surviving spouse and/or children. But in addition to this, any grieving relative may voluntarily taboo to himself some other particular food in memory of the dead. One man told me that he had given up eating breadfruit when his brother died because breadfruit had been his brother's favorite food. More commonly, a person will taboo to himself the food that the deceased had intended to eat just before his death. If a man's wife brought some pandanus home from the garden before she died, the grieving husband often cannot bring himself to eat it. "She brought it home to eat with me," he says. "Now, I would have to eat it alone." He gives it to other people in the longhouse, and henceforth, gives up eating that kind of pandanus. The taboo is voluntary and sentimental. By refusing to eat food that the deceased intended to share with him, by saying in effect, "If I can't eat it with so-and-so, then I won't eat it with anyone," he preserves the integrity of the relationship even after it has been

---

[3]Not to share meat with people to whom one is close is inconsiderate and hurtful of their feelings. "A person who wishes to savor a delicacy by himself, must do so stealthily," two men explained to me as they downed a meal of fish they had brought to eat furtively at my house. The kind of fish they were eating was taboo to their wives and children. But their wives and children loved fish, and to eat it in front of them would only make the wives unhappy and the children cry. Though the husbands could not share with them, they did not want to be thoughtless or unfeeling.

severed by death. Even in death, food remains the vehicle of social relationship.

Food is both the medium through which the Kaluli articulate their social relationships, and the idiom for expressing personal feelings about them. Thus, in speaking of food and hospitality, one is speaking of friends and relatives. Conversely, to speak of hunger implies the opposite: that friends are gone and one is left lonely and vulnerable. It is the latter implications of food, i.e., hunger and loneliness, that underlie and give sense to the imagery of solitude in *Heyalo* songs.

## CULTURAL MEDIATORS AS POETIC METAPHORS

The immense pathos of *Heyalo* songs derives from the interaction through the forms of poetic expression of the two most powerful symbolic mediators of Kaluli culture: place names, the contexts of personal experience and mediators of personal identity; and food, the mediator of (and metaphor for) human relationships. Together they evoke for each individual, in relation to a particular area, his own experience of times past there and relationships with people now dead or absent.

The song frames, through their allusions to food and implication of solitude, pertain not to events but to human fellowship. As conventional formulae, they project typical sentimental poignancies within an overall mood of nostalgia. The names of familiar places, framed in these sentiments and rendered intimate by mention of particular trees, hills, and other details of the locality, evoke for the listeners particular times and circumstances. The mention of a familiar locality set in images of hunger or (where appropriate) of solitary sago trees waving in the breeze recall the people one worked and shared with there. The historical and personal associations of a locality become particularized. "If someone sings of Alimso:k," one man said, "I think of my garden there and my dead wife who planted it with me, and I am sad."

The songs attain additional force because they come as a surprise. Old songs are predictable and people anticipate them before they are finished. Only newly composed songs will move an audience to tears. There is no way for the listener to prepare for them. One does not know in advance what places and circumstances they will evoke or allude to, or what old sorrows will be articulated in new ways.

Sitting in the shadows at the sidelines of the ceremony, gazing on the torchlit dancers, each member of a *Heyalo* audience may turn inward upon himself and attend to his own mood and thoughts. To an observer, it seems as if each listener thinks the dancers are singing only to him. The songs particularize for him his own experience and when he weeps, it is his own sorrows that move him.

# THE STRATEGY OF THE SONGS

The weeping and violence that accompany a *Heyalo* ceremony do not usually begin until about a quarter or a third of the way through the performance. The Kaluli like to develop the intensity of the ceremony carefully in order to work up the mood of the audience to the appropriate pitch. This is not accomplished through the dancing or the dramaturgy of the performance—which remain about the same throughout—but rather through the songs. The songs sung early in the evening, because the dancers are newly arrived in the longhouse, usually do not concern the lands of the hosts, but rather those of the dancers. The isolated bursts of wailing that occur at these times come mostly from women married into the host's longhouse from the longhouse (or longhouses) of the guests. As the evening progresses, the songs gradually concern localities closer and closer to those belonging to the hosts until finally, they cross over onto the hosts' lands themselves, and the weeping and violence begin in earnest. From this point on, the songs, in effect, move back and forth across their hosts' lands producing considerable anguish in the audience until morning comes and the ceremony ends.

To say that the songs move across the hosts' lands is descriptive of the way in which the locality names are given. Place names are arranged in a song as a progression across the area referred to from point to point and landmark to landmark, mapping out a coherent geographical region and thus a series of personal associations for anyone who is familiar with the area.

In one ceremony,[4] the dancers sang:

> At Gudesawel I am hungry, I am hungry at the ba: tree there, I am/
> hungry at Gudesawel.
> At the Masase over there Kabulo: tips are appearing, I am hungry.
> At Gudesawel I am hungry, I am hungry at the ba: tree there
> At Ko:mo:lo: (river pool) the sa:f sago is waving back and forth/
> (in the wind).
> At Gudesawel I am hungry, I am hungry at the ba: tree there
> At Gudesawel I am hungry, I am hungry at the ba: tree there
> At Yalubesi over there, the arrow cane is standing out, I am hungry.
> At Gudesawel I am hungry, I am hungry at the ba: tree there
> At Malosono: over there, the wani palm stands out against the sky/
> I am hungry.
> At Gudesawel I am hungry, I am hungry at the ba: tree there
> At Gudesawel I am hungry, I am hungry at the ba: tree there
> At Sisilip over there, the Uf tree stands out against the sky.
> (Composed by Habe of clan Bono:, November 1968)

The song projects an image of someone passing in hunger from one abandoned place to another, evoking each particular area through reference to its particular trees, weeds, and other features.

[4]Three more *Heyalo* songs are examined in Appendix 2.

The region mapped out is in the vicinity of a low ridge called Gudefili (Figure 1 on p. 142) between the Gudep stream and the Isawa River on land owned by clan Ga:sumisi. The song was aimed at a youth named Minowa. Minowa and his friend Degera had built a small bush shack at a place called Gudesawel, and there they used to "sleep side by side." Degera had subsequently left the Kaluli area to work on the coast. The song was intended to make Minowa nostalgic for his friend whom he now had not seen in some time. At the same time, there were several other people who had associations with Gudefili, The song also referred to Masase, the site of a garden house belonging to two men Isaida: and Wasoba. The house had recently burned down, and the site was already covered with weeds, through which kabulo: (a wild edible cane) was growing up. Opposite the house site (though not visible from it) was Ko:mo:lo:, a pool in the Isawa, with several palms of the safa:, a variety of sago, growing nearby. (The composer did not know whom they belonged to.) Finally, past Yalubesi with its growth of arrow cane belonging to Isaida:, the song passed to Malosono:, the major longhouse of the area, where Minowa, Isaida:, and Wasoba all lived. All these people, and several others who knew the vicinity, were moved to tears by the song and burned various dancers.

## CONCLUSION

When all is said and done, *Heyalo* songs achieve their effect with very little material. Conventional in imagery, abbreviated in reference, their poetry depends largely on the evocative convergence of symbols of land and food, which derive their power from other contexts. To some degree, the effectiveness of the songs depends on the audience's being attuned to this kind of art and knowing what to listen for. To some extent, it depends on the dramaturgy of the ceremonial context: the dim lighting, the buildup of intensity, the element of surprise. But the major element is the songs. The guests themselves sometimes weep over them during practice sessions in their own longhouse on the evenings before the ceremony.

For this simple nonliterate society, where most people deeply share the same values and assumptions within a tightly integrated system of symbols, that poetic metaphor is most poignant and powerful which is couched in terms of those symbols which most widely mediate human relationships, identity, and activity in other domains of cultural experience. Upon reflection, this should not be surprising. Indeed I suggest that symbols which mediate large domains of cultural experience in any given culture may be expected to play an important part in poetic or artistic representation there. In a small group such as the Kaluli where context is closely shared, representation of important meanings need not be very explicit. All that is required of songs is that they formulate appropriately the few key terms or symbols which evoke the set of meanings intended to those who understand them. The result is exactly the kind of abbreviation, or rather economy, of expression that we find in *Heyalo* songs. This economy, in turn, by its very *lack* of explicit representation enables one song to mean different things to the different individuals who hear it, and each individual may find his own allusions in it. Indeed, the Kaluli are keenly attuned to the creativity required for these songs, as old songs sung again will not move an audience familiar with them, and new ones must be composed for each performance to be effective. Newly created songs remodel the relation between land and food by the same procedures, but not in the same ways. The result of each new convergence of locality names and food allusions is newly to evoke (perhaps often the same) particular events for individual listeners. As such, ceremonial songs outline to the Kaluli their version of "history" as a remembrance of things past. It is not history as we know it, organized in causal-temporal sequence. Rather, events are put in relation to one another in terms of geographical locations where one shared his life with others. As one man said of the ceremonies: "This is our memory."

## ACKNOWLEDGMENTS

This paper is based on research undertaken in the Southern Highlands District of Papua, New Guinea, October 1966 to November 1968, financed by Grant #IR04 MH12532-01 and accompanying Training Fellowship 1-FL-MH-31, 120-01 from the National Institute of Health.

# APPENDIX 1

The phonemic orthography follows that established by Murray Rule in *Customs, Alphabet and Grammar of the Kaluli People of Bosavi, Papua,* (unpublished ms., Lake Kutubu, 1964).

*Consonants* are pronounced substantially the same as they are in English with one addition:

        š    Pronounced as 's' in *sugar*

*Vowels* are pronounced as follows:

- a As in English '*fa*ther'
- a: As in English '*ca*t'
- e Similar, but a little higher in the mouth than English '*ge*t'.
- i As in English '*ea*t'
- o As in English '*go*'
- o: As in English '*ou*ght'
- u As in English '*b*oo'
- i As in English 'sister'

# APPENDIX 2

## Three *Heyalo* Songs

All the *Heyalo* songs quoted in this paper were sung at a ceremony performed by the people of Sululip longhouse for the people of the longhouse at Wahalip, in November 1968. (See Figure 3 for longhouse locations.)

The first song was composed by more than one man. The place names are on the land of clan Didesa, some of whose members joined in hosting the ceremony. The area referred to is given in Figure 2.

> Alas, the bol tree, alas, the Wumisen hill, alas the bol tree.
> The ti sago at the Golo spring is waving back and forward in the wind.
> Alas, the bol tree, alas the Wumisen hill, alas the bol tree.
> At the Saliso:no spring the safo: sago palms stand out against the sky.
> Alas the bol tree, alas the Wumisen hill, alas the bol tree
> At the Sia:n spring (Sia:nalip) the ti sago palms are waving against
>    the sky
> Alas the bol tree, alas the Wumisen hill, alas the bol tree
> Alas the bol tree, alas the Wumisen hill, alas the bol tree
> At Goloso:k a yahali tree is waving back and forth in the wind.
>            (Composed by Seli and Dufulu of clan Bono: November 1968)

The song is short because neither of the co-composers had close ties with Didesa or knew its land well. They did not know who owned these particular areas and could give little information about them besides their names and locations. The song was nevertheless effective, provoking one of the most grief-stricken and violent displays of the evening from the Didesa visitors and their in-laws. The tune was catchy and the song retained popularity among young people at Bono: for a week or so after the ceremony. They sang it frequently as they walked the forest trails.

The second song was composed by Hawe of clan Bono:, the area referred to is given in Figure 3.

> Mother ee mother ee mother ee, mother where are you going?
> I am going to stay at Kusa:kini, I am going to stay at the uka tree
>    there
> I am hungry at Kusa:kini, I am hungry at the uka there.
> Come stay at Kusa:kini, come stay at Suguniga, come stay at the
>    sa:l tree there.
> Mother ee mother ee mother ee, mother, where are you going?
> I am going to Wo:ya:na:lip, I am going to the wani palm there.
> I am hungry at Wo:ya:na:lip, I am hungry at the wani palm there.
> Come stay at Wo:ya:na:lip, come stay at Mugumin river pool, come
>    stay at the Ilaha tree there.
> Mother ee mother ee mother ee, mother where are you going?
> I am going to say at the Ibu spring, I am going to stay at the
>    sos tree there.
> I am hungry at the Ibu spring, I am hungry at the sos tree there
> Come stay at the Ibu spring, come stay at Malosono: come stay at
>    the sa:fo sago there.

This song was aimed at Wasoba, Isaida:, and Siga:sa:, three men of two different clans living in the longhouse at Malosono:, who were among those hosting the ceremony at Wahalip. The song was sung as though addressing Siga:sa:'s wife Hiya (a woman from Wahalip), and is supposed to represent the journey of a woman leaving Wahalip to go to Malosono: (though the place names are not really consistent with the path). Hiya, as it happened, was unmoved by the song, but Isaida:, Wasoba, and Siga:sa: all wept since it mentioned lands of their in-laws or close relatives with which they were intimately familiar. Many of the people to whom the places mentioned here actually belonged were not present at the ceremony.

The third song, composed by Dufulu of clan Bono: was intended primarily to serve as the concluding song to the ceremony rather than to cause anyone to weep.

So:lo:so:lo:, gather together, so:lo:so:lo:
Wahalip is sounding (with the sounds of the morning), It is sounding,
  so we are going.
So:lo:so:lo:, gather together, so:lo:so:lo:
Ibulip is sounding, I'm hungry, so I'm going.
So:lo:so:lo:, gather together, so:lo:so:lo:
Dolondosawel is sounding, my stomach is empty, so I'm going.
So:lo:so:lo:, gather together, so:lo:so:lo:
Gagula (ridge) is sounding, I'm hungry, so I'm going.
So:lo:so:lo:, gather together, so:lo:so:lo:
Uwa:k is sounding, it is sounding, so I'm going
So:lo:so:lo:, gather together, so:lo:so:lo:
Desep is sounding, it is sounding, so I'm going
Sululip is sounding, it is sounding, so I'm going.

The gist of the song is that morning has come and the first birds and insects of the day are singing (cf. so:lo:so:lo: = the singing sound of birds and insects). The dancers sing that they are hungry and want to go home. The birds sing at each place mentioned, and the song track leads from Wahalip, the place where the ceremony was held, back toward the longhouse of Sululip, the dwelling of the principal guests and performers.

142

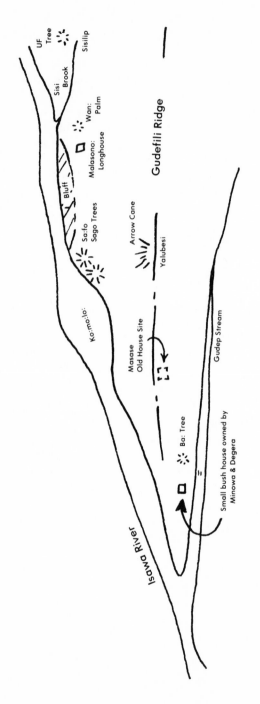

Figure 1

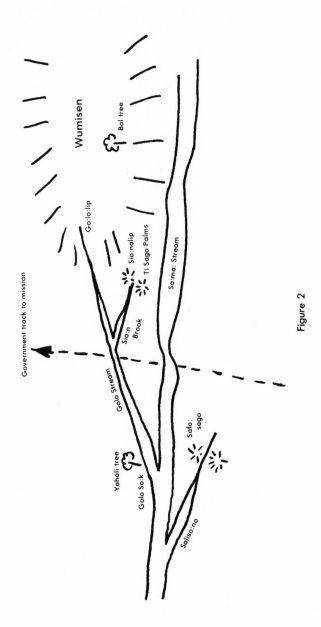

Wumisen

Bol tree

Go:lo:lip

Sia:nalip

Ti Sago Palms

Sa:ma: Stream

Sia:n Brook

Government track to mission

Golo Stream

Yahali tree

Golo So:k

Safo: sago

Saliso:no

Figure 2

143

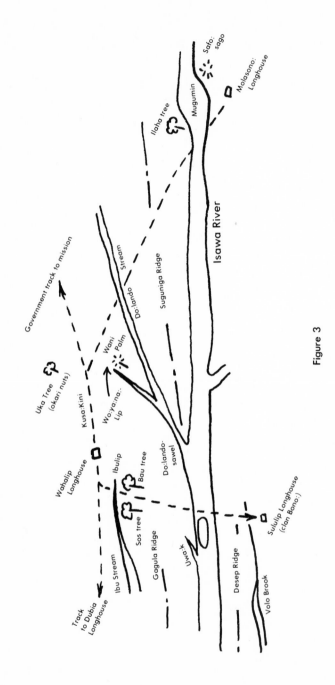

Figure 3

144

# chapter nine

# The Ceremonial System of Savu

James J. Fox

The Australian National University

> How curious: we should like to explain our understanding of a gesture by means
> of a translation into words, and the understanding of words by translating them
> into a gesture. Thus we are tossed to and fro when we try to find out where
> understanding properly resides.

L. Wittgenstein, *Zettel*: 227

This is an attempt at an initial description of the ceremonial system of Savu.[1] In
its entirety, this ceremonial system is one of exceptional liturgical complexity.
Savu (Rai Hawu), including the off-shore islet of Raijua, is located in the outer
arc of the Lesser Sundas in eastern Indonesia midway between the large islands
of Sumba and Timor. Removed and remote from near neighboring islands, the
Savunese preserve on their populous, wind-swept, and eroded island one of the
most integral of indigenous religions to be found in Indonesia today.

Rather than focus on some minor segment of their religious ceremonies, I
prefer, in this paper, to present an overall outline of the Savunese ceremonial
system. Although this does little justice to the intricacy of the entire system, it
provides the basis for further studies later. I, therefore, concentrate on a discussion of (1) the local divisions or states on Savu, (2) the lunar calendar that
determines ceremonial life in each of these states, (3) the descent groups from
which the hierarchy of priests who carry out these ceremonies is chosen. With
this essential background to the system and its priesthood, I examine a single
performance within the ceremonial cycle of Liae: cockfighting as ritual confrontation in the month of *Banga Liwu Rame.*

[1]Since this is an initial description, I wish to make it clear that my transcription of Savunese
words is tentative. For place names, I have adopted well-known conventional designations as, for
example, Savu for Hawu or present Indonesian usage as, for example, Seba for Heba or Timu for
Dimu. There exist only three short studies of the Savunese language: H. Kern (1892), J. K.
Wijngaarden (1896), and M. C. Radja Haba (1958). I hope to be able to make a comprehensive study
of the Savunese language but, in the meantime, I am obliged to rely indiscriminately on the contributions of earlier writers.

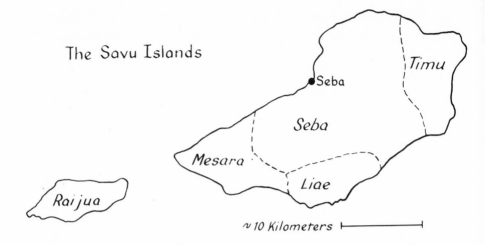

The Savu Islands

~10 Kilometers ⊢————————⊣

## INTRODUCTORY REMARKS

By way of introduction, I would like to raise a problem that is all too often only tangentially broached in symbolic analysis. My concern has to do with the possibility of comparison—the comparison of symbolic systems that are, in their *modalities,* radically dissimilar. Since it is a truism that cultures differ, I wish to indicate, by *modality,* something more than "the grain of the wood," a metaphoric phrase used by the late Professor Evans-Pritchard to describe the idiosyncratic cultural configurations of different societies. By modality, I mean the very manner of expressing symbolic statements, the differing channels and signifying vehicles of particular cultural affirmation. In semiological terms, this modality refers to neither message nor code but rather to the channels by which messages are encoded and communicated and to the effect a choice of channels has on both.

Professor Roman Jakobson has observed "that the most socialized, abundant, and pertinent sign systems in human society are based on sight and hearing (1970:8). He notes, moreover, an essential distinguishing trait between auditory and visual signs. Whereas for auditory signs, time acts as a structural factor in determining sequence and simultaneity, the ordering of visual signs must necessarily involve space. In Peircean terminology, it follows that symbols predominate among auditory signs, icons among visual signs. The combination and patterning of these separate sign systems constitute different forms of discourse.

Evidently, most human communication involves both auditory and visual signs. But what is remarkable, on comparative evidence, is the degree to which particular cultures mute one or the other of these sign systems either pervasively or disjunctively in time or space. The separability of these sign systems goes beyond the often observed cultural patterning of noise and silence and applies to all symbolic expression.

146

Rituals are particularly prone to this kind of modal patterning. Since anthropologists can usually find myths that supposedly justify a ritual or informants who can provide some illuminating explanation of them, this pattern is frequently overlooked. But it seems rare to find rituals that are an equal and coincident combination of auditory and visual messages, despite an anthropological predilection to portray rituals in this manner. The two approaches in anthropology that have recently been developed to deal with the varying forms of symbolic behavior tend to rely on the analysis of different sign systems. The structural approach, dominated by linguistic analogies, focuses on the logical combination and cognitive manipulation of definably discrete units; the "dramatistic" approach examines the sequencing of human actions, physical gesture, and the theatric display of objects, all endowed with emotional as well as intellectual significance. I contend that a choice of one of these approaches reflects more than the personal preferences of individual investigators. In part, it reflects the different modalities of the rituals and different cultures.

To describe semiotic displays involving both persons and specially prepared objects, Jakobson has used the label *ostension,* borrowed from the Czech researcher, I. Osolsobe (Jakobson, 1970:9). For contrast, we can adopt the label *oration* to refer to semiotic systems of production involving predominantly auditory signs. In these terms, to choose two contrasting landmarks in the study of symbolic behavior, the ceremonies of the Nuer are rituals of oration (Evans-Pritchard, 1956); the ceremonies of Ndembu are rituals of ostension (Turner, 1967). Islam, in its orthodoxy, tends toward oration; Hinduism toward ostension. Similarly, Christianity in its Protestant forms relies on oration, whereas Catholicism requires ostension. But instead of overstraining a simplistic polarity, it is more to the point to illustrate these modalities by comparing two island societies in eastern Indonesia that I have been studying since 1965. Since this study has combined fieldwork and archival research, this double perspective provides special insight into the markedly different nature of religious orientation on the islands. The two islands are Roti, on which I have already written a number of papers (Fox, 1971a; 1971b; 1971c; 1973; 1974; 1975), and Savu whose ceremonial system is the particular concern of this paper. The languages of these islands belong to distinct sub-families of Austronesian. In line with these linguistic differences, the social organization and cultural patterns on the two islands suggest historical derivation from different areas of Indonesia. The languages and traditions of Savu point toward western Indonesia; those of Roti to the Moluccas and other islands to the east.

## ORATION AND OSTENSION:
## CONTRASTING MODES OF RITUAL ORIENTATION

In the encounter with new traditions, societies—if granted the grace of time— seem to respond by preserving what is culturally most significant in their social life. An historical glimpse of the responses of the Rotinese and the Savunese to the arrival of the Dutch in the Timor area of eastern Indonesia in the seventeenth century provides the first hint of the underlying differences between these societies.

The Rotinese responded quickly to the Dutch presence; by 1726, the rulers of the states of Roti recognized by the Dutch East India Company began converting to Christianity, began establishing their own Malay language schools, and literally, drew unsuspecting Company officers inextricably into the web of their litigious local politics. But, whereas the Dutch found leaders on Roti with some traditional power of dispute settlement whom they could designate as regents and later rajas, they were at a loss on how to deal with Savu and they could only resort to grafting the alien institution of raja to a ceremonial position from which it later separated. Savu's response to the Dutch was to reject Christianity, to refuse schooling, and virtually to disregard the presence of the Dutch in their area for over 200 years. Only in the second half of the nineteenth century, did the Savunese open their island, within the span of a few short years, to Christianity, to schools. This was soon followed by decimation by smallpox and cholera. Today, most Rotinese consider themselves Christians, but perhaps half the population of Savu would reject this label.

The Rotinese have a tradition of local states, each composed of clans and represented by officials at the court of that state's ruler. The courts, with their interminable debate and argument, are a focus of Rotinese cultural life. Even with the diminution of their judicial powers, these courts still retain their importance. Litigation, at all levels, remains a preoccupation of the Rotinese. As the Dutch first observed, the courts provide a public forum for the demonstration of individual verbal prowess.

Within the local states, residence is scattered and ritually any man can offer to the ancestral spirits. Once a year, after the harvest, there was a ceremonial reunion of clan members who performed common rituals as an invocation of fertility. With a single exception, this ceremony has disappeared on Roti with the spread of Christianity. Only the verbal formulae used at these rituals are well remembered by local elders. The main ceremonial gatherings of the present day involve rituals of the life cycle: first pregnancy, haircutting, weddings, housebuilding, and funerals. They are all occasions for a communal meal. But these feasts are also occasions for elaborate oratory. Much of this oratory consists of a formulaic, stylized, parallel poetry that follows established canonical forms. This poetry, I have described as a *ritual language* because it is a strict and distinctly recognizable form of speaking and because what passes for ritual is usually reduced to the use of this speech.

By any standard, the Rotinese are indifferent ritualists. They have preserved their culture verbally. They can talk a good ceremony, but they are rarely concerned with actually performing one. Speaking represents the life of the spirit and in the chants of their ritual languages, they retain the major architecture of their religious traditions. Ritual language chants are segments of what may once have been a single long epic recounting the deed of two intermarried, yet hostile families: the Lords of the Sky represented by Shark and Crocodile and their descendants and followers. Segments of this indigenous epic are recited; they are never performed as drama. They constitute, however, the basic frame of reference for social life and ritual interaction on the island. On Roti, rituals are primarily acts of oration.

On Savu, the states are ceremonial territories. Within these territories, residence is in specific, named villages, Savu's social system consists of localized male descent groups complemented by membership in one of two island-wide maternal moieties. Each territory has its own hierarchy of priests with their assistants and each month this priesthood is involved in carrying out the ceremonial requirements of the lunar calendar.

On Roti, life is replete with verbal confrontations. But to resort to physical violence to settle a dispute is considered as shocking evidence of a lack of speaking ability and, therefore, physical confrontation is assiduously avoided. On Savu, however, confrontation frequently takes physical form. Litigation and debate are neither institutionalized, elaborated, nor approved as on Roti. And although they provoke fewer disputes, Savunese do not shun physical force in settling them. In the Dutch records, the Savunese were repeatedly singled out not for their verbal but for their martial prowess. For example, in the decisive battle in defense of the town of Kupang, in 1749, of all the native participants from the area, only the Savunese held their ground. For centuries, the Savunese have retained a reputation for firmness, tempered comportment, and resolute action. The ideals of their symbolic behavior are ritualized and epitomized in their ceremonies. One of the most notable manifestations of these is *pepehi wowadu*, the ceremonial rock-throwing contest that marks the transition from the old calendar year to the new. A Dutch missionary, W. M. Donselaar, described this confrontation in 1872:

> On a hilly, stone-strewn area, the male population divides into two groups at some distance from one another. The head is covered with a sturdy cap of waterbuffalo hide and the left hand holds a shield, either round or long in form, of the same material. Already a few days before, the *Deo Rai* has made an offering to *Munkia*, the god of war and now as the combatants stand ready opposite each other, he gives the signal to attack with a few strokes on a great drum. The fight consists of the throwing of stones which have merely to be picked up on the spot and the object of the fight is to put the opposing party to flight. The art of battle consists in speed and accuracy in the throwing of stones and the agility and expertise in covering oneself with a ceaseless movement of the shield, thereby attempting to confuse the opposing party and to drive them from their place. A heavy rain of stones fell on the head-coverings and on the shields of the combatants each of whose side attempts to hold together. On these occasions, light wounds are not infrequent and serious injuries occasionally occur. And if it happens that one group puts the other to flight, the air resounds with the shouts of the winners and the tumultuous performance ends with the general cheering and laughter of the crowd. (1872:317–318)

On Savu, in striking contrast to Roti, ceremonies are not the occasion for elaborate oratory, grandiloquent prayers, or long ritual invocations. A ritual silence is imposed upon the Savunese for half the year, from the time of planting to the time of harvest. During the three months of the High Ceremonial Season, singing is permitted as part of *pedoa* dancing. But unlike Roti where similar forms of circle dancing provide opportunities for the recitation of long narrative poems, *pedoa* dancing features the melodic repetition of brief lines and refrains. All of this is not to argue that there is no verbalization or ancestral recitation in Savunese culture, but rather that the rituals of the ceremonial cycle are not regarded as a proper place for oratory.

Ceremonies, on Savu, require ritual action and hence need little verbal accompaniment. Their ceremonies are not, however, the simple enactment of some eternal mythic pattern. They are in part, as Savunese readily point out, historically determined dramas in which persons act out representative relations among themselves. It is these relations that deserve the most detailed scrutiny, if one is to comprehend the significance of the ceremonies.

On Savu, rituals are primarily acts of ostension. The island's indigenous religion has been preserved by dramatic performance. But for this reason, it now seems more threatened by change. It can be argued that the Rotinese response to the increasing pressure of outside influence has taken form of a retreat into verbalism. Yet this response, if it is such, seems in keeping with the mode of orientation of their entire culture. Talented Rotinese chanters can travel beyond the island of Roti. Some in my acquaintance, who are now living in Timor, have not visited their homeland in decades and yet, on request, can give a verbal performance equal to any on Roti. As Rotinese migrate to other islands, their ritual language can accompany them. But for the Savunese in their migrations, their cycle of ceremonies has not been transported beyond the island. These ceremonies are localized within strict spatial limits and they are specific to relations among certain named descent groups. Moreover, they are seriously endangered by conversion. Converts to Christianity within the local communities that maintain the priesthood and its cult can no longer participate actively in performances. Historically, the evidence suggests that converts to Christianity were forced to migrate from the island. Although this is no longer the case, it is true that a decreasing number of participants gradually diminishes the dramatic effect and comprehensiveness of the ceremonies. For the Rotinese, syncretism is possible and few see any conflict between their present practices and the demands of Christianity; but for the Savunese, the conflict is real and apparent. In certain areas of Savu, the ceremonies still flourish; in others, they are already on the wane. It is important, in this light, to examine the Savunese ceremonial system as it is maintained today.

In examining the ceremonial system of Savu, however, some approach unlike one appropriate to the island of Roti seems necessary. To be deaf on Roti would be to miss the major significance of Rotinese ritual; to be blind on Savu would be to miss almost everything. Minute and exhaustive linguistic analysis is called for on Roti; for Savu, a different method is required. One of the principal objects of this paper is to provide sufficient background to begin the analysis of a single Savunese ritual of ostension.

## THE STATES OF SAVU

The first recorded visit of a Dutch East India Company officer to the island of Savu was in October 1648.[2] At that time there appear to have been at least six autonomous local states on the island: Seba, Mesara, Liae, Timu, Teriwu, and Menia. By 1756, the time of the first and only contract of trade signed with the Company, Teriwu had been conquered by, and incorporated within, neighboring states. Menia, a signatory to that contract, was already threatened by the larger states of Seba and Timu, each of which possessed a harbor that provided access to limited but critical trade. Within fifteen years, it, too, was absorbed by its neighbors.

Following precedent established in earlier dealings with the local states of Roti and Timor, the Dutch in 1756 granted the titled, hereditary offices of raja and of *fetor (weto)* to two prominent leaders in each of the states that they formally recognized. Gradually over the next century, Seba—the north coast state with the island's main harbor—expanded its territory on all sides and eventually came to occupy more than half of the island. As a result, in the twentieth century, the Dutch East Indies government, in attempting to rationalize its relations with the petty states in the Timor area, demoted the rajas of Mesara, Liae, and Timu to the same rank as the *fetor* of Seba and acknowledged the raja of Seba as raja of all Savu. Throughout this historical period, the tiny offshore island of Raijua, considered by the Savunese as the source of their most sacred traditions, retained much of its original autonomy through neglect and inaccessibility.[3]

The Savu islands, including Raijua, have a present population of over 51,000. This gives the islands an overall resident population density of approximately 100 persons per square kilometer. With this density of population, one of the highest in the Timor area of eastern Indonesia, Savu has both an available and accessible populace to perform its continuing rituals.

Administratively, the island is now divided into two *kecamatan,* Sabu Barat and Sabu Timur, within the *kabupaten* of Kupang. For all Savunese, however, the primary though unofficial divisions of their islands remain the four states or former *kerajaan* of Seba, Mesara, Liae, Timu plus Raijua. Each is

[2]The report of this visit can be found in the fragment of the journal of Hendrik Ter Horst published by J. H. Heeres (1895:422–430). For a brief sketch of Savunese culture and society, see Fox (1972).

[3]There is no record of a contract of trade and recognition between the company and a local raja on Raijua; ninteenth-century records, however, name a line of rajas for Raijua.

ceremonially autonomous and possesses its own lunar calendar. (A map is included at the end of the chapter.)


## THE LUNAR CALENDARS OF SAVU

At first impression, the lunar calendars of Savu present a confusing picture: separate successions of seemingly unsynchronized, discrepantly named months.[4] In fact, these calendars form part of a single system that is essentially simple. Each state has its own calendar. The months of each of these calendars name some specific and coincident seasonal occurrence or activity in that particular state. The occurrence of the same natural phenomena at slightly differing intervals and the staggering of similar activities over a three-month period keep the separate calendars in phased conjunction.

These separate annual cycles are unified within a larger ceremonial cycle known as *kelila*. Each calendar includes a month for *kelila* during which certain pig sacrifices can be carried out but only at specified annual intervals in the various states. This entire cycle culminates, after 81 years, in the Great Kelila, *Kelila Rai Ae* at which a major pig sacrifice is held. All Savunese are obliged to return to their island to attend it.

Savunese conceptions of time reflect a recognition of regular intervals and periodic occurrences in nature. Those that figure most prominently in the calendar are (1) the transitions associated with the monsoons, (2) the growing season of the green gram or mung bean, (3) the twice-annual appearance, on the south coast of the island, of a swarming of sea worms, (4) the second blossoming of the lontar palm which signals a time of increasing dryness and a period of intense palm tapping. Underlying all of these and essential to the ordering of all ceremonies is a conception of the moon and a careful attention to all of its phases.

The moon *(weru)* represents a principle of life. Just as the sun rises to the zenith before it sinks and disappears each day, the moon grows to fullness *(hilu)* before it dies *(made)* each month. Identified with the tides of the sea, the moon is

---

[4]There exist two brief studies of the Savunese calendar. The first, based on residence of almost a year on the island, is by the Dutch missionary, J. K. Wijngaarden (1892); the second, by the French scholar, J. Cuisinier (1956), is based on a visit to Savu of several days. In December 1960, a Catholic priest, Father P. Konijn, also had occasion to visit the island of Savu and became stranded there for some time. While waiting in Seba for a boat, he was approached by an elderly Savunese who wished to explain life on Savu to him. The elder was known as Pa Ona and Father Konijn took extensive notes on what he had to tell. In 1965, when I was beginning my study of Savunese culture, Father Konijn showed me these notes and I realized that, although they were sketchy at many points, they represent something of a first course in Savunese cosmology. I used these notes as a guideline in making my own investigations and have continued to rely on them, particularly in regard to conceptions of the moon. I therefore wish to express my gratitude to Father P. Konijn and to Pa Ona whom I never had the opportunity to meet. One observation worth noting is that despite dissimilarities in numerous other aspects of their culture, the Rotinese and Savunese share similar concepts of the sun and moon.

associated with the moist luxuriant aspects of growth, with the quality of coolness, and states of peace, tranquility, and contentment. Yet the moon is inseparably linked to the sun with its steady, unchanging order and its diurnal short-lived peak of heat and intensity. The Savunese equate the sun's daily order with the moon's monthly growth and ceremonies are enacted to conjoin these principles. Auspicious rituals of increase occur during the waxing of the moon, rituals of expiation or propitiation of evil during the waning of the moon. The major rituals of the High Ceremonial Season culminate in a burst of activity while the sun is at its highest on the day when the moon will be at its fullest.

Days of the month are reckoned according to the phases of the moon. The waxing moon is *luha,* the waning moon *hape.* The second quarter of the moon's growth is called *luha ae,* the great *luha;* the fourth quarter is *hape iki,* the small or lesser *hape.* From the first appearance of the new moon to the time of the full moon, Savunese count 15 days of *luha (he peluha, due peluha . . . :* first day of *luha,* second day of *luha . . .).* Similarly, they count the 15 days of *hape.* But this monthly reckoning is adjustable to the moon. The last of *hape iki* can be dropped and the counting of *luha* begun early or *luha* can be counted as 14 days. The critical days of the week of *luha ae* are named as well as counted but one of these days, named *kewore ru kare,* "round as a dedap leaf," is repeated so that any necessary adjustment can occur on the eleventh or twelfth day of the *luha* count.

The Savunese conceive of the moon's development as a cyclical progression. The sun completes in a day the journey that the moon makes in a month. During *luha,* the moon is *weru pa dida.* It is possible to catch a glimpse of the moon during the day. During *hape,* however, the moon is *weru pa da'i* and it cannot be seen during the day. In this cycle, the unseen dead moon *(made weru)* is associated with the west, whence the new moon will arise, whereas the full moon *(hilu weru)* is associated with the east in contrast to the dead moon. The whole of this elaborate conceptual system consists of a series of balanced oppositions. Not only are the sun and moon in conceptual opposition, but each phase of the moon calls to mind its opposite phase within the cycle. Figure 1 is a representation of the moon's cycle based on a Savunese sketch.

Although this account leaves undiscussed Savunese ideas about the relations between the tides and the moon, certain dramatic events recur with an annual regularity to reinforce these associations and to serve as the identification for separate months of the lunar calendar. Twice in the southern coastal states of Mesara and Liae, between mid-December and mid-February, the swarming of the *nyale* occurs. In time with a set lunar phase and according to the tidal rhythms, sea worms *(Leodice viridis)* attached to the undersides of reef rocks release their posterior parts, ladened with genital products (H. M. Fox, 1923; Woodworth, 1907). These free-swimming sexual segments, measuring from three inches to three feet, rise to the surface turning the waters along the shore line into what looks like boiling, slightly green spaghetti. Wading in these waters, Savunese can collect *nyale* by the bucketful.

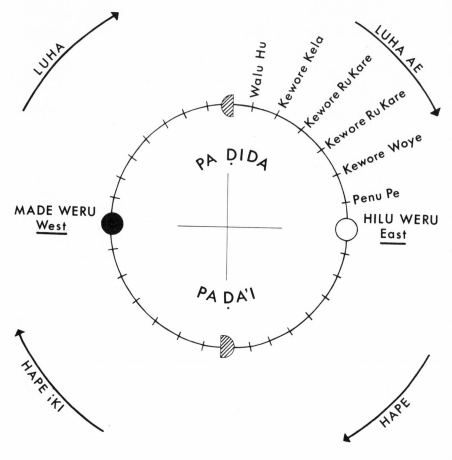

Figure 1

Significantly, there are always two swarmings of the *nyale* and these distinct events have been taken up in different states to identify a month within their lunar calendar. The month known as *Nyale* in Mesara marks the first appearance of these creatures; the month of *Nyale* in Liae signals the last big run before they disappear for the year. This shows that although each lunar calendar is based on the recognition of certain regularities in nature, these regularities have either a periodicity or a duration that allows flexibility in ordering human activities and in naming the months that are in accordance with these activities.

Each state has its own calendar that coincides with the seasonal activity in that particular state. Each of these separate calendars begins with the same month-name: *Koo Ma*, "To clear the fields." But this initial seasonal activity is staggered to occur over a three-month period. Seba is the first to begin the new year with *Koo Ma*, followed in the next month by Mesara and Liae and in the succeeding month by Timu. And just as these calendars begin, so they end: with

154

the same month-name, *Baga Rae/Hae Rae* which occurs successively over a three-month period in the different states.

Certain month-names suggest critical features of the system. Originally and to the present day, even after the introduction of new food crops, the calendar in its early phases is structured to coincide with the growing season of the green gram or mung bean (Savunese: *kebui;* Indonesian: *kajang ijo,* NLi *Phaseolus lunatus*). This is the single most important crop on the island. The month-name *Naiki Kebui,* in the calendars of Seba and Timu, refers to the first sprouts of this bean; *Wila Kolo,* in Seba, Messara, and Timu, refers to its blossoming period. The green gram is of such importance that the high ceremonial season may not begin until after it has been harvested. Rice, a prestige food that is grown only in limited areas where irrigation is possible, has a planting and harvesting cycle that is somewhat at variance with the calendar.

The least reliable of seasonal occurrences is the transition between the monsoons. For the islands of the outer arc of the Lesser Sundas, the period of the west monsoon that brings the rains is a short, fitful, and unreliable time. The rains may begin at any time between late November and January, and once every few years, it is expected that they will all but fail to appear. Determining the precise transition between this irregular season and the onset of the east monsoon is uncertain. The month of *Hanga Dimu* in Seba marks the beginning of this transition, while *Hanga Dimu,* which occurs two months later in Timu, marks the end.

The high ceremonial season—the variously named months of *Daba* and *Banga Liwu*—occurs approximately in the middle of the calendar year. It begins after *Hanga Dimu* in the states on the northern coast or after the last appearance of the *nyale* in the states of the south coast. This season comprises the intermediary months of ritual activity between the harvesting of the green gram and the period of lontar palm tapping. In each of the states, this ceremonial season is followed by two months called *A'a,* Elder and *Ari,* Younger, which indicate the progression of the dry season. Thereafter, there occurs a period of intensive palm-tapping activity that leaves little time for ceremony. Life, on Savu, in its present form, is dependent on the green gram and, more importantly, on the produce of the lontar palm.

The year ends with *Baga Rae* or *Hae Rae.* This is the month of the spectacular ritual confrontations that involve rock-throwing battles in Seba. It is a month when the spirits are said to rise from the sea and must, in the end, be driven from the villages. The final pig sacrifices for anyone who has died during the year are held in this month prior to the renewal of the earth.

In Savunese oral tradition, the south coast is where the ancestors, coming from Raijua, first came upon land. Month-names of several of the ritually most important months, such as *Daba* or *Hae Rae,* denote place names in Liae, suggesting the derivation of certain ceremonies from this region. Liae and Raijua, in turn, have sacred sites, such as Merapu, which suggest links with east Sumba.

The lunar calendars of the states of Savu can be corrected by the insertion of an intercalary month, *Heola*. This additional month is introduced periodically to bring the calendar in line with one of the most reliable seasonal occurrences of the year, the second blossoming of the lontar palm. Between 1889 and 1892, a remarkable young Dutch missionary, J. K. Wijngaarden, managed to live periodically for over a year on Savu and began to learn the Savunese language. In a brief article in a missionary journal (Wijngaarden, 1892), he has outlined the way in which the various calendars on Savu functioned for the year 1890 to 1891. Table 1 sets forth Wijngaarden's information on these calendars in a schematic form. From my own researches in Liae in 1973, I can confirm that this state's ceremonial calendar has continued to operate as Wijngaarden described it in 1890.

## THE STRUCTURE OF THE CLANS AND THE PRIESTHOOD

All the states of Savu are composed of named, localized patrilineal (or rather male-ordered) descent groups *(udu)* that recognize a single common "origin" or "root" village *(rae kepue)*. Some of these are divided into component descent groups *(kerogo)* that occupy subsidiary villages. Occupancy of the origin village defines the leading *kerogo* within the *udu,* and village names can often be used as a convenient linguistic shorthand for describing *udu* or *kerogo* relations. At this point and for simplicity, I shall refer to the *udu* as "clans" and the *kerogo* as "lineages." Yet it must be emphasized that not all clans have lineages and that, therefore, in several instances, a lineage can be the organizational or structural equivalent of an entire clan.

Each state is, therefore, composed of a number of localized clans. But crosscutting these local allegiances on an island-wide basis are the moieties *Hubi Ae,* "the Greater Blossom," and *Hubi Iki,* "the Lesser Blossom." These two *Hubi* are further subdivided into named *Wini,* "Seeds." Membership in one of the two *Hubi* and in their component *Wini* are reckoned through the mother. Although it is improper to speak of or discuss these female-ordered groups, every individual's membership is publicly displayed by means of the design motifs on native *ikat*-cloth that are exclusively owned by each *Hubi* and their specific *Wini.* These female groups determine status, are a prime factor in arranging marriages, and are essential in structuring the rituals of the life cycle. They have, however, virtually nothing to do with the lunar ceremonial system within each state.

In each state, clans are ranked in terms of the priestly offices associated with them. Throughout Savu, the office of *Deo Rai,* "Lord of the Earth" is associated with the leading clan; the office of *Apu Lodo,* "Descendant of the Sun," is associated with the next most important clan. Below this, there is a slightly variable structure in each local state.

To take Seba as an example: the *Deo Rai* comes from the clan, Namata; the *Apu Lodo* from the clan, Nataga; the office of *Do Heleo,* "Overseer," is linked

# Table 1
## The Calendar Year of Savu According to Wijngaarden, 1890–91

| Months | Seba | Mesara | Liae | Timu |
|---|---|---|---|---|
| October | Koo Ma | | | |
| November | Naiki Kebui | Koo Ma | Koo Ma | |
| December | Wila Kolo | Nyale | Kuja Ma | Koo Ma |
| January | Hanga Dimu | Wila Kolo (Pe Netta) | Kelila Aji Lai | Naiki Kebui |
| February | Daba Eki | Hora Kaba | Nyale | Wila Kolo |
| March | Daba Ae | Daba | Daba | Hanga Dimu |
| April | Banga Liwu | Daba Ae | Banga Liwu Gopo | Daba |
| May | A'a | Banga Liwu | Banga Liwu Rame | Rame |
| June | Ari | A'a | A'a | A'a |
| July | Kilila Wadu | Ari | Ari | Ari |
| August | Wadu Ae (Tunu Manu) | Hobo | Kelila Wadu | Kelila |
| September | Baga Rae | Kelila Wadu | Wadu Ae | Wadu Ae |
| October | | Hae Rae | Hae Rae | Wadu Kepete |
| November | | | | Hae Rae |
| December | | | | |

to the next highest clan, Nahoro. These three clans together are likened to the three stones that support a cooking pot. In Seba, the *Deo Rai* is attended by three lesser religious functionaries chosen from his lineage or other lineages of his clan, Namata. Similarly, the *Do Heleo* is assisted by a functionary chosen from another lineage within Nahoro. Finally, in addition to these priests and their attendants, there is a further priest, that of *Rue,* the priest of misfortune, mishap, and bad death. He is chosen from the lowest of the four main clans, the clan Nahupu which has no origin village and whose members live scattered outside the established villages.

Each priestly office in Seba is represented by its own large, hewn, hemispherical stone (*nada*). On these stones sacrifices are made and on these stones, too, the various priests must sit for specific rituals. In Seba, the stones of the three main priests (and their attendants) are grouped together at Nada Ae, a clearing in a precinct near the villages of Namata and Nada Wawi. The *Rue,* however, has his own separate and isolated sacrificial stone at some distance from the stones of Nada Ae.

Thus, in Seba, there is a readily discernible fourfold structure to the order of the clans and to the priestly offices associated with them. There is, in rank order, the *Deo Rai* in Namata, the *Apu Lodo* in Nataga, the *Do Heleo* in Nahoro, and finally the *Rue* in Nahupu. Although the whole of this structure is simple,

157

closer view reveals that each clan with its priest composes part of a tiered oppositional structure with the clan or clans above or below it.

The *Deo Rai* in his person and by his celibacy epitomizes the sacredness of the earth. He represents the highest spiritual authority. By contrast, the *Apu Lodo* is identified with the heavens and is associated with political power. Historically, it was the Dutch who designated the *Apu Lodo* as ruler in each of the states of Savu. In Seba, the *Apu Lodo* became raja and although eventually the office of raja and the office of *Apu Lodo* became separated, the raja has traditionally come from the *Apu Lodo's* lineage of Naluluweo within the clan, Nataga. Strictly speaking, therefore, the concept of nobility is inapplicable to the members of the clan of the *Deo Rai*, Namata, which nevertheless remains ritually superior to Nataga. It applies only to those descended from the raja. Status is of great importance within Nataga and for this reason, Nataga has more component lineages than all the other clans of Seba combined. For Namata and Nahoro, the tendency seems to be to recreate the primary fourfold structure internally among its lineages and to divide the offices of its ritual attendants according to this structure. Below the *Deo Rai* and *Apu Lodo* is the *De Heleo,* "The Overseer." His function as well as that of his clan, Nahoro, is to attend, to serve, and to do what is delegated. The first three clans of the state with their respective priests all stand in sacral opposition to the last and least of the clans, the separate and inauspicious clan of Nahupu which is deputized through its *Rue* to deal with evil. Beyond this, there are two other clans: Kekoro and Teriwu. Both of these "clans" are the coalesced remnants of the former states of Kekoro and Teriwu that were conquered by Seba. Although politically included within the state, they are ritually excluded from its ceremonies.

Table 2 is a list of the clans, origin villages, lineages, and priestly offices of the state of Seba arranged to provide an outline of the social and religious organization of Seba. Similar ritual structures are discernible in all of the states of Savu although the immediate and apparent organization of the clans and priestly offices may vary slightly in terms of names and in specific local arrangements. In my own research, I moved from Seba to Liae accompanied by one of the best-informed men of Seba who had never visited the main villages of Liae during its high ceremonial season. To understand the ceremonial performances that were occurring, his immediate concern was to establish essential ritual equivalences between Seba and Liae. At first genuinely shocked over some differences of names—in fact whispering to me that something was very wrong because Liae had no *Rue*—he persisted in his own inquiries. In discussing matters with the *Deo Rai* and *Apu Lodo* of Liae, he discovered the essentials he was looking for and was able to assure me that Liae's ritual order was peculiar but perfectly correct. A comparison of Liae and Seba illustrates the critical structural equivalences that the Savunese themselves make in organizing their religious life.

In Liae, the *Doe Rai* comes from the clan, Gopo; the *Apu Lodo* from the clan, Napujara. These priests preside over two separate priestly groupings: the

## Table 2
### The Social and Religious Organization of Seba

| UDU (Major Descent Group) | RAE KEPUE (Origin Village) | KEROGO (Component Descent Group) | MONE AMA (Priestly Office) |
|---|---|---|---|
| Namata | Namata | Nabura | Deo Rai |
| | | | Mau Kia |
| | | Napupena | Bawa Iri Deo |
| | | Naudu Ae | Baka Pahi |
| | | Nagalode | |
| Nataga | Nada Wawi | Naluluweo (Raja) | Apu Lodo |
| | | Najingi | |
| | | Naliru | |
| | | Nakaja | |
| | | Nalodo | |
| | | Napubire | |
| | | Napuluji | |
| | | Najohina (Fetor) | |
| | | Napujara | |
| | | Narohaba | |
| | | Nabee | |
| | | Naradi | |
| | | Nawa | |
| Nahoro | Nahoro | Nakahu | Do Heleo |
| | | Napawa | Bawa Iri Dohe |
| | | Nanawa | |
| | | Napuhaga | |
| Nahupu | (None) | | Rue |
| Udu Kekoro | Udu Rae Pudi | | |
| | Udu Melagu | | |
| | Udu Loko Ei | | |
| Teriwu | Teriwu Nadara | | |
| | Teriwu Nagali | | |
| | Teriwu Nahire | | |

*Deo Rai* presides over the *Ratu Mone Telu,* ''The Three Priests;'' the *Apu Lodo* over the *Ratu Mone Pidu,* ''The Seven Priests.'' The *Deo Rai's* group is an exclusive one that consists of his attendants—*Rohi Lodo* and the *Mau Kia*— chosen from his own clan, Gopo. The *Apu Lodo's* group is a heterogenous grouping. The *Apu Lodo* is personally attended by a *Rhoi Lodo* who is chosen from his own lineage, Napulai, within the clan, Napujara. Below him is the *Do Heleo* who is chosen from the same clan but a different lineage of Napujara. This lineage, Napu'uju, occupies a separate village which has, in turn, its own subsidiary village and is seen as structurally opposed to Napulai. In Savunese terms, this is also expressed as an opposition between the origin village, Daba, and its

**159**

subsidiary but now autonomous village, Halapaji. Below these offices, there are four other offices: that of *Kenuhe,* attended by his own *Mau Kia* both chosen from the clan Nahai; that of *Tutu Dalu* from one branch of the clan Nakale; and that of *Gerau* from the clan Nanawa. The *Kenuhe* refers to a great spirit snake that lives beneath the earth and is associated with illness and disease; the *Tutu Dalu,* apparently, refers to ill-omened spirit manifestations that appear as will-of-the-wisps; the *Gerau* is the snake that attempts to swallow the moon during an eclipse. These three priests who represent these spirits are said to be obedient to the *Apu Lodo;* but they perform ominous tasks with which he cannot concern himself. Severally, they perform functions that are equivalent to those performed singly by the priest of misfortune in Seba.

Table 3 sets forth an outline of the names of the clans, origin villages, lineages, and priestly offices of Liae to be compared with those of Seba.

### Table 3
#### The Social and Religious Organization of Liae

| UDU (Major Descent Group) | RAE KEPUE (Origin Village) | KEROGO (Component Descent Group) | MONE AMA (Priestly Office) |
|---|---|---|---|
| Gopo | Gopo | | Deo Rai |
| | | | Rohi Lodo |
| | | | Mau Kia |
| Kolorae | Rae Loko | | |
| Napujara | Daba | Napulai | Apu Lodo |
| | | | Rohi Lodo |
| | Daba | Napulerru | |
| | Halapaji | Napu'uju | Do Heleo |
| Nahai | Ei Ko | | Kunuhe |
| | | | Mau Kia |
| Nakale | Raja Mara | Nakale | Tutu Dalu |
| | Kota Hawu | Lelabu | |
| Nanawa | Rae Wiu | | Gerau |

| | | | |
|---|---|---|---|
| Namata | | | |
| Napawa | | | |
| Narega'uju | | | |
| Narebo'uju | | | |
| Teriwu | | | |

Table 3 does not display as simple or as evident a fourfold hierarchical structure as that to be found in Seba. There are more than four clans. One important clan has no priestly office; another has two offices. For example, one of the month-names of the high ceremonial season in Liae is commonly referred to as *Banga Liwu Gopo* or *Banga Liwu Kolorae*. Gopo is the name of the clan and "origin" village of the present holders of the office of *Deo Rai* and of all the offices of the *Deo Rai's* attendants. The clan, Kolorae, now located in an autonomous village, Rae Loko, is however still popularly recognized as once having had a share in the rituals of the *Deo Rai*. But now by a ritual dialectic, Kolorae has been excluded and has become opposed to Gopo. A similar ritual dialectic is now in process within the clan, Napujara. The lineage of Napulai, in the "origin" village of Daba, retains the office of *Apu Lodo* while another village, Napu'uju, in its own separate village, holds the office of *Do Heleo*. This is more than a mere division of labor within the clan. These offices are opposed as the lineages that maintain them are opposed. By this same process, applied in reverse, there has occurred an opposition within one of the clans that holds an inauspicious ritual office. In Liae, there are three priestly offices that function as the equivalent of the *Rue* in Seba. In the clan, Nakale, there are two lineages. One of these lineages known as *Nakale*, resident of the village of Raja Mara, retains the office of *Tutu Dalu;* the other lineage, Lelabu, in the village of Kota Hawu, is entirely without an office. Therefore removed of the taint of an inauspicious office, members of the Lelabu can, in rituals, assume the side opposed to members of their own clan.

Finally, in addition to what are considered to be the original clans of Liae, there are a number of other named clans. As in Seba, there are descendants of the conquered territory of Teriwu. Members of Teriwu are excluded from the rituals of Liae. But besides Teriwu, there are other clans founded by persons who have come from other states. In Liae, there are the small clans of Namata and Napawa that apparently derive from the clans of Namata and Nahoro-Napawa in Seba. For Seba, the generally stated explanation is that newcomers have been received as clients within Nataga, the clan of the *Apu Lodo*. In Liae, there is no indication of a similar rule and members of outsider clans seem to align themselves in rituals according to their former stations in their state of origin.

In a following section of this paper, I propose to examine, in greater detail, the dialectic process of social alignment within the context of a single specific ritual performance. But the point to be made here is fundamental. The same basic hierarchical pattern of ritual equivalences is to be found in Liae as in Seba, despite minor variations in names and arrangement. Table 4 provides a schematic listing of these religious equivalences for the two states.

The priestly offices of the Savunese, particularly those of the *Deo Rai, Apu Lodo* and *Do Heleo*, exist outside any time dimension. They are a matter of ritual necessity. But whereas the Savunese see as invariable the basic pattern of relationships set by their priesthood, they do not see their states or clans as part of a timeless order. The present holders of priestly office have been determined by a long developmental process. Like a number of other peoples in eastern Indonesia, the Savunese embody this historical development by means of a complex succession of names. In Seba, for example, even after the truncation that

### Table 4
#### Religious Equivalences in the Priesthood of Seba and Liae

| Clan/Lineage | Religious Offices | | Clan/Lineage |
|---|---|---|---|
| Seba | I | II | Liae |
| Namata-Nabura | Deo Rai | Deo Rai | Gopo |
| Nanata-Napupena | Bawa Iri Deo | Rohi Lodo | Gopo |
| Namata-Nabura | Mau Kia | Mau Kia | Gopo |
| Namata-Nagalode | Baka Pahi | — | |
| Nataga | Apu Lodo | Apu Lodo | Napujara-Napulai |
| | | Rohi Lodo | Napujara-Napulai |
| Nahoro | Do Heleo | Do Heleo | Napujara-Napu'udju |
| Nahupu | Rue | Kenuhe | Nahai |
| | | Mau Kia | Nahai |
| | | Tutu Dalu | Nakale |
| | | Gerau | Nanawa |

occurs because certain early powerful names may not be mentioned, there is a succession of between 65 and 70 names from *Deo* to the present *Deo Rai* or *Apu Lodo*. These names, as a kind of mnemonic device, record what has happened over time: the divisions in each state among the primary clans, the segmentation of the clans and transfer of segments from village to village, the movement of individual ancestors from one state to another and the rise of independent clans and lineages, the conquest of Menia and Teriwu, the successive border wars among the remaining states, the various appointments and manipulations which the Dutch effected on the island.

Two distinct but related processes, however, combine to explain the fundamental features of any ritual performance. The segmentary process that, over time, has divided the clans and villages and determined the particular holders of priestly offices and the dialectic process that determines the specific alignment of these segments in each ritual reenactment of the ceremonial cycle.

## THE NATURE OF THE PRIESTHOOD
## AND THE CEREMONIAL CYCLE

The priests of Savu in their activities and in their persons are intimately associated with the agricultural and tapping cycle of the year. In the ritual division of labor in Seba, the *Deo Rai* is identified with the green gram or mung bean, whose growth cycle determines the calendar; the *Apu Lodo* with rice; and the *Do*

*Heleo* with sorghum. In Liae, in the ritual division of labor the *Deo Rai* is identified with the agricultural season and the *Apu Lodo* with the lontar tapping season. Throughout Savu, it is primarily the *Deo Rai* and only secondarily the *Apu Lodo* whose physical person is subject to stringent priestly injunctions. The *Deo Rai* must abstain from all sexual intercourse from the moment of his election. This required celibacy is often achieved by appointing an old man to this office, who, in some instances, may continue to live with his wife but in a separate apartment of the house. For example, in Seba, the *Deo Rai's* house is constructed much like any other Savunese house with its man's half and its woman's half, but in the case of this house, there is no passage between these two halves so that, in effect, it is two separate apartments under a single roof. From the time of the first planting to the time of the harvest of the *kebui* during Daba, the *Deo Rai* and the *Apu Lodo* may not leave the vicinity of their houses; the *Do Heleo,* as their "overseer" must report to them on what is happening to the crops.

Since they are both so closely associated with the forces of life, the death of these priests is ritually denied. Their bodies must be buried secretly, at night, in an unknown and unmarked grave. Their fingernails and tongues are cut off and only after a new *Deo Rai* or *Apu Lodo* has been appointed, can a funeral ceremony be held over these body parts. In Liae, the task of burying the priests is one of the main functions of the two respective *Rohi Lodo.*

Although it is impossible here to enumerate all the activities and sacrifices of the ceremonial year, it is possible to provide some idea of the chief ceremonial duties of the *Deo Rai* and *Apu Lodo.* In order to be specific, I shall deal with the course of this cycle in the state of Liae. The *Deo Rai* and *Apu Lodo* have the right to demand any animal—sex, age, and coloring being important criteria—that they require for their purposes. In addition, individual households must often sacrifice in conjunction with the sacrifices of the priests.

*Hae Rae* is the transition month leading to the new year. It occurs at the end of the dry season and just before the rains are supposed to begin. The *Deo Rai* has principal charge of this month; he must turn the year around and recall the spirits of the green gram, of rice, and of sorghum and, with them, the rain. One of the most important sacrifices is that of a pig. The pig's ear is cut off, perforated, and inserted over the left leg of a chicken. This ritually marked chicken is later sacrificed between *Bu Ihi* and *Hole* in the latter half of the month of *Banga Liwu Rame.*

The new year begins with the clearing of the fields. The chief sacrifice requires two goats (or sheep); the flesh of these animals may not be eaten and their bodies are left on the beach where they were sacrificed. Once the crops have been planted, the year enters a new period: the *Deo Rai* and *Apu Lodo* may not leave their houses, no gongs can be beaten, no singing or dancing may occur, and for the next two months, no animals may be slaughtered. In *Nyale,* the month of the sea worm, animals may be slaughtered again but no major sacrifices may be carried out.

In *Daba,* after the green gram harvest, the high ceremonial season begins. The main religious performances during the three successive months of this season, are cockfights. Organized around this cockfighting are a number of communal and household rituals. First, there is *pedoa* dancing. This is circle-dancing involving men and women that is performed on all nights before and after cockfighting. This dancing is accompanied by singing, but until the middle of *Banga Liwu Rame,* it may not be accompanied by gong or drum. Small baskets are woven into which are placed a handful or two of freshly harvested green grams. These baskets are tied to the ankles of the dancers and the regular shuffling of green grams, in step with the dance, is the only sound that accompanies the chorus in responding to the leader at the center of the circle. At the end of the high ceremonial season, these baskets of green grams are put away until the next planting season when they are opened and their contents planted as seeds.

In *Daba,* the household ritual is *Titu Daba;* children born during the previous year are submerged in water, bathed, and marked on the forehead with betel-areca spittle making the child visible or presentable to *Deo.* The main ritual performance during *Daba* involves, however, two successive days of cockfighting.

In *Banga Liwu Gopo* or *Banga Liwu Kolorae,* there is a single day of cockfighting and this is once more repeated at *Banga Liwu Rame.* In the first of these *Banga Liwu* celebrations, the *Deo Rai* (from Gopo) takes precedence; in the second of these, the *Apu Lodo* takes precedence. At dawn, after the all-night *pedoa,* following the first cockfighting at *Banga Liwu Rame,* gongs may be beaten again and are permitted until the next year's planting. The cockfighting, and *pedoa,* at this time, coincides with the time of the full moon and is called *Bu Ihi.* One week after this, with the waning of the moon, *Hole* is performed; all sickness and misfortune is driven from the island. A small boat or raft is prepared along with various woven leaf containers to represent illness and disease. On the boat, a goat, a dog, and a chicken are placed together with betel and areca nut and the leaf representations of all possible diseases. There is further cockfighting on this day and finally the boat is set adrift.[5]

At *Bu Ihi,* each household holds its own sacrificial meal. A pig is killed and its ear is hung around the neck of a water buffalo. At this same time, the chicken marked with the ear of the pig killed in *Hae Rae* is sacrificed and eaten. Hereafter, until *Hae Rae,* the *Apu Lodo* is in charge of sacrificing and is mainly concerned to insure bountiful fishing and a rich yield from the lontar, both activities concentrated in the dry season. Table 5 presents a simplified outline of the ceremonial year.

[5]In certain respects, this ritual resembles Loi Kratong which forms part of the ceremonial cycle in Thailand.

Table 5
The Ceremonial Year in Liae

| Month | Month Name | Activity | Priest | |
|-------|-----------|----------|--------|--|
| | Baga Rae | | | |
| November | | | | Planting Season |
| | Koo Ma | "Clear Fields" | | Silence |
| December | | | | No Animals |
| | Kuja Ma | "Plant Fields" | | Slaughtered |
| January | | | Deo Rai | |
| | Kelila Aji Lai | "Heavy Rains" | | |
| February | | | | |
| | Nyale | "Sea Worm" | | Animal Slaughtering Permitted |
| March | | | | |
| | Daba | High | | Green Gram Harvest |
| April | | | | |
| | Banga Liwu Gopo | Ceremonial | | Pedoa Dancing |
| May | | | | |
| | Banga Liwu Rame | Season | | Gongs/Drums |
| June | | | | Lontar |
| | A'a | "Elder" | | Tapping |
| July | | | | Season |
| | Ari | "Younger" | Apu Lodo | |
| August | | | | Pig Sacrifices |
| | Kelila Wadu | "Kelila Stone" | | to |
| September | | | | Maja |
| | Wadu Ae | "Great Stone" | | |
| October | | | | |

## THE COCKFIGHT AS RITUAL CONFRONTATION:
### BANGA LIWU RAME

Cockfighting forms the core of Savu's indigenous religion. It is undertaken at successive intervals through the high ceremonial season and is attended by hundreds of intensely serious participants who, in one or two hours, may let loose as many as a hundred or more cocks to fight. It is performed in a ceremonial enclosure, usually on a hilltop, and carried out in enjoined silence or in low whispers broken only by shouts of victory as cocks triumph. It is always a contest involving two sides or two groups but it may never be accompanied by betting. Invariably, the Savunese give two explanations for their cockfighting: it is a struggle between classes of spirits represented by men, the spirits of the land and the spirits of the sea; and it is a substitute for war between clans and villages.

By its nature, ceremonial cockfighting on Savu is decidedly unlike the

Balinese form of cockfighting that Clifford Geertz has so eloquently described (1973:412–453). Ceremonial cockfighting is not a sport; it is not intended for gaming; and above all, it is not organized as an atomistic structure of separate, particular matches. Ceremonial cockfighting is high cosmological drama. Men are free to choose their antagonists only within the bounds preestablished by lineage and clan relations. Each match is sociologically relevant precisely because its participants accept their prescribed role within a larger context and each enters into confrontation with another to decide the unknown. Cocks *(manu lai ae)* embody men but men are the *personae* who represent their lineages and these, in turn, are identified with particular spirits. Fighting does not consist of short bursts followed by periods of vacuity. It begins with the single most important and revealing match and proceeds rapidly—almost without pause— toward a crescendo of action at which point as many as six or more individual matches may occur simultaneously within the circumscribed precinct. This cockfighting is intended to generate a ritual heat and so it must coincide with the rise of the sun to the zenith. To ensure the maximum of intensity, it cannot be allowed to taper off slowly but must end abruptly at midday. The whole of this ritual confrontation is a form of divination, for it reveals the strength of the opposing spirits and foretells the year's future. But it is also propitiatory since, after the fighting is ended, it is the spirits of each lineage or clan who are fed on the flesh of the defeated cocks.

Here I propose to examine the cockfighting ritual that occurs in Liae during the month of *Banga Liwu Rame.* For some comprehension of so spectacular a form of ostension, it is essential to determine the sets of relations among the groups and persons taking part in the drama. For an analysis of the ritual's subtler aspects, it would conceivably be necessary to identify all its oppositions, not only the oppositions among groups but the matching of all opponents and the sequencing of their confrontation. Lacking a means of filming this ritual, however, I found it impossible to record the hundreds of participants who rushed in and out of the enclosure to confront each other. Therefore, as a first approximation, I am concerned here with establishing certain of the higher-level principles for the participation of groups in the ritual.

There are two groups formed on which the ritual of *Banga Liwu Rame* depends: *Ada Mone,* "the Male Group;" and *Ada Rena,* "the Female Group." *Ada Mone* is headed by members of the *Apu Lodo's* lineage and clan, Napujara-Napulai. It can also be referred to as the *Upper Side* or by reference to Napujara's origin village, Daba. *Ada Rena* is headed by members of the *Kenuhe's* clan, Nahai. It is referred to as the *Lower Side* or by reference to Nahai's origin village, Ei Ko. At one level of significance, the *Apu Lodo* representing the spirits of the land does battle with the *Kenuhe* representing the spirits of the sea. The outcome will be an indication of the coming year's prosperity. As Savunese explain, all else could be removed from this ritual except the contest between Daba and Ei Ko.

But to either of these opposing sides, other lineages and clans align themselves. Gopo, the clan of the *Deo Rai,* joins the clan of the *Apu Lodo.* And as would be expected, the clans, Nakale and Nanawa, of the *Tutu Dalu* and the *Gerau,* join the clan of the *Kenuhe.* Beyond this, the other clans and lineages of Liae sort themselves out in accordance with this basic alignment. Napujara-Napu'uju which is opposed to Napujara-Napulai joins *Ada Rena.* Gopo and Kolorae have a common origin, although now Gopo monopolizes all rights to the office of the *Deo Rai.* As a consequence of Kolorae's opposition to Gopo, Kolorae also joins *Ada Rena.* On the other hand, because of the sharp division in the clan Nakale, one of its lineages, Nakale-Lelabu, which holds no rights to the office of *Tutu Dalu,* joins *Ada Mone.* So also, does Namata, a clan of Liae that derives from the *Deo Rai's* clan, Namata, in Seba. In this way, the simple structural division into *Ada Mone* and *Ada Rena* becomes the means of organizing the historically based diversity of clans and lineages in Liae. With the exception of the conquered clans of Teriwu, all lineages and clans and, in this way, all villages take sides in the cockfight. Table 6 gives an indication of the opposing groups at *Banga Liwu Rame.*

### Table 6
Dual Division of Opponent Descent Groups at *Banga Liwu Rame*

| ADA MONE<br>"Male Group"<br>Upper Side<br>DABA | | ADA RENA<br>"Female Group"<br>Lower Side<br>EI KO | |
|---|---|---|---|
| *Ceremonial Leadership* | | | |
| Rohi Lodo : Napujara (Daba) | | Rohi Lodo : Nahai (Ei Ko) | |
| Mau Kia   : Napujara (Daba) | | Mau Kia   : Nahai (Ei Ko) | |
| Piga Rai   : Napujara (Daba) | | Piga Rai   : Nahai (Ei Ko) | |
| *Opposing Descent Groups and Villages* | | | |
| Napujara-Napulai: | Daba | Nahai: | Ei Ko |
| | | Napujara-Napu'uju: | Halapaji |
| Gopo: | Gopo | Kolorae: | Rae Loko |
| Nakale-Lelabu: | Kota Hawu | Nakale-Nakale: | Raja Mara |
| Namata: | Rae Eike Wore | Nanawa: | Rae Wiu |

Both sides are led by three ritually important persons: a *Rohi Lodo,* a *Mau Kia,* and a *Piga Rai.* These persons are chosen for the occasion from Napujara and Nahai. The *Rohi Lodo* and *Mau Kia* should not be confused with the priestly attendants of the *Deo Rai* or *Apu Lodo* who bear the same title. They may or may not be the same individuals. The *Rohi Lodo* and *Mau Kia* are men, the *Piga Rai* a woman. The *Piga Rai,* although she has one of the most important functions in the ritual, never appears at the scene of the cockfight.

Preparation for the ritual begins in the morning. Each side congregates in its respective village: *Ada Mone* in Daba, *Ada Rena* in Ei Ko. In the clan houses of Napujara and Nahai, the two *Piga Rai* have lit fires using only the leaf sheaths of the lontar palm. All the men who intend to let loose cocks in the fight are supposed to warm their hands at this fire. This is the beginning of the build-up of ritual heat. The cockfight itself occurs at midday, the sun at the zenith. By mid-morning, the two sides, each led by the *Rohi Lodo* and *Mau Kia,* set forth, in silence and in single file, toward the hill-top of Kolorae. Men, women, and children join this procession. Men clutch their cocks tightly as they move slowly up the hill. The *Ada Rena,* associated with the lower side, may not depart until the procession of the *Ada Mone* can be seen near the top of the hill heading for Kolorae.

The two *Piga Rai* remain in their respective clan houses, performing the ritual of spinning thread and carrying dried lontar fruit on a stick over their shoulders within the house. These two actions are said to promote the victory of their side.

After the two sides have mounted the hill and entered what remains of the walled fortifications at its top, they align themselves on opposite sides of the ceremonial enclosure. The *Deo Rai* and *Apu Lodo* seat themselves on their stones. With hundreds of people crowded in this narrow confine, men standing, women and children crouching to watch, the two sides wait in silence for the fight to begin. The *Rohi Lodo* on either side, holding above their heads the first cocks that are to fight, do a quick high-stepping dance to the opponent's side and then return to their side. Spurs are fitted and tied to the cocks and the two *Rohi Lodo* enter the center of the enclosure for the first fight. At victory, the triumphant *Rohi Lodo,* with a sudden cry, leaps into his dance carrying the winning cock back to his side.

In the ceremony I witnessed in 1973, Napujara's cock triumphed over Nahai's. There was enormous excitement over the first two matches. In the second, Nahai's cock triumphed over Nakale-Lelabu's cock, balancing the side. Elation and disappointment seemed extreme and genuine. For the next six or seven matches, cocks were paired singly by members of the opposing sides. Gradually this matching escalated, too fast, in fact, to keep any precise record of matches and their procedure. Two matches were fought at once, then three, four, five, until near the end, six and possibly more men were matching their cocks simultaneously in the ceremonial enclosure. With spurred birds flapping about and men crouching, jumping, and dancing as the fights proceeded, the orderly progress of the ritual gave way to organized and excited confusion.

Behind each side, but acting on its behalf, is the *Mau Kia*. At some remove from the fighting occurring at the center, seated on the ground, holding a black cock in his two hands, the *Mau Kia* for either side raises and lowers this bird throughout the fighting. Each man who is to let loose a cock approaches the *Mau Kia* and is given a short piece of red thread. Like the ritual leaders who must all wear red cloth, each cock has this red thread attached to it when the spur is tied to its leg. Someone must accompany or follow each combatant into the center of the enclosure to stomp on the neck of the defeated bird the instant the victorious cock is raised in triumph by its owner. This defeated bird becomes the property of the victor and is carried over to the *Mau Kia* and dropped in front of him. A hundred or more birds are fought and gradually as the fighting proceeds there is accumulated in front of the *Mau Kia* a twitching pile of half-dead cocks.

After the ritual, these defeated birds are redivided among the participants on either side. The first bird defeated by each clan or lineage is the object of special sacrifice. It is cut and cooked at the principal stone of that clan or lineage and its flesh is offered at various ancestral sites. These sacrifices are the afternoon's activity following the cockfight.

But having generated so much ritual heat, ceremonies must continue in order to cool the proceedings. *Pedoa* must be done all night by the light of the full moon. At dawn, after a silence of more than five months, the gongs can be beaten again. The following afternoon there is horse-running which is likened to the dancing. This horse-running consists of a continual circling of a large tree. The horsemen mount women and children behind them and ride in this continual circle to the lively sound of drums and gongs. That night, there is again *pedoa* dancing to dawn. And at dawn, the dancing ground is sprinkled with lontar syrup as the final act of cooling.

## OBSERVATIONS ON COCKFIGHTING
## AS A RITUAL OF OSTENSION

To begin to decipher the significance of this ritual, one must realize that its opponent groups are not those that are opposed in all other contexts. At the level of the priestly congregations, the *Deo Rai* who heads the *Ratu Mone Telu* is opposed to the *Apu Lodo* who heads the *Ratu Mone Pidu*. In contradistinction to the cockfighting of the previous month, *Banga Liwu Gopo,* during which the *Deo Rai's* clan takes precedence in the ceremonies, at *Banga Liwu Rame* the *Deo Rai's* clan joins the *Apu Lodo* in subordination to his ritual initiative. In the cockfighting ritual, it is not the priests themselves but other ritual personnel who assume leadership. Similarly, as has been stressed, various segments of clans that are politically united by descent are opposed in the ritual and the origins, auspicious or inauspicious, of these segments are overridden to construct different dialectic configurations. Named groups, of varying segmentary orders, are recognized as discrete units whose orderly arrangement and hierarchy is determined for the purposes of each ritual. As the purpose of these rituals varies, so does the arrangement of its particular elements within certain limits.

All confrontation rituals on Savu, whether they involve stone-throwing or cockfighting, are characterized by (1) *complementarity,* (2) *markedness,* (3) *parallelism*. Complementarity is the most obvious of these features and one that has often been noted in Indonesian rituals in general. These rituals assume and require a grand *Corcordia Oppositorum,* a balanced reciprocity of action. One side cannot eliminate the other upon which it depends. Nor at a more abstract level is it conceivable that misfortune, adversity, or the provocations of the spirits can be completely eradicated.

Inseparably associated with this complementarity is an unmistakable markedness between the related sides in the ritual. Some of the most elementary of human categories are used to denote this markedness: male versus female; upper versus lower; greater versus lesser. One side is, in some way, distinguished as supraordinate to the other. But what makes these rituals a form of divination, provides an oracular attraction, and creates an inherent excitement is the possibility of reversing this markedness. Of all rituals, cockfighting lends itself to this stirring possibility. The odds are even when each side advances its prize cocks.

The first match is critically important, but in the context of this markedness, the implications of victory are profound. Triumph for the first cock of *Ada Mone* foretells a general prosperity for the whole of the state. A victory for *Ada Rena* negates this holistic forecast of prosperity. It subdivides the society yet implies an enhancement for the victorious lesser half. And even after the first match, successive matches may right the balance or reverse the trend. A careful tally is never kept and it would be difficult to attempt one, especially when hundreds of cocks are brought together to fight in rapid succession. Moreover, the interpretation of the outcome of this fighting may be drawn either sequentially or cumulatively. An initial victory can be considered to outweigh a string of subsequent losses or, conversely, several successive victories may be interpreted as overcoming an initial defeat.

The significance of the fighting is also interpretable at several levels. The first representative cock of one of the two opposing sides may lose and still, overall, a majority of the cocks of some particular lineage on the unsuccessful side may actually win. At another level, an individual's cock may triumph despite the setbacks of his lineage or ritual side. Or, as is more likely to happen, since individuals may engage in more than one match and may rely on more than one cock, a first match may result in defeat, the next in triumph ending in a mixed and inconclusive outcome. Since significance can be drawn at any level and by more than one method, the outcome of the entire ceremony—its ritual statement—is subject to multiple interpretations. The triumphs of one's group may compensate for a personal lack of success, or personal success may lessen the adverse implications of losses by one's lineage or ritual side. The probability of decisive unilateral victory, at all significant levels, is unimaginable. In the end, the final rituals are performed on the bodies of dead and defeated birds, not on some score of triumphant cocks.

In Savunese cockfighting, there also occurs the phenomenon of parallelism. *Parallelism*, the carefully balanced and concordant restatement, in alternate forms, of some initial declaration is as relevant in the performance of ritual drama as it is in the composition of oral poetry. And it would appear to be equally wide-spread (Fox, 1971b; 1975). It is the firm contention of Savunese that all matches at *Banga Liwu Rame* could be reduced on the primary one between Daba and Ei Ko. All subsequent matches, therefore, constitute a successive repetition of the first match. But as in other forms of parallelism, this is no mere reiteration but a form of distinctive repetition. Each individual match retains its own importance yet derives, in addition, a special significance in parallel with the primary match. In Jakobsonian terms (Jakobson and Halle, 1956:76–82), each match is a metaphoric statement because it draws precise correspondences with a prior statement.

The recognition of these three characteristics of Savunese cockfighting—complementarity, markedness, and parallelism—permits a return to the initial concern of this paper, the possibility of comparing symbolic systems that are, in their modalities, radically dissimilar. The Rotinese with their rituals of oration and the Savunese with their rituals of ostension were taken to represent a polarity in the possible modalities of ritual. Since, however, Rotinese ritual language shares with Savunese drama the similar and prominent characteristics of complementarity, markedness, and parallelism, the apprehension of these salient features suggests the possibility of a common theoretical approach in analysis.

Rather than give priority to linguistic analogies by claiming that each Rotinese or Savunese ritual can be considered a "text" to be interpreted, it would be better to view a record of a Rotinese ritual as primarily a linguistic product but a similar record of a Savunese ritual as overwhelmingly like a silent film. Whereas in Rotinese ritual, semantic elements form the essential vehicles of a cultural code, in Savunese rituals, persons constitute the signs of an information-carrying system. On Roti, men, as producers and reactors, are external to the communicative event; on Savu, they are central to the event. As actors, Savunese are themselves the event. A comparison of these differing symbolic systems leads, therefore, in the direction of philosophical goals of Charles Saunders Peirce, toward a unified theory of signs.

One aspect of the cockfighting at *Banga Liwu Rame* remains to be noted. Christian Savunese are permitted by the government to hold cockfights on those days when pagans hold their religious celebrations. So at *Banga Liwu Rame* Christians gather at the foot of Kolorae while the pagans conduct their rituals above. Other Christians come from all over Savu to attend these cockfights. The betting can be high and police must attend to keep order. At the end of their ritual, clutching their triumphant cocks, the pagans must pass this crowd of believers, as they excitedly wager their money on the sport of cockfighting. Here is the beginning of a change in a mode of communication among men.

## ACKNOWLEDGMENTS

The research on which this paper is based was first supported by a Public Health Service fellowship (MH-23, 148) and grant (MH-10, 161) from the National Institute of Mental Health and was conducted in 1965–66 in Indonesia under the auspices of the *Lembaga Ilmu Pengetahuan Indonesia*. The continuation of this research was again supported by a NIMH grant (MH-20, 659) and carried out in 1972–73 under the joint sponsorship of LIPI and the University of Nusa Cendana in Kupang, Timor. For this paper, I must acknowledge my intellectual indebtedness to Derek Freeman, Roman Jakobson, and Rodney Needham.

## REFERENCES

Cuisinier, J. Un calendrier de Savu. *Journal Asiatique*, 1956, *244*, 111–19.

Donselaar, W. M. Aanteekeningen over het eiland Savoe. *Mededeelingen van wege het Nederlandsche zendeling-genootschap*, 1872, *16*, 281–332.

Evans-Pritchard, E. E. *Nuer religion*. Oxford: Clarendon Press, 1956.

Fox, H. M. Lunar periodicity in reproduction. *Proceedings of the Royal Society of London*, 1923, *95*, 523–550.

Fox, James J. A Rotinese dynastic genealogy: Structure and event. In T. Beidelman (Ed.), *The translation of culture*. London: Tavistock, 1971a.

Fox, James J. Semantic parallelism in Rotinese ritual language. In *Bijdragen tot de Taal-, land-en Volkenkunde*, 1971b, *127*, 215–225.

Fox, James J. Sister's child as plant: Metaphors in an idiom of consanguinity. In R. Needham (Ed.), *Rethinking kinship and marriage*. ASA Monograph *11*, London: Tavistock, 1971c.

Fox, James J. The Savunese. In F. LeBar (Ed.), *Ethnic groups of insular Southeast Asia*, Vol. 1, New Haven: Human Relations Area Files Press, 1972.

Fox, James J. On bad death and the left hand: A study of Rotinese symbolic inversions. In R. Needham (Ed.), *Right and left: Essays on dual symbolic classification*. Chicago: University of Chicago Press, 1973.

Fox, James J. Our ancestors spoke in pairs: Rotinese views of language, dialect, and code. In R. Bauman, and J. Sherzer (Eds.), *Explorations in the ethnography of speaking*. Cambridge: Cambridge University Press. 1974.

Fox, James J. On binary categories and primary symbols: Some Rotinese perspectives. In R. Willis (Ed.), *Interpretation of symbolism*. London: Malaby Press, 1975.

Geertz, Clifford. *The interpretation of cultures*. New York: Basic Books, 1973.

Heeres, J. H. *Bouwstoffen voor de Geschiedenis der Nederlanders in den Maleischen Archipel*. Den Haag: Opkomst van het Nederlandsch Gezagin Oost-Indie, *II*, 3, 1895.

Jakobson, Roman. Language in relation to other communication systems. *Linguaggi nella societa e nella tecnica*. Milano: Edizion di Comunita, 1970.

Jakobson, Roman, and Halle, Morris. *Fundamentals of language*. 'S-Gravenhage: Mouton, 1956.

Kern, H. Sawuneesche Bijdragen: Volzinnen Samenspraken en Woordenlijst, met eene Grammatische In leiding. *Bijdragen tot de Taal-, Land- en Volkendunde van Nederlandsch-Indie*, 1892, *41*, 157–196, 513–553.

Radja Haba, M. C. *Havunese phonemes*. Unpublished Master of Arts thesis, Department of Linguistics, Indiana University, 1958.

Turner, Victor. *The forest of symbols*. Ithaca, New York: Cornell University Press, 1967.

Wijngaarden, J. K. Savoeneesche tijdrekening. *Mededeelingen van wedge het Nederlandsche Zendeling-genootschap*, 1892, *36*, 16–32.

Wijngaarden, J. K. *Sawuneesche Woordenlijst*. Den Haag: Het Kininklijk Instituut voor de Taal-, Land- en Volkenkunde van Nederlandsch-Indie, 1896.

Woodworth, W. McM. The Palolo worm. *Bulletin of the Museum of Comparative Zoology*, 1907, *51*, 1, 1–21.

chapter ten

# Synthesis and Antithesis in Balinese Ritual

Mary LeCron Foster

University of California, Berkeley

Little anthropological attention has been given to the semantics of the temporal sequencing of ritual events. As evidence that such sequencing is not random but operates in response to a binary counterpoint of synthesis and antithesis with implications for universal structure, I present here some characteristic Balinese ritual sequences analyzed as representative of a paradigmatic typology responding to a syntagmatic semantic.

Bali has been well studied. A wealth of ethnographic material exists as well as analyses which attempt to extract the significant ethological patterns from various types of ritual behavior, with a high degree of consensus among fieldworkers as to the nature of these patterns. I utilize these materials in my analysis as well as my own observations made in 1973 during the week of Galungan, Bali's major festival. I was interested in exploring Balinese ritual for representations of structures that I had come to believe had universality and found that it provided a catalyst for an expanded hypothesis on the semantics of symbolic sequencing.[1]

Investigation into symbolic dynamics has convinced me that two cognitive principles have major organizational force: analogy and opposition. A natural affinity and spatial "fit" between two separable entities with the potential for either creative unification or conflict provide a binary motivation for the chain effect of the ongoing analogical process. The opposed chains obtain their initial motivation not from the duality of right- and left-handedness as the studies of

[1]For an analysis of certain universal symbolic principles as manifested in Navaho and American ritual, see Foster (1974).

Hertz, Needham, and others might lead us to suppose, but from the human (and animal) opposition and unification of male and female with its mysterious procreative potential (Needham, 1973).

In order to discover the semantic principles of paradigmatic symbolic typology, two analytic steps, or discovery procedures, are necessary: an examination of events for underlying similarities and a determination as to whether like events are similarly scheduled. This syntagmatic scheduling provides the semantic dynamics that governs the relational interchanges between paradigms. Members of a given paradigm are symbols expressing a common underlying meaning or set of meanings by very concrete means, providing an object or act to represent that meaning. Symbolic meanings are always relational, never unidimensional, because they are expressive of social relationships.

A syntagmatic model developed by Bateson after he completed his investigation of Iatmul culture provides a point of departure both because he claims for it some degree of universality and because he denies its validity for Bali (1970). Symbolic duality is a feature of the Iatmul system but Bateson feels that it is not essential to the model, which is also valid for the Western World where duality is not hierarchically predominant.

In a "schismogenic" society such as Iatmul, Western European, or American, tension is released in a climax which follows a build-up of intense social interaction of one of two types, which Bateson terms *complementary* and *symmetrical*. A complementary relationship implies a hierarchically defined role "fit" in which one member is dominant or salient, the other either subordinate or less actively significant in some sense. Examples are master-servant, husband-wife, actors-audience. A symmetrical relationship is between socially conceptual equals who come into competition with one another and express difference through boasting, an armament race, warfare, or the like. If one mode or the other threatens to prevail, the tendency is checked by a negative feedback provided by a schismogenesis of the opposite type. The two types thus represent a contrapuntal symbolic alternation characterized by periodic, climatic release of tension (Bateson, 1958; 1970).

Among the Iatmul, schismogenic sequences take the form of regenerative or "vicious" circles, in the sense that either schismogenic mode tends to operate at ever-increasing intensity (Bateson, 1970:385–386). Other cultures may develop degenerative circles in which a "self-corrective" decrease in intensity occurs at some point in the chain. Sequences of the Iatmul type tend to result in social fission unless some form of restraint is applied. Bateson suggests three possible types of restraint. The first is that degenerative causal loops might be superposed upon the schismogeneses. The second is that factors internally or externally environmental to the parts of the schismogenic circuit might have some restraining effect. A third, and hypothetical, corrective mechanism is integrative: ". . . there may be, in addition to the schismogeneses already considered, other cumulative interactions acting in an opposite sense and so promoting social integration rather than fission" (Bateson, 1970:400).

I argue that ritual integrative mechanisms routinely correct fission and are incorporated into the single symbolic event, rather than occurring as a successive event in one mode countering an earlier event in another. Examination of Balinese instances suggests that there is a syntagmatic swing back and forth between synthesis and antithesis expressed in spatial relationships of two sorts: the first is functional, describing the act itself; the second is modal, describing the relationship between the agents of the action in terms of relative hierarchical position. Bateson's model accounts for the second of these but fails to include the first. The functional relationships and their resolution determine the mode rather than vice versa and unless they are known, it is impossible to ascertain the meaning of the event.

In the syntagmatic sequence each event takes up where the last left off. This means that the succeeding event begins either by starting the modal relationship with which the last one concluded, or by stating a spatial modification which preserves the semantic continuity. Thus a cyclic, unending, self-perpetuating sequence is constituted which is in the nature of a philosophical ritual dialogue about social relationships and their disruptive and unifying force. Bali illustrates this dialogue to perfection because its symbols are ebulliently rich with semantic nuances, layers, and levels, and because their succession is swift, so that the relationship between successive symbols is always clear.

Bateson believes that schismogenesis does not exist in Bali because tension is always muted before it builds to a climax. Children early learn to avoid climax because it is always deflected by a nurturant adult, especially the mother. He claims that Balinese society must be described by some completely different type of mechanism, "for which rules cannot yet be laid down" (Bateson, 1970:401). I hope to show that the rules for Bali are germinal in Bateson's own hypothesis and that no new or different mechanisms are operant. The schismogenic model, however, needs expansion and refinement in ways that will make it more responsive not just to Bali but to the schismogenic patterns of the Iatmul, the Western World, or any other culture. Cross-cultural application of this refined model should serve to point up similarities and differences in symbolic dynamics and lead to establishment of a workable symbolic typology.

In discussing Bali as the "steady state" postulated by Bateson, Geertz says, ". . . social activities do not build, or are not permitted to build toward definitive consummations. Quarrels appear and disappear, on occasion they even persist, but they hardly ever come to a head. Issues are not sharpened for decision, they are blunted and softened in the hope that the mere evolution of circumstances will resolve them, or better yet, that they will simply evaporate. . . . Balinese are not the sort to push the moment to its crisis" (1966:60). Yet the same author offers this other, contradictory passage:

In the cockfight, man and beast, good and evil, ego and id, the creative power of aroused masculinity and the destructive power of loosened animality fuse in a bloody drama of hatred, cruelty, violence, and death. It is little wonder that when, as is the invariable rule, the owner of the winning cock takes the carcass of the loser—often torn limb from limb by its enraged owner—home to eat, he does so with a mixture of social embarrassment, moral satisfaction, aesthetic disgust, and cannibal joy. Or that a man who has lost an important fight is sometimes driven to wreck his family shrines and curse the gods, an act of metaphysical (and social) suicide. Or that in seeking earthly analogues for heaven and hell the Balinese compare the former to the mood of a man whose cock has just won, the latter to that of a man whose cock has just lost (Geertz, 1972:7).

It seems curious that both Bateson and Geertz ignored the schismogenic implications of the cockfight. Complementary schismogenesis, based on a hierarchical relationship, is clearly not involved, whereas symmetrical schismogenesis, a climatic competition between conceptual equals, would seem to characterize it exactly, except for one typically Balinese difference. Schismogenesis, as Bateson defines it, is: ". . . a process of differentiation in the norms of individual behaviour resulting from cumulative interaction between individuals" (1958:175). But in the Balinese cockfight the decisive interaction is not between two human beings but between two cocks. Substitution of the cock for the man is a depersonalization, or what Geertz describes and illustrates as avoidance of direct consociate interaction (1966).

However vicariously induced, both buildup and affective climax are undeniably present in the cockfight. In its climax symmetry moves to complementarity through a degenerative transformation in which the owner of the winning cock improves his status at the expense of the owner of the losing cock, an example of modal feedback within the single event.

A second Balinese ritual with the feature of fission and tension release is Nyepi, in celebration of the spring equinox. In the Den Pasar area, on a day otherwise virtually devoid of activity, a group of boys and girls engages in a tug-of-war game. As Covarrubias describes one such event: ". . . a shouting crowd of boys stood facing a group of girls; the boys charged as in a football game and captured one girl, who then had to be rescued by her friends in a rough free-for-all. Everybody tugged and pulled and the poor prisoner, wild-eyed and with her hair loose, was so roughly handled in the desperate effort to free her that she fainted. But someone walked over to her and unceremoniously emptied a bucket of cold water on her head so she would revive and game could proceed; when the girl was rescued the men captured another" (1937:282). In a similar event in another ward with men on one side, girls on another, a long rattan was pulled from either end until one side or the other triumphed.

The initial relationships would seem to be complementary, and the resolution climactic, but the events are not regenerative because they do not reinforce the complementary relationship which has a degenerative climax, symbolically returning the complementarity to symmetry. Again, the feedback between the two modes is a feature of the climax of the event itself. Thus the cockfight and the tug-of-war games seem to be in reverse relationship; the first a symmetrical relationship leading to a complementary one, the second a complementary relationship resulting in symmetry.

For the tug-of-war games to be understood in a contextual sense, a look at Balinese marriage customs is in order. Marriage is most commonly by abduction. Although the event is prearranged between bride and groom, the bride is expected to kick and bite her abductors, the groom and his friends, in a sham battle of self defense which is climaxed by her submission (Covarrubias, 1937:146). Once the marriage has been consummated and the proper public ceremonies observed, the bride goes to live in her husband's home. She has certain rights and some property of her own, but the husband, as acknowledged master of the household, administers the money and represents the family both legally and religiously. Husband and wife gain status with the birth of the first child. Until that time they are not full adults, freely participating in the adult community.

As a schismogenic event, abduction is complementary and regenerative because it climactically continues and reinforces the initial complementarity. The climax is obviously sexual intercourse. According to Covarrubias;

> Special offerings . . . have been taken beforehand to a hide-out, and once safely there, it is law that the couple must consummate the wedding before the offerings have wilted. This is extremely important as these offerings alone make the marriage binding . . . without them the union would be considered an ordinary, illegal affair. Thus the couple is made husband and wife before the gods, and it appears as if the elaborate ceremonies that follow every wedding are rather the official, public confirmation of it. (1937:148)

In intercourse the superior status position of the husband is emphasized by means of the prescribed position: the woman reclining and the man kneeling above her (Covarrubias, 1937:144). Respect and prestige are expressed in Bali through spatial superiority. On formal occasions an elder or a person of high caste is seated higher than those younger or of lesser rank. Head position marks status. Belo reports that just as it is taboo for the woman to be above in sexual intercourse so, if the clothes of husband and wife must be packed together, those of the husband must be placed on top (Belo, 1970:85–110).

Nyepi observances contrast with normal marriage practice in that sexual intercourse, any kind of work, and especially cooking and the lighting of fires, are taboo. Silence prevails, and in most Balinese villages people are not allowed out of their houses. In Den Pasar traffic is stopped but people do go out visiting (Covarrubias, 1937:282).

Elimination of sexual activity and sex-linked work, such as cooking and the use of fire, women's work, has the effect of minimizing sexual polarization and all its hierarchical aspects. A temporary sexual symmetry is gained, within which the Den Pasar games take place. The contrast is with normal marriage practices which are regeneratively complementary. In the Nyepi climate, complementarity having been cancelled through taboo, the initial game confrontation is seen to be symmetrical and the outcome reinforces that symmetricality. The games and the cockfight, then, are equally symmetrical, the outcomes expressive of a contrast between degeneration, a move to the opposite mode in the cockfight, and regeneration, maintenance of the status quo in the games.

We can now begin to sort out the functional semantics of these three events: the cockfight, the Nyepí games, and marriage abduction. In the initial confrontation of antagonists, an exchange of what may be described as functions of *thrust* and *parry* takes place. In the symmetricality of the cock relationship either animal performs either function. In both abduction and games, thrust becomes grasp and parry either countergrasp or the attempt to evade grasp by whatever means, including counterattack. The thrust of the winning cock's spur into the loser's body is a function of *penetration* and *enclosure* respectively. It is apparent that the alternation between capture and release in the games is another manifestation of this same spatial function as is the successful capture of the abduction. But the final complementarity is reversed, for in the cockfight it is the loser who encloses, in abduction and games, the winner. In both cockfight and abduction the act of penetration: enclosure later becomes reversed and reciprocal as winner eats loser's cock and sexual penetration is accomplished by the bride-groom. In both cases this function changes to *introjection/incorporation* as sperm and food become life-giving within the recipient.

Bateson draws the analogy with orgasm for all schismogenic climaxes, pointing out that all the modes associated with the erogenous zones define themes for complementary relationships. He quotes Homburger as showing how these—intrusion, incorporation, retention, and the like—may be transferred from one zone to another (Bateson, 1970:387). That the transfer may also be from complementary to symmetrical mode is implied but not stated. He says that the "exponential curves" of intensity should be expected to be bounded by phenomena comparable to orgasm in release of schismogenic tension, and calls attention to the "curious confusions between fighting and love-making, the symbolic identifications of orgasm with death, the recurrent use by mammals of organs of offense as ornaments of sexual attraction, and so forth" (1970:388).

It appears that instead of a "curious confusion" it is precisely the analogi-cal, semantic transfer from mode to mode as well as, in different ritual ex-pressions, of the same mode that constitutes the norm. Cultural analogical trans-formation operates in accordance with formulaic conventions to reduce tension and "explain" mysteries. These are the transformations by means of which ritual becomes a communicative act, speaking not to man's intellect but to his emo-tions. Some of them are fairly obvious, others subtly covert. In the replacement of complementary marital abduction by symmetrical Nyepí game the analogy is overt. Transfer of the sexual formula to the cockfight is somewhat more covert.

Complementarity is more fully constituted or regenerated by means of introjection/incorporation, as we have seen in these instances. Penetration/enclosure may be preliminary to this and is reciprocally reversed if introjection takes place; or else the act may end, as in the games, with no reversal from symmetry to complementarity, if introjection is not accomplished. That the symmetry of males is replaced by the complementarity of males as rivals through introjection probably had ancestral beginnings when male dominance over male resulted from sexual greed and thus became linked to sexual success.

The transformational analogy often (perhaps always?) is given metonymic expression. Thus the phallic attribute is substituted for the male whole in the cockfight, and cooking and fire-use for the female whole during Nyepí. At even greater semantic remove, relative position is substituted for the dominance-submission relationship of the sexual act in placement of the husband's clothing above that of the wife, or the requirement of higher head position for an individual of high status.

The interesting reversals of the agent of enclosure to agent of penetration in abduction and cockfight need closer examination. In abduction the first enclosure, of the bride by the groom, does not result in incorporation as does (at least potentially) the second enclosure, this time of groom by bride. This is paralleled by enclosure of the offerings in the place of assignation and their subsequent "enclosure" in the gods who partake of them which gives way to human enclosure (eating) of the same food offerings, all of which proclaims a synthetic relationship of *equivalence* between god and man.

In the cockfight the first enclosure, unaccompanied by incorporation, is death dealing; a real death for the cock and a symbolic death for the man who loses status. When incorporation of the losing cock in the winning owner takes place through eating, it proclaims his symbolic life-increase.

Enclosure without incorporation cannot bring life and the opposite of life is death. This explains very nicely the pollution thought to be conveyed by the menstruating woman in Bali. Because she has failed to incorporate male seed no life has ensued. Hence menstruation equals death.

Syntagmatic sequencing as a form of feedback between the two schismogenic modes may be explored in connection with calendrical events, beginning with the two days of the spring equinox celebration. The day before Nyepí, Metjaru, is the occasion of great purificational offerings, including a morning cockfight during which hundreds of birds are sacrificed. The festival marks the end of the rainy season, time of pestilence and death, and the beginning of spring, time of fertility and life-renewal (Covarrubias, 1937:277–282).

Balinese social structure is intensely hierarchical. Status is inherited rather than acquired; the social niche of the individual is virtually immutable as long as he observes the social rules, plays his inherited role, and produces children. With status as an assured social attribute competition would seem to be redundant. Yet intense competition between social equals from different villages or village wards is the basis of cockfighting. Acquisition of male status at second hand through the valor of one's cock is not just a social but also a religious act. Many temple festivals, and especially Metjaru, require the ritual spilling of cock blood in order that demons may be placated and thereafter exorcized.

Bateson and Mead interpret the bemused preoccupation of the Balinese man with his fighting cock as autoerotic, or "auto-cosmic," narcissistic, and schizoid (Bateson and Mead, 1942). Detachment of phallus, as represented by the cock, from the male body has a counterpart in the bodily movements of the dance in which parts of the body seem to maintain a life of their own, and in the ready detachment of individual consciousness from the social event, especially if it has disruptive overtones. This abstraction may take the form of a waking but dreamy state (called by Bateson and Mead *away-ness*), or of instant slumber or trance.

Geertz verifies the identification of fighting cock with phallus as quite explicit and the basis of much humor (Geertz, 1972:5–6). The cockfight is an event for, and between, men with women excluded. Victory and defeat and their perquisites are vicariously extended from the cock owners to their kinsmen and neighborhood supporters who stand to gain or lose by placing bets on the cock that they favor. Betting at the center, between cock owners and a coalition of their supporters is quiet, almost furtive, and with even money. An outer group of bettors show their support for their favorite by noisy announcement of bets that carry odds (Geertz, 1972:11–15). The larger the center bet, the lesser the odds; equality and uncertain outcome are stressed. In other words, the center stresses symmetry, the periphery complementarity, in anticipation of the complementarity of the outcome. Status acquired from the cockfight is expressed in monetary, or quantitative, rather than spatial terms. The victor does not become formally "higher" but instead richer from having incorporated something from the loser, symbolically identical with the eating of the loser's cock. Money is thus seen as an analogical transformation of semen, the primary incorporative substance, as the initial metaphor becomes more covertly expressed.[2]

The purificatory aspect of spilled male blood stands in contrast to the polluting aspect of female blood spilled during menstruation, when women may not sleep with their husbands, enter temple, kitchen, or granary, go to the well, prepare offerings, nor participate in festivals, all of which are metaphorically associated with fertility. Male blood-spilling is an act of death, but has a redeeming, life-giving aspect that results from the climactic incorporation of betting and cock-eating. The reversal would seem to proclaim social or external creativity of men as opposed to the internal, biological creativity of women; a contrastive conceptualization in which female blood-retention is vital to procreative creativity and male blood-letting vital to social progress.

Demons become analogues of females in their incorporative, blood-ingesting function and of males in the introjection of blood. This is borne out by Mershon's discussion of elemental demonic attributes in which she quotes a priestly informant as saying of the demon called *the second great elemental*, "He is the flow of blood in the body, as well as an element in the semen, for 'there is a blood-making element in the seed else how could it germinate into the body of a child?' . . . the sign of his presence is generally fire . . ." (Mershon, 1970:60–61). The locus of cockfight blood-spilling, the ground, is the site both of demon

---

[2]The analogy of money to semen may well be universal. For us money is seed in the form of "dough" or "bread." Men "make" money and women are the primary users or buyers, incorporating and ejecting it. The Balinese use of strings of ancient Chinese coins in ritual indicates that the metaphor goes beyond the cockfight.

offerings and, in temple ceremonies, of offerings to the Goddess of Earth, Peretiwi (Belo, 1966a:28). Men slaughter and prepare all meat offerings, proffered to demons, not gods.

Through the climax of the cockfight as penetration, man and man become hierarchically separated, but through introjection of blood into the earth as a demon offering man is incorporated into demon who is the equivalent of a goddess, hence female, because the place of both is the earth. Although the social consequences of the cockfight are antithetic, the supernatural consequences prove to be partially synthetic: woman, demon, and female deity are unified (i.e., symmetrical), while man becomes superior to all three. For the movement of blood-spilling is from above, the position of male and cock, to below, the position of female/deity/demon (analogous, of course, to the directionality of the sex act). What had seemed initially to be a clear-cut male/male resolution of the cockfight conflict proves instead to contain a covert female supernatural/male human complementarity by a covert enactment of *equivalence* function.

The equivalence that is covertly made between deity and demon in the cockfight is more explicit in the event that follows it on this occasion, the great purificatory offering of Metjaru as described by Covarrubias (1937:278–281). Offerings to gods are normally placed on high altars within the temple and to demons on the ground outside it; for Metjaru, high altars are erected for offerings to both at the village crossroads, where demons prototypically lurk. The altars face east, the sacred direction of sunrise. On one of these are placed offerings for the godhead, Sun and Trinity (Siva), on another those for the ancestors, and on the third those for the great *kalas,* evil gods or demons. In front of the altars, on the ground, is an eight-pointed star, appropriately oriented with the cardinal directions, constructed from every food, object, or animal of use on the island. To the north of the star and facing it, i.e., in the northeast corner, also on the ground, is an image of Batara Kala, lord of the underworld who created light and the Mother Earth, the demonic or reversed form of Siva (Covarrubias, 1937:7).

Not only is Kala the reverse of Siva but the whole construction reverses temple arrangements, the usual site of offerings. In the temple the northeast altar is that of the godhead, dedicated to Surya, the Sun. Surya's altar faces west, not east, as it does here. Transposition of major god and major demon, east and west, functions as a *coalescence* of sacred and demonic. The two are seen to be but one.

From unity, then, the transformation moves to equivalence represented by equalization of the altars and their side-by-side placement, to supernatural incorporation of man's sustenance as god and demon together partake of the offerings; a reciprocal incorporation because god and demon, in their turn, provide water and fire to man. Vertical relationships are likewise made reciprocally equivalent, for in the altar offerings the supernatural is elevated and in the ground offerings, man.

Taking the complementarity of the cockfight finale as the initial statement of the offerings, we find that through the use of the functions of coalescence, equivalence, and introjection/incorporation, synthesis is triply ensured and god and demon, supernatural and man thoroughly fused. The offering climax is degenerative because it serves to correct the initial fission of male and male, male and supernatural. Male and female are also given equivalence as they present offerings jointly.

After the reiteration of incorporative reciprocity, when the priest gives "new" fire and holy water, the major sacred substances, to the head of each ward, the poor are allowed to loot the offerings for money or anything useful, a transposition of wealth that has the coalescent synthetic effect of identifying rich with poor. Young and old, unimportant child and important adult, are also synthesized in an introjection/incorporation ceremony when after the cockfight ward officials serve a banquet of sweets and cakes to ward children (Covarrubias, 1937:279–281).

Metjaru constitutes a veritable orgy of synthesis of every major polarization. But now a dramatic act of antithesis takes place: the exorcism of demons by means of noise and fire. During the evening, and far into the night, the demons are expelled in a deafening uproar of shouting and firecrackers as the populace, sometimes with painted bodies and faces, rushes through the town in groups, brandishing flaming torches, ordering the lurking demons to "Get out!" (Covarrubias, 1937:281–282).

As the synthesis has been so complete, so the climactic antithesis which follows has all the more dramatic force. Man symbolically "kills" demon with his own phallic fire, rooting him out of the unified structure and ejecting him into outer darkness. The symmetricality that had resulted from making all forces equivalent is resolved by separation into complementarity, as god/man/woman resumes place as the superior (but only temporary) conqueror of the demonic. The human/deity function here is *ejection;* the demon function *withdrawal.*

Note that this rout of demons is both similar to, and contrastive with, the rout of gods and demons at the end of every *odalan,* temple anniversary ceremony. Shouting and exploding firecrackers the people first circle the Sun's throne three times counterclockwise, then the temporary shrine of gods' followers (demons) outside the temple gate, also three times counterclockwise, so that both types of supernatural are eliminated, but at dawn, rather than sunset (Belo, 1966a:64). An *odalan* is a *rite de passage* and, as such, has a liminal structure.

The two-day calendrical *rite de passage* of Metjaru and Nyepi is filled with the reversals and taboos characteristic of liminality phases. The reversal symbolism is every bit as highly structured as that of profane, or nonliminal passages, perhaps even more so since it is elaborately constructed on a transposed metaphor. I believe this to be a universal liminality characteristic and cannot agree with Victor Turner that "In this gap between ordered worlds almost anything may happen'' (1974:13). Ritual liminality is also an ordered world, but of complex reverse order, rather than the chaos that he suggests.

One major island-wide anniversary, occurring every 210 days, regulated by the cyclic *wuku* or permutational calendar rather the *saka* or solar-lunar calendar that governs Nyepí, is Galungan, sometimes called the Balinese New Year, or All Souls' Day. On this occasion, the gods, souls of the ancestors, descend from the mountains to occupy local temples and receive offerings from their living descendants, much as in the *odalan* ceremony but island-wide rather than localized in a single temple. Galungan is the time of the Barong, a fabulous animal-demon, resembling both a dragon and a lion or tiger. Each Barong is animated by two men and accompanied by a troop of dancers. Barongs from many village temples wander about the island to enact the drama of conflict with the female witch, Rangda, in which actors, who are Barong-supporters, and audience become possessed by demons and in trance stab themselves unsuccessfully and without bloodshed with the wavy-bladed daggers called *kris*.

Belo describes this rite as ''climactic,'' and it is another unmistakable case of schismogenesis, overlooked by Bateson and misinterpreted by Geertz (Belo, 1966b). Geertz may be correct from the standpoint of the Westerner, but hardly from that of the Balinese, when he says, ''Even in such a dramatically more heightened ceremony as the Rangda-Barong, a fearful witch and foolish dragon combat ends in a state of complete irresolution, a mystical, metaphysical, and moral standoff leaving everything precisely as it was, and the observer—or anyway the foreign observer—with the feeling that something decisive was on the verge of happening but never quite did'' (1966:60–61). Something decisive for the Balinese had, indeed, happened but was invisible to Western observers who looked for climax in quite the wrong place. Belo assesses it somewhat more insightfully from the standpoint of the Balinese: ''The battle is enacted and reenacted. No one ever wins. What happens is that dozens of villagers, aroused by the excitement held incarnate in these two figures and by the stylized interplay between them, go into trance, go through patterned behavior in a somnambulistic state, attack the Witch with their krisses, and *preferably work themselves to a climax, a true convulsive seizure of hysterical order. After such a performance everyone goes home feeling perfectly great and at peace with the world''* (Belo, 1966b:12; emphasis added).

This climax accords with Bateson's definition of schismogenesis in that differentiation in individual norms of behavior is brought about by cumulative interaction between individuals, but here the individual whose behavior becomes schismogenically differentiated is not one of the two supernaturals who interact, the Barong and the Rangda. This, again, is in the nature of depersonalization of the event or avoidance of direct consociate interaction.

In a hierarchical sense Rangda would seem to have the greater power because she represents an unconquerable, persistent threat to mankind; a *per-*

*sonal* working of evil to bring about disease and death through witchcraft. Native conceptualization of medical causality in Bali has received very little anthropological attention. Covarrubias devotes a chapter to witchcraft and says that *leyaks,* over whom Rangda reigns as queen, who, like vampires "suck the blood of sleeping people and [are] particularly fond of the entrails of unborn children," are held responsible for most of the evils that afflict Bali (Covarrubias, 1937:322). Lansing says that those who practice black magic (i.e., *leyaks*) are generally old and ugly and hope thereby to attract handsome mates (Lansing, 1974). They learn to metamorphose themselves at will into animal form and to fly through the air to wreak destruction. The old have most to gain from witchcraft because of what they have lost in youth and vitality, but particularly the female elderly who no longer have the prestige of childbearing nor the male compensation of influence in village affairs, nor even the prospect of producing more children through additional marriages. Envious of the children of other, fertile women, perhaps even their daughters, jealous of their husbands' favors, frustrated and greedy, they take their revenge. Two informants assured me that *leyaks* are women. Although Covarrubias indicates that it is a role open to either sex he says that women have greater aptitude for it and require less study to prepare themselves (Covarrubias, 1937:344).

That Rangda is said to eat babies, or the entrails of unborn babies, is one indication that procreation is a major source of envy. Others are found in the details of costuming: her sagging breasts, presumably exhausted by the suckling of children, and especially her principal appurtenance, the white sling in which mothers carry babies. Obviously, she has had babies but has them no longer. Her motherhood and the respect that it should entail is her major weapon.

Foster has suggested that babies and the ability to bear them are major causes of envy, and that belief in witchcraft arises in societies in which certain individuals are seen as potentially envious, hence, much to be feared (G. Foster, 1972). Putting this cause and this imputed result of envy together, we have Rangda, frightening not *just* because she is a mother figure of a very particular kind whom the Balinese have very good reason to fear (Bateson and Mead, 1942:34–36). Consumed with envy and frustration over what she can no longer legitimately have, she takes her revenge in whatever way she can. The way that this particular culture provides is witchcraft.

One's first impression is that Rangda and Barong stand in an unequivocally complementary relationship to one another. Rangda is female, Barong male. She is old, he is young. She is bad, he is good. She is a human witch, he is an animal demon. And yet, if we examine their symbolism more thoroughly we find that the opposition between them is not this clear-cut. Clues to an understanding of its nature are found both in Balinese everyday gesture language and in the specialized gestures of the dance drama.

A major kinesthetic contrast between male and female is differential positioning of knees and thighs. Men sit on the ground crosslegged with thighs apart.

Women sit with thighs together, knees bent but uncrossed, and both feet to one side. In dance the most typical male stance is one with thighs, knees, and feet turned outward, that most typically female one in which knees are bent but not turned far outward and with feet close together. In the former position movements are wide, in the latter, narrow. The male posture is typified by the *baris* warrior dancer, the female by the *légong*, danced by pre-adolescent girls. In the *baris* dance the spine is held erect; in the *légong* the spine curves in an arc and the buttocks protrude (McPhee, 1970).

The *baris* dancer walks or strides with knees bent and thighs spread at right angles to his body. He represents fierce and uncontrolled masculinity, is "all" male, passionate and quick-tempered. As the *baris* dance progresses and music grows more violent,

> the *baris* warrior becomes more and more tense, raising himself on his toes until he gives the impression of growing in height; his eyes seem ready to jump from their sockets, his whole body trembles, making the flowers of his headdress shake violently. So raised on his toes and with his whole body at high nervous tension, he slaps his thigh and points an accusing finger at his enemy, as with wild yells of 'Wah! Adoh, adoh!' he draws his *kris* and struts aggressively towards his foe, who comes forward at the same moment; before they meet, the dancers stop defiantly, cursing each other, and when the clash comes, with tiger-like grace they perform a stylized duel to music, in which the routing of one of the characters indicates the end of the dance (Covarrubias, 1937:231).

Since the dance represents a warlike duel, much of the behavior of the warrior is designed to frighten the enemy through threat. Pointing is interpreted as peculiarly insulting in Bali. Rangda, though ostensibly female, adopts much of the kinesthetic behavior of the frighteningly male dancer. Her gestures are also angular and wide, although in a gesture that Belo describes as characteristic, adopted by men possessed by the Rangda spirit in trance, the elbows are held tightly to the sides while the hands are rigidly extended, combining narrow and wide movements (Belo, 1966b:46). Her spine is held tall and erect, her elongated fingernails apart and quivering, her eyes round and staring. She, too, shouts "Wah!" at her enemy in deep tones and extends her arm toward him accusingly as she towers above. Like the *baris* warrior she is tense and sudden in her movements. In addition, the Rangda costume is always worn by a man who becomes possessed by her spirit. One of Rangda's most terrible attributes is an extremely long, pendulous tongue, tipped with fire. This, like her gestures, is phallic, but in contrast to the erect phallic tail of the Barong it is lifeless and impotent, a masculinized counterpart of her exhausted, pendulous female breasts.

Except that the Barong is activated by two men, his masculinity is given visual expression only, and then covertly, in his serpentine body and proudly erect tail decorated with shining mirrors. The shape is similar to that of the *penyor*, a bamboo pole representation of Gunung Agung, mountain and god, placed outside each house and temple entrance at Galungan. The positioning of the Barong is male when he stands above the entranced fighter to restore him to his senses. Other traits point to a feminized identity. Unlike the mouth of Rangda, equipped with a pendulous tongue, Barong's mouth has no tongue at all and would seem to represent a vagina. Unlike the rigid, jerky, phallicized movements of Rangda his are sinuous and circular. His spine describes a concave arc where hers is held rigid. His actions are playful and teasing, like those ascribed by Bateson and Mead to the mother (1942). This is human but also animal-like behavior, as is the greed which he exhibits in the playful parts of the drama, for example, when he snatches a banana from a monkey companion. He is not particularly frightening despite the menace of his constantly snapping teeth and, in fact, often seems timid and tentative rather than decisive.

The smallness of the Barong head in contrast to the length of his body, the height of his tail and the largeness of the head of Rangda make a complex symbolic statement that can be understood only in the larger context of Balinese head symbolism.

We have already seen that the head position is important as a status symbol. Through the representation of the trinity of the godhead in the *ongkara* we find that the crown of the head and the phallus are equated in the upright line at the top of the figure as are eyes and uterus in the half-moon shape below (Covarrubias, 1937:297). Yet the Barong, as animal-demon, nonhuman, nongod, is given a phallic tail, a nonphallic mouth, and an arched (uteral) back, whereas the Rangda as female witch, human but demonic, is provided with phallic head and tongue and an erect back. Rangda gains status with her head, Barong with his tail. The head is the seat of the intellect and the tail that of animality, especially sexuality. The two are partially synthesized through this symbolism. They coalesce in some fashion through the transposition of male and female traits.

Balinese crossing of sex roles was discussed by Belo as a characteristic symbolic phenomenon. Despite this important insight she overlooked the sex-crossing in Barong and Rangda gesture and costuming which seems crucial to understanding the meaning of their conflict. Through it the bad traits of both sexes have been assigned to Rangda and the good to Barong. She embodies male aggressiveness, female old age, desexualized intellectuality or infertile wisdom, hatred and destructive greed which is death dealing. He embodies female lack of aggression, youthful sexuality of both sexes (uteral back, erect tail), female-animal-childlike playfulness and unthreatening animal appetite which is life giving. His strength is in his tail, not in his head.

Because traits of good and evil, male and female, are redistributed, neither opponent has the complete advantage and neither can be permanently defeated. Since both good and evil are inherent in human nature, the evil in the human can be suppressed or transcended, as it is in the outcome of this battle, but not dispossessed. This is a profound philosophical statement, assuredly not completely understood intellectually by the Balinese but certainly grasped emotionally as an effective artistic commentary.

Belo assessed both Rangda and Barong as potentially destructive forces, correctly, I believe (Belo, 1966b:57–59). Although good is on the side of the Barong, it is an animal, childlike good which can easily become destructive. The Barong cavorts about quite selfishly and happily, doing whatever suits his fancy at the moment: snapping quite heedlessly with his fanged teeth, snatching what does not belong to him, acting, in short, in a fashion completely lacking in respect, the foundation of etiquette on which the cohesion of the Balinese social fabric completely depends. Correct, respectful behavior which recognizes rank and age, face-saving etiquette, and sexual and gustatory decorum are never-to-be-forgotten rules of Balinese behavior. Perhaps because his own behavior must be kept under control and his appetites and anger suppressed, the Balinese feels such a strong attraction both to children and to the Barong, a sacred child-animal.

The Balinese adore children, ostensibly because as reincarnated ancestors they are as little gods, but undoubtedly also because they are like innocent, uninhibited demons, permitted some degree of animal-like behavior because of their lack of knowledge, as the Barong is allowed his because intellect is not highly developed in his small head. Barong and Rangda both represent extremes, one more animal and the other more human, one polarized toward life and the other toward death, but both to be held under restraint in the normal adult by the exercise of social ritual.

In the first part of the drama there is symmetry between the two antagonists such that neither is superior and neither can win. When human warriors align themselves with the Barong and attempt to attack Rangda with their krisses, these are ineffective against her passive femininity and flourished baby sling. She is not to be conquered and subdued through penetration, the normal method of establishing hierarchy. Symmetry is equalized and regenerated rather than destroyed by the thwarted penetration, which is actually a refusal of enclosure.

After the cock, the kris is the Balinese male's most valued possession. According to Covarrubias,

> . . . the head of a prominent Balinese family regards his kris as an important appendage and symbol of himself. Today in the old villages it is compulsory for every man to wear his kris to attend a meeting; the kris must be worn at marriage and for all ceremonial or state occasions. Whoever cannot appear in person sends his kris to represent him, as for instance a judge who is sick and cannot attend a trial. In certain cases the marriage of a prince to a woman of the lower castes is performed by proxy in the form of the kris of her future husband. A new kris must be made "alive" by a priest, who blesses it in a special ceremony, reciting magic formulas over it and inscribing imaginary signs over the blade, while its owner dedicates an offering. Ancient krisses are kept alive with offerings of flowers and incense; a neglected and rusty kris is said to be "dead" (Covarrubias, 1937:198–199).

A cock-kris equation is even explicit. A young Balinese male who has been selected by a girl-child in trance to be a fighter for the newly created Barong of his village temple expressed to me his pride over his new role as "one of the Barong's fighting cocks."

Like the cock-owner the Barong is not himself aggressively masculine and requires phallic surrogates for his symmetrical struggle. Hoping that penetration can be effected and symmetricality turned into complementarity as it is in the cockfight, the Barong-fighters flourish their krisses toward the hated Rangda. When the kris proves ineffective they turn it against their own breasts in a suicidal frenzy. What is the meaning of this seemingly insensate act?

The explanation lies in the role of Rangda as a witch; a role she has embraced through the anger and frustration of her infertility and her envy of others more favored. Witchcraft is a reversal. To learn to perform black magic one reads a set of sacred manuscripts in reverse order. *Leyaks* go naked rather than clothed, fly rather than walk, transform themselves into animals. Rather than manifesting the function of enclosure, witches penetrate into the houses of others, but especially into others' bodies, to eat entrails or otherwise destroy through illness. It is not, then, strange that in the drama the Rangda refuses to enclose the death-dealing kris. It is *her* witchly function to provide the penetrating death stroke. Penetration gives her status.

Both Belo and Lansing interviewed participants of the Rangda drama as to their feelings before they went into trance and elicited an intense hate for Rangda and strong desire to kill her (Belo, 1966b:55; Lansing, 1974:80). Lansing attempts to account for this hate by presenting it as the strength to resist evil provided to humans by their Barong-like innocence, symbolized by the Four Brothers, elemental forces present in man from birth, one of whom the Barong is said to represent (Lansing, 1974:81–83). I cannot see that this interpretation, based on an interview with a priest who controls somewhat esoteric lore, serves in any sense to explain the strength of the emotion that Barong-fighters undoubtedly feel. Its source must be sought in the individual life experience of the Barong-fighter.

My single Barong-fighter informant, felt that this experience gave central meaning to his life. The emotion with which he described his participation in the ritual and his pleasure at having been divinely selected for the role attested to the profundity of his attachment to the Barong and hatred of the Rangda.

The only other experience which he related to me with similar emotion was a bewitchment in childhood which caused him and several siblings to fall ill and remain in a sickly condition for several years. His father, a relatively wealthy man, had three wives. The first wife had been supplanted by my informant's mother, no relation to her, whereas the youngest wife was her sister. The older and younger wife, the two sisters, occupied one house together, the other wife lived with her children in the household of a brother of her husband. All these wives were referred to by the Barong-fighter as *mother,* so that it took me some time to sort out the relationships and know who was being spoken of at any given point in the narrative.

When the relationships became clearer to me and I found that incidents involving the older "mother" were somehow entwined with incidents involving the childhood illness, it occured to me that she was very probably the witch. The isolation of the real mother, the reinforcement of the first wife's position through the later acquisition of her own sister as third wife and their occupancy and hold over the family plantation that was the single source of wealth reinforced my initial feeling that the situation was one in which envy could easily have played a part, especially when the second marriage was new and the children young.

As the conversation kept returning to the illness, over which my friend felt an obvious anxiety, I asked him if he knew who had bewitched him. He did, but at the thought of revealing her name, his anxiety increased. When I asked if it was his second "mother" his voice fell to a whisper as he agreed. It was apparent that he felt both surprise that I had guessed and relief that he was now free to speak of it, however secretly, as if we were coconspirators.

If my explanation of Rangda's identity, as personalized by her attackers to such an extent that they can feel real hatred for her, is valid, then it is not difficult to understand the catharsis that this particular young man, who had himself been bewitched, or supposed himself to have been bewitched, by a stepmother, felt over a ritualized release of his pent-up rage.

The judgment of Bateson and Mead that the Rangda symbolizes the mother as the source of childhood fear is partially correct but incomplete (Bateson and Mead, 1942:34–36). Rangda is *a* mother, but not *the* mother. The judgment of Belo that Rangda is the "bad" mother as against the "good" mother, represented by the *tjili* figure of female beauty and fertility comes somewhat closer to the truth as I see it (Belo, 1966b:37–38). Lansing, who even purports to be solving the mystery by means of phenomenology, throws little light on the *individual* meaning of the event, which is really available only through life histories.

A curious inversion in the Bateson and Mead interpretation occurs when they describe frightening *by* the mother as causing the child to be frightened *of* the mother. In order to make him aware that there are dangers she calls out "Snake!" or "Wildcat!" and clutches him against her protectively (Belo, 1966b:51–56). In short, she invokes the snake- and wildcat-like characteristics of the Barong as objects of fear! In truth, it is animality that causes the greatest disgust in the Balinese. Yet the Barong drama shows that which is most tabooed is actually that to which they feel most drawn.

Although men act as the phallic Barong-fighters, both men and women in the audience become possessed and turn the kris in trance against themselves. If Rangda represents a "mother," that she has succeeded in thwarting penetration (interpretable as either murder or incest) by reminding them with her feminine characteristics that she is indeed an older mother, worthy of their greatest respect, the guilt and shame that they must feel as a result of their assault can easily account for the suicidal gesture. This penetration might be successful except for the demonic intercession of the trance, for at that very moment, the kris-wielder becomes possessed by a demon.

Belo terms this spirit a *god* but from her description it emerges as a "follower" of a god, often an animal spirit as "Yellow Tiger" or "Black Tiger," or an "evil god" (Belo, 1966b:46, 52, 55). In any event, in another account she refers to the followers of the gods as *demons* (1966a). In this case (perhaps in all cases?) possession seems demonic. The Barong, often compared to serpent, lion, or tiger, is the demon king. Rangda and her *leyak* followers transform themselves at will into animal form, "birds, pigs, monkeys, snakes, or even tigers" (Covarrubias, 1937:342). Demons would seem to incorporate themselves in *leyaks* through black magic which depends upon many kinds of reversal, and in other human beings on ritual occasions. In the ritual under consideration it becomes imperative that immediately after possession the entranced person be given a kris. The inner demon seems to insist upon this (Belo, 1966b:52).

Since the kris is clearly the phallic element the body under attack must be interpreted as female-like. This is underscored by the typical male krissing stance; body bent backward, kris pressed against breast from above. The demon has been incorporated through prior introjection/enclosure, a reversal of the penetration/introjection sequence in coitus. The body which has already enclosed the male-female-animal demon will not receive the instrument of penetration which unaccompanied by introjection could mean only death. Thus, the demon within acts as mediator in thwarting the self-destruction attempt that must inevitably follow the desire to kill the "mother." He is more powerful than the man, though he is below, a second reversal. The demon without, the Barong, removes the demon within by assuming a sexual position, standing over the possessed person. This is a third reversal from the coitus model in that posture above extracts rather than introjects. The function here is one of *withdrawal/rejection,* which brings the act into analogical cohesion with childbirth instead of coitus. Barong as male, human being as female together bring into the world the beneficial demonic function represented by the possessing demon.

Stated in transformational terms, the succession of schismogenic events in the Barong-Rangda ritual is as follows: a symmetrical confrontation between Barong and Rangda (neither of whom is able to gain advantage because neither is more powerful than the other) is succeeded by a new confrontation between human male and "mother" female, this time complementary. The attempted penetration as *thrust* is countered with a *parry,* either a counterthrust as Rangda raises her phallic fingered arm or her baby sling toward her adversaries, or passivity as she goes limp in their arms. Thrust and parry are regenerative and maintain complementarity, with the Rangda more powerful as she towers above and her adversaries cower beneath her. But suddenly the demon force mediates the conflict by introjection and becomes enclosed in the adversary, a function which equalizes (i.e., provides symmetricality for) Rangda and man, as Rangda and Barong were symmetrical in the introduction. Man then thrusts against himself, but this is successfully parried by the demon within, who through his superior, complementary power prevents penetration. And yet this complementarity is fictive because in the trance man and demon are one. In the final act, either demon mediates to extract demon, where the Barong stands over the possessed man, or god mediates to extract demon, where the priest sprinkles holy water to bring the man to his senses. The use of both techniques is an act of equivalence. Demon and god are as one.

Together Rangda and Barong represent most, perhaps all, of the feared, demonic aspects of human nature which must be checked by culture if they are not to dominate and destroy it. Since they are clearly themselves indestructible they must be turned to advantage; the meaning of the trance and self-stabbing of the climax. The demonic source of fear becomes the means of salvation and evil is, at least momentarily, deflected.

Procreation is an inner, creative event, but so is the reconciliation of conflicting forces within the human breast. That the procreative analogue should be used for such a statement is not surprising. Man usually deals with woman through sex, hence the warrior's desire to stab Rangda with his phallic kris, which is unsuccessful because she thwarts penetration with the respect due her as "mother." The shame that an attempt to penetrate the mother must engender seems capable of expiration only through suicide, a self-penetration. But man is saved from such a death by his own demonic, life-creating instincts, the meaning of possession and trance. Because he has creativity (blood and fire of the demon) within him, suicide, an outer or antithetic penetrative act without introjection, is impossible. He is saved by his inner demon and brought to himself, i.e., given rebirth from his pseudo suicide, by being brought *under* the Barong, or the god, the sources of life, actually one.

As a schismogenic event complementarity (incapable of resolution through penetration/enclosure) is resolved by introjection/incorporation which serves to cancel all the antithetical impulses of the individual and provides him with self-unification. This pacific unity is expressed less violently at Galungan by means of *penyor* and *lamak,* male and female deity representations placed beside the entrance of each dwelling or temple. Into the *lamak*, mat or apron, is woven the *tjili*, a stylized representation with head in the shape of a fan, of Dewi Sri, goddess of rice and fertility. The *lamak* hangs from the floor of a small, raised altar in the form of a house on which offerings are placed, inviting the erect god without to enter and partake of the good within.

Lansing stresses the Balinese need to be *kaikêt,* "tied," to his social and physical world in many complex ways (1974). Knowing his place and that of others in the social fabric, the individual can adjust his behavior and respond appropriately in any social circumstance. But in spite of his many ties he seems, in some crucial sense, socially unsupported and thrown back on his own resources, and is described by many authors as narcissistic, withdrawn, or screened from reality by the symbolic world of drama and social ritual which has come to replace it. The interaction between mother and child in which the mother's attention is withdrawn before climax is reached, which Bateson gives as the typical learning experience which precludes later schismogenesis, perhaps instead provides a model for schismogenesis as an isolated, individual experience, internalized rather than projected (Bateson, 1970:388–389). If this is true then the emotional impact on the Balinese of the act of self-krissing in the climax of the Rangda-Barong conflict is seen to be the most appropriate Balinese schismogenic response. Here the conflict that the individual feels because of his membership in a social group is not projected back on that group as it is in most cultures, but internalized as a matter for individual resolution.

Since the Rangda-Barong drama may take place as a feature of Galungan, otherwise devoted to offerings and entertainment of ancestor-gods, through which man and god become unified by incorporation, the festival emerges as unifying all polarized forces, in contrast to Nyepi, which served to incorporate only man in god and god in man, to banish the demonic and then to unify man and woman through symbolic equivalence. Galungan is, thus, a more powerful or definitive statement than Nyepi. It recognizes, realistically, that the demonic may be temporarily banished, like Rangda, but is still present because human nature contains both good and evil, conceptually male and conceptually female, divine and animal attributes. The climax is a cathartic representation of death (the trance) and resurrection (recovery from trance).

Analysis of Balinese ritual evidence (both that presented here and other, such as the *odalan* and certain dance forms which reiterate the patterns described here without requiring any theoretical readaptation and are not included for reasons of space) lead to a redefinition of schismogenesis which will have the potential of universal applicability and not exclude Bali. Exclusion of Bali from Bateson's model seems to me spurious from the standpoint of climax, which clearly exists. The Balinese material shows, however, that a clearly defined climax that is intensely and obviously affective is not necessary to all sequences which are formally schismogenic on any other ground. Affective potential is always present, else why would the ritual be worth repeating, but may be realized with greater intensity on some occasions than on others, or during some rituals or parts of rituals than others.

*Schismogenesis* may be redefined as an analogical symbolic transformation which, through modal apposition of social relationship and polarization of spatially defined functions categorized as antithetic or synthetic, effects a redefinition of social categories. Modes are symmetrical and complementary. Antithetic functions are thrust/parry, penetration/enclosure, and withdrawal/ejection. Synthetic functions are coalescence, equivalence, and introjection/incorporation.

Analogical transformation stems from the antithesis and synthesis of the male-female relationship, which is complementary and primary. Since both hierarchies and equivalences are potentially open-ended, dualities are not unique symbolic representations. There is, however, a distinct, analogically induced tendency for multiple relationships to be expressed dually. For example, in Bali there are three upper castes and a lower caste subdivision into many subcastes, or *dadias,* "cohesive units of related families" (Lansing, 1974:14). Respect etiquette depends upon knowing each individual's place in this multiple hierarchy. For many purposes, however, the three upper castes are grouped together and polarized against the undifferentiated lower castes. Ritually, dualism is the unique symbolic expression.

Symmetrical symbolism, then, is modeled on complementary symbolism. Symmetrical climaxes and complementary climaxes are induced through exactly the same series of functions, of which penetration/enclosure and introjection/incorporation assume major importance just as they do for sexuality. The motivation for this seems to be the rivalry that develops from a male desire to possess a single mate. Cross-culturally, far more ritualized rivalry is polarized as male-male than as female-female. Our own organized team sports or political parties are cases in point.

A contextual analysis of ritual reveals a semantic matrix in which "Freudian" or sexual symbolism as deep motivation provides a dynamic point of departure for elaboration of facets of many types of social relationship as "surface structure." This is seen especially clearly in the Rangda-Barong rite as an affective experience with both deep and surface implications.

Mary Douglas has suggested that the general assumption that an infinite number of social constructions can be put upon nature because of its variety does not mean that the range of human societies producing these constructions is itself so varied (Douglas, 1973:10). I would add that neither are the constructions themselves infinitely varied if regarded as deep structure, although surface variation is indeed infinite, even within a single culture such as Bali. It is possible that I have not exhausted the total range of deep structural types in this analysis, either for Bali or elsewhere, but I believe that those postulated here will prove themselves cross-culturally as a basis for typological studies.

## REFERENCES

Bateson, Gregory. *Naven* (2nd ed.) Stanford, California: Stanford University Press, 1958.

Bateson, Gregory. The value system of a steady state. In Jane Belo (Ed.), *The traditional Balinese culture*. New York: Columbia University Press, 1970.

Bateson, Gregory, and Mead, Margaret. *Balinese character: A photographic analysis.* New York: The New York Academy of Science, 1942.

Belo, Jane. *Bali: Temple festival.* Monograph of the American Ethnological Society *22* (2nd ed.) Seattle: University of Washington Press, 1966a.

Belo, Jane. *Bali: Rangda and Barong.* Monograph of the American Ethnological Society *16* (2nd ed.). Seattle: University of Washington Press, 1966b.

Belo, Jane. The Balinese temper. In Jane Belo (Ed.), *The traditional Balinese culture*. New York: Columbia University Press, 1970.

Covarrubias, Miguel. *Island of Bali*. New York: Knopf, 1937.

Douglas, Mary. (Ed.) *Rules and meanings*. Middlesex: Penguin Books, 1973.

Foster, G. M. The anatomy of envy: A study in symbolic behavior. *Current anthropology*, 1972, *4*, (2), 165–202.

Foster, Mary LeCron. Deep structure in symbolic anthropology. *Ethos*, 1974, *2* (3), 334–355.

Geertz, Clifford. *Person, time, and conduct in Bali: An essay in cultural analysis*. New Haven: Yale University Southeast Asia Studies Cultural Report No. 14, 1966.

Geertz, Clifford. The Balinese cockfight. *Daedalus*, Winter 1972, 7.

Lansing, J. S. *Evil in the morning of the world: Phenomenological approaches to a Balinese community*. Michigan Papers on South and Southeast Asia, *6*. Ann Arbor: University of Michigan Center for South and Southeast Asian Studies, 1974.

McPhee, Colin. Dance in Bali. In Jane Belo (Ed.), *The traditional Balinese culture*. New York: Columbia University Press, 1970.

Mershon, K. A. Five great elementals. In Jane Belo (Ed.), *The traditional Balinese culture*. New York: Columbia University Press, 1970.

Needham, Rodney (Ed.). *Right and left: Essays on dual symbolic classification*. Chicago: University of Chicago Press, 1973.

Turner, Victor. *Dramas, fields and metaphors: Symbolic action in human society*. Ithaca: Cornell University Press, 1974.

# chapter eleven

# Time and Tune

# in Java

Judith Becker

The University of Michigan

One of the central concerns of the American ethnomusicologist for the last fifteen years has been the examination of the relationship between the musician and his audience, his role in society, and the situation of his music-making. These studies have taught us a great deal, have made us aware that music occurs because someone is doing something *to* someone else, or *for* someone else, and the musical signal is a part, often the most interesting part, of a complex communication system. Although ethnomusicological studies concerning behavior, what might be called *behavioral* musicology, have made us sensitive to the complexity of the musical situation, these studies have not, for the most part, brought us closer to a solution of another problem, namely, what *is* music?

It is clear that *music* can be defined only within a given culture, and that the range of meaning for the term *music* in one culture does not necessarily correspond with the semantic range of the term in another culture (Blacking, 1970; Seeger, 1952). All music systems are infused with the concepts and systems of organization of the surrounding society, concepts which are also manifested in other systems of the society. The same concepts which control the organization of other kinds of experience within a culture control the organization of music and determine the selection of a limited pool of elements from the infinite possibilities of acoustic sound. Music systems are but one way in which the people of a given culture conceptualize and make sense of their world. It follows that music systems do not necessarily relate to the same organizing concepts in all cultures. Governing principles of music in one culture are not necessarily the governing principles of music in another culture.

The specific illustration of this thesis as presented in this paper is the musical system of the Javanese gamelan, an ensemble of from five to twenty-five instruments, most of which are bronze gongs and bronze xylophones. Only after several years of performance of Javanese gamelan music, and research into gamelan music, did I begin to suspect that the underlying assumptions of this music, the way this music is conceptualized, have little in common with the concepts underlying the music I grew up with. I had always assumed that "music was music," anywhere in the world, that musicians were musicians all over the world, and that in spite of surface differences in tone, texture, rhythm, meter, melodic contour, etc., all music derived from common sources, that musicians all over the world used the same kinds of mental processes to produce their melodies. I now feel quite sure that this is not the case, that there is not an abstract "universe of music" which becomes manifest in different ways in different cultures, and the term *music* is a rather sloppy cover term applied to acoustic phenomena which are the result of any number of different mental processes and conceptualizations.

In Java, the fundamental governing principle in gamelan music is the cyclic recurrence of a melodic/temporal unit, which is a musical manifestation of the way in which the passage of time is also ordered. In Java, time is represented as cyclical. Furthermore, time in Java is not represented as a single recurrent cycle, but several concurrent cycles running simultaneously. Important days are reckoned as those points of coincidence between the different, continuously ongoing cycles (Geertz, 1973; Kartodirdjo, 1959).

The five-day-week cycle and the seven-day-week cycle are the two calendrical systems most used in Java for daily affairs.[1] The names of the days in the five-day system are as follows:

1. Kliwon
2. Legi
3. Paing
4. Pon
5. Wage

Running concurrently with the five-day week is the seven-day week. The names of the days are as follows:

1. Ahad
2. Senen

[1]The five-day-week cycle is based on the five-day market system, *pasaran*. The seven-day-week cycle is adopted from Islam and has Arabic words for the days. This calendar replaces an earlier, pre-Islamic seven-day-week cycle which had Sanskrit names for the days. Other cycles not discussed in this paper are the six-day-week cycle called *mawulon* or *paringkelan,* the seven-day-week cycle called *wuku,* (30 *wuku* = 1 year), and the nine-day-week cycle called *pandangon.* For a fuller explanation of all these calendrical systems and others besides, see Soebardi (1965).

3. Selasa
4. Rebo
5. Kemis
6. Jum'at
7. Sabtu

The organization of time into concurrently running cycles of five and seven days each may be mapped onto a circle as in Figure 1.

Any given day must be reckoned by its position in both cycles. Every thirty-five days (5 × 7) the cycles coincide, and this point of conjunction always has special significance. In Figure 1, the day "Jum'at - Legi" recurs every thirty-five days.

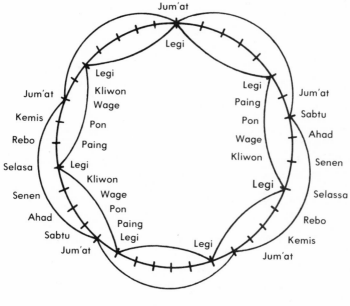

Figure 1

Another calendrical system, less commonly used, but more closely resembling the gamelan system of cycle subdivision, is the lunar-month cycle divided into halves, then into fourths, then into eighths (see Figure 2). This system is called *asta-wara,* or eight turns, after the recurrent eight-day week. The names of the days in this system are as follows:

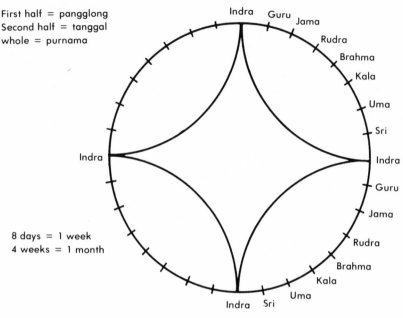

Purnama (full)

First half = pangglong
Second half = tanggal
whole = purnama

Indra    Guru    Jama

Rudra

Brahma

Kala

Uma

Sri

Indra                          Indra

Guru

Jama

8 days = 1 week
4 weeks = 1 month

Rudra

Brahma

Kala

Uma

Indra    Sri

Figure 2

1. Guru
2. Jama
3. Rudra or Ludra
4. Brahma
5. Kala
6. Uma
7. Sri
8. Indra

The organization of time as cyclical units with smaller cycles moving within larger cycles and with points of cycle coincidence marking important moments of time is also the basis of the organization of the music system.[2] Both can be analyzed as closed systems, independent and without reference to each other, but in the sense that they isomorphic with each other, they are also instances of a Javanese way of organizing and making sense of time.

The basic unit of gamelan music is a cycle marked off by a gong, called a *gongan*. This cycle is subdivided into halves, quarters, eighths, etc., by instruments playing at successively greater levels of density, or at successively faster rates of speed. In Figure 3, the cycle *(gongan)*, marked off by gong (G), is subdivided into halves by an instrument called the *kenong* (N), into quarters by an instrument called *kempul* (P), into eighths by an instrument called *kethuk* (T),

[2]The correspondence between calendrical systems in Indonesia and the structural principles of gamelan music was first brought to my attention by A. L. Becker.

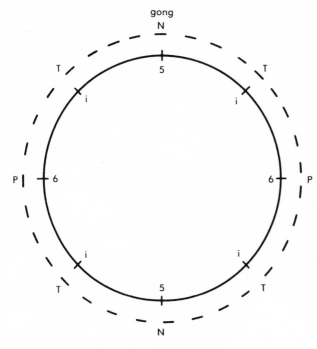

gong
N

Subdivisions of gongan
First: kenong (N)
Second: kempul (P)
Third: kethuk (T) and saron
    (ciphers)
Fourth: ∅ (deleted)
Fifth: bonang barung (-)

**Figure 3**

as well as the instrument called *saron* (ciphers indicate *saron* pitch levels), and into thirty-seconds by an instrument called *bonang barung* (-):[3]

In the largest forms there is a total of ten subdivisions of the gongan. The various kinds of gongan are differentiated from each other not only by their size, but also by which instrument plays at which level of subdivision in any given form. The primary subdivisions of the gongan, the half-way point (first subdivision), the quarter point (second subdivision), are marked not only by the instrument which sounds only at that point, but also by the strong constraints that all

---

[3]Javanese cipher notation indicates the tuned slabs of the *saron*. In one tuning system, *slendro,* the octave is divided into five tones, in the other tuning system, *pelog,* the octave is divided into seven tones. A simple differentiating device indicates visually which tuning system is intended. The five-tone-per-octave system, *slendro,* numbers the slabs of the *saron* as follows:

(A dot below the cipher indicates the lower octave, a dot above the cipher indicates the upper octave)

| 6 | 1 | 2 | 3 | 5 | 6 | 1 |
|---|---|---|---|---|---|---|

Thus there is no slab 4 or 7 in the *slendro* notation system, and the gap between 3 and 5 should not be interpreted as a skipped tone.

melodic lines come together (coincide) on the same pitch at those points. All melodic lines (subdivisions), come together at the same pitch (coincide) at the stroke of the gong.

One is struck not only by the cyclical nature of all gamelan formal structures, but also by what might be called their *rigid binariness*. A whole becomes a half, then each half is divided into halves, making quarters, then each quarter is again halved, making eighths, etc. Like the cyclical conception of time, the basic duality of this music reflects a dual system of classification in Indonesia which astonishes the observer by its constancy and its thoroughness. (Systems of dual classification and their subdivisions found in Java which have their sources in Buddhism or Hinduism brought from India appear to be superimposed upon an indigenous Indonesian duality, e.g., the *asta-wara* calendrical system.) In Java, many aspects of life which our culture does not classify fall into a system of dual classification (Van der Kroef, 1954). Beginning at the cosmic level, there is the cosmic mountain and the subterranean sea. Indonesia consists of a long archipelago of volcanic islands; thus it is hardly surprising that the mountain/sea division is of paramount importance. The mountain is the home of autochthonous Javanese gods, the source of holiness, sometimes the abode of the ancestors, the source of wealth and prosperity. The sea, its balanced opposite (dynamic complementary) is the place of demons, the place of death and evil spirits, the source of malevolence. Over time, the mountain comes to be associated with the sun, fire, heaven, and hornbill bird, the *kris* (ritual sword of Javanese men), the head of a person's body, gamelan, and maleness. The word *gong*, alternate spelling *gung*, is the root form of both the word which means mountain (*gunung* = *gung* + infix *un*) and the word which means great *(agung)*. The sea comes to be equated with the moon, fertility, batik cloth, the watersnake, the feet of a person's body and femaleness (see Figure 4).

| SEA | MOUNTAIN |
|---|---|
| Moon | Sun |
| Earth | Heaven |
| Watersnake | Hornbill |
| Batik | Kris |
| Feet | Head |
| Female | Male |
| Vocal music, stringed instruments | Gong/gamelan |

Figure 4

The dual division of the universe extends from the macrocosmic level, the cosmic mountain versus the sea, to the microcosmic level, the front and back parts of each house, the male and female gongs, the right and left hands, with the two halves in each case sharing the same associations as the cosmic duality.

The classification of space into the four cardinal divisions superimposes a further binary subdivision on the primordial mountain/sea duality. North and east, or the first half of the cycle, come to be associated with the positive aspects of the universe, south and west with the negative aspects. There is no sense of good versus evil in these categories, but rather balanced opposites, or *yin* and *yang*. Directionality, linked as it is with cosmic forces, assumes great importance in Java. "Knowing where north is"—i.e., being oriented within space which has a map drawn on it—for a Javanese, is, equivalent to being a rational, controlled human being.

> Javanese villages, houses, streets and rice fields are aligned with major compass points. Space is square and one moves through it rectangularly. (Geertz, 1960:31)

During a dance lesson, the teacher directs the students by saying "Now move to the east, now take three steps south."

*Binariness* is a quality of Javanese space as well as a principle of organization of things great and small. *Cyclicity* is a quality of Javanese time. Both combine in gamelan music to produce musical cycles divided binarily.

The foregoing discussion concerns aspects of form in gamelan music and temporal relationships within forms. Now, I hope to demonstrate how the concept of melody in gamelan music was originally inseparable from the concept of form.

Any sequence of pitches played on any given gamelan instrument can be perceived as a "melody," can be hummed, and may be even fitted with words. But the process which resulted in that melody may be unrelated to setting a poem or humming a tune, but rather was originally part of the process of cycle subdivision, a conceptual process which is not intrinsically or necessarily a musical process, but happens to be a musical process in this culture.

There is a body of gamelan pieces of great antiquity, which in this article will be called *archaic*. How old they are, no one knows for sure. As a conservative estimate, they were probably played before 1000 A.D. Archaic pieces include the following:

> The genre Srepegan (and by contraction and expansion all
>   Sampak and Ayak-ayakan)
> The genre Kebogiro
> All Cavabalen pieces
> Monggang
> Kodok Ngorek
> Many Lancaran

Several different kinds of evidence point to their antiquity. The simplest, most straightforward evidence is that the Javanese say they are old. Also, several of these pieces form the sole repertoire of archaic gamelan ensembles no longer in regular use today, but played only on special ritual occasions (*Carabalen* pieces, *Kodok Ngorek,* and *Monggang*). The archaic gamelan on which the pieces are played are all owned by members of the central Javanese nobility. Other of these pieces form the core of the musical repertoire of a clearly archaic ritual drama, *wayang kulit,* the Javanese shadow-puppet play. (The genres *Sampak, Srepegan* and *Ayak-ayakan.*) The final evidence for the antiquity of these pieces is structural or internal. They all share certain structural/melodic features, features from which it is possible to derive, by a few simple, ordered rules, all forty-odd formal structures of gamelan music, and a large percentage of the melodic patterns played by the bronze instruments of the gamelan. It is not possible to start with any other homogeneous group of gamelan pieces and derive, with simple rules, so much of the gamelan repertoire (Becker, in press: Appendix 1).

A repeated two-note descending contour is the most frequent contour, sometimes the only contour, found in archaic gamelan pieces. The concatenations of this contour, the transpositions of this contour, and simple derivations from it constitute what can be called *melodies.* Yet it seems clear that the original purpose of pitch differentiation in gamelan music was not related to strictly musical considerations, such as melody and rhythm, but rather to the marking of cycle subdivisions.[4]

*Monggang* is acknowledged to be one of the oldest pieces in the gamelan repertoire. Legend has it that it was given to the Javanese people by the god Shiva (Batara Guru), and it is the only piece played on an archaic ensemble of the same name. The piece consists entirely of a repeated two-note descending contour with a third, higher note inserted between each of the notes of the basic two-note contour. We will call the lowest pitch *pitch 1,* the next higher pitch *pitch 2,* and the third highest pitch *pitch 3.* There are only three pitches on a Monggang gamelan. If the piece is mapped onto a circle, pitch 1 marks the whole cycle (gongan) and the first subdivision of the cycle. Pitch 2 marks the second subdivision of the cycle, the one-quarter and three-quarter points of the cycle. Pitch 3 marks the third subdivision of the cycle, or the one-eighth, three-eighths, five-eighths, and seven-eighths points of the cycle (see Figure 5).

Another archaic ensemble which shares its name with the only piece played upon it is the gamelan Kodok Ngorek. Also like the gamelan Monggang, the gamelan Kodok Ngorek has only three different pitches. With only three pitches one might think it was possible to mark only three levels of subdivision, as in *Monggang,* unless one of the levels is deleted or marked by silence. The only melodic/formal difference between the piece *Monggang* and the piece *Kodok*

---

[4]Pitch differentiation in gamelan music as a function of the marking of cycle subdivisions was first suggested to me by my student, Stanley Hoffman.

(gong)

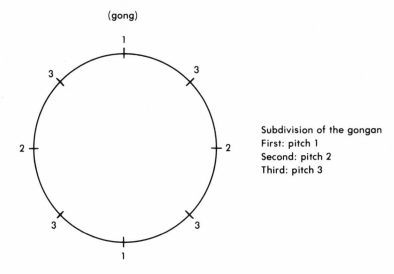

Subdivision of the gongan
First: pitch 1
Second: pitch 2
Third: pitch 3

The melody of the first and second subdivisions is:

2  1  2  1  or:

With the insertion of a third subdivision, the melody becomes:

(3) 2 (3) 1 (3) 2 (3) 1 or:

**Figure 5**

[5]The five tones of the *slendro* system are arbitrarily represented on the western five-line staff as follows:

1  2  3  5  6  1

All examples in this article are in the *slendro* tuning system.

The dotted bar lines used in the transcriptions mark off the contour units or the groups of contour units. The note following the dotted bar line is not a downbeat or stress of any kind. On the contrary, the basic stress unit of Javanese gamelan music is a two-level stress unit with the primary stress on the second of a two-note group, i.e.,

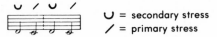

∪ = secondary stress
╱ = primary stress

This stress is not manifested by an accent or a more forceful attack on the second of a two-note grouping, but rather by the fact that more instruments coincide on the second note. The two-level stress unit is called *ding-dong* by Javanese musicians.

**205**

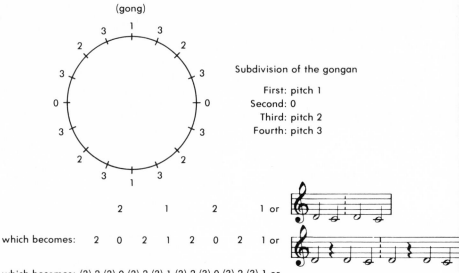

Figure 6

*Ngorek* is the deletion of the marker of the second subdivision in *Kodok Ngorek* which allows a fourth subdivision to be added (see Figure 6).

The same principles manifest in these old pieces of creating melodies by cycle subdivision continue to operate for many centuries. The pieces *Ladrang Agun-agun* and *Ladrang Diradameta* are centuries younger than *Monggang* and *Kodok Ngorek,* but they are still very old. A guess would be that they were played before 1500 A.D. (All the pieces mentioned in this article are still being played today along with many more recent pieces.) The circle mapping of *Ladrang Agun-agun* reveals that in the first section of the piece (circle 1), pitch 2 marks the whole cycle and the first subdivision, pitch 3 marks the second subdivision, or the one-quarter and three-quarter points. Pitch 6 marks the third subdivision, etc. Although the pitches which mark the subdivisions in the second section of the piece (circle 2) differ from those of the first section, the principle is exactly the same (see Figure 7).

The same process recurs in the piece *Ladrang Diradameta* (see Figure 8).

The generation of more complicated contours which occurred throughout the centuries of gamelan playing have largely obscured the basis of pitch differentiation as a redundant marker of cycle subdivision level. Furthermore, the addition to the gamelan ensemble of a host of vocal forms and vocally oriented

Ladrang Agun-agun

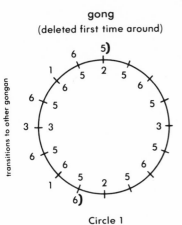

gong
(deleted first time around)

Circle 1

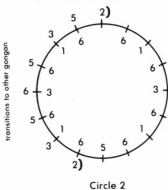

gong
(deleted first time around)

Circle 2

Subdivisions of the first and second gongan (circle 1 and circle 2)

First gongan

First: pitch 2
Second: pitch 3
Third: pitch 6
Fourth: pitch 5

Second gongan

First: pitch 5
Second: pitch 3
Third: pitch 1
Fourth: pitch 6

```
              3     2     3     2              3       5       3       5
becomes:  6   3  6  2  6  3  6  2          1   3   1   5   1   3   1   5
becomes: 5 6 5 3 5 6 5 2 5 6 5 3 5 6 5 2   6 1 6 3 6 1 6 5 6 1 6 3 6 1 6 5
```

or:

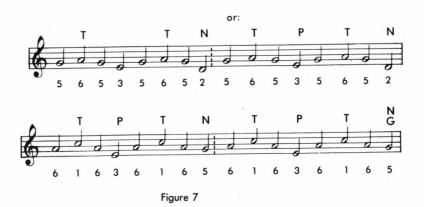

Figure 7

[6]For a discussion of the theory of deleted gong markers in Javanese gamelan pieces see Becker (in press: Appendix 1).

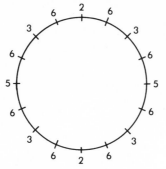

gong
(deleted first time around)

Subdivision of the gongan

First: pitch 2
Second: pitch 5
Third: pitch 3
Fourth: pitch 6

|  | 3 | | 2 | | 3 | | 2 |
|---|---|---|---|---|---|---|---|
| becomes: | 3 5 | 3 | 2 | 3 5 | 3 | 2 |
| becomes:[7] | 6 3 6 5 6 3 6 2 6 3 6 5 6 3 6 2 | | | | | | |

or:

6 3 6 5 6 3 6 2 6 3 6 5 6 3 6 2

Figure 8

instruments has further obscured the original contours of the archaic ensembles and their archaic repertoire. Archaic pieces, however, continue to be played as part of the contemporary repertoire, particularly in theater music and for special festivities such as wedding ceremonies. In addition, many archaic pieces are played in modern style, with all the vocal parts and vocally oriented instruments added. While listening to archaic pieces played in modern gamelan style it is sometimes difficult, but still possible, to perceive the archaic contours beneath the highly elaborated and differentiated acoustic signal. The partial score given below (Figure 9) illustrates an archaic piece (*Ketawang Subakastawa*, Figure 3), in modern guise.[8]

[7]All the pieces described before *Ladrang Diradameta* exemplify the "spreading" process whereby two notes become farther apart to accommodate an added subdivision, i.e., 3    2 becomes __ 3 __ 2, which becomes __ __ __ 3 __ __ __ 2.

Another process, nearly as common as that described above, puts the two-note, original, descending contour at the end of the four-note contour after the "next" subdivision, i.e., 3    2 becomes __ __ 3 2. Then the process reverts to the more usual "spreading" technique for subsequent subdivisions, i.e., 3    2 becomes x y 3 2 becomes __ x __ y __ 3 __ 2.

[8]Other examples of archaic pieces played in modern style are the *umpak* sections of *Ketawang Larasmoyo* and *Ketawang Boyong Basuki,* and *Ladrang Sriwibawa,* as well as many *Lancaran* Irama II and *Ayak-ayakan* Irama II.

## Ketawang Subakastawa

### (Only half of cycle represented in staff notation)

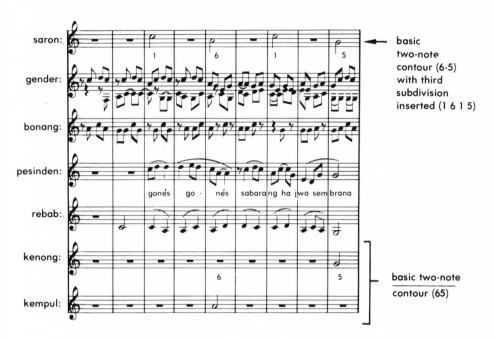

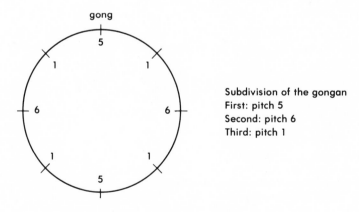

Figure 9

I am not here proposing a linear evolutionary model, but rather describing the development of a single genre, music for bronze gong ensembles played in Java. Few scholars today believe in inevitable, linear development in the direction of complexity, but I believe that a genre can become more complex over time (as well as become more simple over time if a tradition is neglected or if a reverse trend should gain momentum). The evidence indicates that the bronze gong ensembles of Java are an instance in which a more complex musical style has developed over the centuries.

In conclusion, in the gamelan tradition, melody or tune was originally the result of a process of subdivision applied to a concept of cyclical time. Neither cycles nor subdivisions are necessary elements of a music system. In other cultures or societies where cycles, their subdivisions and their coincidences are not so highly valued, one would expect music to derive from processes very different from those described earlier. If music systems are studied in isolation apart from the cultural environment in which they are supported and to which they lend support, a great deal of the meaning of the music is certain to be obscured. Musical thought is indivisible from the thought processes and cultural concepts of the people who produce the music and the people for whom it is played. The implied meanings, the structural meanings, the relational meanings of a music system are often subliminal and difficult to unravel or uncover whether from within a culture or from outside. If, however, we wish to understand music and music-making as a world-wide phenomenon, as a species-specific phenomenon, and as a culture-bound phenomenon, we must accept this challenge.

## REFERENCES

Becker, Judith. *Traditional music in modern Java.* Honolulu: University of Hawaii Press, in press.
Blacking, John. *Process and product in human society.* Johannesburg: Witwatersrand University Press, 1970.
Geertz, Clifford. *The religion of Java.* New York: The Free Press, 1960.
Geertz, Clifford. Person, time, and conduct in Bali. In Clifford Geertz, *The interpretation of cultures.* New York: Basic Books, 1973.
Kartodirdjo, Sartono. *Tjatatan tentang segi-segi messianist dalam Sedjarah Indonesia.* Gajah Mada: Yogyakarta, 1959.
Seeger, Charles. Preface to the description of a music. *International society for musical research,* 5th Congress report, 1952.
Soebardi. Calendrical traditions in Indonesia. *Madjalah Ilmu-ilmu Sastra Indonesia,* 1965, *III,* 1, March, 49–61.
Van der Kroef, Justus M. Dualism and symbolic antithesis in Indonesian society. *American anthropologist,* 1954, *56,* 847–862.

chapter twelve

# Text-Building, Epistemology, and Aesthetics in Javanese Shadow Theatre

A.L. Becker

University of Michigan

> If aesthetics is ever to be more than a speculative play, of the genus philosophical, it will have to get down to the very arduous business of studying the concrete process of artistic production and appreciation.
>
> —Edward Sapir

## INTRODUCTION: SPEAKING THE PAST AND SPEAKING THE PRESENT

In this essay I would like to describe some of the constraints on text-building in a language quite different from our own. The language is Javanese, the kind of text the Javanese shadow play, *wayang kulit,* as I learned to perform it from an East Javanese puppeteer, or *dalang*, Ki Soedjathi Djathikoesoemo, in daily lessons and in watching performances and discussing them together over a period of two years, 1969–71. My goal there was not to become a dalang myself—though that was necessary in order to discover what *not* to do—but to discover how to build a text in Javanese, to explore what text-building revealed about Javanese epistemology, and to learn how to respond aesthetically to a very different artistic medium. I have studied these things and shall describe them within a particular, evolving set of assumptions about what a text is and how it can be said to be meaningful. These assumptions have their roots in traditional philology, modified and expanded by the insights of modern linguistics, ethnography, psychology, and Javanese aesthetic theory itself into what might be called a *modern philology*. These assumptions form a partial epistemography[1]—a specification of

---

[1] I owe this term, and much of my understanding of it, to Vern Carroll.

211

*what* it is important to write about concerning Javanese shadow theater, and how one achieves coherence and completeness in writing about it.

As an intellectual discipline, *philology* can be defined as the text-centered study of language. Philologists have traditionally set themselves the task of making ancient and foreign texts readable. Only part of this task is simple translation, since any careful philologist knows that few foreign words have translations. Words and phrases must be described, often in great detail, not merely mapped onto a foreign term. This description traditionally takes the form of masses of footnotes which explain the contextual relations of words, phrases, sentences, and larger units of the text. These relations ideally include the following:

1. The relations of textual units to each other within the text, which establishes hierarchy and coherence in the text.
2. The relations of textual units to other texts, since part of the context of any text is, more or less, all previous texts in a particular culture, especially texts considered to be in the same genre; readable literature is structurally coherent with its own ancestors.
3. The relations of the units in the text to the intention of the creators of the text, with *intention* defined as the relations of the creator to the content of the text, the medium, and to the hearers or readers.
4. The relation of textual units to nonliterary events with which units in the text establish relations of the sort usually called *reference*.

The *meaning* of a text, then, is a set of relations, by no means all of which are listed above. The information necessary to describe the kinds of relations just listed must be known, discovered, or reconstructed before one can know the essential meaning of a text, any text. For contemporary English works—except for the most esoteric or specialized literature—contextual relations have been presumed not to require philological explication for English-speaking readers. However, texts whose contexts (or epistemologies) are distant from the best-trained readers require philological notes as an essential foundation for interpretation. In a multi-cultured world, a world of multiple epistemologies, there is need for a new philologist—a specialist in contextual relations—in all areas of knowledge in which text-building (written or oral) is a central activity: literature, history, law, music, politics, psychology, trade, even war and peace.

The specific activity of the philologist is contextualizing conceptually distant texts. For many philologists in the past that was the only goal, an annotated edition of a written or oral text. Some philologists, however, in the course of this activity and based upon it, have sought generalizations about the major constraints on text-building itself, the laws of grammar, poetics, narration, etc. Nowadays philology has been partitioned and distributed among various specialists. In the study of literature, there has developed a gulf between those who study particular texts (especially written texts) and those who study constraints[2] on the activity of creating texts: the former is usually part of the humanities (literary scholarship), the latter a science (linguistics).

In the study of texts, however, these two activities correct each other, since any meaningful activity is a conjunction of preexisting constraints (or rules, or structures, or laws, or myths) with the present, the unpredictable, particular *now*. In this way a text always—but to varying degrees—contextualizes the present in the past.[3]

One can roughly specify for any language activity the degree to which the speaker/writer is speaking the past or the present. Repeating is almost entirely speaking the past, whether it be repeating something said a moment ago, or written a millenium ago—a repeated remark, a prayer, a song. Yet in these activities there is always something of the present, some variable of the communicative act which is free to express the *now*, be it only the voice quality of the speaker, the variations of tempo and pitch and resonance that express the repeater's attitude about what he is repeating. Furthermore, each repetition of a text (or bit of a text) is in a new context and takes new meaning from its context. One can

[2]I am using the term *constraint* here in a special way which may puzzle some readers. The basic notion is from information theory. It is given wider relevance in Gregory Bateson's essay, Cybernetic explanation (1972:399–410). There Bateson uses the term *restraints*. I use the term *constraints* since it is current in linguistics and appears perfectly compatible with Bateson's term. The linguistic term first appeared to me in the work of John R. Ross and George Lakoff, where linguistic variables were not subject to rules but constraints with differing scope and force. Bateson writes (p. 399): "In cybernetic language, the course of events is said to be subject to *restraints,* and it is assumed that, apart from such restraints, the pathways of change would be governed only by equality of probability. In fact, the 'restraints' upon which cybernetic explanation depends can in all cases be regarded as factors which determine inequality of probability." Later, "Restraints of many different kinds may combine to generate this unique determination. For example, the selection of a piece for a given position in a jigsaw puzzle is 'restrained' by many factors. Its shape must conform to that of its several neighbors and possibly that of the boundary of the puzzle; its color must conform to the color pattern of its region; the orientation of its edges must obey the topological regularities set by the cutting machine in which the puzzle was made; and so on. From the point of view of the man who is trying to solve the puzzle, these are all clues, i.e., sources of information which will guide him in his selection. From the point of view of the cybernetic observer, they are *restraints*" (p. 400). In a text, or any unit of artistic expression, "constraints" are different in different languages and in different cultures. That is, the area of significant variation is not the same in all languages, in all cultures, but it can be discovered by finding what the constraints on the text are, which is what this essay endeavors to do for *wayang*.

[3]The notion of speaking the present and speaking the past came to me from Maurice Bloch. Speaking the past is a particular kind of speech act or mode of communication, which Bloch defines for the Merina of Madagascar, who themselves describe certain ritual speech making as "speaking the words of the ancestors" (Bloch, 1974). Bloch is wrong, I think, in contrasting formalized speech acts and everyday speech acts, on a scale of most to least formalized language. Everyday speech acts are also highly formalized. I feel that the poles of this scale range from repetition (most formal, speaking the past) to imagination or internal discourse (least formal, speaking the present), and I argue that neither pole is ultimately attainable. For an early view of wayang as "speaking the words of the ancestors," see W. H. Rassers (1959).

never wholly speak the past.[4] Even in those ritual repetitions when we speak the past as intently as possible in a kind of temporary trance, there is always something of the present communicated.

Likewise, one can never wholly speak the present. Even everyday language is highly conventional, far more constrained than we normally recognize. Consider how small talk varies from language to language in both content and form. Most conversations begin with repeated conventional content which is not meant to be discussed truthfully (i.e., in the present): How are you? (English); Where are you going? (Javanese); Have you eaten yet? (Burmese), etc. At this point in a conversation relationships are being established, between speaker and hearer first, then between speaker and other—the people or things referred to. Some conversations never get beyond this stage, and the pace at which one moves conversationally from the conventional, predictable past to the present varies widely from language to language.

Notice that language, in these instances and always, communicates on at least two levels, the actual surface content of the message (the proposition being asserted, requested, questioned, etc.) and the relational statements that are conveyed simultaneously, more often by intonation, posture, facial expression, and the like, than by direct statement. This relational communication has been called *metacommunication* by Gregory Bateson and others—communication about relationships, about the context of the message.[5] Hence in speaking the past, in prayer or small talk, too, we are communicating our relations to the hearer and the people or things referred to in the lexically expressed message. Ritual language speaks the past on the surface, but conveys the present at the metalinguistic level.[6]

How, then, does one most fully express the present? Only by decreasing the redundancy (the predictability) at either the lexical level of the message (L) or at the metalinguistic level (Lm), or at both. In short, by spontaneity. *Completely* spontaneous linguistic activity is impossible. Rather, other people could not understand it—or even recognize it as language: the uncompromising position of the schizophrenic, the lonely alienated poet, and the foreign language learner. As Wittgenstein put the paradox: "if lions could talk, we couldn't understand them."[7] One can increase, however, the spontaneous, the *here and now* in communication. One way is to speak directly what is in your mind right at the time you are speaking, speak right from what Ernest Becker calls the "inner

[4]The implications of this notion are explored in Jorge Luis Borges' short story, "Pierre Menard, author of Don Quixote" (1962). Menard, by coping Cervantes' novel word for word in the twentieth century (i.e., by changing the context of the text act), produces a very different work. (Brought to my attention by Susan Walton.)

[5]A similar, multi-channeled view of language has been developed by Kenneth L. Pike, see especially (1963).

[6]This is most apparent in trance communication and hypnosis. The latter is described in these terms in Jay Haley, How hypnotist and subject maneuver each other (1963:20–40).

[7]The quotation—and the idea behind it—were presents from Shelly Errington.

newsreel,'' the impressions, observations, musing, and rehearsing of embarrassing moments in the past or yet to come which constantly occupy the idling, otherwise not preoccupied mind, the background noise of living—an area of linguistic activity studied at present mostly by Freudians and Buddhists (E. Becker, 1962:77–79; Lacan, 1973; Waldo, 1975). We might revive an old term and call this the *imagination*. Many (e.g., Croce, Sapir, Freud, Lacan, Ernest Becker, Emile Benveniste) have argued that the imagination is an aspect of language, or at least "structured like a language" (Croce, 1970; Lacan, 1973; Benveniste, 1971; Wilden, 1972:29). It is obvious to us all that we *imagine* constantly, waking or sleeping, yet it is very difficult to get at our imagining and examine it, and it takes considerable skill and confidence or wildness or naivete to brush aside enough of the conventional to speak from the imagination. Literary conventions create situations in which it is possible.

All language activity, including literature, involves, then, variation between spontaneity (present) and repetition (past) and communicates on at least two levels, the lexically expressed message (L) and the relational message (Lm). Of course the lexically expressed message may be about the relationship, in which case a new relational communication is conveyed, leading, if repeated, to the sorts of linguistic involutions exposed by R. D. Laing (1970).

Various forms of indirect speech complicate the act of communication further by at least doubling every variable. Take a statement like the following:

"'You sound nervous,' she said, ironically."

This statement involves at least two speakers ("she" and the writer), two hearers ("you" and the reader), *two lexical communications* ("You sound nervous" and " 'You sound nervous' she said, ironically") and at least *four metacommunications* ("she" relating to "you"; "she" relating to the statement "you sound nervous"; the writer relating to the reader, pointing out the irony; and the writer relating to his statement: does the irony refer to "she" or to the whole statement, or, was she ironic or is the writer being ironic?). The writer here is speaking the past or only pretending to speak the past (it may be either fiction or reporting—or fiction disguised as reporting—present disguised as past—or vice versa). The ambiguous term *ironically* may be a comment from the present in which the writer is writing, or a reported fact about "she." If "she" is being intentionally ironic, then "her" statement is probably not a spontaneous remark to "you" but perhaps a repeating of something said to her by "you" ("You" may have told "she" she sounded nervous a few days before, and "she" is now ironically repeating the remark back to "you"). Fuller context is necessary to resolve *some* of the ambiguities; others are resolvable only in the imagination of the reader. As complex as this seems, all these relations and many more are necessarily part of the understanding of the statement.

To summarize, then, the analysis of a text requires, minimally, that the modern philologist describe several kinds of relations in order to recreate a conceptually distant context. A minimal set of these relations includes:

1. The relation of words, phrases, sentences, and larger units of the text to each other (i.e., the coherence of the text),
2. The relation of this text to other texts; the extent that it is repetition or new (speaking the present or the past),
3. The relation of the author to both the text and the hearers/readers of the text—seen from the point of view of the author or from the points of view of the hearers/readers (i.e., the intent of the text-builder),
4. The relation of units in the text to nonliterary events (i.e., reference).

Context, then, includes coherence, degree of repetition/spontaneity, intent, and reference. Sorting out the *sources* of constraints on all these relations is a further task for the modern philologist: to what extent are the constraints on these relations human (i.e., universal to all texts)? Or are they operative only within a single language family or cultural tradition, or within a single language, or only in a specific genre, or only in the works of one author? Any work is constrained at all these levels.

The methodology of this essay will be to describe, in the order just stated, the various sorts of relations a particular kind of text, the Javanese shadow play, has with its context. I have been able to isolate some of the generic constraints on contextual relations, and some of these above the generic, particularly at the level of the Javanese language itself. By implication, too, I reveal something of that area of variation constrained only by the individual performer (the dalang) in a particular place and time (A. Becker, 1974; Young, Becker, and Pike, 1971).

## TEXTUAL COHERENCE IN A WAYANG:
## PLOT AS SYMBOLIC ACTION

Textual coherence can be examined at any level of structure in the hierarchy of structures that make up the text. One might examine the structure and categories of words in a wayang, isolating the special vocabulary and distinctive phonology of the language of the puppeteer (basa padalangan). At the level of sentences, and across sentences, there are kinds of coherence unexploited in most Western languages, coherence based not on tense (which is the basis of Western narrative coherence) but upon a system of person (in its grammatical sense) elaborated far beyond similar systems in other languages. I have described this system elsewhere in relation to Old Javanese (Kawi) literature (A. Becker and Oka, 1976; Zurbuchen, 1976). These are constraints which are used in building many other kinds of Javanese texts as well. Here I would like to focus on a higher-level system of constraints, a level intermediate between the usual sentential (i.e., sentence-based) concerns of the linguist and the global concerns of the literary scholar, the level of plot.

The plot of a story or a play is a set of constraints on the selection and sequencing of dramatic episodes or motifs.[8] These constraints are like the rules of a game, say tennis, which constrain the selection of possible acts in the game (i.e., defining illegal acts) and the arrangement of acts in the game (i.e., defining what may not be done at certain times within the context of the game). Plots, like tennis rules, do not allow one to predict—except in very general terms—what will happen in a play. Rather, plots tell us what cannot be done appropriately. They also, like scientific theories, tell us one other important thing; what the relevant variables are in the things one can do in the play. There is no rule in tennis against scratching my head as much as I want to in the course of a game. There is a rule, however, against serving with my feet across the base line. Head-scratching is, by implication, an irrelevant variable, but foot-faulting is a constraint on position: it tells me where I may not stand, not where I must stand. Likewise, a set of constraints on a plot specifies what areas of variation are particularly relevant and what are insignificant. If I may borrow from a closely related medium, music, we may note that melodic variation is highly relevant to some kinds of Western music, but rather insignificant in some kinds of Javanese music.[9] An American who is looking for melodic variation in gamelan music will be bored; a Javanese looking for dense musical texture in a symphony will also be bored. Likewise in drama, an American who seeks character development in wayang is going to be disappointed in all but a very few wayang stories, and a Javanese who seeks complex coincidences in all but a few American movies (those few being comedies, like the Marx Brothers' *Animal Crackers*) is also going to be disappointed. Plot (i.e., constraints on the selection and arrangement of dramatic episodes) includes constraints on the *kinds* of variation that are relevant.

For the most part, in most cultures, knowledge of plot constraints is un-stated background knowledge, like the knowledge of grammar and syntax. It is learned indirectly, first through fairy tales and nursery rhymes (and their equivalents in other cultures), and then from the various media that have access to children. Some Greeks, however, were self-conscious about plots. Aristotle's *Poetics* includes a description of plot which still holds for most Western drama and narrative.[10]

Aristotle calls plot *fable*: "The imitation of the action is the fable," he writes. "By fable I now mean the contexture of incidents, or the plot." He lists the six major variables in a drama:

1. fable or plot,
2. manners or character,

---

[8]The notion of a text as a selection and ordering of motifs (or motives) is derived ultimately, from V. Propp (1958) and Kenneth Burke (1969).

[9]This point is supported and illustrated in Judith Becker, Time and tune in Java, in this volume.

[10]The text used here is Aristotle's *Politics and poetics,* translated by Jowett and Twining (1969), especially book 2, ch. I–IX and book 4, ch. VI.

3. diction or metrical composition,
4. sentiments or speeches,
5. decoration,
6. music.

Aristotle continues, "Of all these parts the most important is the combination of incidents or the fable." Fable or plot is most important because it imitates what Aristotle held was the most important referential content of the drama, action (or imitation of action).

Among the constraints on plot which Aristotle lists are the following. Note that they are all phrased negatively—i.e., as constraints.

1. A proper fable must not be incomplete: "The poet who would construct his fable properly is not at liberty to begin and end where he pleases. . . ." A fable should, he explains, suppose nothing to precede it, and require nothing to follow it (book 2, chapter IV). Completeness here is completeness of linear (i.e., temporal) causality, a powerful constraint on selection *and* arrangement.
2. Coincidences are to be avoided. Sequences should follow as probable and necessary consequences. Nothing improbable should be admitted, or, if necessary, it should arise out of the fable. Perhaps Aristotle's most famous comment on plot makes just this point: "Impossibilities, rendered probable, are preferable to improbable, though possible" (book 2, chapter VI; book 4, chapter VI).
3. No part of a proper fable may be transposed or omitted without destroying the whole. Anything that can be left out, should be (book 2, chapter V). Again there is emphasis on linear (temporal-causal) sequence.
4. The time in the text should not be more than a single day (book 1, chapter IX).

These basic constraints all have to do with unity and causality, above all with temporal unity and linear causality—two aspects of the same thing. All of them are rooted in the simple fact that intersentence coherence in Indo-European languages is achieved primarily by *tense*. Clarity and coherence *means* to speakers of these languages linear temporal/causal sequencing. Tense is seen as iconic: that is, past, present, and future are taken as facts about the world, rather than facts about language. Tense is not iconic in all language-cultures and hence temporal-causal linearity is not the major constraint on textual coherence in all languages.[11]

[11]The notion of iconicity is derived from Kenneth Boulding (1961), a basic text in the study of comparative epistemography. The centrality of tense in establishing textual coherence in English narrative is demonstrated in William Labov, Transformation of experience in narrative syntax (1972).

What I call the *narrative presupposition* is the presupposition in English (and other, but not all, languages) that in two succeeding clauses with past tense verbs, unless otherwise marked, the events referred to happened in the same order as the clauses. That is, the sentences, "The man looked at the clock. He sat down." mean, in part, that the man looked at the clock before he sat down, although this order is presupposed, not *marked* in the structure of these sentences. In many languages (e.g., Old Javanese, Burmese) this presupposition does not hold and narrative order is a *marked* strategy. This is an example of a basic linguistic difference in languages which affects text-building strategy. These basic differences usually concern iconic linguistic facts, facts assumed by native speakers to be about the nature of the world, not about the nature of language. For a discussion of non-Western iconic facts, see A. L. Becker (1975).

The linearity of Aristotle's constraints can be stated in another way. If meaning comes from temporal-causal sequences, then epistemologies do not, and cannot, change from episode to episode, or, as stated in a recent study of plot,

> Semantically standard universes always have consistency in the interpretation of several connected ambiguous episodes. (Hahn, 1973:8)

That is, Jay Gatsby, Godzilla, Agamemnon, John Wayne, and Charlie Chaplin do not and may not appear in the same plot.

What emerges in the episodes of Western serious drama are the disambiguating causes of actions. These causes are at base represented as character defects, often minor ones. The episodes lead to a catastrophe and a climax, a reversal of expectations, all of which leads on to the end of the causal chain.

Nearly all these constraints are violated by wayang plot structure. It is not that wayang plots may not have temporal unity, causal linear sequences, catastrophes, reversals and all the rest. These do appear in wayang plots, particularly in those plots most admired by Western viewers, such as the plot of *Dewa Ruci,* a linear search for the water of immortality, or the plot of the simplified and shortened versions of the Ramayana, a search for a stolen wife. These Aristotelian constraints, however, are not *necessary* to a good wayang plot, and to focus on, for instance, causal sequences and character development is to miss the area of relevant variation in wayang theater and to miss the subtlety and depth of good wayang.

Wayang plots are built primarily around coincidence, a word which we in the West use to explain away things of no meaning. "A mere coincidence" cannot, in the West, sustain prolonged scrutiny and analysis. In wayang theater coincidence motivates actions. There is no causal reason that Arjuna, the frail wayang hero, meets Cakil, a small demon, in the forest, as he (or a counterpart) does in each wayang. It is a coincidence; it happens (jadi), and because they are who they are, they fight and Cakil dies, but not forever; he will be killed over and over again in each wayang. When Arjuna and Cakil meet, two worlds, two epistemologies coincide for a moment, Cakil is purely physical. He attacks Arjuna because Arjuna makes him uncomfortable. Arjuna's meditation has raised the heat of the forest higher than the creatures who live there can bear. Cakil responds instinctively to this thermal pollution. On the other hand, Arjuna attacks Cakil because he recognizes him as evil (i.e., other), not because of anything he has done, but because he knows—by thought, not instinct—that it is his duty (dharma) to combat evil. He kills coolly, dispassionately, the passionate Cakil, who is defending his forest home against the intruder. Arjuna controls nature by killing it, but it renews itself again and again. There are other interpretations of this motif. Not every observer of wayang will agree with this interpretation of it. It does seem evident, however, that Arjuna and Cakil live in different conceptual worlds and that their meeting is not caused but is rather an accident, a coincidence of these worlds. Nothing in the prior events of the text nor in the succeeding events made it a necessary part of the plot in Aristotle's terms. Yet this motif is necessary (obligatory) within the constraints of wayang plot.

This is but one coincidence, one intersection in the interwoven, cyclic actions that inform a wayang plot—unmotivated, unresolved, meaningless within a chain of causes and effects, but symbolically very rich.

The name for a wayang plot derives from the root *laku* "step or act" plus the suffix *-an,* which normalizes the root, giving us, by vowel sandhi, *lakon* "an action, a way, an event, a plot." A lakon includes three major divisions, within each of which a certain range of voice pitches and a valuing of particular pitches is maintained, and within each of which there is a prescribed internal structure. These divisions, called *pathet,* include combinations of scenes called *jejer* (audience scenes, before a ruler or holy man), *adegan* (scenes outside the audience hall, e.g., *adegan wana* "forest adegan," *adegan gapuran* "gate adegan," *adegan gara-gara* "turmoil adegan," etc.), and *perang* (battle). The meanings of these names for the parts of a wayang are richly metaphoric. Understanding them as words helps to contextualize them within the Javanese semantic world. *Jejer* also means "what exists," "the subject of a sentence," and "the handle of a kris," as well as "an audience before the King." *Adegan,* the scenes outside the audience hall, means also, "propped up," "standing," "door-frame" and "the punctuation of a sentence" (two vertical, parallel lines). The linguistic metaphors suggest a paradigmatic, associational link between sentences and plays, within whose structures experience is shaped and expressed.[12]

A wayang plot, then, is built hierarchically in structures made up of three basic units. A lakon (event) is divided into three *pathetan* or acts, each with the same internal structure. Each *pathet* is made of three basic scenes: (1) the *jejer* (static audience in a court or a hermitage where a problem arises and a plan is formed); followed by (2) two or more *adegan* derived from that audience, and always involving a journey away from the audience place; (3) a *perang* (battle) at the end of the journey.

Each scene, in turn, has three basic components: (1) description of a situation (either *janturan* "description of a place" or *carios* "description of prior action"); (2) dialogue (ginem); (3) action (sabetan). The *minimal* structure of a play—or an event is:

---

[12]These Javanese terms are partially described in Probohardjono (1966) currently being translated from the Javanese by Susan Walton (J. Becker, ed., forthcoming). The conceptualization of a sentence as a drama, with actors, agents, scenes, actions, etc., suggests that traditional Javanese philologists shared a metaphor, at least, with modern linguists (e.g., Pike's Tagmemics, Fillmore's Case Grammar) and literary critics (e.g., Kenneth Burke's dramatism).

LAKON (EVENT)

Pathet Nem      Pathet Sanga      Pathet Manjura

Jejar   Adegan   Perang    Jejer   Adegan   Perang    Jejer   Adegan   Perang
/ | \    / | \     / | \      / | \    / | \    / | \      / | \    / | \    / | \
1 2 3    1 2 3    1 2 3     1 2 3    1 2 3    1 2 3     1 2 3    1 2 3    1 2 3

(Key: 1 = description, 2 = dialogue, 3 = action or motion)

Any given wayang allows for three basic operations on this minimal structure: permutation (reordering units below the level of *pathet*), conjunction (repeating units below *pathet*), and embedding (putting units within units below the level of *pathet*). Pathet structure was fixed in the tradition I studied.[13]

The only permutation regularly evident is in Pathet Sanga, within which the *adegan gara-gara* "turmoil scene" (a clown scene during the world turmoil created by the power of the meditation of the hero) *may* precede the *jejer* (the *jejer pertapan* "meditation audience" or *jejer pandita* "audience with a holy man, usually Abiasa"). This inversion is perhaps constrained by dramatic rhythm, particularly impatience among the viewers for the clown scene.

Conjunction may be the repeating of a scene or a whole sequence. That is, there may be more than one *adegan*, or *perang*, or the whole sequence *jejer* + *adegan* + *perang* may be repeated. *Jejer* are not repeated unless the whole sequence is repeated. In the first *pathet* (act), called *Pathet Nem*, there are frequently, not always, two or three complete sequences, though each succeeding sequence is shorter in time and complexity than the one preceding it. Seldom does this occur in the other two *pathet*. There are often up to three *adegan* in a sequence, however, and two *perang*. This may occur anywhere in the play. This derived structure might look like the following:

*Jejer* + *adegan* + *adegan* + *adegan* + *perang* + *perang*. These different *adegan* and *perang* are given special names, as are the various *jejer*, and the contents of each is constrained by its place in the entire *lakon*. In the repertoire of a puppeteer are at least the following scenes:

[13]*Pathet* in music means something slightly different, closer to our notion of mode. See Probohardjono (1966), translated by S. Walton, in J. Becker (forthcoming). In a wayang performance, music from the final *pathet (manjura)* is played before the play begins, creating a cyclic musical structure, since it is the first and last mode one hears. This musical redundancy is not reflected in the foregoing representation of *lakon* structure.

221

## A Basic Repertoire of Scenes

### 1. Kinds of Jejer (Audience Scene):

| | |
|---|---|
| jejer kraton | "palace jejer" |
| jejer sabrangan | "foreign jejer" |
| jejer sabrangan rangkep | "second foreign jejer" |
| jejer pertapan | "jejer before a meditating person" |
| jejer pandita | "jejer before a holy man" |
| jejer tancep kayon | "closing scene in which the Tree of Life (kayon) is stabbed (tanceb) into the banana log with the other puppets arranged around it." |

### 2. Kinds of Adegan (Outside Scene):

| | |
|---|---|
| Adegan gapuran | "gate adegan" |
| adegan kedatonan | "inner-palace adegan" |
| adegan paseban jawi | "outer court adegan" |
| adegan kareta | "choriot adegan, i.e., assembling the army" |
| adegan gara-gara | "turmoil adegan" |
| adegan wana | "forest adegan" |
| etc. | |

### 3. Kinds of Perang (Battle):

| | |
|---|---|
| perang ampyak | "gang rumble" |
| perang gagal | "unsuccessful battle" |
| perang simpangan | "crossroads battle" |
| perang kembang | "flower battle, i.e., forest battle between small, refined hero and small demon" |
| perang gridan | "slow-motion, very refined battle" |
| perang tanggung | "middle battle" |
| perang tandang | "everyone-rallies-together battle" |
| perang amuk | "wild, frenzied battle" |

Each of these scenes involves certain kinds of characters and characteristic choreography. One could not present a shadow play without knowing how to do these basic scenes, though the list is not by any means exhaustive. Individual dalangs may invent additional scenes (usually scenes involving newly invented demons, one of the most common areas of innovation over the past three hundred years) and are frequently known for the kinds of scenes they do best. For instance, a dalang may be famous for his monkey battles, for his adegan gara-gara (clown scenes) or for the depth and pathos of his meditation scenes (adegan pertapan).

Within any given scene (jejer, adegan, or perang) the structure is, as stated: (1) description, (2) dialogue, (3) action. There are two kinds of dialogue, *janturan,* the description of a place and the people there, and *carios,* the description of a prior action. Only the *janturan* is accompanied by music. After the description, one or more suluk (described later) are sung and the dialogue begins. When the mood changes or a new character enters, other *suluk* are sung. Finally the dialogue ends and an action occurs, a movement of the puppets—e.g., a journey or a battle (there is different music for each, *srepegan* for journeys, *srepegan* or *sampak* for battles). All of this follows specific rules for the speech and movement of each different puppet, and for each puppet in relation to each other puppet.[14]

The suluks—sung poetic passages in Old Javanese—are of three kinds: *pathetan* (descriptive verses, accompanied by several instruments, including the rebab, gender, gambang, and suling); *sendon* (lyric emotional verses, accompanied only by a few instruments, usually gender, suling, and gambang); and *ada-ada*—verses which build excitement, accompanied by gender, and the knocking of a small mallet against the puppet box or a set of metal plates— (Probohardjono, 1966, in J. Becker, forthcoming). There are, in turn, three possible versions of pathetan and ada-ada: a short version (jugag), a long version (agung), and a normal version (wantah). The pitch center or mode of the suluks changes (i.e., gets higher in pitch) in each succeeding pathet (nem, sanga, manyura).

Within scenes, as well as between them, there are variations in structure; however, no permutation is possible in scenes, and conjoining is rare. Embedding is the common practice. For instance, during the dialogue of a scene, a new character may enter, in which case there will be an embedded description + dialogue + action, after which we return to the previously interrupted dialogue. This produces structures of the following type:

*Scene/Adegan*

Description (with suluk) + Dialogue [description (suluk)
+ dialogue + action] + Dialogue (continued) + Action

Here the bracketed sequence is an embedded scene.

As night goes on, different parts of the scenes are foregrounded, that is, some parts are shortened, others prolonged. In the first act (pathet nem) description usually takes more time than dialogue and action combined. In the second act, dialogue—mostly jokes, but also very heavy spiritual instruction from a holy man—is foregrounded. In the third and final act (pathet manyura), action—usually battle—predominates. When one part of a scene is dominant, however, the other two always appear, albeit often briefly.

One may notice that in describing the structure of a dramatic event, the words used are all Javanese not Sanskrit. Though stories are often imported into wayang, chiefly from Sanskrit epics, plots appear to be uniquely Javanese.

Having seen something of the sequencing of events or motifs in a wayang play, let us turn now to the paradigm of events themselves and the kinds of coherence that appear within the structure that has been described. It is often very difficult for the viewer, foreign or Javanese, to know just where he is in the story

[14]These rules are described in numerous handbooks for dalangs. Among the more complete ones are Nojowirongko (1960) and Sajid (1958). There are also numerous *pakem* (scenarios) for individual plays. See James Brandon (1970) for an English translation of one of the best of these, which combines a handbook and *pakem*, the *Serat Tuntunan Padalangan*.

being presented, i.e., in knowing that polarities between protagonists and antagonists are being established. One always knows, however, where one is in the plot—the structure defined earlier. The story may be very obscure, much of the action may take place off the screen or be assumed by the dalang to be well known, and there may be all sorts of loose ends left after the plot cycle has finished. It is primarly the clowns who try to tell the audience what is happening. Certainly little of the *motivation* for action appears in the plot. The clowns, using modern language, modern ideas, and modern behavior, step among the heroes and demons and gods like wideawake men in a dream world. They bring the present into the story (i.e., they always speak the present), and with the paradox of forethought, contextualize the present within the tradition, changing both, as usually seems to happen when epistemologies are allowed to coincide.

In the coincidence of epistemologies, as just noted, the real subtlety of wayang appears. The major epistemologies are (1) that of the demons, the direct sensual epistemology of raw nature, (2) that of the ancestor heroes, the stratified, feudal epistemology of traditional Java, (3) that of the ancient gods, a distant cosmological epistemology of pure power, (4) that of the clowns, a modern, pragmatic epistemology of personal survival. All these epistemologies coexist in a single wayang, and others may be added (most usually the epistemology of the Islamic saints, that of the modern military, or that of some strange foreign land where one of the clowns goes to be king, like Gulliver among the Lilliputians). Between each of these epistemologies there may be—and usually is—a confrontation and a *perang,* a battle. No one ever wins conclusively, but rather a proper balance is restored. Each epistemology, each category of being, exists within a different concept of time, and all the times occur simultaneously. That is, nature time, ancestor time, god time, and the present are all equally relevant in an event, though for each the scope of an event is different. Throughout the wayang, each is kept distinct, even in language (which will be discussed later). The constraints on wayang plot sustain the notion of multiple time and multiple epistemology.

The differences with the Aristotelian notion of plot should now be apparent. What in the wayang plot are significant coincidences, in the Aristotelian plot are crudities, violations of the basic notions of unity and causality. In wayang, we might say that Gatsby, Godzilla, Agamemnon, John Wayne, and Charlie Chaplin—or their counterparts—do appear in the same plot, and that is what causes the excitement; that clash of conceptual universes is what impels the action.

As far as I know, the wayang tradition has no Aristotle, no one who has attempted to articulate the set of constraints which underlie the tradition. I cannot, as an outsider, do this with any depth or hope of adequacy. I am not even sure that in Javanese eyes it is worth doing, but the symmetry of this essay, the plot we are caught within at this moment, seems to demand it. A wayang plot, then, seems to be constrained in the following ways, all stated *by contrast* to Aristotelian constraints.

1. A wayang plot can begin at any point in a story. It has no temporal beginning, middle, or end. Indeed, a wayang plot is very similar to a piece of traditional Javanese music, in which a musical pattern is expanded from within, producing layer upon layer of pattern moving at different times.

   A wayang plot, however, must begin and end in certain *places;* it cannot begin and end anywhere, though it can begin and end anytime. It must also pass through a certain place in the middle. Thus wayang plot has a spatial, rather than temporal, beginning, middle, and end. It must begin and end in a court, the first the court of the antagonists, the last the court of the protagonists (to use the Greek *agon* terminology, which seems appropriate here). The middle section must be in nature, usually in the forest on a mountain, but sometimes, too, in or beside the sea. It is movement out and back, a trip. This structure may well reflect the origin of wayang as an instrument of communication with the dead via trance (Rassers, 1959).

   Like an Aristotelian plot, a wayang must not be incomplete, but incompleteness is not temporal or causal, but rather spatial.

2. Coincidences, far from being avoided, impel action, for they induce cognitive puzzles or paradoxes. Coincidences are the way things happen, and the way communication between unlikes occurs. In Javanese and Indonesian, the word used to describe what we call a coincidence (a causeless interaction) is *kebetulan* (or *kebenaran*), literally a "truth" (an abstract noun derived from the adjective *betul/benar* meaning "true"). There are many related terms (e.g., *dadi* "happen, become," *cocok* "come together, fit") which make up a semantic set used to describe events none of which imply linear causality. Likewise, a piece of music is structured by the coincidence of gongs occurring together, and a holy day by the coincidence of simultaneous calendrical cycles.[15]

3. Any scene in a wayang plot may be transposed or omitted, except for the constraint that the plot begin in a court, have its center in nature, and return to the court. Transpositions and omissions of story material do not destroy or even change the whole. Almost anything can be left out or brought in.

   When something is brought in, however, it must follow the paradigmatic and syntagmatic constraints of the *lakon* structure described above. This structure defines an event (lakon) as made of three acts (pathetan), which we can now on the basis of the spatial constraint just discussed call the *pathet* of the antagonists (because the first scene is located in the antagonists' court, the antagonists dominate the action and win the battles), the *pathet* in nature, the *pathet* of the protagonists (because the final scene is located in the protagonists' court and the protagonists dominate the action and win the battles). Each act, in turn, is made up of three scenes (jejer, adegan, perang), which may be permuted and conjoined in limited ways. Each scene, in its turn, is made up of three parts (description, dialogue, and action) and scenes are frequently embedded one within another. There are further constraints on the sets of characters (demons,

---

[15]For a description of time reckoning in Bali (and traditional Java) see Clifford Geertz, Person, time, and conduct in Bali (1973). See also Soebardi (1965). These structural principles are applied to the description of music in Judith Becker, Time and tune in Java, in this volume.

heroes, gods, clowns) in relation to one another (e.g., how they speak and how they move) which will be described later. All of this makes up what might be called the *grammar* of a wayang plot.

4. Aristotle suggests that the time of a serious drama should not be more than a single day. He meant the time enacted within the plot on stage, not the whole story. Here is his most stringent constraint on temporal unity, one not always followed by Western playwrights but rather held as an ideal, even by such modern American dramatists as O'Neill, Miller, or Albee. Indeed, it may be one of the reasons for identifying these as good, serious playwrights in the Western tradition.

The *time* enacted within wayang is unconstrained, except that it must be multiple. Coincidences are timeless. But, the *performance* time of a wayang is *symbolically* a single day. It is necessary to explain this rather strange phenomenon. The division of scenes is marked by a large image of a tree (or a mountain) called a *kayon* (or *gunungan*). During the play, which is usually performed at night, the *kayon* marks the imaginary progression of the sun from east to west by the angle at which it is set against the screen (which is properly set up on an east-west axis, or if necessary, north-south, in which case north substitutes for east).[16] The kayon is a dramatic clock which marks only the progression of the *plot,* not the times in the story or the time on the wrist watches of the viewers.

These are but a few of the features which define the coherence of a wayang plot, particularly those few which contrast most sharply with Aristotle, whose writings about plot well define the unconscious constraints on plot that most of us in the West have absorbed since childhood. I now turn from discussion of the structure or coherence of a wayang to consideration of the relations of the text with its context, from inner to outer relations, with a full awareness that there is much more to be said, particularly at more technically linguistic levels of focus, about Javanese textual coherence in general, and wayang coherence in particular.

## TEXT WITHIN TEXT: THE JAVANESE ART OF INVENTION

The distinction between story and plot is very important in studying the structure and development of a wayang text. The *plot* has been defined as a set of constraints on the selecting and ordering of episodes or motifs. The story is a prior text, fictitious or factual or both, which is the source of these episodes or motifs; it is a prior text to some degree known by the audience. Literature, in this sense, is mostly about prior literature. For example, in our own tradition any cowboy movie tells the story of the past more in the sense that it repeats episodes and characters of previous cowboy movies and novels than that it recounts "real" events that occurred in the American West. The "truth" of a cowboy movie is much more a matter of its correspondence with a mythology (a body of prior

---

[16]For a description of the Old Javanese-Balinese semiotics of space, see C. Hooykaas (1974). I am indebted also to unpublished work on the five directions by Patricia Henry.

literature) than with any events recognizable by nonfiction cowboys in their own experiences.[17]

Wayang has reference to a mythology accessible to us in Old Javanese or Sanskrit literature, primarily the two great epics, the Ramayana and the Mahabharata. Javanese, of course, have access to this mythology in many less literary ways: in names of people and places, in other theatrical performances and oral literature, in comics, in the very language itself (Resink, 1975; Anderson, 1965; Emmerson, forthcoming). A wayang plot, however, *need* not draw on this mythology, though it almost always does. That is, a dalang may well turn to Islamic or Christian or autocthonous Javanese mythology, wholly or in part, as a source of the motifs and characters for his performance, and he can do so without violating any of the plot constraints discussed earlier.

The story, whatever its source, provides *content* and *context* for the plot. To introduce Arjuna, the hero of the Mahabharata, as a character into a particular plot establishes as a context for that particular plot all the prior texts (mythology), oral or written, related to Arjuna. Arjuna has done certain things, relates in certain ways to other characters, and is associated with many details of appearance, dress, behavior, speech, etc., which have been established in prior texts (Anderson, 1965; Hardjowirogo, 1968; Kats, 1923).

What happens to Arjuna in a particular plot may either repeat episodes from prior texts or it may be new, although consistent with prior texts. The new creation fills in more details of the growing text or mythology related to Arjuna, new episodes in his life, only hinted at previously, or a return to the world by Arjuna across time, into, for instance, an ancient Javanese court. The Arjuna mythology (or Rama mythology, or Hanuman mythology, etc.) is a living expanding text in Java. Two examples of this sort of text expansion may help to make this process of invention clearer.

During the Indonesian national elections in 1971, one dalang who supported the incumbent military government created a wayang in which Krishna, when he realizes that he must direct the Pandawa armies (the armies of Arjuna and his brothers Yudistira, Biam, Nakula, Sadewa, and their allies), in the great war of the Bharata, seeks out the old clown-servant Semar. Krishna asks Semar what he should do and how he should behave as a military leader. Then, in the center of the play, in the forest, Semar instructs Krishna in his duty, the common man in an era of democracy instructing the ruler. The text for these instructions was the *Sapta Marga*, the official Code of Behavior for modern Indonesian soldiers. This brilliant new story, *Bagawan Ismojo Sandi*, conceived by Ki Hari Puribadi, very deftly contextualizes past in present and present in past simultaneously; the Sapta Marga is sanctified as a modern Bhagavad Gita, and the ancient mythology is given rich current relevance.

---

[17]This sense of mythology is explored in Roland Barthes (1972), particularly in the final essay "Myth today," in which Barthes writes, "Mythical speech is made of a material which has *already* been worked on so as to make it suitable for communication" (p. 110).

Another kind of invention involves no overt innovation at all, but rather lets the audience infer the connection with current events. This second example was performed in 1971, too, but this time by a dalang opposed to the military government, a supporter of the PNI, the political party associated with former President Soekarno. This dalang performed the old text nearly without change, except that the clowns did say they were volunteer workers at the PNI party headquarters and made several jokes about campaign activities on a day-to-day level. The story was *Kangsa Adu Jago,* a traditional Sanskrit story of a powerful villain (Kangsa/Kamsa) who usurps Krishna's kingdom and drives Krishna into the forest. Krishna seeks the aid of his cousins, the Pandawas, particularly Bima, in defeating and driving out the powerful Kangsa. No one missed the political statement.

It is interesting to note that in those national elections the most powerful public statements against the government were made by dalangs, using just this technique. Every other medium of communication, including other forms of theater, was noncritical. It is also interesting that two sides, the government and the PNI, recognized the same mythological context; the difference lay in whether Krishna represented the modern Ksatria or the deposed king.

One of the most important differences between traditional artistic expression and modern individualistic artistic expression is that in a traditional medium the artist is consciously expanding a prior text, an open corpus of literature, art, or music, whereas an artist whose intent is self-expression creates and develops his own text, his own mythology, so far as he can and still communicate. When an artist can no longer work within the inherited mythology and plot constraints, he seeks new mythology and constraints, often from his own imagination, and he works in alienation from his own society. This same distinction appears to have been made by Levi-Strauss, this time in distinguishing the shaman and the psychoanalyst:

> . . . the shamanistic cure seems to be the exact counterpart to the psychoanalytic cure, but with an inversion of all the elements. Both cures aim at inducing an experience, and both succeed by recreating a myth which the patient has to live or relive. But in one case, the patient constructs an individual myth with elements drawn from his past; in the other case, the patient receives from the outside a social myth which does not correspond to a former personal state. To prepare for the abreaction, which then becomes an "adreaction," the psychoanalyst listens, whereas the shaman speaks. Better still: When a transference is established, the patient puts words into the mouth of the psychoanalyst by attributing to him alleged feelings and intentions; in the incantation, the shaman speaks for his patient (Lévi-Strauss, 1963).[18]

No dalang is in this sense a modern artist (or psychoanalyst). It is as if he were performing a new act of Hamlet, or relating a new episode from the Gospels, working on an expanding text which extends through space and time far

[18]This passage was brought to my attention by Shelley Errington.

beyond his own imagination. In this kind of traditional creation, the skill of the dalang is revealed in his ability to recreate the past, which he must do at the beginning of each wayang and at certain points throughout the performance, most particularly in singing short descriptive passages from Old Javanese (Kawi) texts. Here he speaks directly *to* the past of his own culture in words almost entirely unintelligible to the dalang or his audience.

These suluk occur at dramatic transitions in the plot, at any point where there is a descriptive passage (one of the three requisite components of a scene, description + dialogue + movement). The content of these Old Javanese quotations is usually unrelated in any easily discernible a priori way to the particular plot, except that the dalang can substitute relevant names, if he wishes. A bit of another story is recited, and it coincides mysteriously with the evolving plot, linking old text with new. Here is part of the first suluk in most performances:

> Leng leng ramyanikang, sasangka kumenyar, O. . . .
> Mangrengga rumning puri, O. . . .
> Mangkin tanpa siring, halep ikang, umah,
> Mas lwir murub ring langit, O. . . .
> Tekwam sarwa manik, O. . . .
> Tawingnya sinawung, O. . . . , O. . . .
> Saksat sekarning suji, unggwan Bhanuwati, O. . . .
> Ywan amrem alangen, mwang Nata Duryuddana, O. . . .
> Mwang Nata Duryuddana, O. . . .

Very few dalangs are aware of the erotic nature of this quotation from section V, verse 1 of the Old Javanese *Bharatayuddha,* composed in Kediri (Daha) by Mpu Seddah in approximately 1157. Krishna has come to the palace of the Kaurawas, enemies of the Pandawas, in order to try to avert war; at least on the surface that is what is happening. After the initial audience with Krishna, King Duryuddana retires to the inner palace. It is early night, and the moon has risen. Then comes the passage quoted:

> Beautiful was the moon that shone over the palace where the women lived. More and more it grew golden, an incomparable golden house against the sky. And so too its curtain of gems, like flowers on an embroidered fabric. And here was the chamber of Queen Bhanuwati where she slept with King Duryuddana. . . .

Here prior text is being quoted directly, the history of the genre is being displayed, and the Javanese art of invention exemplified. One must interpret the actions of the present in the mysterious context of this scantily understood passage.

The art of invention for the dalang, working within the plot constraints of his medium, involves selection of motifs and characters from the body of mythology he believes in. This is not unlike the Aristotelian art of invention, which was primarily the selection of quotations and ideas from the classics—a kind of information retrieval—in order to interpret the present (Young and A. Becker, 1966).

A political change in Indonesia can be reflected in wayang as a change in mythology, as it has been described in the penetrating studies of Donald Emmerson (forthcoming), and Benedict Anderson (1965), and G. J. Resink (1975). One generation of heroes may replace another, or one set of gods may replace another, as was the case in a village wayang I saw in Lombok in which the Hindu gods were the villains who were defeated by Moslem heroes. This is, however, essentially new wine in old bottles, or what we might call *surface change*. Deep change, in terms of this essay, would be change in the plot, change in the constraints on selecting and ordering the characters and motifs. Deep change would be change in the Javanese conception of time and event, change of epistemology.[19]

## INTENTIONALITY IN A TEXT: THE USES OF TEXTURE

One of the first things a dalang learns is that not everyone will respond to a wayang in the same way. There is no assumption that everyone will be interested in the same things at the same time; someone will always be dozing. The setting for a wayang is noncompulsive, more like a Western sports event than serious theater. It is not shameful or embarrassing to sleep through what someone else is enjoying. Jokes, philosophy, action, poetic language, each has different appeal to different people, depending on their own mental makeup, which is often described in a way parallel to the Indian theory of rasa and guna (Coomaraswamy, 1957), a theory parallel, in turn, to the archaic theory of humors in the West. One responds according to his makeup. There can be no single, intended correct response to a play, no one complete interpretation. This multiplicity of events and perspectives builds the kind of thick texture that Javanese favor. As an old man responded when asked why he liked wayang,[20] "Asalnya ramai!" ("Above all because it is bustling/complex/busy/beautiful!") *Ramai* < Old Javanese *ramia* < Sanskrit *ramya* "pleasing, beautiful." Notice the semantic change in Java from "beautiful" to "beautiful because bustling and complex." Sanskrit words, like Sanskrit stories, are recontextualized in Java.

Within the variety of responses—too thick to be untangled here—there are always two separate audiences at every wayang, an essential audience, without whom the play is pointless, and a nonessential audience, who may or may not be present and who in some sense overhear much of the drama. It is the nonessential audience that we have described so far, the various people who have various responses to a noncompulsive event, which is noncompulsive precisely because they are the nonessential audience.

The essential audience of a wayang is normally unseen: spirits, demons and

---

[19]Ironically, most attempts to "preserve" traditional drama require deep change. This "irony" is discussed in A. L. Becker (1974).

[20]Reported to me by Patricia Henry, personal communication from Malang, East Java.

creatures, gods, and ancestors. To whom does the dalang speak in Old Javanese and Sanskrit if not to those who understand these languages, which are unintelligible to the nonessential audience? Archaic language is not merely embellishment or mystification, else it would have been lost long ago. Rather it is essential language addressed to the essential audience, the ancients, the dead. All drama, as we have noted, speaks from the past, the unseen sources of power which are the widest context of the play.

The first words of a wayang—prior even to the *lakon* itself—are uttered softly to unseen hearers, "prayers" or mantra to the sources of power. Before the puppeteer arrives at the place of performance he establishes relations with this wider spiritual context, including his own, nonhuman brothers (kanda empat) who guard and extend his senses and provide buffers in an unpredictable, often hostile environment (Hooykaas, 1974).

There are several prayers uttered by the dalang between his home and the place of performance, all seeking safety and support. The words of these prayers are not repeated exactly each time, but they are highly constrained variants of the Javanese-Sanskrit phrase which begins literary works:

Awighnam Astu "Be there no hindrance."

This initial phrase of a wayang text is called the *manggala* in Old Javanese (Kawi) written literature. A *manggala* is anything—word, god, or person—which has the power to support the poet. The *manggala* is invoked, praised, and then relied upon to sustain the poet/dalang in his effort. Here is a point of choice, then, for the puppeteer, who is likely to turn his mind to several sources of support. For the dalang, unlike the poet in the kakawin (poetic literature of the Old Javanese period), it is a private act, invoking the widest context of the shadow play, the earth, the light, the wind, the mountains.

The language of the manggala-prayers is usually a single expanded sentence which includes a descriptive subject and an imperative predicate. The sentence is preceded by the original syllable, *Om,* which establishes the parameters of all language sounds, in Sanskrit linguistics. In structure, the *manggala* is very similar to a Vedic hymn:

Om. O' (insert name of the *manggala* and phrases describing him/her/it) + Imperative predicate.

For example, as he adjusts the lamp (kerosene or oil), the dalang may softly say:

Om. Be there no hindrance. God of spirit, center of all, God of light—let the flame of this lamp illumine the world.

The phrases of the prayer linguistically are parallel. All prayers follow the general pattern just given, except that the phase "Be there no hindrance" is not always stated. The language is a blend of Sanskrit and Javanese, the subject in Sanskrit (the language of the gods, the remote past), and the predicate in modern

Javanese (the language of the himself, the immediate present). The words bridge past and present, and must be uttered with full attention.[21]

Perhaps here is the place to note an extraordinary fact about the language of the wayang, a fact of great importance in understanding what is happening at any given moment. A wayang includes within it, in each performance, the entire history of the literary language, from Old Javanese, pre-Hindu incantation and mythology to the era of the Sanskrit gods and their language, blending with Javanese in the works of ancient poets (the suluks), adding Arabic and Colonial elements, changing with the power of Java to new locations and dialects, up to the present Bahasa Indonesia and even a bit of American English (in which one clown often instructs another). I do not just mean here what might be said of English, that it reflects its history in vocabulary, syntax, and phonological variation. That is also true of modern Javanese. The difference is that in the shadow play, the language of each of these different eras is separate in function from the others; certain *voices* speak only one or the other of these languages and dialects, and they are continually kept almost entirely separate from each other. One could even say that the content of the wayang is the languages of the past and the present, a means for contextualizing the past in the present, and the present in the past, hence preserving the expanding text that is the culture. I shall point out these different kinds of language as they appear, though we have already seen that the prayers (mantra) to the gods and other sources of power use Sanskrit and modern Javanese, the *suluk* use Old Javanese (Kawi), and the clowns use all modern languages, Javanese, Indonesian, Dutch, English, Japanese, French, neatly reflecting the context of modern Indonesia. Clowns speak the older languages only to mock them.

Like the manggala-prayers, the *suluk* speak to the ancients (not the gods but the Javanese ancestors) in their own language at the beginning of each scene. In many cases the chanted *suluk* are addressed to the individual characters represented by the puppets in the wayang. Like Vedic hymns they invoke the character in his own language by a kind of word magic, in which to state a thing properly and effectively, even without intent (as in a casual Brahmin's curse, which cannot be revoked), is to effect power in the world, bridging time and space.

It is here that wayang becomes an education in power. Wayang teaches men about their widest, most complete context, and it is itself the most effective way to learn about that context. There has been much written about the mystical communication in wayang, and its details are best left to Javanese themselves to write about. For us in the West it might be called *trance-communication*. The dalang is above all a man who can be "entered," a "medium," though to use our own terminology is to invoke all the wrong associations. *Trance speaking* can be defined as communication in which one of the variables of the speech act

---

[21]These mantra are being translated by Susan Walton and will appear in J. Becker (Ed.), in press. Some of the mantra also appear in Hooykaas (1973).

(I am speaking to you about $x$ at time $y$ in place $z$ with intent $a$) is denied, most frequently the variable $I$ is paradoxically both speaking and not speaking, or speaking involuntarily or nonintentionally. Trance is a kind of incongruence between statement and intent (I/not I am speaking to you/not you. . . .), and covers a wide spectrum of linguistic experiences, from the minor trance of singing the national anthem—or any song you *believe*—to the major trance of hypnosis and schizophrenia (Haley, 1963).

In any case, it is as trance communication as a means of relationship with an unseen, essential audience that wayang can be linked to the Barong drama of Bali, the autochthonous trance ritual of the other islands (e.g., the ma'bugi in Sulawesi),[22] and the use of puppets and dolls as spirit media throughout Southeast Asia.

What is the use of communication with the ancients, besides preserving the text of the culture, which is probably not a primary goal but a constant effect of this communication? Two uses are implied in the instruction books for the dalang: to exorcise danger or potential danger, and to contextualize the present in the past. There are many well-known myths about the origin of wayang as a way of subduing or at least calming down dangerous power, the power of Siva amuck or the power of his demon son Kala (time) who formerly dealt out death indiscriminately.[23]

How does wayang *control* power gone amuck, madness, demons, disease, and stupidity? By nature all these are sources of chain-reacting, linear power,

[22]The ma'bugi trance ritual of Sulawesi has been beautifully filmed by Eric Crystal in *Ma'bugi: Trance of the Toraja.*

[23]Versions of this myth appear in Sastroamidjojo (1964:142–163), Rassers (1959), and Holt (1967). The basic source is the Tantu Panggelaran, written during the latter days of Majapahit. Claire Holt translates the text as follows:

> As for Lord Guru, never before was he seized by wrath, now however, he was overcome with fury; therefore, he cursed himself and became a *raksasa* [giant]. Then the Lord Guru took on the shape of a *raksasa* with three eyes and four arms; since then he has been called Kala-Rudra. All the gods were stunned, as was the whole world, when they perceived the shape of the Lord Kala-Rudra who was bent on devouring everything on earth.
>
> Directly, Icwara, Brahma, and Wisnu tried to prevent Lord Kala-Rudra from devouring the world; they descended to earth and played *wayang;* they told about the true nature of the Lord and the Lady (his consort) on earth. They had a *panggung* [an elevated place] and a *kelir* [screen]; their *wayangs* were carved out of leather and were extolled in beautiful *panjangs.* The Lord Icwara was the *udipan* [*dalang?*], Brahma and Wisnu protected him. They wandered about the earth, making music and playing *wayang,* since then there exists the *bandaginahawayang;* thus was the origin according to the old tale.
>
> Another means of defense by the Lords Icwara, Brahma, and Wisnu against the Lord Kala was they went about the earth and sought out Lord Kala who, pale-faced, agitated, moved around his *bale* [pavilion], . . . . Icwara became *sori,* Brahma became *pederat,* Wisnu *tekes;* they went around singing songs *(mangidung)* and playing *(hamenamen);* since then there has been the *bandaginamen* men.

which accelerates by repeating more and more of the same. Someone who is amuck kills and kills *without intent* until he in turn is killed. Likewise disease and madness feeds upon itself. The closest answer to the question of how wayang subdues power gone amuck came to me from a Balinese friend, who answered, "You know, it's like the doors in Bali." (NOTE: an entrance in Bali and traditional Java is backed by a flat wall or screen (Javanese *wrana*) a few feet behind the entrance gap in the outer wall, so that one cannot go straight in but must pass right or left. Demons and people possessed or amuck move in straight lines, not in curves like normal human beings.) My friend continued, after I looked mystified, "The demons can't get in. The music and shadow play move round and round and keep the demons out." Then he paused and laughed heartily, and added, "As you might say, demons think in straight lines!"

Clearly, from this point of view, it is not the story or the archaic words or the puppets but the whole thing, the *texture* itself, the maze of relations, that is most important. The structure of the medium itself subdues power gone amuck, inducing paradox and coincidence, anathema to those who think in straight lines.[24]

In summary, then, the dalang speaks as himself and as the past through himself to an unseen, essential audience and to the immediate, nonessential audience, each containing a wide variety of perspectives on the action being performed. And he is playing with fire. If, for the immediate audience, the event is noncompulsive, for him, it is powerfully compulsive. Once begun, he may not for any reason (illness, storm, violence, power failure) stop until the play has finished. Hence, he must be careful not to begin anything he cannot end.[25]

## REFERENCE: ON LANGUAGE AND THINGS OF THIS WORLD

The first sentence of Hardjowirogo's *Sedjarah Wajang Purwa* (*History of Traditional Shadow Theater*, 1968), like the book itself a subtle blend of Javanese and Indonesian, sets the perspective of the book: "Wajang purwa adalah sebagai

---

[24]The term for this texture is *ruwat*, which is often translated as "liberation," but it is "liberation" in the sense that Br'er Rabbit is "liberated" from Br'er Fox within the safety of his tangled briar patch. Wayang is a kind of conceptual briar patch. The active verbal form for *ruwat* is *ngruwat*, the term used for performing a shadow play in order to exorcize spirits. *Ruwat* is part of a series *ruwit, ruwed, ruwat*, "little, delicate tangle," "medium-sized tangle or complication," and "large physical or conceptual tangle, or liberation."

The word *ruwat* is rich in folk-etymological associations, due to its phonological associations with *ruwah*, "spirit, soul of the dead" and *(w)ruh* "to see or know." See the following section for discussion of the importance of this etymologizing (Cf. evolution of Sanskrit *ramia*, "beautiful" > Javanese *rame* "complicated, tangled lively").

[25]My teacher tells the story of his first wayang performance in which he insisted on performing a story which was too "heavy" *(berat)* for him. All the oil lamps died mid-performance, so his grandfather pushed him aside and continued the performance, and all the lights came on again.

On Mount Kawi, near Malang, a wayang performance goes on every day and every night, nonstop year round, performing for the essential audience and preserving the spiritual texture, the *ruwatan*.

perlambang kehidupan manusia didunia ini'' (Traditional shadow theater is a signification of the life of man in this world). Part of the statement is that it is our present life as men in this world, not our ancestors in the ancient world, nor a spiritual world, nor an imaginary literary world, but this world that *wayang* signifies. To understand how that can be so is to understand the referential meaning of wayang, the relation of the text to the present-day non-wayang world. This aspect of the meaning of wayang is both the easiest and the most difficult to describe. It is easy because interpreting the present relevance of shadow theater is a ubiquitous kind of discourse, oral and written, in Java; hence there are countless examples of wayang hermeneutics. It is difficult because the linguistics of wayang commentary—the constraints on it as a language activity or speech art—are as yet unexamined. And it is difficult, too, because there are major epistemological differences in the way people of different cultures relate language to nonlinguistic phenomena. That is, we all too frequently apply our own current Western assumptions about how linguistic reference works— particularly how reference works in *fictional* literature—to a non-Western text. A study of the way a wayang text relates to "this world" ought to begin, then, with a study of *how* words are thought to refer in Javanese. Once again, as with Aristotle and the notion of plot, the strategy will be to begin with some features of the dominant Western notion of reference and then try to show how wayang epistemology differs.

In the dominant Western notion of reference (the one assumed in introductory and popular books about linguistics), there are three categories which can be labeled roughly *words* (language), *thoughts* (or concepts), and *things* (objects in the sensible world). These are assumed to be separable (though slightly overlapping) categories of being, since concepts appear to be stateable in different languages, and there appear to be different, unrelated names for the same things in different languages. The relations of language to concepts and things are therefore felt to be fundamentally arbitrary. If anything, natural language gets in the way of clearly seeing things as they *are* (Bacon's "idols of the market"), and gets in the way of clear, logical thought (based as it is for us now on measurable identities and differences). Thinkers in the West tend to give priority to concepts or things and treat language as a "tool" to be shaped to our ends, or discarded and replaced. Not for many centuries in the West (until recently in the works of Foucault and Lacan and with the development of modern linguistics) has language itself been given priority as a source of highly valued knowledge.

Opposed to this notion of the arbitrary nature of reference is one familiar in American thought in the work of Emerson, particularly in his essay "Language." In this earlier view, the relation of words, thoughts, and things is not arbitrary, though it has been confused by the multiplicity of languages. The laws of Nature govern thoughts, words, and things alike. Emerson could, therefore, make his essay "Language" a subsection of his larger work, *Nature. Signified* and *signifier* are constrained by the same laws. To know is to interpret either words or things or concepts. All three—signifier (words), signified (things), and the relations between them (concepts)—offer themselves to men to be deciphered in order to discover the "text" of the world. As Emerson wrote, "The world is emblematic. Parts of speech are metaphors, because the whole of nature is a metaphor of the human mind" (Emerson, 1948:18; A. Becker, 1975).

A favored form of discourse in this epistemology is the commentary or the essay, a decipherment or interpretation of language and nature. In commentary, etymology is an important strategy, not as an attempt to discover the original meaning of words, but rather as an attempt to discover the "intrinsic 'properties' of the letters, syllables, and, finally, whole words." One of the things that strikes us about the text of a Javanese shadow play is the pervasiveness of etymologizing as an explanatory strategy. Javanese call this etymologizing *djarwa dhosok* or "forced" (imposed) interpretation.[26] My own first impulse was to dismiss etymological commentary in wayang as "folk" linguistics, rooted in ignorance about the true history of the words explained, for many of which I knew the Sanskrit etymons. I dismissed etymologizing, in spite of its frequency and obvious importance as a text-building strategy, since it did not give the "true" origin of words. Even more, it appeared to me as an embarrassing and silly aspect of wayang. What I failed to see then was that, since the meanings of words constantly change, etymologies must be reformulated (like genealogies), based upon what one now, in the present, sees as the "intrinsic" meaning of the word under consideration. A brief example: etymology A of the word *history* traces it to French *histoire,* then to Latin *historia* "a narrative of past events" to Greek *istoria* "Learning by inquiry" and back to *istor* "arbiter, judge" and hence back in time to a possible Indo-European root. Etymology B of the same word divides it into "his" and "story," and interprets the elements of the word in the present. "His-story" is also an account of past events, but an account relating primarily to men, with women in a secondary role. Which etymology is correct? It is impossible to answer, for the question is wrong in insisting that we reject one or the other conceptual strategy, etymology A or etymology B. Certainly etymology B tells us more that is relevant and true to current thought than etymology A. In traditional Javanese discourse, including wayang, but also including history and commentary, the strategy we have called *etymology B* is held to be serious and an important part of a text, a basic way of deciphering this world.

Etymologizing of this second sort is known to us, in part, as *explicating,* and the object to be explicated is usually a text clearly recognized as literary or religious or legal, and we have specialists who explicate each of these kinds of text. What they do is relate the words of the text (and the phrases and sentences, etc.) to the current context. Precisely in this sense, though less specialized, the

---

[26]This term was pointed out to me by Susan Walton, who observed that the pervasiveness of etymologizing in Javanese texts is closely related to the high value placed on coincidence. Both are considered nonarbitrary.

dalang relates the old words to the current context. What differentiates the dalang from the explicators of texts in our society is that he explicates primarily proper nouns, names for things, whereas we tend to feel that names are the most arbitrary words of all, given to people and places before they really "are." Etymologizing about names is not unknown in our culture, of course, but it is not particularly highly valued as a way of understanding people and places. What can we know by explaining the name "Detroit," via etymological strategy A or B?

There are two structural points in a lakon when etymologizing, as a text-building strategy, is appropriate: in description or dialogue. (It never occurs in *suluks*, where it is most needed.) Etymologizing is the descriptive part of a scene (either *janturan*, "description of a place," or *carios*, "description of prior action") is done by the dalang directly and it is serious. Etymologizing in a dialogue is done by one of the characters, and may be serious and "academic," if spoken by Krishna or Abiasa, or only half-serious, if spoken by a clown. A major skill in puppetry is the ability to etymologize in all these ways. Let us examine a few instances.

After the mantra and a set musical interlude, the dalang brings out the puppets for the first scene, and begins the description of the first scene of the first *pathet* of the lakon, using fixed phrases:

> Once there was a land. Many are god's creatures that walk the earth or fly the air or swim in the water. Many are the beauties of the world. Yet none can equal those of this land, Manikmantaka (here the name of the particular place in the particular story is inserted). Among a hundred there are not two, among a thousand not ten like Manikmantaka. . . .

Then the dalang describes the kingdom following the strategy of moving from widest physical context to narrowest, from the place of the kingdom among all kingdoms, the mountains around it, the sea, the town itself, the houses, the people, narrowing to a specific person, the king and those about him. All this is set language, though phrases can be left out or reordered slightly. In these passages, the skill of the dalang in controlling the rhythm and pitch contours of his voice in relation to the gamelan is established (or not).[27] In speaking the past almost entirely his legitimacy as a dalang is being proved in one area. At some point in the description, usually as a transition from the description of the kingdom to the description of the king, the dalang begins his first etymology, either on the name of the country or on the name of the king, or both. Here another skill is brought to the foreground, for the etymologies are not set, although one may borrow them from wayang promptbooks called *pakem* (at the risk of being

---

[27]See Gregory Bateson, for further examples (chiefly Balinese) of the role of skill as a basic element in aesthetics: "Style, grace, and information in primitive art." Bateson writes, "Only the violinist who can control the quality of his notes can use variations of that quality for musical purposes." (1972:148).

known, condescendingly, as a "book" dalang).[28] The dalang displays his skill at explication; he must be authoritative and informative. He does not, however, explain words by consulting a dictionary of Sanskrit roots, but interprets the elements of the words as Javanese words:

> The king who ruled this land is called Maha Prabu Niwata Kawaca. And his name means "one who wears armor that may never be pierced" which, in our time, means "one who could not be defeated," for he and all his people believed that, and acted as if that were true. His name is made of three words: Ni, Wata, and Kawaca. Ni or nir is from the word *nirwana.* Nirwana means freedom from desires, freedom from the past, freedom from the future, something which cannot be likened to anything. In other words, the Great God. *Wata* means blind, without vision. Kawata comes from *Kaca,* which means mirror. Hence, his name, Niwatakawaca, means a mirror that is broken, a mirror which has lost its ability to reflect the truth, the Great God. When he was young he was called Nirbito, which comes from Nir and bito. Nir is, as was said, from *Nirwana.* Bito means afraid. For although all feared him, he was himself a coward and turned away from the Great God.

This is a version of the first etymology from the story, Arjuna Wiwaha, as I learned it. Notice that the name is explicated more than once, and that the meaning as a whole ("one who could not be defeated") is not the same as the meaning of the parts ("a mirror blind to nirwana"). Both are true and both, along with the childhood name of the king, tell us about him. If he had other names they would be interpreted here, too. Clearly, words here are not arbitrarily related to people and things.[29]

I do not intend here to go into the ritual and magical potentialities of this language, chiefly because I only very dimly understand them.[30] It is enough to say that the shadow play is a text nonarbitrarily related to the world outside the play, and that explication of the language is a means to cut through the hidden nature of things. The dalang is a skilled explicator, who demonstrates that complexity and obscurity can be unmasked and, hence, provides a model for understanding the world.

Others (Anderson, Resink, Emmerson) have described how the present world looks within this model. Events in Indonesia really are interpreted by some Javanese as lakon, the lakon plot does have psychological reality as a kind of meditation, names of political leaders are taken as revealing character and role, changes in stories or mythologies from which motifs are drawn to parallel social and religious changes. That is, each way that the text relates to its context (see

---

[28]A book dalang is insufficient for most Javanese because he fails to perform one of the important functions of a good dalang, contextualizing (the present in the past, and the past in the present).

[29]Thus foreign borrowings are *information* about nature. Almost all Sanskrit borrowings into Javanese (and Kawi) are nouns, the names for things. Javanese (and others) borrow from Sanskrit (or Arabic or Dutch or English) not primarily to appear elegant and learned—though these are secondary motivations sometimes—but to gain information. See J. Gonda (1973).

[30]There are many difficult Javanese books about the mystical meaning of the language of wayang. For a sample, see Holt (1957), which is a translation of Mangkoenegoro (1973).

the first section) is emblematic of the world and defines a way of interpreting the world, once one believes, knows, or pretends that reference is nonarbitrary.[31]

## CONCLUSION: TOWARD AN AESTHETIC UNDERSTANDING OF COMMUNICATION

The methodology of this essay has been to describe the various sorts of relations a text (or a part of a text, a word, a sentence, a passage, an episode) has with its context. Parts of a text relate to the whole under the constraints of what we called *plot coherence*. The motifs or episodes of a text relate to their source in a cultural mythology under the constraints of invention. The text and its parts relate to the participants in the linguistic act (direct or indirect speaker, direct or indirect hearer, direct or indirect beneficiary, etc.) under the constraints of intentionality. The text and its parts relate to the nontext world under the constraints of what we have called *reference* (either naming or metaphoric reference). In the previous sections of this commentary, these relations have been examined, not in terms of their specific content, but at the more general level of constraints on specific content.

By no means have all the relations of text to context been explored here. The complex grammatical and phonological constraints on wayang language have so far only been hinted at. The semiotics of voice qualities and typologies of dialect and style, for example, relate a character to particular attributes. The dalang learns to reshape his mouth and alter his entire vocal mechanism systemat-

---

[31]That the Javanese view wayang emblematically in this way is supported by frequent allusions in literature and by constant references in conversation. Here is a well-known and frequently quoted example from the Serat Tjentini, translated and explained by Zoetmulder (1971). In a discussion about wayang and its relation to Islam, a Javanese host says,

> The illuminated screen is the visible world. The puppets, which are arranged in an orderly fashion at both edges of the screen at the beginning of the play, are the different varieties and categories created by God. The *gedebog,* the banana trunk into which the dalang sticks his puppets whenever they have no role to fulfill in the play, is the surface of the earth. The *blentjong,* the lamp over the head of the dalang behind the screen, which brings to life the shadows on the other side, is the lamp of life. The *gamelon,* the orchestra which accompanies the play with its motives and melodies fixed in accordance with the various persons and events projected on the screen, represents the harmony and mutual relationship of everything that occurs in the world.

> The creatures, which appear in the world in uncounted numbers and in an astounding variety of forms, may become an obstacle to true insight, impeding understanding of the deeper meaning of all that is created. He who refuses to be led by one who is wiser than he [that is: the uninitiated who is unwilling to put himself under the guidance of a guru] will never see that God is in and behind everything. He is deceived by form and shape. His sight becomes troubled and confused, and he loses himself in a void, while the true significance of the universe remains hidden to him. He goes astray on a path full of obstacles for, lacking the right knowledge, the true meaning of all that appears before his eyes continues to evade him.

ically to distinguish certain characters and types of characters. Pushing the points of the articulation of sounds forward in the mouth suggests refinement and culture, pushing them back toward the throat suggests roughness and raw nature. Between these two extremes is an unmarked area, where characters most like the "us" defined by the dalang speak. Steady, even pitch and rhythm suggest control; wide pitch and rhythm variation suggest impulsiveness, a dimension of character very important to Javanese. It is interesting that gods speak outside the system of evenness versus irregularity; in wayang they have their own semiotics. Nasality is tied to cleverness, and *latah,* a version of the speech pathology echolalia,[32] is related to a wild and powerful inspiration in both gods and men. Each character speaks in a certain way, in a certain range: taken together, the voices of the set of characters reveal the semiotic polarities of Javanese phonological variation.

Nor have the visual constraints, the constraints on the shape and color of the puppets (called *wanda*) and their movements (called *sabetan*) been explored here (Mellema, 1954; Hardjowirogo, 1968). The voice qualities of the puppets are supplemented (or contradicted for humor) by labeled, recognized variations of eye shape, head angle, ornamentation and clothing, stance, arm and body movement, speed, etc. Furthermore, certain puppets and styles of puppets are attributed to particular people in history,[33] and keen observers of wayang can recognize the different *wanda* of, for instance, Siva as *Bartara Guru wanda Karna,* attributed to Senapaten Mataram I in the Javanese year 1541 (A.D. 1619), or *Batara Guru wanda artja,* attributed to Susuhunan Mangkurat in 1578 (A.D. 1656). The fire-haired demon (Kala Dahana) is attributed to Sultan Agung Hanjakrakusuma of Mataram in 1563, and the eggplant demon (Buta Terong) is attributed to Susuhunan Paku Buwana II at Kartasura in 1655. This lore adds further kinds of meaning to the total text, relating it to particular people, places, and things in the history of Java. And beyond sound and vision are the other perceptions of the wayang night, the smells, tastes, and feelings which add further layers of meaning, more and more particular, to the context of the wayang text.

Commentary here approaches closer and closer to the performance itself and the total responsiveness of the ideal, Javanese audience.

The goal of the philologist is to guide outsiders (here non-Javanese) to what might be called an *aesthetic* understanding of a text. To achieve an aesthetic understanding it seems reasonable to say that in interpreting a text, the outsider must be aware of his own differences—particularly those most "natural" to him—and must learn to use new conventions of coherence, invention, intention-

---

[32] See Hildred Geertz (1968), one of the very few explorations of the cultural context of speech pathologies.

[33] Some of these attributions are listed in Sastroamidjojo (1964: 265–273). Attribution is itself an interesting linguistic act. Who attributes what to whom under what circumstances? We attribute texts mostly, whereas Nukuoro attribute some words to certain individuals, as Vern Carroll pointed out to me.

ality, and reference. For an aesthetic response to be possible, a text must appear to be more or less coherent; the mythology it draws upon and presupposes must be more or less known; the conventional intent of the creator or speaker of the text in relation to one's own role as hearer/reader/interpreter must be relatively well understood; even the more basic assumptions about how words relate to thoughts and the things of the world need to be more or less shared. If any of these kinds of meaning is not understood, then one's responses to wayang are either incomplete or contradictory. Never fully to understand and constantly to misunderstand are linguistic pathologies that characterize a wide range of phenomena from the strategic understanding of the schizophrenic to the persistent confusion and uneasiness of one who is learning to use a foreign language; all these pathologies subject one to a world in which language and metalanguage are incoherent, where, to take an extreme case, people say ''I love you'' and at the same time reveal contradictory messages, even ''I hate you,'' in a look or a slap.

The universal source of language pathology is that people appear to say one thing and ''mean'' another. It drives people mad (the closer it gets to home). An aesthetic response is quite simply the opposite of this pathology. It is opposite in the sense that the same constraints are relevant to both, but there is one difference. That is, opposites are things which are in the same class but differ in one feature (Hale, 1974). Schizophrenia, foreign language learning, and artistic expression in language all operate under the same set of linguistic variables, constraints on coherence, invention, intentionality, and reference. The difference is that in madness (and in the temporary madness of learning a new language or a new text) these constraints are misunderstood and often appear contradictory; whereas in an aesthetic response they are understood as a coherent integrated whole. Shadow theater, like any live art, presents a vision of the world and one's place in it which is whole and hale, where meaning is possible. The integration of communication (art) is, hence, as essential to a sane community as clean air, good food, and, to cure errors, medicine. In all its multiplicity of meaning, a well-performed wayang is a vision of sanity.[34]

[34]This essay, taken together with Judith Becker's *Time and Tune,* suggests the possibility of a single set of constraints running through the whole of the traditional Javanese epistemology, in music, calendars, texts, rituals, and social relations. Of course, this unity may be in part the oversimplification of an outsider, but if true, this unity is probably a rather rare situation in a culture, as it is in a person. In both it has great power. The complex of changes we call *modernization* necessarily fragments this unity. Social change alters one by one, and in no particular order, it seems, those relations of a text to its context which constitute its meaning. Modern single time (Greenwich Mean Time, manifest in the modern necessity of life, the wrist watch) thus strongly affects plot coherence by devaluing multiple time. If multiple time is devalued, coincidence ceases to be ''truth'' (kebetulan), and is replaced, usually, by narrative/causal ''truth.'' (In music the strategy of expanding cycles gives way to linear theme and variation.) Likewise the mythology may change and a whole new set of characters and motifs may come into currency. The unseen audience may fade, and trance communication become just entertainment. Words may lose their naturalness and hence etymologizing its purpose. Thus conceptual worlds slowly disappear, just as new ones emerge.

# ACKNOWLEDGMENTS

I wish to acknowledge the important contributions of several people with whom I discussed this essay or parts of it: Gregory Bateson, Judith Becker, Maurice Bloch, Vern Carroll, Soedjathi Djathikoesoemo, Donald Emmerson, Shelly Errington, William Foley, Patricia Henry, Peter Hook, Robin and George Lakoff, James and Susan Matisoff, I Gusti Ngurah Oka, Kenneth Pike, Charles Pyle, Soewojo Wojowasito, Richard Wallis, Susan Walton, Aram Yengoyan, and Mary Zurbuchen.

# REFERENCES

Aristotle. *Politics and poetics* (B. Jowett and T. Twining, trans.). New York: Viking Press, 1969.

Anderson, Benedict R. O'G. *Mythology and the tolerance of the Javanese*. Data Paper No. 27. Ithaca: Cornell University Southeast Asia Program, 1965.

Barthes, Roland. *Mythologies*. New York: Hill and Wang, 1972.

Bateson, Gregory. *Steps to an ecology of mind*. New York: Ballantine, 1972.

Becker, Alton. The journey through the night: Some reflections on Burmese traditional theatre. In Mohd. Taib Osman (Ed.), *Traditional drama and music of southeast Asia*. Kuala Lumpur: Dewan Bahasa dan Pustaka, 1974. (Also in *The drama review*, Winter 1970.)

Becker, Alton L. A linguistic image of nature: The Burmese numerative classifier system. *International Journal of the Sociology of Language*. 1975, *5*, 109–121.

Becker, Alton and I Gusti Ngurah Oka. Person in Kawi: Exploration of an elementary semantic dimension. *Oceanic linguistics*, 1976, *13*, 229–255.

Becker, Ernest. *The birth and death of meaning*. New York: The Free Press, 1962.

Becker, Judith. *Karawitan: Source readings in Javanese music*. Center for South and Southeast Asian Studies, University of Michigan, forthcoming.

Benveniste, Emile, Ch. 6: Categories of thought and language. Ch. 7: Remarks on the function of language in Freudian theory. In *Problems in general linguistics*. Coral Gables, Florida: University of Miami Press, 1971.

Bloch, Maurice. Symbols, song, dance, and features of articulation. *European journal of sociology*, 1974, *XV*, 58.

Borges, J. L. *Ficciones*. New York: Grove Press, 1962.

Boulding, Kenneth. *The image*. Ann Arbor: University of Michigan Press, 1961.

Brandon, James (Ed.). *On thrones of gold: Three Javanese shadow plays*. Cambridge, Mass.: Harvard University Press, 1970.

Burke, Kenneth. *A grammar of motives*. Berkeley: University of California Press, 1969.

Coomaraswamy, A. K. Hindu view of art: Theory of beauty. In *The dance of Shiva*. New York: Noonday Press, 1957.

Croce, Benedetto. Ch. XVIII: Identity of linguistic and aesthetic. In *Aesthetic: As science of expression and general linguistic* (D. Ainslie, trans.). New York: Farrar, Strauss and Giroux, 1970.

Crystal, Eric. *Ma'bugi: Trance of the Toraja*. 16 mm. film, 22 min., color. Private collection.

Emerson, R. W. *Nature*. New York: Liberal Arts Press, 1948.

Emmerson, Donald. The Ramayana syndrome. Forthcoming.

Geertz, Clifford. *The interpretation of culture*. New York: Basic Books, 1973.

Geertz, Hildred. Latah in Java: A theoretical paradox. *Indonesia*, April 1968, 93–104.

Gonda, J. *Sanskrit in Indonesia* (2nd ed.). Sata-Pitaka Series, vol. 92. New Delhi: International Academy of Indian Culture, 1973.

Hahn, Edward. Finite-state models of plot complexity. *Poetics: International review for the theory of literature*, 1973, *8*.

Hale, Kenneth. A note on a Walbiri tradition of autonymy. In D. D. Steinberg and L. A. Jakobovits (Eds.), *Semantics: An interdisciplinary reader in philosophy, linguistics, and psychology*. New York: Cambridge University Press, 1974.

Haley, Jay. *Strategies of psychotherapy*. New York: Grove and Stratton, 1963.

Hardjowirogo. *Sedjarah Wajang Purwa*. Djakarta: Balai Pustaka, 1968.

Holt, Claire. *On the wayang kulit (purwa) and its symbolic mystical elements*. Data paper no. 27. Ithaca: Cornell University Southeast Asia Program, 1957.

Holt, Claire. *Art in Indonesia: Continuities and change*. Ithaca: Cornell University Press, 1967.

Hooykaas, C. *Kama and Kala (Materials for the study of shadow theatre in Bali)*. Amsterdam: North Holland Publishing Co., 1973.

Hooykaas, C. *Cosmology and creation in the Balinese tradition*. The Hague: M. Nijhoff, 1974.

Kats, J. *Het Javaansche Jooneel I Wayang Poerwa*. Weltrveden, 1923.

Labov, William. *Language in the inner city*. Philadelphia: University of Pennsylvania Press, 1972.

Lacan, Jacques. *The language of self* (A. Wilden, trans.). Baltimore: Johns Hopkins Press, 1973.

Laing, R. D. *Knots*. New York: Vintage, 1970.

Lévi-Strauss, Claude. *Structural anthropology*. New York: Basic Books, 1963.

Mangkoenegoro. Over de wajang-koelit (poerwa) in het algemeen en over de daarin voorkomende symbolishe en mysticke elementen. *Djawa*, 1973, *XIII*, 79–95.

Mellema, R. L. *Wayang puppets: Carving, colouring, symbolism*. Amsterdam: Koninklijk Instituut voor de Tropen, 1954.

Nojowirongko, M. Ng. *Serat tutunan padalangau*. Jogjakarta, 1960.

Pike, K. L. The hierarchical and social matrix of suprasegmentals. *Nabitka zprae filologicznych*, 1963, *XVIII*, 1, 95–104.

Probohardjono, R. Ngb. S. *Sulukan Slendro*. Solo: 1966.

Propp, V. Morphology of the folktale. *International journal of American linguistics*, 1958, *24* (4), Part III.

Rassers, W. H. On the origin of the Javanese theatre. In *Panji, the culture hero*. The Hague: Mouton, 1959.

Resink, G. J. From the old Mahabharta-to the new Ramayana-order. *Bijdragen tot de Taal-Land en Volkenkunde*, DL 131 II/III, 1975, 214–235.

Sajid, R. M. *Bauwarna Wajang*. Jogjakarta, 1958.

Sastroamidjojo, Dr. Seno. *Renungantentang Pertundjukan Wajangkulit*. Djakarta: Kinta, 1964.

Soebardi. Calendrical traditions in Indonesia. *Madjalah Ilmu-Ilmu Sastra Indonesia*, 1965, *14* (1), 49–61.

Waldo, Ives. Metaknowledge and the logic of Buddhist language. In *Loka: A journal from naropa institute*. Garden City: N.Y.: Anchor, 1975.

Wilden, Anthony. *System and structure: Essays in communication and exchange*. London: Tavistock, 1972.

Young, R. E., and Becker, A. L. Toward a modern theory of rhetoric: A tagmemic contribution. In J. Emig, J. Fleming, and H. M. Popp (Eds.). *Language and learning*. New York: Harcourt, Brace and World, 1966.

Young, R. E., Becker, A. L., and Pike, K. L. *Rhetoric, discovery and change*. New York: Harcourt, Brace and World, 1971.

Zoetmulder, P. J. The wajang as a philosophical theme. *Indonesia*, Oct. 1971, *12*, 89.

Zurbuchen, Mary. Kawi discourse structure: Cycle, event, and evaluation. *Rackham Literary Studies*, Winter 1976, 45–60.

chapter thirteen

# Dahlan and Rasul: Indonesian Muslim Reformers

James L. Peacock

University of North Carolina

Encouraged by the opening of the Suez Canal and the expansion of steamship travel, great numbers of pious Indonesian Muslims began to make the pilgrimage to Mecca during the late nineteenth century. By the beginning of the twentieth century, the Indonesian community was the largest among the pilgrims residing in the holy city, and many Indonesians who traveled to Mecca remained in the Near East for study in Cairo. A number of these students came under the influence of the great teacher of Muslim reformism, Muhammad Abduh of Cairo's Az-har University. Returning to Singapore, the port of embarkation and disembarkation for the Mecca pilgrims of Southeast Asia, these disciples of Abduh founded schools, journals, and associations to perpetuate the doctrine of reformism. Spreading into the islands of the Indies and, to a limited extent, into Malaya, they became known as the *Kaum Muda* (New Faction) of Malayo-Indonesian Islam.

The Kaum Muda reformists pressed for a return to the fundamental truths of the text and tradition, the Qur'an and the hadith, for the Qur'an was believed to record verbatim the word of Allah and the hadith to record accurately the actions of Muhammad. Other authorities, including the venerated Muslim teachers and scholars who taught ornate philosophies and the law of medieval Islam, were rejected on the grounds that their schemes were of merely human origin. Believers were exhorted to pursue the method of *itjihad,* to analyze and dissect the original Arabic scriptures in order to read for themselves the divine message.

Paradoxically, a return to the ancient text implied an advance toward modernity, for the holy scripture did not mention the animistic and Sufistic rites and beliefs cherished by the majority of Indonesian Muslims; such superstitions must therefore be excised from the lives of the pious. Properly analyzed, the scripture was believed to contain an understanding of economics, science, medicine, law, politics, and education that was fully adequate for the modern world. Through reformism, then, the pious Muslim sought to rediscover a bedrock of ancient and pure identity which was adaptive to modernity.

Propagated by several Indonesian organizations, the reformist viewpoint has been most successfully implemented by the Muhammadijah. Founded in 1912, the Muhammadijah has expanded steadily until today it boasts some 200 branches distributed throughout the islands of Indonesia. Muhammadijah is certainly the most powerful reformist organization ever to exist in Southeast Asia, perhaps in the world. Essentially a missionary movement, striving to convert the syncretist Muslims of Indonesia is pure, reformed Islam, Muhammadijah has made impressive social and educational contributions as well. Its clinics, orphanages, and hospitals, together with some 4,900 schools make it easily the most important private and non-Christian welfare and educational organization in Indonesia. Muhammadijah's women's organization, 'Aisjijah, is probably the most dynamic of any in the Islamic world. The political party, Masjumi, with which Muhammadijah was affiliated until the party was banned by Sukarno in 1960, was for a time the most powerful in Indonesia. In short, Muhammadijah has gained significance in Indonesian, Southeast Asian, and Muslim history; an investigation of the lives of its founders is relevant from a historical as well as psychological standpoint.

K. H. A. Dahlan founded Muhammadijah, and H. Abdul Karim Amrullah, also known as Hadji Rasul, was perhaps its most charismatic early leader. If Dahlan was the most important Islamic reformer on Java, Rasul played an equally critical role in that other major birthplace of Indonesian reformism, Sumatra. When one deals with their biographies, it is important to be aware of the complementary Java/Minangkabau patterns that the two men express.

A pervasive theme in the revolutionary and reform movements of modern Indonesia has been the drawing of complementary leaders from two *bangsa* or "ethnic groups," the Minangkabau of Sumatra and the Javanese. The fifty million or so Javanese who populate the crowded wet-rice-growing villages and industrial or court cities of the central island, Java, have provided the hierarchical civilization and aristocratic, quasi-feudal values against which movements act. They have also supplied the leaders to move them, the figures with mass appeal and organizational might. The five million Minangkabau have elaborated a matrilineal *adat* ("custom") and society stimulating to the spirit yet oppressive to the status of the males with the result that they have long made a practice of fleeing abroad, going on the *rantau*, and this flight has often taken them to Java. From these immigrants have come many of Indonesia's leading intelligentsia. One thinks of Tjokroaminoto, the Javanese aristocrat who led Indonesia's first mass nationalist movement, and his partner the shrewd Minangkabau ideologue, Hadji Agus Salim. Sukarno, the Javanese "Great Leader of the Revolution," found his counterparts in the rationalist Minangkabau economist, Muhammad Hatta and the socialist, Sjahrir. Nor is this pattern lacking in the Muhammadijah. Founded and organized by the Javanese Dahlan, it found a theologian and teacher among the Minangkabau, Rasul.

Standing as two towering figures during the founding period of Muhammadijah, Dahlan and Rasul have both been honored by biographies in the Indonesian language. Rasul's was written by his son, Hamka, himself the most prolific and famous of Indonesian writers of the santri persuasion. It is called: *Ajahku: Riwajat Hidup Dr. H. Abd. Karim Amrullah dan Perdjuangan Kaum Agama di Sumatera (My Father: Life History of Dr. H. Abd. Karim Amrullah and the Struggle of the Religious Faction in Sumatra)* (Amrullah, 1957). For Dahlan, the official Muhammadijah biography is by an influential leader of that organization, H. M. Junus Anis: *Riwahat Hidup K. H. A. Dahlan, Dan Perdjoangannja (Life History of K. H. A. Dahlan, His Action and Struggle)* (Anis, 1962). It is supplemented by a popular work, Solichin Salam's *K. H. Ahmad Dahlan, Reformer Islam Indonesia (K. H. Ahmad Dahlan, Indonesian Muslim Reformer)* (Salam, 1963).

These texts will be confronted historically, ethnographically, and psychologically. The first task is simply to report the biographical facts, few of which are known in English. The second is to indicate the Javanese and Minangkabau sociocultural contexts within which these events must be interpreted. The third task is to construct, insofar as the materials permit, the subjective processes by which the action unfolded, in a word, *verstehen*. Yet throughout we must remember the literary form. A biography, after all, is not a life but a portrayal of life, and due regard must be shown for the author's style and purpose. The first question, then, is whether one may even apply the term *biography* to documents coming from civilizations whose narratives, from the Babad Tanah Jawi to Pramoedya Ananda Toer, embody exotic conceptions of time and history. At the surface level, these works are straightforwardly chronological and topical in a conventional Western-like format. Junus Anis divides his "life history of K. H. Ahmad Dahlan" into five phases: "Time of Infancy and Education," "Childhood," "Education," "As Husband and Father," "Struggle," and "The End of his Life." Since Hamka's organization is essentially the same, though his style is more melodramatic, this sequence will be followed in comparing the two accounts.

## INFANCY AND CHILDHOOD

### Dahlan

"Jogjakarta is known inside and outside the nation as a city of struggle *(perdjoangan),*" writes Junus Anis, "though from its location one would assume that it is a region of peace." Anis goes on to observe that this court city of

Mataram, nestled in the agrarian rice bowl of Central Java and revered for its refined and syncretic *(abangan)*[1] civilization is "distant from the crowds and noise of the outside world." Yet Jogja was the natal home of the first revolutionary Indonesian nationalist, Diponegoro, and the revolutionary capital of the new Indonesian republic. "Thus it is proper that Jogjakarta be termed a *City of Revolution.*"

In Jogjakarta is found the "Kampung Kauman . . . situated near the palace of the Sultan, famed as a residence of the pious." Writing not long after Dahlan's death, the eminent Islamologist Pijper elaborates Junus' image of the Kauman at this time. Pijper (1934:1) describes these crowded but affluent ghetto or casbah-like quarters as the place of residence of pious batik (fabric) manufacturers and mosque officials. Owing to an old privilege granted by the sultan, only santri (Muslim Javanese) live here; Chinese and Christians are excluded, as indeed is the world, in the form of such abangan (non-Muslim) pleasures as the *gamelan* music and *taledek* dance, and during the fast month no one would dare eat, drink, or smoke during the day in the Kauman. In the evenings, the sound of qur'anic chanting issues from houses while on the streets men and women scurry to places of prayer. This pious, commercial quarter was to be the lifelong residence of K. H. A. Dahlan and the birthplace of Muhammadijah.

In this Kauman, "in the nineteenth century there lived an *alim* (religious teacher) named Kijahi Hadji Abubakar bin Kinjahi H. Sulaiman." *Bin* means "son of," reflecting a patrilineal emphasis among santri which is lacking in the bilateral kinship of abangan. Junus is setting the stage for the birth of the son by telling the pedigree of the father. Hadji Abubaker held the office of *chatib* (religious official responsible for the Friday sermon) in the Great Mosque of the Sultanate of Jogjakarta.

"In the year 1868 (Christian calendar) or 1285 H. (Muslim calendar), the family of H. Abubakar was blessed by God with the birth of the fourth son. He was named Mohammad Darwisj." The biographer apologizes that only the year of birth, not the day, is known, throwing in relief Darwisj's deviation from the traditional abangan who frequently remembers the day but not the year. The abangan calendar is cyclical and punctuate, emphasizing not the passage of time but periodic meshing of simultaneous cycles, such as seven- and five-day weeks, and since the days of meshing are suspicious they are celebrated, remembered, and serve as the reference point for such occasions as birth (C. Geertz, 1960:31). The santri calendar is more linear, as is reflected perhaps in this passage of the biography, emphasizing the passing of unrepeatable years—in a word, history—rather than the repetition of days.

Both the patrilineal and the historical are revealed in the biographer's genealogy that traces Darwisj's ancestry for eleven generations on his father's

---

[1]For explication of this and other Indonesian terms and concepts, a general source is C. Geertz (1960).

side and four generations on his mother's. Again, this pattern rather resembles that of some santri in the Jogjakarta area, who trace their membership in patrilineal clans. Anis mentions Darwisj's mother, but only to say that her father, like the father of Darwisj, was a chatib of the Great Mosque: "From this we know that the child named Mohammad Darwisj was born into a pious family and lived in a religious atmosphere."

A lack of interest in remembrance of childhood (which may be typical of either traditional narrative or official biography but also of the santri as opposed to the syncretists) is reflected in the lack of information on this period. We are told only that Darwisj was "diligent, honest, and helpful," and that he was "exceptionally clever and industrious with his hands, with which he constructed play-things that made him popular among his playmates." In place of experience, then, we are given morality and technology, a bit of *Wert* and *Zweck rational*. The mention of the use of hands and construction of toys is unique among Javanese biographies or autobiographies that I have read, which place more emphasis on the social than the technological orientation of childhood. As one Javanese youth once put it to me in a somewhat forced analogy, "Instead of building things, we like to ride toy horses—thus learning how to mount to higher status [*naik pangkat*]." Dahlan's alleged interest in crafts and Junus' mention of it probably reflect the somewhat greater santri interest in technology, as illustrated in the concentration of small craftsmen and fabric manufacturers within the Kauman. Dahlan's manual dexterity as a child foreshadows Junus' characterization of him as a man, not of words but of work.

### Rasul

Hamka's biography of Rasul is four times as long as Anis' of Dahlan, yet the order is similar. After a long sketch of Islam among the Minangkabau, Hamka turns his attention specifically to Rasul with his second chapter, "Ancestry of my Father." As in the case of Dahlan, the genealogy is patrilineal. Hamka identifies his great-grandfather, lists each of his several wives, the sons (but not the daughters) borne by each, and the children of that son who is the father of Hamka's father. The patrilineal emphasis reflects the title of the entire work: "My Father."

"My Mother's Brother" might seem more appropriate in light of traditional Minangkabau culture. In the matrilocal, matrilineal household of the traditional Minangkabau, the son lives not with his father but with his mother's brother. Even after marriage, a man remains in his mother's house, known as the *womb*, together with his sisters and their children. As the brother to these sisters he is more directly responsible for the care and guidance of their children than for that of his own children, who look to their own mother's brother. Hamka does not describe the type of household in which Rasul was reared, and he mentions only one mother's brother, a certain Hadji Djala. Hadji Djala was so delighted that Rasul was a boy that, upon his birth on 10 February, 1879, he erected a prayer house in hope that Rasul would grow up to teach religion.

Nothing else is said about matrilineal kin, yet much about Rasul's father. The father is described as a religious teacher of unusually great sanctity, so revered by the people that they preserved the water in which he made his ablutions and scraps he left on his plate. And his prayers were believed to be efficacious; as one old man told Hamka, when his grandfather once said Allah would send a curse, a mosque immediately burned down.

The biography begins, then, by tracing the religious power that descended from Hamka's grandfather to his father, and it ends as the mantle is taken by Hamka himself. The text can be seen as reflecting a pattern of patrilinealization that emerged in Minangkabau society because of the creation of Islamic schools (Abdullah, 1966). Domestic spheres remained matrilineal, but the headships of these schools were typically passed from father to son.

Despite the patrilineal nature of religion, Rasul must have been raised in a matrilocal, matrilineal household, surrounded in his early childhood by his mother's kin and separated from his father. Some, like Hagen, have theorized that reformists originate from authoritarian fathers, which Rasul's father may, indeed, have been. But he was not around the house, and much of his authority must have been usurped by Rasul's mother's brother. Intriguing as this variation on Hagen's theory may be, the oedipal facts are absent. As in the case of Dahlan, little is said about the childhood of Rasul. A suggestive contrast is that Hamka does not portray Rasul as "good, diligent, and helpful" in the benignly moralistic imagery applied to Dahlan, but emphasizes the reverse, that he was "naughty" (*nakal*, a term which itself is a somewhat stereotyped label that Indonesians frequently apply to their childhood to denote a mischievous "real boy"). Rasul delighted in such mischief as goading chickens to fight and taking home the winner. Dahlan would become the steady, pious organizer, but it was Rasul who grew to be the fiery rebel.

## EDUCATION

The maturation of a pious Muslim boy follows a common pattern throughout Southeast Asia: centrifugal movement from the female to the male, the domestic to the public, and the playful to the Islamic. The santri boy moved from the cozy, female-dominated household, the matrilocal "womb" in Minangkabau, the so-called matrifocal household in Java (H. Geertz, 1969: 76–82), out to the male-dominated school and mosque, finally on the pilgrimage to the distant Mecca.

What few facts are provided suggest that Rasul and Dahlan probably followed this typical pattern; they began to learn the elements of Islamic doctrine and chanting from their parents and neighborhood or village schools, were circumcised probably before age ten,[2] and began to join their male kinsmen in praying at the mosque. Before their teens, they became students at the austere Islamic schools *(pesantren* or *surau)* (Selosoemardjan, 1962:25) which typically cement attitudes of independence, male solidarity, and commitment to the Islamic cause. Certainly their schooling gave a break from the local community, whether it be the matrilineal, adat-dominated clan system of Minangkabau or the hierarchical, Hinduist court complex of Jogjakarta.

The next move was the pilgrimage to Mecca, which both boys were requested to make by their fathers. Darwisj's biographer reports that when he was "rather large" he was "ordered" (disuruh) to go (his expenses paid by a businesswoman aunt). Hamka reports that when Rasul was age sixteen his father said to him:

> Rasul, you must go to Mecca to study religion; you may not return home until you complete your study. You should emulate your ancestor Sjech Abdullah Arif, . . . who filled the mosque when he preached. The voices of persons reciting qur'an were like the buzzing of bees!

Rasul, it is reported, greeted this request with joy.

Of Darwisj's time in Mecca, it is stated only that he lived in the sacred land several years in order to pursue religious studies such as *tafsir* (qur'anic exegesis), *tauhid* (theology), *fiqh* (religious law), *tasauf* (mysticism), and *ilmu falak* (astronomy). Hamka's account of Rasul's experience details not what he studied but with whom: Ahmad Chatib, a famous Minangkabau teacher who had become imam (head) of the Shafiite school of the mosque of Haram in Mecca. Chatib had married into a wealthy Meccan family, adopted the Arab style of life, and decided to remain in Mecca forever because he disapproved of the matrilineal adat of Minangkabau. Studying with this expatriate seven years, Rasul became one of his favorite pupils, and Hamka makes much of Rasul's pride, for the rest of his life, in being a pupil of Chatib. Hamka does not, perhaps because of his reformist ideology, depict any "mystical" bond between pupil and teacher such as has traditionally been felt to exist between *santri* and *kijaji*. At the most mundane level, the relationship must have been intensified by the identity of ethnicity in a foreign land; the so-called *Jawi*—Malays and Indonesians—were the largest pilgrim population in Mecca at this time, and there had emerged a coterie of *Jawi* teachers, Chatib being one of the most famous, who mediated between the Arab world and the homeland of their students.

Eventually the pilgrims came home, Rasul at twenty-three in the company of Minangkabau comrades with whom he shared a reformist zeal inculcated by doctrines of Abduh broadcast by Chatib; Dahlan, too, must have been influenced by the writings of Abduh, as works by him were found in Dahlan's library. As was customary for returned pilgrims, names were changed: Rasul to Abdul

[2]Hurgronje (1924:111–249) reports this age of circumcision for Java and Sunda around 1890, which is during the period when Dahlan and Rasul would have been circumcised.

Amrullah, and Darwisj to Ahmad Dahlan. Dahlan's biographer refers to him henceforth as Dahlan, but Hamka continues to use Rasul. I shall do likewise, for brevity deviating from Indonesian custom by referring simply to these "last" names.

Both later made the pilgrimage again, returning to the locale of their youthful study. Dahlan went back at age thirty-three or thirty-four, partially (according to sources other than the official biography) because he was exiled by the sultan of Jogjakarta on account of his reformism. Rasul went back at age twenty-five, to accompany his cousins. Now Chatib told him that he could teach Islam, and when his pupils could not squeeze into his house he began to teach in a mosque but was ordered out by the *mufti* (high religious advisor) of Mecca. Rasul's protest of this action is romanticized by Hamka as the prickly courage of a *nakal* young rebel, who, despite being a lowly Indonesian, stood up to the stuffy Arab official of the holy city.

## AS HUSBAND AND FATHER

### Dahlan

Junus Anis begins his description of the post-pilgrimage phase of K. H. A. Dahlan's life by stating:

> . . . K. H. Ahmad Dahlan for his entire life was chatib . . . of the Sultan Mosque of Jogjakarta, replacing his father. It is no secret that the Sultan Mosque of Jogja has 12 chatibs. . . . As a chatib, he received a monthly salary of 7 guilders. In addition, the honored-he manufactured and sold batik fabric. His trade took him to East Java, West Java, and nearby islands.

From observation of the Kauman today, one can imagine Dahlan's life alternating between cozy and pious routine in these cramped quarters and travel, by outrigger boats, coal-burning trains, horse-drawn wagons, and foot among the noisy and competitive marketplaces of the towns and ports. Though Dahlan would deliver occasional sermons in the Great Mosque under the shadow of the Sultan's palace, and he doubtless enjoyed evening study-sessions *(pengadjian)* and dawn-prayers followed by the sipping of coffee with his fellow worshippers of the Kauman, much of his time must have been spent on the road. This peripatetic pattern remains a core of santri life and of Muhammadijah.

"K. H. Ahmad Dahlan married Siti Walidah (later famed as Njai Dahlan), daughter of Kijahi Penghulu Hadji Fadhil." Siti's father, a religious teacher was Dahlan's mother's brother. Later he was to marry four additional wives, divorcing each after a short time but retaining "Mother Walidah" until his death. Such serial/simultaneous polygamy was typical of religious leaders of his day.

## Rasul

Like Dahlan, Rasul returned to "replace his father." During Rasul's second visit to Mecca, his young wife and infant son died, and his father summoned him home to "lead the umat." In 1906, after two years abroad, Rasul returned "feeling most sad, sad to leave the teacher who had adopted him as a son, sad to leave the grave of his own wife and son. . . ." A certain ambivalence about return is reflected further in Rasul's account of nearly accepting an offer to become religious teacher in the distant island of Ternate. He agreed to accept the post if his father gave him permission, but either did not ask it or was not granted it.

Instead, Rasul soon found himself comfortably settling into a respected status in his home village. His charisma, reinforced by news of such events as his protest against the Mufti of Mecca, soon attracted pupils, and he became known as the "young teacher" alongside his father, the "old." He taught in prayer houses and married again—the younger sister of his dead wife, then another wife as well. In those days, marriage to an Islamic teacher was highly desirable, and Rasul was probably much sought after.

"Sadly, his father Sjech Muhammad Amrullah . . . could not long observe the development of his son." He died in 1907. "But exactly 9 months and 10 days after the father died . . . Rasul's wife Safiah gave birth to a son." Though found elsewhere in Indonesia, this notion of equilibrium achieved by substitution of the third generation for the first is alien to the Western attitude that an individual is unique and therefore irreplaceable. This same principle of substitutability is reflected too, perhaps, in the phenomenon of one's teacher becoming a more significant figure than one's father (the "guru" syndrome) and a new wife replacing the old one (the pattern of serial or simultaneous polygamy, to be illustrated shortly). Relations of kinship, marriage, and authority or comradeship have a quality of bureaucracy, of the mechanical rather than the personal. A logical result is that Indonesian biography (and indeed other literary forms as well) tends, on the whole, to treat social relations and individual consciousness with a schematicism embellished only by the melodrama of a Hamka.

Rasul married several wives, whom Hamka describes perfunctorily (even though one of them was his mother): the first, who died in Mecca, her half-sister (same mother, different father), a third, apparently preceding this half-sister marriage though not mentioned except in the summary; a fourth, his mother's uncle's daughter; and briefly, three additional women. The second wife was associated with Rasul longest (thirty-eight years, until he died), the third and fourth divorced in 1920 and 1929, respectively, and the fourth accompanied him into exile years later. The biography gives no details of living arrangements, but presumably the traditional Minangkabau pattern was followed: each wife stayed in her natal home while Rasul lived in his, except that when he went into exile his wife and he lived together.

# STRUGGLE

"Struggle" *(perdaungan)* is the standard category in modern Indonesian life histories, following the usually perfunctory account of childhood, youth, and marriage. The "struggle" is usually in a collective context, a movement, and it is against something, some broadly conceived force or condition. It is the struggle that is one's calling, that gives one's life meaning, that culminates in retirement and death.

This formula is closely followed in both biographies under study, each of which entitles a section "perduangan" and casts it in the context of the Muhammadijah movement and against a set of rather stereotyped forces and conditions. Outlined more subtly by Hamka, these are schematically listed by Anis as Mysticism, Hindu-Buddhism, Feudalism, and Colonialism. According to the reformist viewpoint, each led to the decline of Islam, for different reasons. Syncretic mysticism led to preoccupation with the "inner life and the after life" at the expense of social problems. Hindu-Buddhism contaminated the purity of Islam. Feudalism deified royalty in place of Allah. Colonialism encouraged Christianity and oppressed Islam. Hamka describes the additional factor of the matrilineal, anti-Islamic *adat* of Minangkabau.

Rasul's struggle against these things was fiery, individualist, and entangled in the web of kinship. Dahlan's was calm, bureaucratic, and less of a protest than a reform.

## Dahlan

Only a single instance of direct protest against the established order is described in the biography of Dahlan, and this is omitted from the section entitled "His Struggle." Indeed, as though to signal its deviancy from the thrust of his effort, it is relegated to a catch-all section entitled "Several Anecdotes." The incident occurred soon after Dahlan's return from his first pilgrimage. Trained in astronomy, he teamed with some students to demonstrate the unorthodox compass orientation of the Great Mosque by chalking in the correct one. This act incurred the wrath of the chief Penghulu of the palace, who burnt down Dahlan's prayer house during an evening of the fast month. Stricken, Dahlan prepared to catch a train out of Jogja but was intercepted by his older brother who persuaded him to stay.

A second incident, also reported among the "several anecdotes," suggests that Dahlan kept a polite and humble attitude toward the Jogja court. He wished to bring before the Paduka Sri Sultan a suggestion concerning the holding of the Gerabeg feast. So that Dahlan could "speak freely and convey the contents of his heart without being dazzled by the Paduka Sri Sultan and the nobles of his staff," this personage received Dahlan in a darkened room at midnight. Although the biographer relates the incident to show Dahlan's "daring" *(keberanian)* in speaking to exalted royalty, the incident was hardly so rebellious as Luther's "Here I Stand" uttered in the presence of princes, but then it is reported that Luther himself was barely audible on his first day at court.

In order to envision Dahlan's position, the nearly divine status of the sultan of Jogjakarta should be recalled. He was Kalifatullah, successor of Mohammad, Apostle of Allah, and king of one of the three remaining courts of the empire of Mataram. The sultan's birthday must be celebrated every five weeks, and through such ceremonies as the Islamic-Hinduist Gerabegs he was believed to sustain the sociocosmic order; were the rites neglected, "the heavenly guardians of the mountains and the state pusakas (relics) might feel offended, and evil would befall the State and its People" (Selosoemardjan, 1962:28). Though deprived of true military power, the sultan was at the apex of the sociocultural hierarchy in Jogjakarta, backed by the colonial government and supported by a corps of noble officials, the prijaji. Dahlan was himself merely an employee, one of the Islamic officials whose duties included performing the Gerabegs.

Under the circumstances, it is remarkable the Dahlan was permitted to remain chatib. Dutch reports portray more forcefully than Anis his differences with the authorities. Rinckes, not Anis, reports that Dahlan's chalking of the proper direction of the Great Mosque resulted in his exile to Mecca (Mailrapport 1096/13, 1913), and he describes Dahlan's small Arabic school as "in the middle of the arch-conservative palace complex, an abomination to the native authorities (Mailrapport 1782x/14, 1914). Yet Rinckes' report of January 27, 1914 (two years after the founding of Muhammadijah) states that Dahlan is still chatib, and he apparently remained so until his death.

The other establishment against which Dahlan could have revolted is the colonial, and Salam Solichin depicts Muhammadijah in this light:

> . . . . the birth of Muhammadijah was a response to the challenge thrown down to the Indonesian people in general and Indonesian Muslims in particular . . . its birth was to free the Muslim community and Indonesian peoples from the snares of colonialism, conservatism, dogmatism, formalism, traditionalism, and isolationalism. (1965:64)

But no specific anticolonialist protest by Dahlan is mentioned, either by Salam or accounts of Muhammadijans offered in interview during 1970. Various clues against the Salam's statement, written at the height of the Sukarno era, was designed largely to assert the pro-Sukarno, anticolonialist posture of the suspiciously un-nationalist movement of which Salam himself was a member. Classified Dutch reports written during Dahlan's lifetime suggest that he was highly regarded by the colonial regime. Indeed, the official, Rinckes, idolized Dahlan in 1913, as a kind of Indonesian epitome of the Calvinist ethic, an

> energetic, militant, intelligent man some 40 years of age, obviously with some Arab blood and strictly orthodox but with a trace of tolerance. . . . Personally H. Dachlan makes a good impression: one notes a man of character and a will to *do* which is not seen *everyday* in either the Indies or Europe (Mailrapport 1096/13, 1913).

In contrast, Hadji Samanoedi, founder of the mass movement, Sarekat Islam, is to Rinckes a dissolute boor:

> of about 35 years of age, with sensuous not unattractive face that shows his years. Rumor has it that earlier he gambled and ran with loose women, or changed wives in the meantime, while his fortunes derived from producing batik and lending money to the prijaji of Solo. . . . That this man, who is wholly uncultivated, also poorly educated in Islam, and apparently possesses merely the good merchant's savvy, should have purpose and expectation that his association should expand is difficult to understand. . . .

Nine years later, after the Muhammadijah was in full motion, the Dutch opinion of Dahlan remained excellent, according to the well-known sociologist and official, Schrieke (Mailrapport 195x/22, 1922), and even the Catholic missionary, Bakker, one of Muhammadijah's most adamant opponents, wrote that Dahlan himself was a man of tolerance toward Christians (Bakker, 1925).

Concerning the movement itself, the Dutch reports consistently regard it as rational and safe; thus, one report notes approvingly that Dahlan has "avoided the tactics of independence movements, late night, secret meetings with Dzikir (trance-inducing chants) and the like" (Mailrapport 1782x/14, 1914), which were associated with uprisings elsewhere in the colony. Schrieke advises the government not to oppose the organization so long as it sticks to its original missionary and educational objectives (Mailrapport 195x/22, 1922). And in fact, although more politicized organizations—such as the PKI (Indonesian Communist Party), PNI (Indonesian Nationalist Party)—were crushed or crippled by the colonial government, Muhammadijah was permitted to function despite general fears of the revolutionary potential of Islam.

Dahlan's struggle, then, was not a violent and revolutionary protest. What was it, and how did it start?

Anis depicts Dahlan's movement as beginning when he traveled about trading but also contacting religious teachers to cooperate in "spreading Islam and improving the Muslim community" through such activities as study conferences and qur'anic chanting contests. During these early years, Dahlan also participated in the syncretist-Javanist organization, Budi Utomo, in Jogjakarta, and he associated with theosophists, mystics, even Christians: "All of this was used as a means to bring about an orientation for the development of a Muslim missionary organization."

Dahlan's early nucleus was his own students, which, as we shall see, was also true of Rasul. Twelve individuals, including students and fellow teachers from the various schools at which Dahlan was teaching, reportedly urged Dahlan to organize an association to carry forward the reformist ideals. Dahlan agreed, and when they asked him the organization's name, he replied, "Muhammadijah." On November 18, 1912, when Dahlan was approximately forty-four years old, he founded the Muhammadijah in Jogjakarta.

Conventions of Javanese life history seem frequently to accord the role of initiating action to forces other than the motives of the central character. Note that Dahlan was "ordered" to go to Mecca, and then he was "urged" to found Muhammadijah. How much of this is Javanese modesty and indirectness in recounting behavior and how much reflects a stereotyped notion of prophetic calling is impossible to say, but once the founding was accomplished the role of Dahlan is portrayed as a highly goal-oriented and systematic one. Regardless, at this point the account ceases to be of his individual life and begins to portray the collective movement; it is now the *organization's* goals and plans that are enunciated.

Summarizing the thrust of the struggle after 1912, Junus Anis outlines the Muhammadijah goals (essentially to restore pure Islam), its "committees" (missionary, youth, etc.) and its "periods" (depending on who was head), the number of its branches, schools, clinics, and hospitals, and congresses. He summarizes the "endeavors" ('amal usaha') of Dahlan and Muhammadijah under three headings: religious, social, and educational.

Much of this activity is rather bureaucratic and reveals little about Dahlan except his organizational skill and diligence. Of more interest, however, are Salam's remarks about his view of the role of women; this view reflects both the rationalizing implications of reformist psychology and the traditionalist patriarchal conception of sexuality.

Reasoning that the education of women was of critical importance since it was they who educated the young, Dahlan organized a school to teach women Islam, he encouraged them to speak in public and to organize, in short, to become effectively functional instruments within his campaign. Yet while encouraging women's organizational emancipation, Dahlan also intensified their sexual segregation. Thus, he encouraged his pupils to become doctors in order that they need not reveal their private parts to male doctors, and he took pains to get the Kauman women to give up jewelry and dresses that advertised their feminine charms, while teaching them to cover the head with the *kudung*.

Dahlan's efforts at education and evangelism were not universally greeted by applause. He was called infidel, even Christian, by conservative santri, and he was reportedly threatened with murder at least once. His biographers stress that in the face of all obstacles, he was a model of calm determination. This image is expressed also in remembrances of Dahlan that are the lore of the movement today.

### Rasul

Driving toward a more violent struggle than that of Dahlan, Hamka's account of Rasul's struggle is set in an atmosphere of black forces of sorcery. When Rasul's first wife rejected a headman of a certain clan in favor of Rasul, the headman took revenge by using magic to make the wife repulsive in smell and appearance to her husband. As a result, Rasul became impotent. Later sorcery caused the wife to suffer an almost fatal tumor.

These incidents so "pressured the feelings" of Rasul, that he began the study of magic before his second trip to Mecca. But in that holy city, his teacher Chatib reassured him that faith and piety (imam and ibadat) were sufficient protection against the threat of sorcery. Rasul was instructed to rise in the middle of the night, perform a special prayer (nawa'fil), and chant a request-prayer (doa) to the prophet. Said Chatib: "Then no spirit can oppose you. If you are attacked anyway, give the sign by remembering God. Believe!" After Rasul returned to his village, he made Chatib's formula his routine, and Hamka reports the pleasure (perhaps not unalloyed) which villagers felt upon hearing the mellow voice of Rasul chanting the *doa* at 3 A.M. each day.

Though it is difficult to reconstruct the emotions and ideas embodied by Hamka's terse statement that animism "pressured the feelings of Hadji Rasul," general knowledge of Indonesian culture suggests that he was, indeed, deeply troubled. He must have felt the presence of tangible, powerful, and pervasive dark forces such that Islamic faith and ritual were not merely symbolic frameworks but supernatural weapons to defend against these threatening forces. Thus one can explain Rasul's diligent, almost obsessive implementation of the instructions of his counselor, Chatib.

Even more essential than faithful ritual was strong belief; the best defense against pantheism is monotheism. Resisting the general Malayo-Indonesian custom of placating the plurality of spirits, Rasul rigidly placed his trust in a single transcendent being in whom was concentrated all spiritual power. Not accidentally, the single writing of Rasul which Hamka chooses as most representative of his thought is "Only Allah," a tract written to Japanese authorities during the World War II occupation to explain that Muslims could not worship the emperor of Japan because all power was due to the one God, Allah. Practicing what he preached, Rasul became a hero at risk of his life by publicly refusing to bow in the direction of the emperor; he explained, "I fear Allah more than the Japanese."

Deep-seated, culturally grounded anxieties concerning the dangers of swarming spirits may have combined with the Muslim doctrine of monotheism *(Tauhid)* to reshape Rasul's personal theology, but his earliest public reforms followed directly the admonitions of modernist ideology transmitted by his teacher Chatib and the Kaum Muda movement in general. His first blow was struck against Minangkabau mysticism of the Sufist type that was felt by modernists to undermine Islam by mixing magical, ecstatic, and animistic practices with the pure obedience to Allah taught by the original Islam. Rasul's own father was a leader of the local Sufist order, Thariqat Naqusjabandijah, and apparently for this reason Rasul kept his silence for a time.

Then one day Rasul and several other young reformists of his village attended a gathering of older religious teachers in another village. At a certain point in the evening, the host asked all teachers present to give an opinion concerning Thariqat. Drawn into the discussion, Amrullah in a "clear voice" beat down every argument the old teachers could muster in support of the Sufi orders. By midnight, he had become "angry and impassioned" and finally insulted his elders by asserting that even a child could understand his arguments. Soon neither Rasul's friends nor opponents had much to say, and only his own voice was heard, loud and unceasing. The host finally proposed that the debate be postponed until 9 o'clock the next morning, and the group dispersed. When morning came, rumor had it that a physical fight would ensue, and the young reformists decided they had best hop a train home.

Hamka adds that "In spite of his [Rasul's] harsh attitude regarding Thariqat and the spread of news of the debate through all Minangkabau, when he returned to his village he did not alter his behavior toward his father." He remained respectful, although he was now known as leader of the Kaum Muda in Minangkabau.

Rasul's second major reformist protest could, like the first, be construed as opposing his father though it is difficult to separate ideological from oedipal motives. When Rasul's father died, the villagers planned to honor him in the Minangkabau tradition by a series of funeral feasts, on the third, fourth, seventh, fortieth, and hundredth day after his death. Rasul did help to bathe his father's corpse, but he refused to participate in the feasts sanctioned by animism rather than Islam. A brother disputed his view, and the issue was brought before the Taunku Laras, the official who regulated customary practice and administration, and he ruled in favor of the brother. Rasul was now despised by many villagers who felt he had been disrespectful to his father. The situation becomes complex, when one remembers that, in the adat context, it was Rasul's mother's brother against whom he should have felt oedipal resentment of authority, but within the Islamic stream, his father did indeed have force. Yet it is within the adat context that the objection is being raised.

Rasul's action was supported, however, by students who were devoted to him as a charismatic teacher. As one put it, "We valued a person whom we felt was of high status, at least we wanted to receive sacred blessing (berkat) from his knowledge . . . although we were his students we were also his friends, kinsmen, and assistants." During the one hundred days of feasting by villagers, this group joined Rasul in praying at their own prayer house as an alternative, Islamic ceremony. The satisfaction of spearheading reform was recalled by one, who states, "We were happy for we were still youngsters. Always we read the saying (hadis): 'Whoever loses something to Allah will receive better from him in return.' "

In a preface to Salam Solichin's biography of Dahlan, the former Indonesian Minister of Information, Rosihan Anwar, describes Dahlan's life as a rhythm of "joy and sadness, ups and downs." Actually such a pattern seems more characteristic of Rasul, whose "struggle" was not subsumed under a single organizational effort and whose life alternated between sickness and health, triumph and exile. The "ups and downs" were metaphorically expressed by the geography of his life during the months following his father's death. Increasingly in demand, Rasul taught alternate weeks in the hot, coastal city of Padang and the cold, mountain town of Padjang Pandjang, pursued back and forth by his devoted students and apparently setting up separate households with separate wives at the two levels. Note the alternation of hill and coast, frequent also in the travels of heroes of Southeast Asian mythology. Eventually, "because of the incessant work . . . he became dangerously ill, to the point he was forced to go home to Manindjau (his home village), where he lay in bed for months."

But the "thin but well knit" Rasul, athletic to the point of expertise in the Malayo-Indonesian karate (penjak-silat), bounced out of bed to spread reformism even further afield. At the age of thirty-seven, he carried the campaign to Malaya. There he aggressively opposed a golden-robed, silken-turbaned, dagger-carrying, automobile-driving, and lustful polygamous official of the Sultan of Johore. Rasul made a point to perform reformism at precisely those places where this *mufti* spread conservatism, and he was gradually "persuading the people" until the threat of action by the establishment drove him home.

In 1917, Rasul journeyed to Java, where he met K. H. A. Dahlan, who gave Rasul "new inspiration." When Rasul returned to Minangkabau, his struggle came, like that of Dahlan, to center around education. He founded a religious school on the *madrasah* rather than *surau* pattern; the circle of chanters was replaced by a sequence of classes in an organized and graded curriculum on the Western model. Working and teaching without rest, he organized the famous school system known as *Sumatra Thawalib,* which came to form the backbone of the Minangkabau Kaum Muda; as in the case of Dahlan, Rasul's movement was grounded in support by his students.

Such support included the physical. In 1920, an Arab teacher who was regarded by the conservatives as possessing spiritual powers was in Minangkabau preaching against reformism. When at one gathering he insulted Rasul, a pentjack expert named Mak Adam who was a student of Rasul, challenged the Arab to fight. Hamka writes with glee that the teacher panicked, ran, tripped, and fell in a pond. He then developed a paranoid fear of attack and began carrying an axe into the *mimbar* (pulpit) for defense. Hospitalized, he was released and last seen in the Medan marketplace, "singing, chanting, excoriating the Kaum Muda, and selling amulets."

Rasul's school system became politicized, then fell under the influence of Communism, and Rasul resigned in 1923. Disappointed with the rise of Communism, revival of the Kaum Tau, and personal difficulties, Rasul spent much of 1925 and 1926 traveling, in Java and Egypt, but returned at the age of forty-seven ready for what Hamka termed his "new struggle." Since his home in Padjang Pandjang had collapsed, he moved back to his village, built a house and study, and here began a stringent routine which Hamka says he followed until his exile in 1941. The Calvinistically methodical schedule, parallels to which can be found among other santri teachers, reveals a rationalizing power within the Islamic ritual framework.

Before dawn, Rasul would go to the prayer house to await villagers whom he would lead in prayer. After they went to their fields, he would go to his study to write, read, and chant. At noon he would again summon the villagers to prayer. After prayer he would lunch with one of his two wives, then nap until the afternoon prayer, after which he would teach study groups until time for the evening prayer. Following this he would chant and do an optional prayer until the night prayer, which he would follow with another optional prayer before retiring to sleep for those hours before rising again to pray before dawn. In his spare time, Rasul aided the Minangkabau Muhammadijah.

Rasul did not, however, officially join that organization, partly because he could never completely agree with its doctrine. One of the issues on which he deviated concerned the role of women. He opposed the 'Aisjijah (women's branch of Muhammadijah) practice of letting women participate in public meetings, and when a congress was to be held in Minangkabau he opposed the Javanese leader, Mas Mansur, who planned to let an 'Aisjijah leader address a mixed-sex audience. Rasul had argued that this was *haram* (forbidden), but he finally had to admit that his position was personally motivated since in Islamic law this action was *makruh* (permissible if necessary under the circumstances). In other respects, too, Rasul was more stringent regarding women than was Muhammadijah, for example in opposing their wearing of the short (Javanese-style) blouse rather than the long (Minangkabau-Malay-style) type that more fully concealed feminine contours. Yet, like Dahlan, Rasul encouraged feminist activism, and two of the most activist female organizers in Minangkabau Islam were his former pupils.

Around 1928 Rasul became involved in protest against the colonial government. When the government proposed to introduce a "guru ordinance" that would limit the activities of religious teachers, Rasul deliberately made a fiery speech at a meeting attended by a Dutch spy and he accepted chairmanship of a radical committee. After years of activities of this kind, he was imprisoned and then exiled to Sukabumi, West Java. When the Japanese occupied Java in 1942, he moved to Djakarta, accompanied by his young wife, Darijah, and his youngest daughter, who "guarded him faithfully."

## THE END OF LIFE

### Dahlan

When Dahlan became ill in his fifites, he was advised to seek a change of climate at a retreat near Mount Bromo. "But even there he continued to work [doing missionary organization and preaching], until he got worse instead of better"; his industriousness is suggested by seventeen out-of-town trips for Muhammadijah which Dahlan made during the year before he died. When his wife begged him to rest, he replied:

I must work hard, in order to lay the first stone in this great movement. If I am late or cease, due to my illness, there is no one who will build the groundwork. I already feel that my time is almost gone, thus if I work as fast as possible, what remains can be brought to perfection by another.

"What he said was apparently true, for not long after he could not rise from his bed," writes Anis. When Dahlan's death was near, he summoned friends and his brother-in-law to delegate tasks to his successors. He died February 23, 1923 at his home, Kauman 59, Jogjakarta.

### Rasul

Rasul, who was born some ten years after Dahlan, lived twenty years after his death. He was in Djakarta in exile in 1943 when Hamka, at his father's request, visited the ailing old man. Moved by his coming, the father who normally detested the traditional Islamic santri custom of children kissing the father's hand simply "gave it to me, and said, 'My child . . . my child! Your father still lives to await your arrival.' "

Hamka's account of his visit emphasizes the pride with which his father realized that his "child" *(anak)* had become a "person" *(orang),* indeed, what is even more reason for pride in the Malayo-Indonesian culture, a "person of stature" *(orang besar).* What would strike the Western reader as unsubtle namedropping in these passages by Hamka apparently has the effect of affirming that the son has arrived, that he is an *orang besar.* As the father's death draws closer, the son takes up his role of prominence in the biography.

At this point, too, the father is portrayed as mellowing, and for the first time in the biography, the relation of father and son is depicted with emotion. As the father temporarily revived in health, Hamka himself fell ill, and the father nursed him. Hamka recalls how he would awaken him for morning prayer, calling in a sweet voice "Lik, lik [affectionate nickname for Hamka's name, Malik], get up . . . morning prayer, morning prayer!" Then, says Hamka, "We would pray, snack, and drink coffee together Praise God!" In a somewhat melodramatic style, the biography portrays what would seem a typical and plausible psychology of rationalization; the mellowing of relationships that the harshly rationalizing reformist had denied himself throughout life but permits now with the approach of death.

The golden days ended with Hamka's departure from Sumatra. He had suggested that Rasul return with him, to end his days in his natal village among old friends. Rasul refused, saying that Java doctors were required to control his illness, and because God gave no care to where one died, he need not return home. Hamka nevertheless saw signs of an "inner struggle" in Rasul as he made his decision to stay in the alien city of Djakarta. As Hamka boarded the train, he called out to Sukarno (who was to become president of the republic and is here portrayed as a comrade of Hamka, one of the *orang besar* with whom he rubbed shoulders): "Take care of our father! The *Bung* replied in the language of nationalism: "Do not fear, comrade!" Again, the exit of the old man is signaled by the entrance of the son, of secular nationalism in place of pure Islam.

Hamka never saw his father again, but he describes his last days as reported in a letter from Rasul's son-in-law Nur Sutan Iskandar. Though having difficulty breathing owing to asthma aggravated by smoking, Rasul persisted even in his deathbed in giving rulings *(fatwa)* to those who sought counsel. Friends were staying overnight to keep him company but he had already turned his attention to the beyond: "What touched us was that he did not turn his face toward the world, i.e., his wife and children, friends and relatives, but to God. . . ."

After making his dawn prayer at 7:10 A.M. on June 2, 1945, Rasul died at the age of sixty-six. He was buried in an Arab graveyard with a simple funeral "as he would have wished it."

## COMMENTS: REFORMIST PSYCHOLOGY

The biographies of both Dahlan and Rasul conclude with the biographer's own assessment of the "character" (Kepribadian or Pribadinja) of the subject.

Of Dahlan, Salam Solichin writes

> His type of personality was *sepi ing pamrih* (Javanese language for "lacking self interest") yet *rame ing gawe* (Javanese for "active in work"). He was a man who was *ichlas* ("stoic, devoted, steadfast") . . . Kiai Dahlan had the spirit of the *satria* (the Hindu-Javanese conception of the warrior who, like Ardjuna in the Bhagavadgita, carries out the code or dharma of his station, waging the struggle while at peace inside).

Precisely the same terms—*ichlas, sepi ing pamrih, rame ing gawe,* and *satria*— are applied by Junus Anis, and these terms are typical also in the teachings of syncretic mystical philosophies and in Javanese "philosophy of life" in general. In the end, Anis sums up his fellow Jogjarkartan by a set of virtues more Javanese than Islamic.

As associated Javanese value is the hierarchical one, *hormat,* reverence for statutes higher than one's own and for hierarchy as such. Though a reformist, Dahlan had *hormat,* whether in his custom of speaking the stratified Javanese language, in his courtesy to the Sultan and the Dutch government, or in his inner humility *(isin).* No "protestor" in the ill-mannered sense, throughout his career he remained the faithful servant of the hierarchy. Within his status, he happened to lead a pragmatic and positive movement to purify the faith, but the movement never attacked the status system, which explains how he, a reformist, could remain *chatib* of the court, deeply conservative, until he died.

Least Javanese and most Islamic about Dahlan was his stress on hellfire and damnation. Anis' first quotation from Dahlan's "Teachings and Pearls of Wisdom" is:

> We humans are given as a trust only one life in this world. After you die, will you be saved or damned?

Other quotations carry the same message, which of course reminds us of the driving force of Weber's Calvinists. Yet this theology does not surface as a *leitmotif* in the biographies; indeed, it is not mentioned except in this isolated section on the "Pearls." Quietly the concern with salvation must have played a role in the struggle, but all that is depicted is the steady dedication of a man determined to carry through the precepts of a reformist mandate; neither the motivational nor the metaphysical basis of the struggle of Dahlan is given so much weight by his biographers (or in recollections by Muhammadijans today) as the organization and its creed.

Among Indonesians, Minangkabau are frequently stereotyped as less reserved than the Javanese, and Rasul's origin as well as his biographer's being his son and a novelist rather than an official may explain the greater intimacy of description of his personality. Thus, Hamka relates how Rasul was stingy, careful, and aggressive. Every book that he had ever owned, he carefully encased in cabinets. He washed and mended his own clothes, to ensure that they were neat and clean. He would become angry if interrupted in the midst of arranging his things and angry if even a speck of food were wasted. During travel, he would keep his mouth working constantly, muttering passages from the Qur'an, and only after finishing a passage would he join in conversation, whose subject would frequently be his arguments in defense of his views and pleasant memories of crushing opponents in argument. In actual debate, he would easily become enraged, bombarding his enemies with invective and even violating Minangkabau *adat* to the extent of pointing at them with his left hand.

Rasul could also be brutally legalistic, as in one incident where he was visiting a couple whom he had counseled when they were on the verge of divorce. As they were in the midst of cooing happily about their reconciliation, Rasul suddenly informed them that they were living in sin. He reminded the husband that he, in anger, had stated that the wife was divorced if ever she set foot in the mother's room. The wife had done so, therefore, under Islamic law, they were no longer married.

Stinginess, cleanliness, orderliness, legalism, and a certain violence that underlies and occasionally breaks through this orderliness bears strong resemblance to the classical anal-aggressive, obsessive-compulsive personality which some identify with Protestantism. Indeed, it is plausible that in any type of rationalizing effort, the systematization and organizing of behavior would result in a certain amount of suppression, repression, and frustration of impulse, which could then find expression in outbursts or general irascibility. That Dahlan apparently had the orderliness without the anger is explicable in part by syncretic Javanism, which so deeply and subtly inculcates a code of courtesy and hierarchy that aggression is typically expressed only indirectly or in such extreme conditions as trance and battle.

Hamka himself agrees that the reformists of Minangkabau shared common traits of personality: "harshness, dictatorial, spirit of leadership, simple, concerned wtih ablution, thrifty but generous.'' As throughout his biography of Rasul, he emphasizes their feisty pride: ''They would humble themselves to those whom they respected, but were haughty to those who snubbed them.'' And he stresses the fiery bravery and charisma of Rasul, which he says are visible in the fire of his eye. It is this defiance and dashing charisma which differentiates Rasul from Dahlan, though the latter's steady dedication worked at least equal effect.

Despite personality differences reflecting their separate ethnic values and stereotypes, Dahlan and Rasul shared a basic psychology which logically flows from reform and rationalization. Methodical, orderly, struggling continuously for cultural purification, both mistrusted sensuality and the giving way to forces of the id, the notorious *hawa nafsu* of Malayo-Muslim psychological theory. This is exemplified in their drive to stifle the sensuality of women. Although some might reduce this motive to some unconscious fear of the woman-power of their many wives, any such emotion is subordinate to the broader logic of rationalization; the reformist struggles to purify the world of magic, mystery, and sensuality in the name of law, scripture, and the supreme God, to control the hawa nafsu through *achlag* and *akal,* which is to say, subordinate id to superego and ego.

Now one deals with the question of how Dahlan and Rasul compare to the type of reformist known in the West. Useful for our purposes is Erikson's analysis of Martin Luther (Erikson, 1958). Despite the numerous difficulties in systematically comparing figures so different in historical context and biographical record as Luther and our reformists of Indonesia, the comparison can at least highlight certain qualities of these men and their biographies which are salient to analysis of the distinctively Indonesian life history.

Apparently absent from both Indonesian personalities was the intense inner struggle of a Luther whose autobiographical accounts depict a person obsessed by the need to achieve justification by purging himself of guilt and sin (Erikson, 1958:101–104). The surface results of Dahlan's and Rasul's reformation were not unlike the results of Luther's, the stripping of ritual down to its essentials, delivery of sermons in the vernacular, reliance on the book instead of the priest. But Luther's formulation, though meaningful only within a culture imbued with the concept of original sin, was apparently an original solution to a torment peculiar to himself. And the historical effect, if one accepts the analysis of Erikson, was radically to reorganize the psychological configuration of guilt-imbued Western man. Less subjective in either origin or direction, the reformation of Dahlan and Rasul was borrowed from outside—a legalistic attempt to impose a Middle Eastern ethic on a Malayo-Indonesian society.

Like Luther, Dahlan and Rasul emerged as reformers after an experience of isolation, in Erikson's words, a ''moratorium.'' Luther's monastery was Rasul's and Dahlan's pesantren (religious school) and pilgrimage. During these years of study, they, as Luther apparently did, also, must have undergone profound psychological transformations of emotion from parents and kin to teachers and teachings. But their experience was within a more objective and social framework. Luther entered the monastery prompted by his own compelling needs and against the wishes of his father.[3] Dahlan and Rasul took the haj at the command of their fathers and with the fullest sanction of their *santri* culture and community; they were doing what every good Muslim boy should do.

Their return, too, was securely within the local, social system. Each took his father's place, in familial, occupational, and Islamic spheres, and by their thirties they had large families, prominent positions, and many students. At the same age, Luther was a celibate monk. He had inherited from Christ the tradition of celibacy and isolation while changing the world, whereas Rasul and Dahlan could follow Muhammad's example of polygamy and community in the midst of reform.

The concept of biography is itself alien to the syncretist culture; biography was introduced by Islam. Syncretist writings today include the biographical, especially when dealing with heroes of the revolution, which exemplifies the syncretist's own paths of rationalization, but biographies are still most in evidence among the santri; the Muhammadijans appear to be the only Indonesian movement to publish an ongoing biographical series, in which the work on Dahlan is a number, and the syncretists have no parallel to the biography of Muhammad. Despite the biographical emphasis, however, the santri biographical form is not identical to that familiar to the West. The linear, chronological format of the biographies of Dahlan and Rasul is divided into the familiar phases of childhood, education, and struggle. But little attention is given to the development of personality through these experiences. Especially in what we are accustomed to term the *formative* years, the sketchy and episodic treatment makes one think that the biographer is simply reporting a few events to express a conventionalized category of time rather than to work though a process of personal development.

This apparent lack of cohesion expresses another level of meaning. The scattered episodes of personal experience are replaced by the integrated frame of reformist Islam. Through the systematization of doctrine, ritual, preaching, teaching, and above all, the perdjuangan, life becomes meaningful and focused. Critical in this synthesis is the word. Like young Muhammadijans today who discuss their evangelistic campaigns with the same fervor as Western athletes talk about their sports, Rasul and Dahlan integrated their lives around evangelism, the communication of the word. Rasul was so devoted to it that he muttered it constantly to himself in the midst of conversation and travel. A life of the word transforms the *Zweckrational* into the *Wertrational* and reflects a critical emphasis of Islam, which is scripturalist and legalistic; Islam, brought to its logical perfection in reformism, is based on the Qur'anic law by contrast to Christianity

---

[3]Erikson notes, however, that Luther's eventual marriage was justified as "to please my father" (1958:91).

which is more quintessentially biographical in that its root-metaphor is not the law but the life sacralized in the biography of Christ.

Noteworthy is the *local* and *familial* focus of these reformists. Unlike the Western-education, secular intelligentsia who, as Taufik Abdullah has noted, were frequently "absorbed into the rantau society permanently" (1971:11), these Islamic reformists came home. Each centered his movement in the very community of birth, Dahlan in Jogjakarta Kauman, Rasul in his Minangkabau village, and as Alfian observes (1970:261–400), they rooted their struggles in a nexus of blood and ethnicity; many of the earliest targets, members, and leaders of the movement were kinfolk of the two reformers in their respective clan and city milieux. Though drawing on pan-Islamic, modern philosophies, their early reforms were directed against those customs and beliefs which were the core of existence of their own neighbors and kinfolk, such as the matrilineal adat in Minangkabau and the abanganism of Jogja.

In interviewing contemporary, secularized Malayo-Indonesians, men who, though devoutly Muslim, earn their living as bureaucrats, businessmen, or workers, I have been struck by the large number who claim inspiration through figures who resemble Dahlan and Rasul. In the life histories of many of these Muslims appears some *keras* ("strict") and *sutji* ("pure") Islamic teacher, frequently the informant's own father, who, in a bygone time of colonial domination, stubbornly championed a faith which the son now follows in a paler form. The same two-generational pattern appears in the consciousness of the Muhammadijah organization, crystalized in the official memories of the founders. Indeed, one could see the biographies of Rasul and Dahlan as mythical charters for each of the two streams in the contemporary Muhammadijah movement.

Muhammadijans today perceive a certain complementarity between the official headquarters, which is the provincial court city of Jogjakarta, beside the Kauman neighborhood on 99 K. H. A. Dahlan Street, and most important branch office, which is in the national capital of Djakarta, on bustling 62 Menteng Raya. In 1970, the biography of Dahlan, but not, as it happened, that of Rasul, was on sale in Jogjakarta at the office of the Kauman-Javanese–dominated headquarters. In Djakarta, the leaders are Minangkabau more than any other single ethnicity; they include Hamka himself, they are intellectuals and activists, and expatriates, and on sale is *Ajahku,* displaying on its cover a memory, the lean, fiery-eyed, sharp-faced Hadji Rasul.

Whatever the merits of this particular argument, it is clear that the authorized lives of the founders embody a psychology that follows from the logic of reformism and rationalization. Their ancestry is patrilineal, abstracted from the richer context of matrilineal and bilineal kinship recognized by tradition. Their lives, too, are lineal, shaving away irrelevance and organized methodically toward the goals of reform and salvation. This struggle takes precedence over the intimacy and nostalgia of childhood, the sensuality of women, and the ecstasy of mysticism, all of which distractions are opposed in the interest of the straight and narrow.

Despite these strong thrusts toward rationalization, they show less individualism and inner exploration and development than a figure such as Luther. Though the pesantren and haj required the youths to quit their homes, they did so in the company of friends, under the sanction of the community, with the guidance of esteemed teachers, and in enclaves of their own ethnicity. When they returned home, they replaced their fathers, settled into networks of kin and neighbors. Their friends and especially their students seem to have initially prompted them to mount their "struggle," and to have supported them throughout. Even, as in the case of Dahlan, where the enemy was spiritual, it was socially motivated as in sorcery by a rival chief, and the entire reformist campaign was a social tug-of-war, between the Kauman (the Islamic people) and Kraton (the palace), the Kaum Muda (the new faction) and the Kaum Tua (the old faction).

## REFERENCES

Abdullah, Taufik. Adat and Islam: An examination of conflict in Minangkabau. *Indonesia,* October 1966, 161–184.

Abdullah, Taufik. *Schools and politics: The Kaum Muda movement in West Sumatra (1927–1933).* Modern Indonesia Project, Southeast Asia Program. Ithaca: Cornell University, 1971.

Alfian. *Modernism in Indonesian politics: The Muhammadijan movement during the Dutch colonial period, 1912–1942.* Ph.D. dissertation. University of Wisconsin, 1970.

Amrullah, Abdul Milik Karim, hadji. *Ajahku: Riwajat Hidup Dr. H. Abd. Karim Amrullan dan Perdjuangan Kaum Agama di Sumatera* (3rd ed.) Djakarta: Djajamurni, 1957.

Anis, H. M. Junus. *Riwajat Hidup K. H. A. Dahlan, dan Perdjo ang annija.* Jogjakarta: Pusat Pimpinan Muhammadijah, 1962.

Bakker, F. L. P. De opleving vanden Islam in Djokdja. *De Macedonier,* 1925, *29,* 161–170.

Erikson, Erik H. *Young man Luther.* New York: Norton, 1958.

Geertz, Clifford. *Religion of Java.* New York: Free Press, 1960.

Geertz, Hildred. *The Javanese family.* New York: Free Press, 1969.

Hurgronje, Snouck. Breiven van een Wedana Pension. *Verspreide Geschriften* (Vol. 4, Pt. 1). Bonn and Leipzig: Kurt Schroeder, 1924.

Mailrapport. Departmen von Kolonien. Ministerie van Biunenlandse Zaken. 1096/13, 1782x/14, 195x/22.

Pijper, C. F. *Fragmenta Islamica.* Leiden: E. J. Brill, 1934.

Salam, Solichin. *K. H. Ahmad Dahlan, reformer Islam Indonesia.* Djakarta: Djajamurni, 1963.

Salam, Solichin. *Muhammadijah den Kebangunan Islam di Indonesia.* Djakarta: N. V. Mega, 1965.

Selosoemardjan. *Social change in Jogjakarta.* Ithaca: Cornell University Press, 1962.

# Part Four
# INNOVATION IN TRADITIONAL COHERENCE SYSTEMS

chapter fourteen

# Balinese Temple Politics and the Religious Revitalization of Caste Ideals

James A. Boon

Cornell University

> By looking closely at what happens on this peculiar little island over the next several decades we may gain insights into the dynamics of religious change of a specificity and an immediacy that history, having already happened, can never give us.
>
> (Geertz, 1964)

Bali-Hindu religious concerns find expression largely in rituals performed at the island's innumerable temples, its most conspicuous ethnographic feature. An enormous primary and secondary literature discusses the often obscure Hindu cosmology of temples, a brand of esoteric knowledge traditionally restricted to Brahmana experts. More recently, specialized literati interested in the formal exegesis of Balinese religious practices have codified these interpretations for popular education. Dutch colonial archaeologists and ethnographers, seeking information germane to the administration of the island, focused on sacred legends legitimizing royal dynastic temples and other major shrines. In contrast, this paper discusses more local sociopolitical aspects of lesser ancestor temples and reveals how the caste-status implications of revitalized temple networks have influenced recent political developments.[1]

---

[1]Many cosmological interpretations of temples are reviewed in Miguel Covarrubias (1937) and J. L. Swellengrebel (1960), especially the introduction. Recent Indonesian language summaries of the Hindu significance of temples appear in *Upadeca: Tentang Adjaran-adjaran Agama Hindu* (1968) and I Gusti Gde Ardana (1971). A sample of the vast Dutch colonial work on temples is translated into English in Swellengrebel (1960) and Hooykaas (1964). The standard Dutch work on Balinese religious and legal customs is still V. E. Korn (1932); a handy summary is J. Kersten (1947); and more recent materials on temples are found in J. L. Swellengrebel (1948). There is much data on the ceremonial forms within and around temples in Jane Belo (1953), Jane Belo (1960), Beryl de Zoete and Walter Spies (1939); and on the function of irrigation temples in F. A. Liefrinck (1927). The translocal significance of temple legends was pointed out in Gregory Bateson (1937); and the importance of nonnoble ancestor group temples is cited in Clifford Geertz (1967). But there has been little work on local status and political implications of temples and temple networks or on the more recent political uses of temples.

Temples are basically walled-off sacred spaces reserved for periodic visitations by gods and spirits influencing a particular aspect of social life. Each level of Balinese spatial organization, economic organization, and social organization is designated by a variety of temple. Individual houseyards, village-area localities *(desa)*, entire districts, and pan-Bali are all commemorated in different temples whose congregations crisscross and overlap. Every market, wet-rice irrigation cooperative, watershed division, and profitmaking voluntary association corresponds to the supporters of a particular temple, and every Balinese has numerous temple affiliations for different purposes. Moreover, sets of households tracing their members to the same ancestral source can be organized into an ancestor temple group. Its temple might in turn be thought to relate to other distant temples, all conceived as offshoots of an original temple founded by the arch-ancestor of these descendants. Bali's three upper caste categories (Brahmana, Satrya, and Wesia) are idealized as such expanded ancestor groups, defined by a temple network, and complicated by an ideology of hierarchy. According to upper caste sacred manuscripts, Brahmanas should constitute such an island-wide temple network, Satryas another, and Wesias (more problematically) a third. Each caste *(warna)* is believed to descend from a founding Javanese ancestor initially ranked by his function in society (priest, king, or warrior-administrator). The ancestors are sanctified as once-worldly representatives of Hindu divinity. By some accounts these castes are in turn internally differentiated into ranks based either on the birth position of the ancestor's sons who established the regnant collateral lines or on the different caste-statuses of the ancestor's multiple wives who produced his descendants. In these high caste accounts Sudras are largely ignored; they are merely "the rest." This ideological scheme reveals little about complexities in the actual working of Balinese caste-statuses (Boon, 1973:III). And one must remember that in Bali, social hierarchy is essentially a religious concept of ritual purity, not intrinsically tied to other social props. Thus commoner ancestor groups can be richer, more powerful, more artistic, more educated than higher-ranking groups, while remaining their inferiors in the ritual and etiquette expressions (most prominent in temple ceremonies and death rites) that are the primary index of caste standing. Nevertheless, the traditional *warna* scheme relating different kinds of power to different ranks of society remains indicative of values still important in Bali, even among so-called Sudras, values central to the way temple networks symbolize caste-statuses and enter into contemporary politics.

To demonstrate the persistence of these values and how they affect religious change, we describe three cases which illustrate some political and status components of current Balinese religion: first, a particular ancestor temple which commemorates the interlocal and cross-caste ties of its congregation, symbolizes its traditional status pride, and reflects recent bids for renewed prestige and influence. Second, a contemporary quasi-political movement to organize a pan-Bali temple network by emphasizing ancestral connections (both actual and legendary) between congregations. Finally, a local area which, by participating in this movement, has effectively introduced the germs of a new range of caste-statuses into its daily affairs.

Just as real as the cosmological and ritual significance of temples are the political strategies and status ambitions they mediate. One role of temples in Balinese society is to amalgamate goal-specific strategies and general religious-mystical concerns in a single institutional framework. And recent developments in Bali reveal how Weberian "rationalization" and traditionalist revitalization need not be either/or dimensions of religious action.

## AN ILLUSTRATIVE TEMPLE

Many Balinese ancestor temples are nodes in composite webs of temple networks that interrelate the religious well-being of different congregations in widespread locales. The most immediate significance of a temple's component shrines is the political and status relations they symbolize, which may or may not be elaborated according to high Hindu cosmology. The potential complexity of native sociopolitical explanations for their sacred structures is illustrated by the temple of a large Sudra ancestor group in southwest Bali. The group today (1972) includes over five hundred members who live mainly in the court center of Tabanan district and in two other village areas, each about 30 kilometers away. In pre-Dutch Bali its members performed important administrative duties in the kingdom and were apparently granted many high-caste prerogatives by the radja. Their influence in governmental and political affairs continued through the colonial period, and has not diminished since independence in 1948 (Boon, 1974).

Our present interest in the group, however, concerns what its ancestor temple reveals. This temple—visually a shambles, yet ritually in perfect order—consists of a score of shrines which, in partial imitation of royal dynastic temples, reflect the group's legendary history and chart its ties to other shrines and congregations supporting them. Unlike many royal and noble temples, no sacred palm leaf text records a Hindu iconographical significance for these elaborate pedestals. But the combined efforts of several ritual specialists from the group—who peruse the brick and thatchwork, concretely recalling which offering is placed where by which agnatic faction on what occasion—yields the following tally of more pragmatic exegeses:

1. Two pedestals *(pelinggih)* enable the group to propitiate some of its controlling spirits at distant temples purportedly founded by its ancestors on their heroic migration out of eastern Bali. The group still maintains portions of those temples and enjoys friendly relations with the local groups that share them. But these pedestals enable the group to render the spirits a kind of long-distance homage with minimum expense and energy.
2. One monument is reserved as the visitation spot of the spirit of the classical radja who was the group's principal benefactor. Members of the royal house themselves are said

still to come here occasionally to leave offerings. Another marker symbolizes the general relations between this group and the royal palace; yet another commemorates its relations with a lesser radja's house, which received several of the group's women in marriage.

3. There are the vessels for offerings to ensure familial peace, and the standard focal shrine *(kamulan)* for the group's own ancestors (also interpretable in Hindu fashion as Vishnu-Shiva-Brahma).

4. Also sacred is an ancient fruit tree, reputedly planted by the former, upper-caste *(Gusti)* inhabitants of this houseland before their exile.

5. One standard throne is for goddess Saren, divine aspect of sacred ancestral heirlooms (ceremonial swords, spears, etc.). Three others are for the deities of health, economy, and agriculture; their Hindu names are known, but it is the functions themselves that are stressed, since they represent official classical duties which the group still considers to be its professional specializations.

6. Two pedestals connect the temple with the gods of mountain shrines once important in the group's affairs; today they receive only token offerings. Another pedestal, however, refers to a northern irrigation headwater temple, and two small thrones receive the spirits from forest shrines erected by the group's ancestors when searching for the spring this temple commemorates; this connection has recently been revitalized and will soon be discussed.

7. Finally there are the offerings platform, kitchen, evil spirit retaining wall, elevated threshold, and orchestra pavilion standard in Balinese temples.

In some respects the ancestor temple represents the ideal unity of its congregation. Its principal structures—the orchestra pavilion and entrance threshold—are maintained, financed, and outfitted with offerings by all the women of the group equally. No offshoot temple can be built with a taller entrance, which would imply it outranked this sacred ancestral source of all legitimate members of the group. General cyclical and life-crises rites culminate here, from the optional elevated ceremony of auspicious marriages to the recent extra offerings made to assure ancestral benefit for the group's candidates during the 1971 elections. These latter measures were, again, taken by the women as a whole, and it is their concerted ritual activity—each female contributing the same share—that effects in actuality the unity symbolized by the temple.

In other respects the temple represents the internal differentiation of the group, and even the implicit ranks dividing it. Each of its idealized collateral divisions is responsible for repairing different shrines; the size of the shrine reflects the status of the division, and any laxity in upkeep provokes censure. If one of several brothers receives a larger paddy inheritance, he is likely to accrue heavier responsibilities for financing temple festivals. The ordinary adult male's knowledge about his ancestor temple pertains not to esoteric religious lore but to his share of costs of upkeep and finances for ceremonies. By making meticulous calculations to distribute fairly the practical monetary burden of maintaining an ancestor temple, the men assure that any collateral divisions claiming higher prestige must pay for it. (The many thousand temples of "the island of the gods" do not rely on the fabled "Balinese religiosity" alone.)

Beyond symbolizing its own congregation's unity in diversity, the temple is the program for the group's participation in its immediate sacred surroundings. Holy water for its festivals must be collected at a nearby river shrine built by the group at the radja's classical bathing spot. On certain temple holy days, offerings for the ancestors must also be placed at another temple called *pura melanting,* the general designation for marketplace shrines. This *pura melanting* however, lies within a haunted bamboo forest which, suitably eerie at sacred-dangerous noon, because of the piercing shrill of sun-sensitive locusts, provided a handy hideout for the group when the Japanese first occupied Bali. The significance of this temple is obscure; an ancestor from one of the collateral divisions built it as a meditation site, and it is connected with the spirits of another temple important in the migration legend of Tabanan's royal house. The general view is that the ancestor was a man of special mystic powers, was considered by the radja to affect the economic prosperity of the kingdom, and accordingly was licensed to build a *pura melanting.* Thus the group still maintains it, and many unrelated market women stop by the bamboo forest on the temple's festival day to leave offerings.

These connections between the ancestor temple and other shrines, although of dubious social utility, are perpetuated, as are those sacred traditions just itemized which align the group to the now powerless royal dynasty and other parties. Obligations to maintain such shrines are often vestiges of the classical period; much of their significance (e.g., royal baths, meditating for economic prosperity) has grown obscure and politically irrelevant. The group's concern with the shrines is thus instructive in that, for whatever old and new reasons adduced, the concern persists. For example, it built the riverside and bamboo forest monuments in accordance with its active role in the sacred power structure of Tabanan kingdom. Yet when in 1906–1908 the political basis abruptly disappeared, the temple duties remained. Occasionally these seemingly hollow, tenacious ceremonies and legends about past obligations can, if need arise, facilitate the renewing of social ties that have long lain dormant.

A case in point involves the recently revitalized ceremonial activity for the spirits of an irrigation temple in the distant mountains. Interest in the relevant shrines (point 6, p. 274) was revived by a district assembly councilman from the collateral division which once supplied irrigation officers for the kingdom's mountain region. The councilman had suffered a serious illness marked by tormented semiconsciousness; he eventually arose from his sickbed displaying untutored spiritual knowledge, determined to become a ritual specialist in acknowledgement of his cure. Legends credited his division's ancestors with once winning a competition commissioned by the radja among Brahmanas, Sengguhus (exorcist priests), and themselves to explore for new irrigation sources. After meditating in the forests they discovered a spring and, having won the contest, built a new temple there. Today this headwater temple for one of the district's broadest watersheds brings together during its festivals leaders of all irrigation societies which receive paddy water from the river fed by this source. To emphasize his group's special involvement with this headwater temple, as manifested in its ancestral shrines there, the councilman promoted more vigorous participation in the temple's climactic postharvest rites. No longer does it suffice merely to place offerings on the pedestals at home that commemorate these ancestral accomplishments. Now every 210 days an impressive contingent of a dozen or so descendants, predominantly from the councilman's division but including the group's other political figures, makes the tortuous journey to spend the night in a prestigious pavilion reserved for their witnessing the intense ceremony. They are officially recognized by the head priest; trancers receive messages from their ancestors which commend the attendance of these descendants and bid them return regularly. The town group takes little part in the ceremony; its presence simply constitutes another part of the offerings. The councilman himself is subject to trance and climbs to the more distant meditation shrines to pay homage. Divine messages advising how to improve irrigation facilities and remedy troubles between cooperatives issue from trancers through the long night. Some of the councilman's more skeptical kinsmen attribute this aspect of the proceedings to empty emotionalism. Nevertheless, they all value the right to be honorably received at this event, where they make contact with the whole network of irrigation officials and enhance the ceremonies that help ensure bountiful subsistence throughout the region.

The group's renewed interest in its classical involvement with a remote headwater temple cannot be reduced to any single reason. Motivations range doubtless from genuine mystical convictions of the councilman, to the open curiosity of the younger generation, to the at least partial opportunism of the group's more astute politicians. For part of the group's success in the 1971 general elections resulted from the enthusiastic support its campaigners enjoyed throughout the watershed area whose headwater temple it helps sustain. Their reputation in the area has clearly profited from their ancestrally licensed attendance at ceremonies like the one just described. Thus, capitalizing on the social relations implicit in old temple shrines can be, at least indirectly, politically advantageous, yet individual motives vary. Some members of the group favor a rationalized, streamlined role in the irrigation temple rites, a token participation that does not interfere too much with professional obligations and religious duties nearer home. Those who are more interested in the conspicuous presence of their prestigious group than in the rites themselves might be suspected of more outright opportunism. Finally, some of the latter's brothers advocate a fully revitalized commitment to the distant temple rituals, which should ramify through all divisions of the group and help enhance connected religious rites at other shrines on other sacred days.

To summarize, in the case cited a single ancestor temple of a fairly corporate group serves as a catalogue of covert trans-local ties kept in ritual reserve until conditions warrant reactivating them for various advantages, both pragmatic and religious. Later we shall note a more complex social and political significance of temples where traditions of pan-Bali temple networks arise, yet it works on the same principles of cross-referencing distant shrines just illustrated.

## THE POLITICAL RENEWAL OF STATUS PRIDE

*Pasek* is a traditional Balinese (non-Sanskrit) term which designates groups traditionally holding local administrative offices. The "Pasek people" *(Warga Pasek)* refers today to an entire organization of elevated Sudra ancestor groups which, like high castes, trace their origins to the Javanese Madjapahit epoch or before. The fourteenth-century vanquishers of Bali reportedly brought with them Paseks, experts in war, local government, and religion, to serve as village-area officials. Pasek traditions relate that the founding hero of Hindu-Bali, Gadja Mada, originally licensed Brahmanas to oversee the island's local administration, but they proved incompetent and were replaced with Paseks. These Paseks eventually came to employ the personal title I Gde, their purified ceremonial specialists bore the honorific Empu, and like the high castes, they never used teknonymous-looking systems of naming as did "indigenous Balinese."[2]

This ideology which enables members of the Warga Pasek figuratively to assert "I am Brahmana," does not characterize all groups called *Pasek*. There are, for example, Pasek Kaju Selem with their own temples who trace their ancestry to plant categories. But true Warga Pasek traditions are correlated with a set of sacred shrines called *Tjatur Paryangan,* devoted to several legendary brothers who bore the once-Brahmana honorific Empu. A Pasek religious expert enumerates the sacred landmarks as follows:

One shrine located in the heart of classical Hindu-Bali (Gelgel) and maintained by nearby Paseks commemorates Empu Gana who had no descendants. Another shrine in Karangasem (East Bali) is dedicated to Empu Kuturan who possibly begat one daughter who remained in Java. Pasek literati are currently researching such matters, in particular another shrine in Java traced to Erlangga's tenth century reign and dedicated to Empu Berada, thought to be the progenitor of Brahmanas and Satryas. Thus Paseks refer to a pre-Madjapahit era to legitimize their status. A third shrine at the Balinese state temple Besakih is for Empu Sumeru, who also had no descendants. Finally, there is a fourth shrine in Bali for Empu Gde Djaja, who begat the seven descendants who in turn presumably generated the whole current population of Balinese Warga Pasek Sanak Pitu (Pesek People of the Seven Forbears). A sacred genealogy traces their progeny down to a contemporary assortment of local Pasek ancestor groups.

[2]One version of the Warga Pasek traditions is compiled in Sugriwa (1957). Van der Tuuk's 1897 dictionary glossed *pasek* as "'the name of a class of people said to be descendants of the Dewa Agung' (the King of Klungkung, the suzerain of the other Balinese Kings) 'by a *shudra* (common) woman; many *paseks* and *mangkus* (guardians of the village sanctuaries). They presume to be higher in rank than the *perbalis* and to belong really to the third caste' " cited in Pigeaud (1962), IV, 260–261.

Thus, like Satryas, Paseks believe they are descended from Brahmana stock, but they never had the power to rule, only to administer. They currently comprise the island's largest category of elevated commoners and enjoy a popular reputation for cleverness in governmental and military matters, suggested by the envious remarks such as: ''If you're a village leader, you've got to be Pasek! They're smart all right; why Sukarno was of Pasek blood by his mother.''[3]

Recent efforts to revitalize ideas of the special social role for Paseks have sometimes been denigrated by non-Paseks as ''smelling of politics'' *(berbau politik)*. Even before the elections of 1955, there were rumors of Paseks bickering with ordinary Bendesa groups (those with the right to head customary village-areas) over their relative ranks. But the movement to unify the ''true'' descendants of the seven Pasek ancestors gained momentum after 1965, during the confusion produced by the anticommunist massacres throughout Bali following the unsuccessful coup attempt in Djakarta (GESTAPU). Before the elections of 1971, leaders even moved to secure a Pasek seat in the general assembly of a central Balinese district, arguing that the region's numerous Paseks represented its largest constituency. Their effort failed, possibly because of the worries by the Nationalist Party (PNI) over any potential split in its ranks. Informants say that before the GESTAPU the Paseks included many communists, but after it they were largely PNI. By 1971, many were joining the ''functional groups'' (GOLKAR) created by Suharto's administration to replace ideological parties (Nishihara, 1972). Several district-wide meetings of Pasek groups were planned in different regions, and all-Bali Pasek conventions took place in 1969 and 1970. In 1971 a Pasek leader at the movement's central office in the Balinese capital tried to form a stronger Pasek branch in a neighboring district by requesting the support of a well-known elder from the classical Pasek ancestor group there. The latter's initial refusal was interpreted by some observers as an indication that the Pasek movement would wane under the new GOLKAR antiparty political system of Indonesia.

Regardless of the movement's long-term success, that an organization can aspire to a broadly representational base by employing an idiom of exclusivistic caste principles to authenticate its supposedly restricted membership is suggestive of the (persistently disowned) flexibility characterizing Balinese social status, religion, and politics, all—especially in the Pasek case—approximately the same thing. To appreciate this, we must consider the source of the movement's grassroots appeal. The attraction to Pasek status stems from the fundamental Balinese premise that most troubles arise from neglecting, or worst of all forgetting, the ancestors. Typically, because of some misfortune such as illness or crop failure, several brothers might seek the advice of a magician-healer *(balian)*. He diagnoses a failure properly to propitiate the ancestors and recommends that they go in quest of their true origins. He might specify a particular

---

[3] A sample of other sorts of elevated commoner groups is listed in C. Geertz (1967:222). And contrasts in such groups' reputations in different regions are suggested in Boon (1973:232).

Pasek temple worth visiting on its fesitval day, to determine whether it is their ancestral source. The brothers could also hire a Brahmana priest—well-informed about the legends relating that many Paseks forgot their status after the collapse of Bali's old central kingdom—to detect from manuscripts' clues illuminating their true origins. If the elders in the Pasek temple receive them, the brothers make a payment—perhaps a bit of gold and three meters of white cloth—and they become Pasek, although not necessarily acknowledged as such back home. This same chain of events can characterize people who rediscover their place in a higher caste-status (especially Gusti), but their claim might well require direct confirmation by a traditional upper-caste group. Much more accessible to ordinary Balinese commoners is the category of Pasek, to which nearly any commoner may aspire in perfect confidence that he merits this embellished designation with its implications of superior religious standing.

A doubtless exaggerated report on the scope of rediscovery of Pasek origins appears in *Warta Duta Warga,* a mouthpiece of the Pasek organization. The magazine's contents, in Indonesian and Balinese, include traditional Hindu texts, articles on Bali-Hindu philosophy, a printout of the chronicle collected from palm leaf manuscripts which legitimizes Pasek claims to authority, and general information on the well-formed Pasek houseyard: the proper construction of houseyard temples, distinctive offerings, etc. Each issue also includes a section of a progressive compilation of Pasek ancestor temples *(ring pura-pura paibon, panti, dadia).* Every entry itemizes the temple's location, information on its source in the form of a sacred founder or the prior temple it sprang from, and the names of its religious custodian, chief elder, and chairman of its council. Finally, the number of family heads supporting the temple is noted, a figure ranging between ten and two thousand per temple. By temple sixty-three the Pasek movement was already counting among its followers around 5 percent of the family heads in Bali. And judging from the potential redefinition of old temples and old statuses, no end was in sight.[4]

Differences in the social composition of localities affect the feasibility of converting to Pasek status. The existence of several ancestor groups in a given area with precedent claims to traditional Pasek standing might discourage recognizing new aspirants, since a group admitting newcomers is apt to be disparaged by its status rivals. On the other hand, it is economically advantageous to have more family heads financing a temple's costly ceremonies and repairs. A possible compromise, which allows for a continued aura of exclusivity while meeting practical financial needs, is to restrict local affiliations of a given Pasek temple

---

[4]The journal was issued bimonthly throughout 1971. Later it folded, only temporarily according to some. The Pasek organization also issued a calendar with notes on the festival dates of—from its point of view—important temples; another guide to Pasek privileges in Balinese and Indonesian is *Bisama Pasek* (ed. I. N. S. Atmanadhi, 1970). For the thirty Pasek temples whose figures I have, 7,870 family heads are tallied, and for the incomplete list of 63 temples as of issue ten, we can guess around 14,000 (out of a total population of over 2 million or around 250,000 family heads).

but to welcome affiliations of geographically distant "kinsmen" who, although not part of the death-contamination *(sebel)* group, help out in maintenance costs. In some conservative regions traditional overlords might retain a voice in authenticating ancestral "memberships" of any caste-status, as might a strong village-area or hamlet organization. Thus, the Pasek movement has the greatest potential for sweeping local effects in areas characterized by few distinctions in caste-status (see below).

Each case is particular. For example, in Sangolan village-area sixty family heads support the Pasek ancestral temple in the neighboring locale Pangkong Prabhu. Not long ago there were only fifty, but then ten more began frequenting the temple because of illness in their families. According to informants: "They remembered they were Pasek descendants, and now they are well received in Pangkong Prabhu." Sangolan also boasts its own ancestor temple for the twelve family heads who consider themselves a Bendesa-type group, with the traditional authority to serve as leader of Sangolan. Thus, Sangolan's upper crust contains both the Pasek group and the Bendesa group which, as yet at least, does not consider itself Pasek. These two local groups claim sole rights to a minor honorific *(Pan)* rather than the ordinary peasant appellation *(Nanang),* a privilege articulated several years ago by a Pasek who was the area's only salaried civil servant. Paseks and Bendesas vie over who merits the more prestigious spot in the graveyard and similar matters of rank. Of particular interest here is the story that in classical times, the radja split Sangolan into three divisions, each apportioned to a different guru who provided ritual holy water. Two of these divisions were the holy water clients *(sisia)* of Brahmana Siwa priests. The third division, however, became clients to the holy man in Pangkong Prabhu, a mystic in charge of the Pasek ancestor temple. This situation is susceptible to at least two different retrospective interpretations. Either the Sangolaners were seen as kinsmen of these Pasek, since a Pasek holy man *(Empu)* generally sanctifies water only for his own kinsmen, or the royal house considered the Pasek holy man as equivalent to a Brahmana priest, the kind of ritual specialist who generally can have a non-kin clientele. Regardless, it is noteworthy that the Sangolan-Pangkong Prabhu relationship, which is retrospectively primarily coded as a guru-client bond, is today coded in terms of kinship relations of an inter-local Pasek ancestor-group.

Thus at the local level, participation by certain houseyards in the Pasek temple system—which is theoretically an interrelated network of locales sacred to an enormous group descended from a single Javanese Empu—may involve that area in the greater Hindu strain of Balinese culture, in this case the sacred cosmography of the Pasek Sanak Pitu. New Paseks gain potentially practical benefits of a wider network of often influential associates, but they also assume financial responsibilities to support the temple and its ceremonies. Sometimes brothers are split, some claiming Pasek status and others not. By joining ranks with the Paseks, a commoner accumulates more ancestral spirits to watch over his interests, spirits enhanced through commemoration in sacred texts. If enough houseyards in a particular locale agree on their status and discover which Pasek temple they issued from, they can in turn construct an ancestor temple, whose members might tend then to marry within the temple congregation. (Some observers contend that Pasek-type houseyards can build an ancestor temple with fewer members than other kinds of commoners, since they have automatic links with Paseks in other areas.) The new congregation, whose core group manifests mutual religious contamination, represents an additional sacred source in the expanding Pasek network.

Unsurprisingly, opponents of the Pasek movement challenge its legitimacy. They point out that Sengguhu and Pande ancestor groups (the first are traditional specialists in exorcist rites, the second in metalwork) contain no false members: "There are no new Sengguhus." This classical caste scheme again is invoked to challenge a Pasek's right to bear witness to another man's status. Traditionally, it is argued, only the radja could legitimize a Pasek line, and there were only a few Pasek source groups in each kingdom. Even the Dutch are said to have allowed only true Paseks to become village-area officials. The movement's opponents scoff at those who profit materially by admitting outsiders to their temple festivals and ceremonial banquets. "Seventy-five percent of Bali seems to be Pasek," they joke. They point out the political jockeying involved when officials agree to sanction the re-dedication of a group's temple as a Pasek temple. One such event in Tabanan district was attended by a district chief official *(Bupati)*, the district leader of the national department of religion, and by an officer from Parisada, an organization spearheading the rationalization of Bali-Hindu religion and its expansion into other areas of Indonesia. Opponents deny that such an affair constitutes what its participants feel is a valid continuation of classical precedents, whereby the then district chief (the radja) and his temple experts always supervised the dedication ceremonies of new shrines.

Even when the authenticity of a new or refurbished "Pasek" temple cannot be doubted, any obviously opportunistic political overtones provoke cynicism among non-Paseks. Consider the case of an important civil servant whose group was the primary source of Pasek officials in classical Tabanan kingdom. He recently acquired a government house in the capital where he now keeps his first wife (a Sudanese) and their children; back home a second wife, his patri-cousin, looks after the elders. A new dwelling requires a new house-temple, and on the propitious day a group of elder ritual specialists from his ancestral home were trucked forty-odd miles to conduct its dedication ceremony. They sat outside cross-legged upon grass mats squeezed onto the front stoop. The guests—a cosmopolitan array of professionals—sat inside on aluminum folding chairs, smoking Kansas cigarettes, and drinking beer and palm wine to the recorded tune of "Two Lonely Flowers Surround my Heart with Tears," before eventually consuming the traditional ceremonial feast being prepared back in the kitchen. Outside were the skeletal elders from the sacred source. Inside was the corpulent power contingent which included—and this is what mattered—the head of Badung district, himself a Pasek who came to witness the sacred dedication of a bureaucratic bungalow to the ancestors he shares with this up-and-coming member of his constituency.

As this example suggests, the Pasek movement involves efforts to fit a rising professional sector of society into a traditional Balinese cultural framework. Sometimes civil servants employed far from their customary *(adat)* rights and obligations can pay fines to cover the inevitable neglect of duties. Policies vary, however, according to the fanaticism of each hamlet council, and often there are no exemptions from cremation witnessing. A more extreme strain on adat relations arises when, as just described, a member of the bureaucratic elite obtains housing in a town. He might help finance a customary hamlet near his new residence, but his own life-crisis ceremonies *(suka-duka)* continue to be executed in his original houseyard and hamlet. A prominent civil servant can in fact maintain what is called a "double hamlet membership." But the surest way to perpetuate home ties is to belong to a strong temple group which can protect a man's local rights even in his absence; such groups are traditionally less dependent on local hamlet organizations for carrying out the rituals central in Balinese life. Thus, with the burgeoning mobile civil service, any tightening of temple-groups and the Pasek movement in general reflect a refusal to sever local ties which lends a distinctive shape to Balinese "urbanization."[5] A cluster of motives is involved:

1. Belief that the ancestors are linked to a sacred point of origin, part of the rich symbology of the religious source of important groups;
2. Maintenance of rights in houseland owned by the hamlet (and as of land reform in the 1960s, and maintenance of rights to own agricultural land in one's home subdistrict);
3. Care for the elders, sometimes keeping a patri-cousin "country wife" at home, and another outsider wife in town;
4. Perhaps most importantly, sustaining good family and hamlet relations that insure a final resting place and proper ceremonies after death, the ultimate religious ideal in Bali.

Membership in a strong ancestor-group—a "Pasek" congregation, for example—allows an individual greater flexibility in forwarding a career, while delegating his *adat* tasks to other members of his group who represent both his practical and religious interests in local affairs.

There are differences of opinion among Pasek and non-Pasek alike concerning the ultimate goals of their movement. The organization seeks unity, a familial feeling among all Paseks, both old and newly rediscovered. Some hope to convert this solidarity into a means of controlling a vote bloc at various levels of government. Others proclaim these ambitions exaggerated and view the

---

[5]Contrast, for example, the situation in neighboring Java where "townsmen, particularly the pegawai [civil servants] and merchants, rarely have houses in villages" (H. Geertz, 1963:41).

movement merely as an effort to coordinate Pasek control within the Balinese bureaucracy. After independence, it is explained, Paseks were fragmented and their lines grew obscure, since an agency no longer verified descent claims as in the colonial period. Now, since they number many government employees, Paseks want to organize to make the bureaucracy more efficient, to control access to white-collar positions, and thus to endow the traditional category of Pasek with pragmatic advantages. A Pasek pedigree is one of the surest ways to win a salaried position in contemporary Bali.

Thus we find both in the upper echelons and at the grassroots of the Pasek movement a combination of aims and motives. It is as much a revitalization of cultural principles advanced to unify all true Paseks as naturally endowed administrators, as it is an opportunistic political maneuver to coordinate a bureaucratic in-group and extend the Pasek category to build an effective vote bloc as (prior to 1971, at least) an alternative to the Nationalist Party. The combined political, social, and religious aspects of the Pasek phenomenon—this modern lateralization of a prestigious Sudra caste-status—are neatly subsumed in an informant's traditional Balinese commentary:

> Paseks are looking for their source, for family connections. They are seeking their deified ancestors *(kawitan)*. Now the *lontar Jatua Sarasamuscaja* disproves the kawitan theory; it says there is only one kawitan, God *(Tuhan)*, which has been broken up because of the various social functions. But people still search for their own kind, in order to eat with them; yes, in order to have someone to eat with.

## RELIGIOUS HIERARCHY EMERGING

Antosari is the name of a governmental local unit in western Tabanan district. It is a progressive, commercial area situated on the Dutch-built road between Java and the Balinese capital. Around four hundred families inhabit the vicinity which contains twelve hamlets, whose members are distributed into four customary village-areas and fragments of other village-areas *(desa adat)*. In recent years some eighty households have transmigrated to Sulawesi; they represent one of the rare successful episodes in the government's faltering transmigration program. Sulawesi's advantages are, in contrast to Sumatra, hilly terrain and enough water to support a traditional Balinese irrigation system. In 1971–72 the national transmigration office sponsored return trips to Bali for the most enthusiastic migrants, and the Antosari contingent persuaded another score to join them in Sulawesi. Among those convinced were many prosperous Paseks. A transmigrant generally sells his paddy to kinsmen, but must contribute enough land to cover his share of costs for cremating any ancestors not yet exhumed. The achievement of the national program in Antosari is a good indication of the progressiveness of the area.

West of Antosari stretches a region first opened by the Dutch in 1913.

Classical Antosari was situated beyond the subkingdom of Krambitan, which was ruled by the Tabana radja's collateral and marked the western extreme of pre-Dutch courtly society. Even due east there were no Satrya-Wesia noble houseyards and, judging from present-day ranks, only a few Brahmana houses (*griya*). The only glimmer of Hindu hierarchy in classical and colonial Antosari apparently centered on a group of highly ambiguous status, reputedly descended from a noble exiled from classical Tabanan's courtly neighborhood. There is an elaborate legend about the group's founding hero: how his shameful exile was transformed into a legendary trek; how by white magic this mystic sage foiled the radja's men, achieved miracles, and finally settled beside a river on magical ground normally deemed uninhabitable in the Balinese scheme of things. His descendants still live there and use this legend to explain how an exiled noble's house (*Gusti* caste-status) came eventually to be designated by the Brahmana courtyard label *griya*. They say the founder's healing powers won the devotion of surrounding ordinary people, who began relating to him as clients (*sisia*) to *guru*. In this way, it appears, a great traditional caste configuration slipped into commoner Antosari behind the radja's back, and a controversially "Brahmana" house was born replete with providers of holy water for loyal supporters and its own graveyard for exclusive cremation ceremonies. In the colonial period the group's holy men sought official recognition as Brahmana *pedandas* by the courts, but were refused. Today, however, even officially legitimate Brahmana priests agree that the remarkable feature of the riverside house is its capacity to attract and maintain outsider *sisia*.[6]

Although it lies 2 kilometers away, this isolated group participates in Antosari's northeast hamlet, also the source of many transmigrants and populated largely by Paseks, at least recently. Elaborations of the hierarchical principles apparently introduced into Antosari by the riverside group are occurring within the area's Pasek ranks. There currently reside here four Pasek branches with these ancestral titles:

1. Pasek Gelgel
2. Pasek Tangguntiti
3. Pasek Toh Djiwa
4. Pesak Antosari.

The only other Hindu religious pattern characterizing Antosari is the *sisia-guru* relations just described, and many Paseks support one of the anomalous holy men as their ritual specialist. The first two Pasek groups trace their origins to the traditional Pasek sources in southwest and central Bali named in their titles. The Pasek Toh Djiwa claim to derive from a Pasek group in another subkingdom which provided administrators for the royal house. Finally, Pasek Antosari is a laughable title to some, since Antosari is obviously not a traditional local Pasek

---

[6]Marriage strategies in such elevated groups of anomalous caste-status will be discussed in a separate study on flexibilities in Balinese marriage values.

source. This admittedly new group first felt it originated from Toh Djiwa and then leaned toward either Emas (a Pasek source in Gianjar district) or Gelgel. Its members are still examining chronicles but now frequent the festivals in Emas. Whether they are Gelgel or Toh Djiwa might appear a moot point, since the latter themselves arose from Gelgel before moving to another subkingdom and still have a shrine in the Pasek Gelgel temple (cf. offshoot shrines described earlier). But the issue is potentially vital for discerning the *relative rank* of Pasek Antosaris *among Paseks*. Apart from the Paseks, there is a Pande group (traditional smiths) with its own minor temple, offshoot of a larger one in a neighboring subkingdom. There are as yet no Pasek temples, not even a partially independent *pura pemaksan,* which is actually the highest-level temple that could be built here, since the only legitimate larger Pasek *panti* temples in Tabanan district are still considered to be in Tangguntiti and Wanogiri.

In spite of their still obscure origins, the Pasek groups have been busily correlating their status claims with specific functionary rights. For now Paseks express their superiority in Antosari society less by corroborating distinctive religious origins than by apportioning among themselves rights to temple duties and protocolar forms. Only the four Pasek Tangguntiti families do not yet participate in the division of offices. Although they have theoretically the easiest status claims to verify, they have not researched their rights in the sacred texts. They do, however, claim the privilege of using burial and cremation towers. Based on the eastern Balinese archetype of hierarchy, the Pasek Gelgel should merit the highest biers and the most honorific speech forms from other Paseks, since the eastern Pasek Gelgel are considered descendants of the highest-ranked legendary brother documented in the chronicles. But Antosari's Pasek Gelgel have yet to assert these privileges.

As might be expected, Pasek Antosari (Emas) is the least protocol minded group; in light of its legendarily subordinate descent, it has more to gain by stressing the exclusive tasks outlined in Pasek traditions. Its members claim rights to special official roles at a nearby prestigious temple sacred to the general population of Tabana district, regardless of village-area or ancestor group. The fifteen Pasek Antosari family heads organize and oversee the festivals here, and they are responsible for all-night watches when the gods descend. Other Paseks are not forbidden from assisting, but this group is in charge; it is already educating one of its members to replace the old temple priest-custodian. People in Antosari observe that practices here still fall short of the exemplary East, where the prescribed group must fill its specified office, even if none of its members desires to. If such a case arose in Antosari, the position would be likely to pass to another group. They confess there is still much confusion in these matters; yet the ideal of special offices for each Pasek rank is strengthening. As for the other Paseks, the Gelgel and Toh Djiwa titles are considered rightful suppliers of priests for the *desa* temple set, where certain duties in the preparation of offerings are given over to the Pande group as well.

Antosari thus demonstrates caste-statuses in parturition, born of the consolidation and redefinition of temple groups articulated by the Pasek ideology. We can speculate that soon local competition over relative rank will be thriving, especially in the ultimate sphere of Balinese religion, differential funerary privileges. A locale achieves hierarchy; Antosari arrives. As neighbors increasingly compete in matters of religious rank, there is little danger of exhausting the supply of exclusive offices which help express status differentiation, since new temples can always be erected. For example, sixty northern households recently decided to break away from the Antosari village-area to build an independent origins-temple where (a religious expert divined) a long-forgotten temple once stood. The new temple will theoretically provide more meticulously differentiated religious offices for the ranks of Paseks.

The emergence of a debatable hierarchy of temple functions that must at some stage be legitimized by government officials, with the accompanying costly ritual protocol and expensive shrines, has been facilitated by the area's commercial prosperity. Moreover, one could relate the recently successful transmigration program to the growing sense of Pasek status identities. This glaring exception to the general stereotype (as pervasive inside Bali as outside) that no Balinese could bear to abandon his island can possibly be explained by the hope of some Antosarians to extend their distinctive ancestor groups to a new sacred locale. Transmigrants to Sulawesi appear more willing to leave behind their kinsmen and local customary obligations and privileges, because they know that their family and collaterals in Antosari constitute a thriving group well-connected in a temple network, a group that can attend to the absentees' religious interests in Antosari, always remaining there in the event they wish to return home, physically or spiritually.

Temples are thus playing somewhat the same role in modern Bali as in fourteenth-century Java when, as legend has it, the establishment of Bali's first Hindu-Java ancestor temple brought civilization to the rustic Bali Aga. Antosari's Pasek enthusiasts are very receptive to the view that as the generals of Gadja Mada once implanted in Bali sacred Madjapahit standards of courts and temple, so now Paseks have established in lowly Sulawesi new temples whose congregations trace their divine origins to Bali. From Java to Bali and Bali to Sulawesi, the classical process of Hinduization continues, however altered its scale.

## CONCLUSIONS: IS BALINESE RELIGION CHANGING?

Not all recent developments affecting Balinese temples so neatly complement traditional high Hindu ideals by realigning political associations and status ambitions. In 1971–1972 a scandal reverberating all the way to Jakarta exploded over a seaside shrine that lay in the path of the projected expansion of an important tourist facility. After the area's district leader announced his intention to demolish the temple, resistance spread among local residents and officials in a neighboring district as well. The leader offered a compensatory payment for the temple and its lands and promised to rebuild it nearby. This proposal was rejected, since the significance of a temple is the sanctity of the actual space it occupies which, together with the productive lands "owned" by the temple, is supposedly inviolable. When the demolition squad was eventually dispatched anyway, its members lost their nerve, and the priest who had agreed to sanctify the proceedings (even temple-*un*dedications are religiously dedicated in Bali) reportedly became powerless, and two days later his wife died. To abate the growing protest, the district leader backed down, and the hotel extension was built elsewhere (*Tempo* . . . , 1972). Thus, this particular temple still stands, but the conflict reflected in the episode persists, especially where tourism is growing fast.

The exact contrary to this leader's apparent neglect of sacred shrines arises where an official's conspicuous devotion to temples and ritualism is denigrated by his opponents as a deflection from his true responsibilities. A vivid instance of this situation concerned a recent district leader in southwest Bali who had a reputation for religious fanaticism. His obsession with refurbishing district temples and elaborating their ceremonies was in sharp contrast to his predecessor's interest in improved roads, expanded electricity, and thriving commerce. The leader, previously an active military officer, was personally devout and observed the ritual precautions of mystic specialists. He managed to reconstruct the district center's market temple and death temple into impressive edifices, especially for this part of Bali. But his most disputed project involved an obscure set of shrines near his headquarters which, according to local traditions, was once sacred to the royal house of the kingdom but had been neglected since the radja was first deposed by the Dutch in 1906–1908. He laid the groundwork for having the shrine complex acknowledged as a district temple so it would qualify for government financing. The temple was expanded, and fuller participation in its ceremonies was offered first to some of his political favorites; all this indirectly enhanced the status of the leader's own ancestor group houselands which adjoin the temple. Yet even the commercial Chinese sector of town was assessed for temple funds, as if it were a general public shrine. In 1972 the dispute continued; some parties accused the leader of taking advantage of his office to elevate the ritual status of his own ancestor group and related lesser nobel houses by outfitting a temple at public expense that might eventually be construed as theirs alone and help them overshadow other noble groups. This case suggests the intensity of renewed status competition even among the upper caste-statuses of commercial towns.

Although diametrically opposed, both cases reflect the same rift that has appeared in Balinese experience which splinters the traditional amalgamation of religious, economic, and political affairs. Traditionally (at least retrospectively) any bald conflict between sacred ceremonialism and some other activity would have been improbable, since ritual provided the backdrop and often the actual realization of any political, economic, or otherwise pragmatic measure. The two episodes just described instantiate the new sentiment among some Balinese—first described for Bali in 1957–1958 by C. Geertz—that rituals are irrelevant to certain aims or even in competition with other areas of life (C. Geertz, 1964). The forefront of the perceived "rationalization of Balinese religion" is the Parisada organization which attempts to compartmentalize ritual practices and explain them by some kind of individual-internal value typical of religious reform movements and to codify a Bali-Hindu doctrine for easy export. This budding attitude of reformism spearheaded by urban elites, many of them Brahmana, can be perceived behind both the attempted desecration of a temple and the criticisms of an official for religious fanaticism just outlined, since both episodes imply a sense of separation of religious from other kinds of action.

Any hint of reformism in Balinese religion raises the question not only of rationalization and nationalization, but of Javanization (Geertz, 1972). The specter of the apparently devastating effects post-fourteenth century Islamic reforms had on traditional Javanese religious life arises in any consideration of the implications of reform in neighboring tiny Bali, which always appears somehow defenseless. Ardent Balinese reformists themselves expect rapid results in rationalizing their "feudal," archaic compatriots. The post-Independence reform movement has in recent years, however, suffered some setbacks. Participation in the unusual temple constructed in the heart of the capital city by the Parisada organization has become politicized. Opponents say that only coerced school groups now attend the dogmatic sermons preached there; they recall the heavy-handed, partisan promotion of the original dedication ceremony some years ago and point out that its site was originally a favorite haunt of prostitutes. Parisada did help to win Jakarta's recognition of Bali-Hindu as a legitimate religion and to design the systematic religious education of Bali's masses. But its efforts to normalize the island's complex and variable temple system and to give precedence to village-area origin temples as mosque-like corporate confraternities appear to have faltered. At least the widespread renewed emphasis on ancestor group temples and networks, inevitably detracting from village-area temples, partly undermines this aim.

If the religious tendencies highlighted by the Parisada reform organization had reached the proportions of a genuine reformation, then parts of the Pasek movement and other efforts we have described to reinstate the social and political underpinnings of elaborated ancestor temple ceremonies would constitute something of a counter-reformation—a reenchantment of the world, in this case by revitalizing some of the social and political dimensions that were part and parcel of the enchantment in the first place. But such sweeping macrohistorical formulations are too bold to depict the Balinese developments, which illustrate reenchantment occurring before disenchantment has made much headway. Bali suggests how a Weberian rationalization of religious organization and intensification of ritualism keyed to a hierarchical cosmology are not intrinsically opposed; nor need either necessarily advance by denying the legitimacy of the other (*Upadeca,* 1968) to ingratiate it in a national bureau of religious affairs, to extend it beyond its centuries-old confinement in a very small island, and to re-legitimize an urban elite as professors of a dogma. Simultaneously the Pasek movement and other resurgences of caste-status have promoted the propagation of status-laden ritualism, in order to replicate traditional caste ideals and to claim old forms of mystical and ritual expertise for local commoner charismatic figures.

If the classical higher statuses move to systematize and rationalize their religious concerns and sacred roles in society, their traditional inferiors tend to assimilate any older patterns almost at the moment they are discarded. Consider, for example, the efforts of the Balinese religious bureaucracy to outline and limit the role of Brahmana priests, to streamline their exclusive rituals, to dictate their character traits and demand exemplary behavior *even in nonritual matters,* and to test their achievement in mastering the sacred literature, often reinterpreting classical texts to legitimize these new policies. One general Balinese response has been to tolerate this reform of Bali-Hindu's ultimate ritual specialists, but on the other hand to increase support of ritual practitioners from other statuses who can continue with unfettered, unreformed ceremonies. We see this in the revival of charismatic Pasek Empus with new temples as ritual settings; and the Pasek case is just part of the tendency for all old or newly defined ancestor groups to support their own ritual specialists, calling less often on Brahmana priests or even outsider commoner *pemangkus.* It appears that if Brahmana priests ever become a truly routinized religious elite, concerned more with edifying internal character than with ritually juxtaposing the propitious elements of the sacred universe, then this latter task will have proliferated among other caste-statuses.

To conclude, Balinese religion is indeed changing. The changes appear somewhat ''heterogenetic'' where the ritual duties temples require are considered by religious reformists to conflict with other needs.[7] But the developments in our case studies are more ''orthogenetic''; in large measure Balinese religion as manifest in temple rituals is changing just as it always has. The expansion of temple networks—whether at the level of a once-powerful temple group refurbishing old inter-local ties commemorated in its shrines, or of a program to consolidate an islandwide network of Pasek statuses—is in perfect continuity with the precolonial history of the extension of Bali-Hindu courtly ideals and ritual centers into new territory. Evidence documented earlier suggests that any wave of reform in Balinese religion also generates many eddies of ritualistic revitalization. An alternative to speculations by Indonesian reformists, and by

[7]For a review and explanation of the concepts of heterogenetic and orthogenetic social and cultural change, see Singer (1972: chap. 9). Many of the developments described in this paper could be plotted against Singer's more schematic theories of enclavement and compartmentalization, vicarious ritualization, ritual neutralization, etc.

those fearing them, that traditional Bali-Hindu ritualism could (analogous to Java) be almost eliminated by a sweeping reform movement is that ritualism will experience a change in the social strata specializing in it. It is at least worth observing that some two decades after a nationalist religious reform policy was launched and institutionalized by urban elites, in less elevated spheres of society—individual resurgent ancestor groups, enhanced commoner temple networks, and newly enlightened rustic locales—Balinese temple ceremonies continue to facilitate the redefinition of political allegiances under the rubric of traditional caste-status relations, and to imbue recent social change with the religious aura of the very old and ritually preordained.

## ACKNOWLEDGMENTS

This study is based on fieldwork carried out in 1971–1972, largely in Tabanan district, Bali, Indonesia, first as a Ford Foundation Consultant, and under N.I.M.H. grant (1 F01 MH 51800-01); it was revised with the help of a grant-in-aid from the Wenner-Gren Foundation for Anthropological Research. Thanks to the other participants in the conference and especially to O. Boon, H. and C. Geertz, and S. Ortner for helpful comments.

## REFERENCES

Ardana, I Gusti Gde. *Pengertian pura di Bali*. Den Pasar: Projec Pemeliharaan dan Pengembangan Kebudajaan Daerah Bali, 1971.

Atmanadhi, I. N. S. (Ed.). *Bisama Pasek*. Den Pasar: Maha Gotra Sanak Supta Rsi, 1970.

Bateson, Gregory. An old temple and a new myth. *Djawa*, 1937, *17* (5, 6), 291–307.

Belo, Jane. *Bali: Temple festival*. Monographs of the American Ethnological Society, 22. Seattle: University of Washington Press, 1953.

Belo, Jane. *Trance in Bali*. New York: Columbia University Press, 1960.

Boon, J. A. *Dynastic dynamics: Caste and kinship in Bali now*. Doctoral dissertation, University of Chicago, 1973.

Boon, J. A. The progress of the ancestors in a Balinese temple-group (pre-1906–1972). *Journal of Asian Studies*, November 1974, *34* (1), 7–26.

Covarrubias, Miguel. *Island of Bali*. New York: Knopf, 1937.

de Zoete, Beryl, and Spies, Walter. *Dance and drama in Bali*. New York: Harper's, 1939.

Geertz, Clifford. Internal conversion in contemporary Bali. In J. Batson and R. Roolrirk (Eds.), *Malayan and Indonesian studies*. Oxford: Clarendon Press, 1964.

Geertz, Clifford. Religious change and social order in Soeharto's Indonesia. *Asia*, 1972, *27*, 62–84. Ithaca: Cornell University Press, 1967.

Geertz, Clifford. Religious change and social order in Socharto's Indonesia. *Asia*, 1972, *27*, 62–84.

Geertz, Hildred. Indonesian cultures and communities. In Ruth T. McVey (Ed.), *Indonesia*. New Haven: Human Relations Area File Press, 1963.

Hooykaas, C. *Agama Tirtha: Five studies in Hindu-Balinese religion*. Verhandelingen der Koniklijke Nederlandse Akademie van Wetenschappen, Afd. Letterkunde, LXX, 4. Amsterdam: N.V. Noord Hollandsche Uitgevers Maatschappij, 1964.

Kersten, J. *Bali*. Eindhoven: Uitgeversmaatschappij "De Pilgrim" N.V., 1947.

Korn, V. E. *Het Adatrecht van Bali*. 's-Gravenhage: G. Naeff, 1932.

Liefrinck, F. A. *Bali en Lombok*. Amsterdam: J. H. de Bussy, 1927.

Nishihara, Masashi. *GOLKAR and the Indonesian elections of 1971*. Modern Indonesia Project 56. Ithaca: Cornell University Press 1972.

Pigeaud, T. G. Th. *Java in the 14th century*. The Hague: Martinus Nijhoff, 1962.

Singer, Milton. *When a great tradition modernizes*. New York: Praeger, 1972.

Sugriwa, I Gusti Bagus. *Babad Pasek dalam Bahasa Indonesia*. Den Pasar: Balimas, 1957.

Swellengrebel, J. L. *Kerk en Temple op Bali*, 's-Gravenhage: W. van Hoeve, 1948.

Swellengrebel, J. L. *Bali: Studies in life, thought, and ritual*. The Hague: W. van Hoeve, 1960.

Swellengrebel, J. L. *Further studies in life, thought, and ritual*. The Hague: W. van Hoeve, 1969.

*Tempo, Madjallah Berita Mingguan*. Bali jang Berubah: Bila waktu Mendjamah Bali, May 27, 1972.

*Upadeca: Tentang adjaran-adjaran agama hindu*. Den Pasar: Parisada Hindu Dharma, 1968.

chapter fifteen

# From Purity to Pollution? The Balinese Ketjak (Monkey Dance) as Symbolic Form in Transition

Philip F. McKean

Concord Academy

How is a symbolic form, which may undergo a variety of interpretations, to be understood in its different expressions? Among the plethora of symbolic forms which exist in Bali one, the *ketjak* dance, has at least two distinct meanings, depending on the social context, the intention of the sponsors, and the nature of the audience. On one hand, the dance is a religious performance used during times of peril and pestilence to exorcise evil. On the other, it is an increasingly popular tourist attraction, featured on the pages of *National Geographic* and the American Express travel magazine, a dance every international visitor who "does" Bali in two to five days is likely to see and hear.

The contrast between sacred and profane is obvious and leads to more difficult predictive questions. Does the profanation of Balinese culture by tourism mean the triumph of *Homo economicus,* even on that island so traditionally devoted to the divine world? Does the coming of an international economy, with market transactions, competition for wealth, and concern for capital accumulation and profit, mark the triumph of one symbol system over another older one, which has traditionally been rooted in devotion to the sacred pantheon of Balinese Hinduism?

Over thirty years ago, Ernst Cassirer encouraged a new appreciation of symbolic forms. He termed myth, art, language, and science, *symbols:*

> . . . each of which produces and posits a world of its own. . . . Thus the special symbolic forms are not imitations, but *organs of reality,* since it is solely by their agency that anything real becomes an object for intellectual apprehension and, as such, is made visible to us. For the mind, only that can be visible which has some definite form; but every form of existence has its source in some peculiar way of seeing, some intellectual formulation and intuition of meaning. (1953:8)

Two Balinese legong dancers, in costume and form similar to the sangyang dedari, indicating the synchronous motions when the dancers perform together, accompanied by the ketjak chorus. Here they are not in trance, but dancing for a tourist audience.

Assuming that the *ketjak* is a form which embodies a "peculiar way of seeing" for Balinese, what "intuition of meaning" can be ascribed to this symbol over the course of decades past and present?

The *ketjak* proper refers to the sounds voiced by a male chorus, similar to the rhythms of a *gamelan* orchestra, which is normally absent in this performance. It is an ancient accompaniment to several kinds of dances which are initially intended both to stimulate trance states in individuals and to promote the purification *(sangyang)* of a village. This chorus can accompany several different kinds of sangyang ceremonies and consists of the adult males who were tied to a particular temple *(pura)*, hamlet *(bandjar)*, or kin group *(dadia)*.

The meaning of the term *ketjak* is subject to different folk interpretations. First, several Balinese told me that they thought the call of the house-lizard *(che-chuk*, named onomatopoetically) was being imitated in the *ketjak* dance. The house-lizard is believed to be a messenger of good fortune, and many Balinese folktales link the lizard to beneficent spirits. Thus the *ketjak* might be an invocation of the name of the house-lizard, bearing good fortune for the village or clan. Alternatively, the word *ketjak* may be related to the Balinese word *tjak*, meaning "to break or separate" (compare the Indonesian word *petjah* with a similar meaning). In this sense, *ketjak* would be a shout at malevolent spirits, pleading or demanding that the evil powers bringing plague, bad luck, or infertility to a region be broken and separated from the place. Knowing that *ketjak* is essentially an exorcist ceremony, for Balinese use it when danger or disease are threatening, we may conclude that the latter interpretation of *ketjak* also seems reasonable.

In contemporary Bali, the *ketjak* is still used for exorcism, and in March 1971, my wife and I, along with several students and friends, witnessed the ceremonies on three occasions at Tjemenggawon, 20 kilometers (12.5 miles) to the east of Denpasar on the main "tourist road" to the mountains. The ceremony started in December and was performed nightly for four months, then every fifth night for another month. On the meeting hall of the hamlet *(bale bandjar)* was posted the following sign, in both English and Indonesian:

### ATTENTION

This is a ceremony to call down Sangyang Bhatara Ratu Widhiyadari with her *whisperings* for health and prosperity. It is not allowed to take photographs. Visitors and lookers-on are urgently requested to take notice which means supporting the holy Dewa Yadna.

The Community of Tjemenggawon Village                    9 December 1970

The ceremony had begun when we arrived at 8:00 P.M., with a local priest *(pemangku)* preparing offerings and incense, seated next to two young girls, perhaps fourteen years old, the persons in whom the spirits would incarnate themselves as long as the ceremonies continued. These girls were the bodily recipients of *dedari*, or heavenly nymphs, and provided the name for this dance intended to exorcise evil and bring a blessing: *Sangyang Dedari*. After undergoing tests to establish that they were genuine representatives of the spirit realm, the girls were secluded for special treatment appropriate to heavenly beings. Each evening they joined the priest and villagers at the temple and became entranced. They served as mediators of the divine realm, sprinkling holy water *(air tirta)* on sick infants, reporting what must be done by the local community if the divine world is to be pleased, and dancing well into the night before emerging from the trance. The *dedari* was sumptuously dressed in *kain pradja,* a hand-painted gilded cloth, and each wore a double-peaked helmet covered with blossoms. During the first hours they heard requests for aid and blessed persons suffering from various illnesses. Then the *dedari* were lifted onto bamboo thrones, mounted on carrying poles. Eyes shut, hands moving gracefully as their fans and fingers circled and wove into patterns that mirrored each other, they were borne aloft by teams of chanting boys. The rest of the villagers, men and women singing antiphonally, followed behind the nymphs on their thrones, all walking by torchlight. They went from the center area of the village toward the south, stopped for prayers at the border, then turned around, and the whole procession returned through the center of the hamlet to the northern perimeter, where prayers were again offered. The chanting group returned to the meeting hall at about 10 P.M. The temple *kulkul* (wooden gong) was rung to indicate that the *dedari* were in residence. The girls, still in trance, were seated slightly higher than the rest of the villagers, on raised chairs, with closed eyes and calm, dreamy faces. Occasionally their heads would nod, and it appeared that they were about to topple from their thrones, but one by one, and then together, they would rise and dance graceful *legong* patterns.

It was during this dancing at the *balé bandjar* that the *ketjak* itself began. It continued for several hours. A chorus of thirty men was seated to one side of the central stage where the girls danced and rested opposite the priests. A soloist provided the lead note, which was reinforced by the chorus, reached a crescendo, and then diminished before the cycle began again.

By midnight the *dedari* had ceased dancing, the *ketjak* chorus was finally quiet, and the *pemangkus* had begun to waft incense towards the girls, who were beginning to return to "everyday life." The golden attire was removed and packed in cases for the next evening, holy water *(air tirta)* was sprinkled on them and on the outstretched hands of the villagers, who then rubbed it over their faces, hair, and sipped it from cupped hands. Finally, flowers from the ceremonial garb and offerings were tossed to the surrounding crowds who scrambled to acquire a blossom. The successful tucked a flower behind an ear before wandering off to sleep.

This condensed description of the context in which the Balinese still use the traditional *ketjak* dance contrasts sharply with performances viewed by tourists. Two kinds of tourist performances employ the *ketjak.* One is a simplified version of the *Sangyang Dedari,* with tourists gathering to view the *legong* dancing for about half an hour. They do not watch the prior temple ceremonies during which the girls enter trance. In Bona, not far from Tjemenggawon, the *Sangyang Dedari* is immediately followed by a *Sangyang Djaran,* during which a single male dancer riding a hobbyhorse repeatedly charges through the coals left by a bonfire of coconut husks while the *ketjak* chorus chants. A brief ceremony of blessing by a *pemangku* begins and closes the performances, which lasts just over an hour. There were weekly performances of this ceremony in 1971, and they were given, not in response to the requests of villagers, but in order to accommodate the plans of hotels and tour agents who paid the performing group Rp. 8,000 (about U.S. $30.00) each time. In Bona, three *sekaha* (voluntary groups) compete for the profits of performing for tourists, and the income is not distributed to the entire hamlet. The time of performance was condensed from the four or five hours of an exorcist ceremony to one hour, photographs were permitted, and the seats of the tourists were as high or higher than the *dedari*. At Tjemenggawon the heads of the worshippers were never higher than those of the sacred nymphs, nor were the other actions allowed. These details indicate that the villagers gathering around to watch the *Sangyang Dedari* at Bona were not so much worshipping, as joining the crowd of tourists to watch a spectacle, before trying to sell souvenirs to the visitors.

The presence of tourists at the Tjemenggawon ceremonies was not really desired, as the public signboard indicated, and I felt rather unwelcome, even though the local priest *(pemangku)* who was also a village leader *(perbekel)* had earlier issued a formal invitation to us and a group from Udayana University. Even the "native" anthropologists acknowledged that they felt like "marginal men" at the ceremony. Rather than being ushered to positions of honor with a clear view of the proceedings, we were relegated to sitting on the outside rows of the closely packed villagers. These villagers did not wish to answer questions I put to them about the ceremony. Later on, the village leader told us that he had seen five *Sangyang Dedari* in Tjemenggawon during the past fifty years. We asked him whether it was not a difficult task for villagers to carry on these exorcist rites every night for months. "No," he replied, "because it is our belief that this is good for the health of our village, and because we all believe it is important, the task is made easy."

The Tjemenggawon ceremonies were believed to have a power which was primarily religious, and although the people could have advertised and attracted "paying tourists," they clearly thought it was important to keep the activity "pure," and not mix up religion and economics.

On two other occasions I witnessed *Sangyang Dedari* and *Sangyang Djaran* ceremonies which were intended for the divine world, not tourist audiences. On June 5, 1971 in Peliatan, in the Gianyar District just to the south of Ubud, both these dances were performed in connection with an *odalan,* or temple anniversary, at the *Pura Dalem*. An outside stage was constructed with mats strung over bamboo supports located in a hollow between two low hills in front of the main temple complex. An electric generator provided lighting. A procession, let by the two *Sangyang Dedari* carried on their thrones, entered the stage, and shortly thereafter a *ketjak* chorus began. The *dedari* danced together, then individually, and again together, and attendants helped them to revive while the *ketjak* chorus continued unabated. After about an hour after they were finished, a bonfire was lit, allowed to burn down until piles of glowing coals remained, and then a *Sangyang Djaran* dancer appeared, accepting holy water and the smoke of incense from a priest as he went into trance. The hillsides, meanwhile, had become packed with thousands of Balinese, but apart from Stephen Lansing and me, no other Westerners were present. The *djaran* rider mounted his hobbyhorse, a brightly painted almost carousel-style horse's head on a stick, and began to "gallop" around the stage. Suddenly he turned toward the fire, dashing repeatedly through the blazing coals in his bare feet, sending showers of sparks into the air. At last the coals were nearly extinguished, the *djaran* rider "trotted" to the perimeter again, knelt to receive a priestly blessing, and slowly emerged from trance. It was only after these two ceremonies were finished that the *ketjak* chorus gave way to the *gamelan* orchestra, and a *legong* dance began. At that point, about 9:00 P.M., a dozen or two tourists appeared from the nearby Ubud hotels. They had been told that a "temple ceremony" would begin at 9:00 P.M. at which they would be welcome. And that was not wrong; it simply was not the "whole truth," since they had missed the spectacular *Sangyang Dedari* and *Sangyang Djaran* dances.

The dances were being performed, according to at least one informant, because the national elections were looming ahead in early July; the political parties in the vicinity of Ubud and Peliatan were engaged in some rather intense competition and people were being intimidated. To forestall further trouble and bring harmony to the villages, these exorcist rituals were introduced as an *odalan*. One note of importance to our study was the reaction of children present at the *Sangyang Djaran*. When the "hobbyhorse" had finished his dance through the coals, and retreated to the sideline, the hundreds of children began to applaud, and a flood of handclapping swept across the audience on the hillsides. I had never seen this in Bali. Certainly it was behavior copied from the tourists, who were often in the region at performances. Applause for the dancers may change the performance subtly, away from the "divine world" toward the "village audience"; it also indicates that a certain "climax" in emotional expression *is* reached and acknowledged, quite in contrast to the Bateson-Mead thesis (Bateson and Mead, 1942:47–48).

The other indigenously organized performance at which the *ketjak* chorus figured predominantly was in the midst of the city of Denpasar, in Bandjar Bon on July 1, 1971. Several thousand residents from this distinctly urban neighborhood, together with Ngurah Bagus, a number of visiting scholars and interested nonnative residents gathered to witness this ceremony. After a prelude of offerings and chanting at the local temple, two young men performed a kind of *legong* in trance, wearing peaked hats decorated with flowers. A fire of coconut husks was lit in an open courtyard beneath a huge *waringan* (banyan) tree, and a chorus of men started to sing a rather imprecise and rough version of the *ketjak*. Half a dozen young men, apparently in trance, rushed from the temple area and began to toss blazing coals into the air with their hands. They raced through the coals, kicking them aside, picked up handfuls, threw them up into the air, showering sparks on themselves, and sometimes onto the surrounding crowds. A hobbyhorse was kept at the edge of the wildly moving men, but was not "ridden." After thirty minutes, the coals were extinguished and the dancers returned to the temple, where they quickly emerged from trance, and walked quietly into the crowds, rubbing their charcoaled hands. In the meantime women were receiving holy water from a priest and reaching for flower blossoms which had been affixed to the dancers' hats. The ceremony was to continue every fifth day for a month, according to the informants, and since it was held during the period immediately surrounding the national elections, it was suggested that the ceremony might ensure safety and peace in an intrinsically upsetting time.

From these accounts of how the *ketjak* is used in modern Bali it should be evident that this symbolic form is a tradition which still has believed-in power and significance among a variety of populations. The *ketjak* chorus is far more than a "tourist production"; but it is *also* that, with groups in a number of locales ready to accept invitations by tour agents.

The tourist *ketjak* seems to have had its earliest development in the village of Bona. The creator of one of the first "tourist" productions is Ida Bagus Mudiara, who was born about 1900 in Singaradja on the north coast, but moved to Gianyar in 1927, and to Bona in 1930. When the royal house of Gianyar asked him to prepare an orchestra for ceremonies in 1930 he was already "producing" a dance called the *djoged kraton,* a kind of social dance which encourages onlookers to dance with the soloist and has certain flirtatious overtones. But Mudiara decided to use his knowledge of the *gamelan* orchestra, which seems to have originated in the north, like so many other innovations which have been developed and refined in south Bali. He began to blend the *suara gamelan* ("voice" *gamelan*) of the *ketjak* with the epic Hindu poem, the *Ramayana,* which was at that time enacted through *wayang wong* (human actors acting legendary parts). Accompanying these *wayang wong* performances was a *gamelan* orchestra with percussion instruments called *gender wayang Ramayana,* and according to Mudiara he decided to substitute the voices of the *ketjak* chorus for the *gamelan* using the chorus as actors in the story as it seemed appropriate, and then selecting portions of the *Ramayana* for performance. The reigning leaders of Gianyar were much taken with this innovation and asked for it repeatedly. About 1932, the German painter, author, and entrepreneur, Walter Spies, who was then living in Bali, saw the *ketjak* performance with the *Ramayana* story and immediately commissioned performances for tourists (de Zoete and Spies, 1938). That was the beginning of the shortened version, as the epic was edited to last only an hour, preserving only a portion of the *Ramayana* story, along with a dramatic accompaniment of voice and movement by the *ketjak* chorus.

The story of Prince Rama, his bride Sita, and brother Laksmana is retold, emphasizing the abduction of Sita by the wicked King Ravana, and his struggles, aided by the monkey-king, Hanuman, and the bird, Jatayu, to recapture his bride.

I. B. Mudiara of Bona dislikes the title "Monkey Dance," since its main theme deals with human beings and only incidentally with animals. He reported that some tourists come to Bona looking for the "monkey man" and he vehemently argued that he was not the "father of the monkeys," even though he was pleased to acknowledge authorship of the "tourist *ketjak*." He noted that President Sukarno had seen the Bona *ketjak* in 1950 and had asked that it be taught in neighboring villages. Both Mudiara and Sukarno evidently believed that it would help to unite villages and would bring many foreigners pleasure. He added that it was considered a useful activity in Bona, since the more it was performed, the more likely it would be that health, prosperity, and peace would follow. He did not think that doing it too often could ever harm its meaning, and affirmed that it was still considered powerful in Bona.

I asked Mudiara what he thought *ketjak* meant and he gave an interpretation quite different from that of other informants. "Ketjak," he thought, "was derived from the Sanskrit term for 'voice' [compare the Indonesian *tjakup*, "talk," "speak"] and this was a 'voice' orchestra." The other interpretations, when I reported them, were not so much countered as simply shrugged off. His explanation was satisfying to him and seemed reasonable. Time and again I had the experience in Bali of receiving a variety of interpretations for a single phenomenon, and there was little sense that another "meaning" was necessarily wrong, so long as the one proposed seemed right to its advocate.

Mudiara said that, because he had taught the *ketjak* to so many villagers in the past two decades, the Bona group performs only once or twice a month now, and is not on the main "tourist route." His own home contained a small souvenir shop, but without the handsome appointments of more prosperous shops on the central tourist thoroughfares. While we talked, his son-in-law joined us and told us that he was operating the guide service at one of the luxury hotels in Sanur. He noted that the *ketjak* is performed weekly by a local group on the hotel grounds and that the story follows exactly that of Bona. He added that in the Balinese elementary schools, children are now taught the *ketjak* as a part of their formal education. It has become one of the characteristic cultural items which he considered truly representative of a Balinese!

One location where the "tourist *ketjak*" was introduced by Mudiara and has recently become an important institution is in the village of Mas, on the main "tourist route." It was organized by a young Brahman, Ida Bagus Ambara, who is a carver and entrepreneur, operating one of the nine shops lining the main road between Denpasar and tourist attractions to the north—Ubud, Tampaksiring, and the mountains. In the *bandjar* an organization of forty men and half a dozen women prepare costumes, decorate the grounds, arrange props, and perform about three times weekly for tourists. The "shows" are held in the forecourt of the *pura dadia,* a clan temple associated with the early Brahmanic traditions in Bali, or in case of rain, in a specially constructed pavilion by the roadside. The pavilion adjoins art shops operated by the two older brothers of Ambara. Ambara's father, Ida Bagus Gelodog, is a carver, a masked dancer in *Topeng* performances, a local priest *(pemangku),* and a puppeteer *(dalang).* He serves as the ritualist for the opening ceremonies at the tourist *ketjak* in Mas. One of his daughters, a younger sister of Ambara, was dancing the role of Rama in early 1971. An observer, entering the courtyard complex in which Gelodog and Ambara live just before a tourist *ketjak* in Mas, would see the main actors in the *Ramayana* story and the producers making preparations, and discussing last-minute arrangements in the context of a family group. But the income from the performances, which amounted to about Rp. 35,000 per week (nearly U.S. $100.00), was incorporated in the total communal wealth of the *bandjar* and not distributed to individuals or families. The family itself did not make a profit directly from the performances, but it was able to make a reasonably good living by the production and sale of *objets d'art.* Using its traditional skills in art and religion, the priestly family of Gelodog has moved from control of sacred ritual to control of income-producing performances, and its position in the community continues to be an honored one.[1]

The *ketjak* in Mas is a recent addition to the dance repertoire, having been established in 1970. It is used only for tourist performances and has never been associated with purification or exorcist ceremonies, and I found no indication that it was considered especially useful for that purpose. It was developed primarily as an income-producing event to bring added wealth to the *bandjar,* which depends on two major sources of income: growing rice and carving wooden statues for sale to tourists.

In conclusion, the symbolic form of the *ketjak* is one which may have two meanings, depending on context and intention. Both, apparently, can coexist without one (economic gain) replacing the other (religious obligation). But will the belief-system of the Balinese, which I believe is the key to their continued cultural identity and viability, be maintained in the face of the empiricism and materialism associated with "modernization"? Shall the Balinese retain their pure devotion to a hierarchy of gods, demons, spirits, and wraiths which are acknowledged to have power or control over their lives, in contrast to technology—the symbolic form dominant elsewhere—through which men seek control over their natural, social, and even cosmic environment? The continuing power of the *ketjak* as a symbol organizing and motivating Balinese is a partial answer, in the affirmative, to a perplexing and, I believe, fundamental question about whether symbolic forms may undergo change and transformation without becoming broken, destroyed, and emptied of a previous "intuitive meaning."

True, the Balinese described in this article have become adept at perform-

[1]Similarly, Clifford Geertz has described high-caste families elsewhere in Bali seeking to retain their status by entrepreneurial means (1963:82–121).

ing for money as well as for love, and the tourist productions add materially to the cash resources of many villagers, yet there remains an "intuitive meaning" for the *ketjak* which is deeply rooted and is celebrated at special times. Like Christmas and Hanukkah in the Euro-American tradition, the commercial aspects do not completely vitiate the authentic symbolic power of the *ketjak* for Balinese. In conclusion, interpreters of a symbolic form must learn again and again to pay special attention to context, to the particular persons inventing and reinventing a form, to the historical precedents and the multiple layers of meaning for a range of people to which a symbolic form may communicate.

## ACKNOWLEDGMENTS

The research on which this article is based was conducted in 1970–1971 supported by a grant from the National Institute of Mental Health (#3 F0 1 MH 47221-0151 CUAN, U.S. Department of Health, Education and Welfare), administered by Brown University. I wish to express my thanks for advice and support to a few of the many generous persons who assisted both the research and the writing of this article: Drs. I Gusti Ngurah Bagus of the Bali Museum; Dr. Koentjaraningrat of the Lembaga Ilmu Pengetahuan Indonesia; I G. P. Riyasse and Merta Pastime of the Department of Tourism, Bali; Professors Robert Jay, Philip Leis, Dwight Heath, George Hicks, Edward Bruner, and A. B. Hudson. Also Deborah McKean, Judith Hudson, Stephen Lansing, Kitty Axelson, and Gale Brown for their companionship, criticism, and typing of manuscripts. Discussion at the Conference on Symbolic Systems further contributed to refinement, but any errors I alone acknowledge.

## REFERENCES

Bateson, Gregory, and Mead, Margaret. *Balinese character*. New York: New York Academy of Sciences, 1942.
Cassirer, Ernst. *Language and myth*. New York: Dover, 1953.
de Zoete, Beryl, and Spies, Walter. *Dance and drama in Bali*. London: Faber and Faber, 1938.
Geertz, Clifford. *Peddlars and princes*. Chicago: University of Chicago Press, 1963.

# chapter sixteen

# Zaman Dan Masa, Eras and Periods: Religious Evolution and the Permanence of Epistemological Ages in Malay Culture

Robert McKinley

Michigan State University

> And this period—what are its essential features? How does it differ from other periods? What are its characteristic ways of history making?
>
> C. Wright Mills (1959:7)

## A TIME WHEN TREES COULD TALK

On one of the very few occasions when I have been treated to the Malay art of story telling, I was standing on the second-story veranda of a large public housing block in Kampong Baharu, the central Malay neighborhood of the city of Kuala Lumpur, and the center of my field research activities from 1970 until 1972. Residents of the housing project were not much in the habit of reciting traditional tales to each other. They were more inclined to pass their evenings watching television or visiting around the neighborhood to help edit the local gossip. But on this one brief occasion, I was given a small sample of the lore which most Malays learn as children.

The story I was told concerned the casuarina tree, or *pokok ru,* and how it was cursed by Allah. But first let me describe the setting in which my story was told.

It was shortly before sundown prayer time and my host and I had just finished bathing after a long hot day. We had changed into comfortable sarongs and were ready to relax for the evening. The baby of our household, my host's one-year-old son, wanted to be picked up and held, so his father gathered him up and we stepped out onto the veranda to survey the sights of the neighborhood at its time of changeover, change from Western-style dress and urban occupational roles to Malay-style dress and village forms of visiting and interaction.

Across the way we could see the usual parade of people making their way home along the top of a large dyke which protected the immediate area from the recurrent flooding of the Kelang River. The Kelang serves as the boundary between this part of Kampong Baharu and an area of Chinese settlement to the south, and Malays refer to this dyke not simply as a "dyke," *bendung,* but rather as a "fortification," *benteng.* The dyke itself consists of a steep man-made embankment with a very flat top. On its near side, people from the apartments have put in some small gardens and chicken coops; on top is a well-worn path lined by a row of stately casuarina trees. This path furnishes the main route to the Muslim cemetery which lies on the opposite side of the river, and local Malay funeral processions must pass this way before crossing a small bridge into the cemetery. In this regard the dyke becomes a fortification of a very special kind. For not only does it separate the land from the water and the Malays from the Chinese, it separates the living from the dead.

Each of these three separations had immediate importance in 1970. Many of the families in the first and second levels of the buildings which made up this complex were still seeking government relief for losses they had suffered during a very serious flood which came just two months before my arrival. And memories were still all too fresh regarding the bitter race riots which had broken out in and around Kampong Baharu in May of 1969. Finally, there were rumors in the air of sorcerers who would sneak into the cemetery late at night to steal blood from the corpses of murdered men. With their blood they could raise up vampire spirits to do their evil bidding.

Surveying this familiar scene of people, space, and metaphor, my host was prompted to tell me that the casuarina trees across the way, which I found so handsome, were a "cursed" species. I wondered for a moment if he meant that one of the individual trees in our sight was haunted by some vagrant spirit. "No," said he, "this was something that happened long long ago, before our time, before the growth of the present trees, and even before the birth of the prophet Muhammad. The tree was cursed by Allah because it had sinned." The story he then related was that in an age when trees could talk, some evil men planned to kill the prophet Jesus. They wanted to do this upon a wooden cross. So a call went out to all the trees in the world to see which one would be willing to supply the wood for the cross. At first all the trees refused, but finally the casuarina, which at that time had beautiful broad leaves and not the dry needles we see today, decided that sooner or later these men were going to take one of the trees willing or not. So, innocently enough, the casuarina volunteered to be the one. But this betrayal of the prophet so angered Allah that he put a curse on the casuarina. From that time on its leaves have only been able to form as thin needles and not as the lush broad leaves it once had.

This legend explained what my friend meant by a cursed tree. And, appropriately enough, the needle-bearing casuarina does seem a bit deprived and out of place among the many full-leafed trees of the Malaysian environment. Perhaps Malays see this kind of logic in the tale my friend related. But the point which most interests me about this story has to do with the telling of the tale and not with the tale itself. All stories must be located in a special time or framework of meaning, otherwise we could not participate in what is special about them. But my host was particularly emphatic, apparently for my benefit, that no one would expect trees to talk today, and that the story therefore took place in a *zaman* ("age") "before the prophet Muhammad when trees could talk." In other words, our narrator's comment tells us that before the truth of Islam there were truths of another kind. Of course, the exact time of this mythic age is not the crucial point here. What matters is that knowing "then" and knowing "now" are two different things. Furthermore, since the story itself is able to transport us "back" to the mythic age and its conditions of knowing, we can be certain that time as such is not what "then" and "now" are really about. "Then" and "now" represent alternative ways of knowing; they are epistemological ages.

Still, there are reasons why the life of Muhammad was a good choice for the watershed separating the present from the mythic age of this story. To appreciate this we must consider the situation in which the story was told. Seeing the casuarina trees before us, my friend wanted to let me in on an alternative way of knowing about this class of trees. Since the knowledge he wanted to give me was quite remote from our immediate viewing of the trees, he needed to locate it in a more distant time. He could not let me think that Allah had cursed the tree at three o'clock that afternoon. He wanted me to know the story but he did not want me to think that he believed that trees could talk. Clearly the time of Muhammad seemed remote enough to imply different possibilities in what could be known about trees. Yet it was not so remote as to be inappropriate to a story dealing with the prophet Jesus, who is recognized by Islam as a forerunner of Muhammad. Furthermore, since Muhammad had founded the religion of Islam, he had indeed profoundly changed people's knowledge of God and man. The *zaman Islam*, or "age of Islam," represented one system of knowledge as opposed to all others, therefore the mythic age when trees could talk belonged on the other side of the Islamic age. A final reason for this choice had to do with the casual way in which the story was told. I do not think that the specific mention of a time before Muhammad was a fixed part of this story. My host wanted to provide something definite for me, his audience, to latch onto at the start of his rendering of the tale. He had often discussed with me the growing importance of Islam in his life, and I can imagine him thinking to himself, "Surely by now my European friend has heard of Muhammad!"

## TIME AND KNOWLEDGE

It is quite obvious that in tales such as this, the ages of myth and legend are epistemological ages, that is, alternative views of reality, and not a chronology of past events. But what is not so obvious is that much the same can be said for any named period of human history: the Elizabethan Age of England, the era of European colonialism, or the period of independence in Malaysia. The only difference is that with historical ages the departures between what can be known "then" and what can be known "now" are not expected to be quite so dramatic as is the case with myth. All ages are inherently epistemological propositions. We seem destined to know the past of social life only in terms of what we regard as timeless about it. And the most timeless qualities of any age are its socially constructed meanings, its system of knowledge and view of the world. For this reason, matters of religion and political outlook play such a prominent role in the naming of historical periods. For both religion and politics have a great bearing on what people conceive as being possible or impossible in social life. Noteworthy changes in religion or politics, therefore, become suitable metonyms for the mood of an age. These allow us to get to know the past as a multiplicity of ways of knowing.

In this sense, mythical tales and historical periods may be viewed as reciprocals of each other. They stand in an inverse relation to the terms *time* and *knowledge*. In telling a story, time often serves as the metaphor for what is unusual about the knowledge contained in the story. The story must happen "once upon a time." Even the tale presented earlier was forced to become history, in that it had to be located at a time before the birth of Muhammad. In the case of historical eras, this process is reversed: a certain time from the past must now be given a name and a distinctive mood or outlook which contrasts with the mood of today. An assumed difference in ways of knowing becomes the primary means of representing an earlier time. In short, with stories (myth), another time is used to represent another way of knowing, whereas with history, another way of knowing is used to represent another time.

In the rest of this chapter, I address two problems about the relations between time and knowledge. The first concerns Malay notions regarding their own past, especially as these are expressed in the concepts of *zaman,* "era" or "age," and *masa,* "period" or "time." The second concerns the evolution of religious cosmologies in Southeast Asia. These two problems are indirectly related in that Malays consciously attribute many of their own religious beliefs and symbols to different ages of past religious influence. My point on Malay attitudes is that the different eras and periods of which they speak are not strictly a matter of historical time in the linear sense. Rather, like the eras of myth and like religious beliefs themselves, these historic ages represent different ways of knowing what is possible in human affairs. They are epistemological ages. Moreover, the assumptions they contain regarding human knowing and acting are part of the present. They remain permanently available and access to them is conditioned by current contexts of religion, social relations, and art.

For example, there are times when Malays find it appropriate to restage certain aspects of the colonial period, as when trying to appear especially diplomatic to a European employer or guest. Likewise, in the area of national politics it is almost essential, if one wants to gain popular support, to employ the rethoric of the early days of national independence, with its further allusions to the precolonial supremacy of the indigenous Malay rulers. In the area of folk religion, Malays are called upon to make continual reentries into the symbolic orders of their pre-Islamic past. From wedding ceremonies to magical spells, we meet the Hindu pantheon and indigenous notions of spirit essence. Nor do these reentries come in an entirely haphazard manner. Malay charms and spells seem to be framed on the outisde with calls for the blessings and curses of Allah; then further in they are fortified with appeals to the royalty and rank of the Hindu deities; and finally there is a core of direct address to the spiritual make-up of whatever force or entity is being manipulated through the spell. It may be thought that this is merely a symptom of religious syncretism, but I suspect there is more to this. Rather than producing a random mixture of religious idioms, I think the Malay magicians have employed their own idiom of moving through all known religious eras to deal with that which they regard as primordial and therefore as permanent, namely, spirit essence or *semangat*.

The question of the evolution of religious cosmologies in Southeast Asia puts the relationship between time and knowledge in a rather different form. Instead of asking how past ages are conceived, it asks how ideas once present in a society come to influence those of later times. The point to be made is that the ideologies found at any one time among the historic cultures of Southeast Asia have always been actively engaged in a dialogue with other ideologies from earlier times. This dialogue has not been a simple matter of the survival of certain ancient beliefs; it has been a form commentary, through new meanings, upon the ways in which earlier meanings have lost plausibility in the face of profound social change. So I am not speaking, as does Coedes (1967:54), of the possible similarities between pre-Hindu and Hinduized features of Southeast Asian religions. For it is in the very nature of dialogue that contrasts rather than carry-overs or similarities should receive the most attention. Thus, where Coedes (1967) makes much of the parallel between the indigenous practice of building artificial mountains to represent the center of the universe, I would stress that the former were built *outside* tribal villages while the latter were built *within* the walls of royal cities. By social and cosmological context, the two types of shrines are very different. The one helps mediate contact between the human community and the powers which surround it; the other makes all the surrounding universe dependent upon human control at its center. It is, of course, no surprise that this shift in cosmology came with the growth of trade and the formation of the state in Southeast Asia around 200 to 400 A.D. Yet there is another difficulty with the interpretation which views this shift only in terms of the ideological function of legitimizing rule. For this interpretation uses contemporary social functions and interests to account for religious change, and therefore usually fails to see any meaningful interaction with the past. My solution to this problem is stressing that, in response to social change, new meanings address not only new conditions, but also whatever seems to be missing among older meanings. The new meanings must compensate for the fact that specific features of new actions have no place among earlier views of reality. The dialogue here is not just between meanings and conduct, rather it is between two sets of meanings which contain different views of conduct.

This reformulation of the problem of ideology raises several important questions for the sociology of religion. Most speculation on the evolution of religious symbols has been confined to matters of social function *given* the fact that society itself is always changing. The theme of ideological legitimatio.i has been major in such considerations. But there are two variations on this theme: one, the Durkheimian, sees symbolic legitimation as a kind of buttressing of the ontological status of society (and culture) itself, a way of capping the collective process of the social construction of reality; the other, the Weberian approach, sees legitimation as the indirect rationalization or justification of specific modes of acting and of other actor-oriented experiences, such as suffering and injustice. At first glance it would seem that the second view would be the one most applicable to the study of religious change since it relates religious meaning to the *direction of social action* and not just to the *representation of social essence*. Ironically, however, a more serious consideration shows just the opposite to be true. For the ultimate yield of an analysis which seeks to match each mode of action with a particular "spirit" or legitimizing rationale and each set of beliefs with an implicit plan of action is a series of synchronic profiles. We are shown something of the functional relations between ideology and conduct at different points in time, but we are provided with no developmental model for the actual process of change. This, we note, may be one reason that Weber himself placed so much emphasis on the role of the charismatic leader as the bringer of social change. In order to move society from one synchronic pose to the next, Weber's theories require an heroic actor of this unbound type.

The Durkheimian model, on the other hand, reminds us that, phenomenologically at least, society as a whole is always capable of a complete crisis in plausibility and must therefore maintain a constant discourse with itself about the meaning of things. This allows us to deal more precisely with the fact that religious symbols must interact with other social phenomena primarily in terms of meaning and only secondarily in terms of function. Using this approach, I shall continue to ask: "How have the conditions of both religions and society at any one time been a product of conditions and meanings that have gone before?" In answering, I shall assume that the meanings of each new age must first be put in touch with those of its predecessor before the process of legitimation can become complete. This will allow me to propose a series of new interpretations of major shifts which historians have often noted in Southeast Asian cosmologies. In particular, I shall consider:

1. contrasts between indigenous tribal cosmologies and Hindu cosmology
2. the role of Hindu cosmology in the formation of the early Southeast Asian states
3. the decline of the Hinduized states in the thirteenth and fourteenth centuries and the subsequent spread of Islam and Theravada Buddhism.

## INTERSECTIONS OF BIOGRAPHY AND HISTORY

During fieldwork in Kampong Baharu, I often received a very standardized response to my routine questions about people's ages and about the lengths of time they had lived in various places. People in the age brackets above forty-five years would give a brief recitation of the major political events which had touched their lives. They would make a counting gesture by placing the thumb of the right hand against the little finger and then begin counting off by moving the thumb against each other finger in succession. The enumeration always stopped at the index finger, as only four times or events were named. A strict counting cadence was maintained as the verbal accompaniment to this gesture. The four period names went as follows:

|     |               |                                                                                      |
| --- | ------------- | ------------------------------------------------------------------------------------ |
| (1) | *masa orang puteh* | "period of the white people" (before 1941)                                      |
| (2) | *masa Jepun*  | "period of the Japanese" (1941–45)                                                   |
| (3) | *merdeka*     | "independence" (1957)                                                                |
| (4) | *tiqabelas Mei* | "May thirteenth" (1969) (This was the date of a serious outbreak of violence between Malays and Chinese.) |

This gesture, in fact, is a slight modification of the standard Malay counting gesture. Usually the sequence "one to five" goes from the thumb to the little finger and not from the little finger to the thumb. Apparently this reversal is regarded as kinesthetically more appropriate to chronological reckoning. Accordingly, the time most distant from the present is given to the finger most distant from the thumb. Each step marked in time comes closer to the thumb. The thumb itself, which could conceivably represent a fifth period, or the present, is kept busy doing the actual counting. In a teleological sense, it supplies the movement toward itself. If the thumb in this gesture does represent the present, then I might suggest, in keeping with the main argument offered here, that it is a very nimble present. Like Malay attitudes towards past ages, it can move quickly to recontact its past.

A closer look at the specific periods and events named shows that they are not simply temporal periods or chronological landmarks. Each refers to a distinct condition of politically constituted social reality. This is most clearly true for the *masa orang puteh* (European colonialism) and the *nasa Jepun* (the Japanese occupation), but it is also true for *merdeka* (independence), and *tigabelas Mei* (May thirteenth). For the events of national independence in 1957 and those of violent racial confrontation in 1969 both led to radically new assessments of the locus of power in Malaysian society. By naming these events, people imply new sets of assumptions about what could be possible in social relations. The linguistic context supports this interpretation because even though neither *merdeka* nor *tigabelas Mei* is explicitly called a *masa,* the position of each, coming at the end of what might be called a "*masa* series," implies that each of them is as much a *masa* as are the other members of the series. If mentioned alone, both independence and the riots would be no more than outstanding events, but as part of this series they are metonyms for contrasting political conditions.

Of course, all this was presented to me in the context of biography, not history. Still, these data give us an interesting glimpse at the nature of informal understanding of the connections between biography and history. My informants were not just telling their ages, they were indicating that they were in a sense "survivors" of the four *masas* named. And indeed they had lived through some very profound changes in world and national politics. The magnitude of these changes can be appreciated when we consider that the *masa orang puteh,* which had just ended during their lifetimes, had begun as far back as 1511 with the Portuguese takeover of Malaka. It later embraced the rule of the Dutch in Indonesia and that of the British in Malaya; and since many of my informants had migrated from Indonesia during the years before World War II, they could claim direct experience with both of these later manifestations of the *masa orang puteh.* At the same time, it may seem that my informants were being overly subjective in treating the conditions following the 1969 riots on the same scale as all of European colonialism. Yet their impressions here are not without foundation, for racial matters have become the primary concern of their government. Nor is it wrong to assume a relationship between the current racial situation in Malaysia and the conditions which developed on the peninsula under colonialism.

Quite significantly, in fact, the four periods just named do reflect differing constraints upon ethnic relations. To state the details on this as briefly as possible, we must note that British colonialism created a so-called plural society in Malaya; one in which differing ethnic groups, many of whom were recent immigrants, tended to fill different roles in the colonial economy. They tended to live rather separate social lives as well. Direct confrontation and competition between the major Asian communities was kept to a minimum through the intervening authority of the British.

When the Japanese entered Malaya in 1941 this situation changed. The Japanese were already at war with China and they viewed the Chinese in Malaya as potential enemies. Meanwhile, they claimed the Malays as their newly liberated Asian brothers. Armed conflict between Malays and Chinese became both direct *and directed* under these conditions. After the defeat of the Japanese and with independence from Britain, things changed again. Ethnic relations were now managed by a group of moderate Westernized leaders who headed several ethnically based political parties. These leaders had all been in the forefront of the negotiations for independence, and this had won them great respect among their followers. Their policy was to seek compromises on any matters where there were conflicts of interest between the major ethnic groups. Politically, of course, the Malay leaders had greater bargaining power in these compromises, but the economic influence of the Chinese community could not be denied. The national constitution reflected this situation. Malays were given recognition of their claim to prior rights as citizens in the new nation; even Malay royalty would be allowed to continue enjoying many of its traditional privileges. The Chinese and Indian minorities, on the other hand, were given the right *to become* citizens, and they were given the assurance of safety for their many business interests. Finally, things changed again with the 1969 riots. By this time, the spirit of mutual accommodation which had surrounded the independence movement had lost its focus. Younger citizens of all groups were no longer content with the compromises worked out by elite figures. The general elections of that year brought on the first really direct political confrontation between Malays and Chinese; ultimately, this political confrontation provoked the physical confrontation known as *tigabelas Mei.*

Following the riots there were changes in leadership and in the government's policies on racial matters. Since that time there has been a much stronger assertion of Malay rights both politically, in banning any discussion of the special privileges of the Malays, and economically, in the use of employment quotas and special training programs designed to benefit Malays. In addition, many new public meanings have been created which draw attention to the issue of ethnicity. Slogans of goodwill and national loyalty pervade the mass media, and there is much talk of building a "national culture," the content of which is very markedly Malay rather than Chinese or Indian.

In short, since independence, the central problem of Malaysian social life has been that of ethnicity. More exactly, it has been that of the contradiction between political democracy and a racially ordered political economy. But given this problem, the attempt to deal with it has gone through two phases of management: first, a phase of open democracy with compromise between ethnic factions; second, a phase of closed democracy with affirmative action programs favoring Malays. My point is merely that the folk labels for these two phases are *merdeka* and *tigabelas Mei.*

Contrasting political constraints are not the only features of the four recent *masas.* Each *masa* had its own particular set of public meanings as well. Everything from monies and postage stamps to monuments of five-year plans could be included among these significant meanings. But in addition, each ensemble of public symbols had attributed to it a degree of coherence which implied a sense of permanence about the existing social order. It is this sense of permanence and not duration alone which makes for a *masa* in Malay views of the past.

A striking illustration of this point is that none of my informants ever mentioned the post-World War II period of Communist insurgency as a *masa*. British officials at the time called this period "the Emergency." It lasted from 1948 to 1960, and it has loomed very large in the writings of Western observers of modern Malay history (e.g., Purcell, 1954; Clutterbuck, 1966; O'Ballance, 1966; and von Vorys, 1975). Yet despite its long duration and the distinct hardships of a social life subjected to terrorism, curfews, and resettlement, the Emergency did not register as a *masa* in the everyday categories of Malay thought. I think a reason can be given for Malays' not experiencing the Emergency years as a distinct *masa*. Politically this was a very confused period; the British had returned to power, but they were not really in control. The military situation remained indecisive for almost a decade, and people's loyalties were also confused. Some Malays had joined the insurgents in their militant push for independence; others became bounty hunters against them. Furthermore, the closer the British came to controlling the situation, the further they had committed themselves to granting independence anyway. So even in victory, they would not quite be the victors. Everything had become tentative, and in Malay views of the social past this is not what makes for a *masa*.

By contrast, the Japanese occupation, which lasted only a little over three years, showed every sign of becoming a permanent situation, and because of this it made a much deeper impression on Malay consciousness. In trying to consolidate their rule, the Japanese had printed a new currency, bundles of which still remain hidden in some Malay homes, and they had begun educating people in the Japanese language and system of writing. People's memories of this period are interesting. Many speak freely of their cooperation with the Japanese, but all lament the oppressions of military rule. A few cultural innovations of that time are favorably recalled, for example, some of my informants thought that the Japanese syllabary alphabet was ideally suited to the sound structure of Malay. But the clearest impression one gets is that Malays experienced the Japanese takeover as something which could become every bit as permanent as the British regime it had replaced. I suspect that this attitude had a great deal to do with their initial acceptance of Japanese rule. It is also the reason why this brief period was given the status of a *masa*.

A sense of permanence seems implicit in the concept of a *masa*. But since no social or political condition is ever really permanent, we know that a *masa* is a very subjective classification. Likewise, the coherence of meaning implied by the notion of a *masa* must be based on subjective impressions, since public symbols are never fully coherent. Yet the conditions of power in society can make some structures seem more permanent, and some meanings more coherent than others. So, in being a sign of how history is subjectively experienced and known, the *masa* classification is not unrelated to what, as the saying goes, really happens to a society. In identifying a *masa*, Malays lift a way of knowing out from the events of politics and history. And it is, again, as a way of knowing that the constituted logic of society during a given *masa* becomes permanently available for reliving and remembering in the present.

## THE RELIGIOUS AGE

If, in everyday understanding, a *masa* is a way of knowing lifted out from the events and structures of political life, then a *zaman*, or religious age, is a way of knowing which can encompass these same events and structures. Since it refers directly to the religious views predominant at a given time, the *zaman* starts as a way of knowing and is imposed on the rest of history. It is the epistemological age par excellence. Though less immediate than the political *masa*, the religious or philosophical *zaman* has greater magnitude.

Again context is important. Whereas the four recent *masas* are usually mentioned in the context of biography, the various *zamans* tend to be brought up in the course of discussing Malay folk religion, or *adat*, customary observances. They provide a framework for the past and present of all Malays as a people and are only indirectly linked with the individual's place in history. In explaining the non-Islamic features of *adat* observances, people will indicate that first there was the *zaman dahulu*, or "early era"; then there was the *zaman Hindu*, or "Hindu era"; next came the *zaman Islam*, or "Islamic era"; finally there are times when it is now necessary to speak of the beginnings of a new era, the *zaman modan*, or "modern era." During the *zaman dahulu* the beliefs and customs of the pagan ancestors of the Malays were formed. These traditional beliefs are often called *kepercayaan orang duludulu*, "beliefs of the early people," with the implication that they cannot now be fully understood because no one within historical memory created these beliefs. It is assumed, however, that the contemporary pagan peoples of the Malay peninsula still possess something close to the original understanding of these beliefs. Malays have an especially great respect for the powers of the shamans among the aboriginal groups. The *zaman Hindu*, of course, was the age in which many Hindu and Buddhist concepts entered the Malay world. Much of state ritual is still influenced by Hindu symbolism, and many other rites, such as the Malay wedding, in which bride and groom are worshipped as royalty, are based on Hindu models. Even more ancient rites, such as those concerned with protecting and strengthening the soul of an infant, are discussed in Hindu terms. A general gloss given for the purpose of these rites is *puja semangat*, "to worship or invoke soul essence," even though the Sanskrit notion of *puja*, or "worship," seems a bit out of place here. A favorite example of Hindu influence offered by informants is that of the use of benzoin incense during ritual invocations. Whether this attribution is historically accurate, the comment seems to be a way of saying that even though there is no need to burn incense in prayers to Allah, it is still helpful to do so when addressing other aspects of the spirit world, that is, spirits, souls, and ancestors. And indeed, it is in the verbal address of the spirit world, with its heavy use of Sanskrit vocabulary, that we find the most active presence of the *zaman Hindu*. Few Malay charms and spells are uttered without some reference to Hindu cosmology.

The *zaman Islam* begins with the revelations of Muhammad and with their eventual spread to the Malay world. It is significant, in fact, that Malays recognize Islam as having an earthly center and origin outside their own cultural domain. This means that Islam has allowed them to claim a special place among all other peoples only in terms of their devotion to the general principles of the religion, and not by virtue of being at the mystical center of any new cosmos. Because Islam has become a central element in Malay ethnic identity, the *zaman Islam* is viewed as the most immediate of the religious eras.

The *zaman modan* is currently emerging as a new philosophical era, and it is seen as being in potential conflict with outlooks derived from the other three *zamans*. Superficially, the *zaman modan* would be little more than technological change, such things as the presence of rock bands at Malay weddings. But more seriously, it includes a technocratic approach to public life, an emphasis on secular learning, and a kind of willingness to make changes. The concept of modernity also includes a vague sense of keeping pace with the rest of the world, and this leads to many negative judgments about attitudes derived from the past. For the individual, modernity is associated with the goal of salaried employment, or *makan gaji*, "eating by wages." The specific content of the *zaman modan* is extremely diverse and is increasingly influenced by the emerging mass culture of Malaysia.

Table 1 lists the four major *zamans* along with the four most prominent *masas* in order to show the relative chronology among them. As epistemological ages, however, none of these has completely disappeared, so the chronology must not be taken in an absolute linear sense. The table does not represent divisions of historic time so much as it represents two cycles of meaning, one religious and philosophical; the other, political. Malay curers, for example, will at times turn to their pagan counterparts to extend their magical knowledge. This puts them in touch with the *zaman dahulu*. Likewise, classical drama and ritual language reorient people to the *zaman Hindu*. The *zaman Islam*, on the other hand, is so massively present that one need not "return" to it. Yet there are occasions when it requires defense, or reinterpretation in light of changing conditions. For this reason, one finds much talk about the applicability of Islam to modern life. It is argued that Islam must be the final guide to social justice in the modern world. Religious leaders remind that Islam has never been provincial in outlook, nor should it be made an excuse for cultural conservatism. As for the *zaman modan*, its signs are everywhere, from the latest five-year plan to government subsidies for the pilgrimage to Mecca.

## Table 1
Relative chronology of religious eras and political periods.

| Time | Zaman (religious era) | Masa (political period) |
|---|---|---|
| late | Modan (modern era, emerging mass culture) | |
| | ---------------------------------------------------------- | |
| | | Tigabelas Mei (May 13) Merdeka (independence) Masa Jepun (Japanese period) Masa Orang Puteh (European period) |
| | Islam | |
| | Hindu | |
| early | Dahulu (early times) | |

In all cases but the *masa Jepun* the reminders of the presence of the four recent *masas* are equally near at hand. The Malaysian monetary system, its parliamentary government, the continued involvement of European interests in the economy, the style of bureaucratic interaction, the club memberships and residential preferences of the upper classes, the school examination system, and many other things all point to the continued importance of the *masa orang puteh*. But the *masa Jepun* has left fewer traces. It is only recalled, never relived. Yet there is a tendency for Malaysians to view the increasing role of Japanese capital in their economy as a kind of rebirth, in peaceful form, of the *masa Jepun*. The continued presence of *merdeka* and *tigabelas Mei* requires no further comment.

## RELIGIOUS EVOLUTION IN SOUTHEAST ASIA

It should be apparent that Malay views on past religious eras follow the same sequence as is recognized by historians of Southeast Asia. This being the case, I would like to conclude this chapter with a brief reappraisal of religious evolution in Southeast Asia. I realize that this problem is somewhat removed from the ones covered so far, but it is still a problem of the relation between time and knowledge. So far we have been asking how different ways of knowing can be recognized in past social experience; we turn now to the question of how past forms of knowledge can influence later ones. More basically, we ask how the conditions of both society and knowledge at any one time have been a product of preceding conditions.

Each major shift in religious symbolism comes in response to some significant change in social relations. Yet, in tracing the connections between such events, it would be an error to reduce the new meanings in question to nothing more than a rationalization of new experience. Both the process of social change and that of ideological legitimation are more complex than this. And the reason for this complexity is fundamental: long before any new shift in social relations can ever produce a change in ideology, it has, itself, already undergone a partial absorption into a previous and more established system of meanings. The new social form cannot exist as a raw condition; it exists only as something which has been redefined at birth by an existing system of meanings. The result is that new meanings always come in response to old meanings, as well as to new social forms. They come in response to things which the older meanings could not quite contain regarding the new social forms.

Applying these assumptions to major shifts in Southeast Asian cosmologies, such as Hinduization and the spread of Islam, we are directed to view each new orientation in ideology as a kind of commentary on its predecessor. This gives us a fuller awareness of the dialectical nature of the process of legitimation. For example, those who have invoked the concept of legitimation in trying to account for the importation of Hindu cosmology to Southeast Asia have taken a somewhat narrow view of the advantages of Hindu symbolism to the ruling elite. Van Leur, speaking in this vein, tells us that:

> Southern India was the trading region for Indonesia, the shipping to the east went especially from the southern Indian ports. By means of that trade . . . the Indonesian rulers and aristocratic groups came in contact with India, perhaps seeing it with their own eyes. In the same sort of attempt at legitimizing their interests involved in "international trade" (in the first place vis-á-vis Indian traders themselves), and (though this was probably of secondary importance) organizing and domesticating their states and subjects, they called Indian civilization to the east— that is to say, they summoned the Brahman priesthood to their courts. (1955:98)

Again, he argues: "The Indian priesthood was called eastwards—certainly because of its wide renown—for the magical, sacral legitimation of dynastic interests and the domestication of subjects, and probably for the organization of the ruler's territory into a state" (1955:103–104). Wheatley offers a similar reconstruction of the indigenous response to trade with India:

> Those individuals with the most compelling reasons to change the old order of society . . . would have manipulated the new alternatives or inconsistencies thus created in the indigenous scheme of values in an effort to strengthen their own prestige and ultimately to achieve some degree of freedom from the restrictive bonds of tribal custom. For these chiefs too, as for chieftains dealing with seasonal

traders, wherever customary sanctions inhibited the extension of authority to validate the power required for supra-village rule, the concept of the god-king would
have proved especially attractive. The assumption of divinity, by translating the
ultimate source of authority from—in Weber's terminology—consensus to
charisma, freed such chieftains from the traditional restraints of tribal custom and
simultaneously afforded a basis for stratifying the tribe, henceforth to be divided
into rulers and subjects. (1975:242)

Both these authorities are correct in linking Hinduization to the formation of the
state in Southeast Asia, yet one suspects that they have made the attractions of
Hindu ideology almost too transparently the interests of aspiring chieftains and
rulers. Thus, although van Leur recognizes that the Brahman religion had the
broader function of allowing for "the organization of the ruler's territory into a
state," his main emphasis is on the "legitimation of dynastic interests." And
though Wheatley, for his part, draws attention to "inconsistencies . . . created in
the indigenous scheme of values," he does not show how the concept of the
god-king helps to make sense of these inconsistencies. He merely argues that this
idea helps tribal chiefs "to strengthen their own prestige" and so allows them to
manipulate the situation to the point of creating a new society. In this scenario,
we might say that the magic attributed to the king is given the power to create the
kingdom, an admittedly Weberian point of view.

A somewhat different interpretation is possible if we stop to compare
Hindu cosmology with its tribal predecessors. Without mentioning details, it is
characteristic of indigenous Southeast Asian cosmologies to express a felt tension
between culture and nature. For the Semang foragers of Malaysia this tension is
represented vertically in the conflicts between human beings and the sky being
Karei, or Thunder, who uses violent storms to punish people for mocking animals and for other offenses against the normal order of life (cf., Needham, 1964;
and the contributions to this volume of Benjamin and Endicott). For the many
swidden farming peoples of the region, this same tension is expressed in the
opposition between village and forest. In either case, shamans, who can be in
touch with powers beyond the morally secure but physically and spiritually weak
human realm, are required to balance out this tension, thus legitimizing human
encroachments on nature. All this is much the opposite of the Hindu cosmos
which allows human beings to exert ritual control over the universe at its sacred
center, which itself is located in the middle of a kingdom. Judging from this
difference, one suspects that among the attractions of Hindu ideology was its
presenting the idea of a centered realm, not just its bestowing magnificence upon
the ruler.

In offering this alternative view, I am not trying to minimize the role of
Hindu symbolism in legitimizing dynastic rule, rather I am trying to bring out its
value in compensating for the absence of any definite ideas about the relationship
of ruler and realm in indigenous cosmologies. In other words, the acceptance of
Hindu cosmology had as much to do with presenting the idea of *a kingdom* as it
did with justifying the king. It is likely that chiefs and leaders of various types

had been present for some time in Southeast Asia, but kingdoms able to impose their rule on peoples of diverse origin, what Wheatley calls "supravillage rule," were new. In this light, it is not surprising that the Southeast Asian importers of Hindu ideology, stressed its special version of the microcosm-macrocosm idea. The state not only became the universe, but its capital city became the center of the universe (Heine-Geldern, 1942). By implication, all that lay around this sacred center could be subordinated to it, a situation not known prior to the early states, yet something which was becoming more and more a part of everyone's experience. No doubt, indigenous cosmologies had also placed one's own tribal village at the center of the universe, but as I have tried to indicate, they did so in a rather different way. The mystically charged points in the tribal universe tended to lie *outside* the village deep in the forest, or in the upper-world or the under-world. Shamans were required to bring the sacred power of such outer zones back into the village. But the Hindu cosmos, with its central shrines and monuments, was just the opposite of this. It had its sacred center *in the middle* of a kingdom, and it required the priests of a royal cult to activate the radiating influence of this mystic point. Moreover, the full development of this idea as expressed in the plans of the classic Southeast Asian shrines and cities seems to go well beyond the Indian originals. I doubt that this exaggeration was merely for the glorification of rulers, it also provided what previous ideology had no reason to provide, namely, a meaning to go with the subjugation of conquered peoples to a central authority. The idiom of spatial symbolism, which seems always to have had great importance in Southeast Asian cultures, was now used in a new way and to a new purpose, the legitimation of supravillage rule.

This analysis may also help us to understand the extent to which Hindu ideas received popular acceptance throughout the region. Many writers still treat the Brahman religion as having been primarily a court religion, but as Wheatley (1975:246) has recently emphasized,

> the transformation was not confined to the differentiation of bureaucratic roles and modes. In Indian civilization the spiritual and the temporal were so closely inter-woven that the adoption of specific political and social institutions was impossible without some measure of adherence to Indian religious norms. [He continues,] Surely the peasants called to labor on national temples or the shrines of the aristocratic families could not have returned home totally ignorant of Indian iconography. And there is no doubt that . . . they often adopted the gods of that tradition in modified form into the pantheon of the village (1975:249).

We might add to this that although not everyone participated in building monuments or conducting state ritual, anyone could invoke the names and titles of the Sanskrit deities and heroes when calling in secret upon the powers of the spirit world. In these and in other ways, the *zaman Hindu* took hold on the popular mind as well as among the elite.

The next major shift in the religious cosmologies of this region came in the thirteenth and fourteenth centuries with the decline of the great Hindu and Mahayana Buddhist states. The Mongol invasions of the late thirteenth century had been an important factor in creating certain political changes at this time. But Coedes, who marks this period as the significant turning point for the Hinduized states, points to some deeper reasons for the change.

> The underlying causes of the decline of Indian culture lay in the ever increasing number of indigenous peoples who adapted it and in doing so adopted it to their own cultural traditions, and also in the gradual disappearance of a cultured aristocratic class, the members of which had been the guardians of the Sanskrit cultural tradition. Hinduism and Mahayana Buddhism, as practiced in the form of the worship of kings and other individual persons, were religions with little appeal for the masses; and this explains why the masses so quickly and so readily adopted Sinhalese Buddhism. (1967:133)

The main point here seems to be that with the assimilation of Sanskrit culture, religious ideas began to be selected for their vernacular appeal. Sinhalese Buddhism had this appeal because it could reach the laity in a closer way than did the royal cult. The same can be said for Islam which was also gaining acceptance at this time. Both were more egalitarian in outlook than Hinduism, based as they were on universally conceived notions of morality and justice. All people regardless of their standing in society were in need of salvation, everyone could respond by performing acts of merit, and if diligent enough, any peasant from even the most humble village could one day achieve the pilgrimage to Mecca.

Yet the popular appeal of these universalist doctrines does not fully account for the loss in plausibility of the divine-king cult. After all, there were still rulers and subjects. Why was the old means of legitimation less suitable now? Why were the rulers themselves converting?

Here, of course, many political and economic factors were involved. On the mainland rival political factions had often favored different religious schools, and Sinhalese Buddhism had now become the most stimulating source of new ideas. In the Indonesian islands, Islam offered the added advantage of promoting better trade opportunities with the rest of the Muslim world to the west. But despite these advantages of the new creeds, the loss of plausibility of Hindu ideology had a different source. In my view, the crisis for the Hindu states occurred because too many rulers and too many competing realms were appearing to allow the idea of ''one kingdom, one universe'' to seem realistic. Coedes' summary of the situation on the mainland presents just such a picture.

> If we now cast a backward glance over the events of the thirteenth century and attempt to assess their consequences for the Indochinese peninsula, we see that they brought about a decline of the Indianized kingdoms and at the same time the growth, at their expense, of a number of petty principalities and one or two kingdoms all ruled over by the T'ais. (1967:131)

Obviously, a historical situation of proliferating and competing states is very different from a period of the first formation of states within a region. The ideologies which could legitimize power in one situation may not work equally well in the other. This was the case with the shift from Hinduism to Theravada Buddhism and Islam. The idea of a centered universe, which had at first been exaggerated within Hindu cosmology in order to compensate for the lack of any indigenous theory of a controlling center of political power, now seemed out of place. With kingdoms of approximately equal might on all sides, the claim of any particular kingdom to being the absolute center of the universe was greatly weakened. If the authority of religious truth were again to be used in legitimizing rule, it would have to find a new form. That new form, borrowed from Ceylon and the Near East, emerged as a kind of ''church-state'' structure in which the official religious institutions stood separate from the state as such. Though church and state were usually in support of each other, the ruler no longer claimed divinity. Instead, his dignity was to be enhanced by shows of piety. He would be a patron of the religious institution, but not a god.

Although court ritual tended to remain elaborate, it no longer had a monopoly on sanctity. The separation which had been made was a major step in the secularization of politics. But as the king moved away from the center of religious life, organized religion moved out into the villages of the realm. The village *wat* in Buddhist areas and the mosque and prayer house among the Muslim converts brought the peasant population into almost daily contact with some expression of the official religion. In this sense, the disenchantment of the capital had become the enchantment of the village.

The shift of the center of gravity of the sacred cosmos from king and court to church-like institutions appears in the need for all Muslims to acknowledge Mecca as the earthly center of their religion, and for most Buddhists to accept Ceylon as their major center of religious learning. Any local pretense to being the sacred center of a symbolic universe was thereby diminished, though not entirely precluded, by one's secondary place in religious geography. This was almost a declaration that the new religions would not legitimize rule by the same symbolism as had the old one.

If we were to diagram the basic cosmology of the early Hinduized states, and then to compare this model with another one representing the situation under Islam and Theravada Buddhism, the contrasts would be somewhat as follows: The first model would have a large pyramid or point in its center, around which would lie several rings of smaller and smaller pyramids or points; the whole configuration would be oriented to the cardinal directions. The second model would have an array of cones standing about in an irregular pattern, with no one cone being central and with none greatly superior in height to any other. Crosscutting all the cones would be a single plane. The cones would represent the many competing states which arose as political power became decentralized throughout Southeast Asia. The plane would stand for the independent religious institution, or church, and its universalist moral ideology. The ruler who occupies the center of the first model can rightfully claim to be a deity upon whom all else depends. But the rulers occupying the tops of the cones in the second model, which has no center, can hardly make this same claim. They can only declare their piety with respect to the universal values of the official religion. Meanwhile, in the secular competition for political power, they may be using every means at their disposal to prevail against one another and against internal rivals.

In his work on the sociology of religion, Peter Berger (1967:10–11) has argued that for every active system of beliefs there must be a supporting social "plausibility structure." The contrasts I have just pointed out show that by the fourteenth century, the central ideas of Hindu cosmology had lost their plausibility structure in the kingdoms of western Southeast Asia. This loss had little to do with whether people still *wanted* or finally *did not want* to believe in divine kings, it had simply become a fact that *it was no longer plausible to do so*. The god-king concept was an idea that could remain artistically true but not socially true in any direct sense.

Indeed, we might reflect for a moment on the meaning of this shift for Balinese culture, since Bali, which held onto the Hindu cosmology, would seem to be the exception to my analysis. Yet it is the exception which proves the rule, for in maintaining Hindu culture the Balinese transformed society into art (Geertz, 1966; 1975). They perpetuated the Hindu cosmos at a level where it could not lose its truth, in drama, dance, and personal identity. In the absence of Islam and Theravada Buddhism, the Balinese thoroughly vernacularized Hindu ritual. In doing this they made the microcosm-macrocosm model portable. It is said that Hindu temples cover the Balinese landscape even more thickly than do the *wats* and the mosques in other parts of Southeast Asia. None of these is treated as the absolute center of the universe; everything has been relativized to fit with the infinite permutation of ritual contexts. Each minor center is approached in its turn, and any social grouping may found or appropriate such a center; no literal kingdom being required (Boon, 1977:98). Ritual and artistic context, including such things as temple anniversary dates, determine which particular portable universe is most relevant at any given time. It appears that the general Southeast Asian concern for spatial idioms and contextual meanings has allowed the Balinese to vernacularize this nonchurch religion and cause it to fill the same sort of vacuum as that which was filled by Islam and Theravada Buddhism in the other areas. The product, of course, is unique, but the process was similar. My point is that this distinctive outcome should not be attributed to some special quality of the Balinese psyche or cultural ethos. Once the idea of "one kingdom, one universe" began to lose its plausibility, some adjustment had to be made. In most areas this meant turning to the world-rejecting and universalist religions, in Bali it meant replacing the idea of "one kingdom, one universe" with that of "many dramas, many universes." Hindu ritual could now be used to commemorate the importance of any level of social grouping, and kingdoms were relativized to the point of being no different from ancestral groupings, irrigation cooperatives, or any other group.

# CONCLUSION

To summarize the results of this inquiry into problems concerning time, knowledge, and society, three points may be made. First, there is a degree to which both stories and histories are each other's best metaphors. Mythic tales, which offer alternative ways of knowing about things present in everyday reality, must be placed in a "mythic age"; whereas periods of past social history must be treated as different ways of knowing, different ways of knowing what can be possible in human social experience. In either case, we are confronted with the phenomenon of epistemological ages. Perhaps, in calling both mythic ages and named historic periods *epistemological* ages, I have offered no more than an understatement. Nevertheless, it has been useful to explore the qualities of these ages. For in doing so, we have been reminded that whether through narrative or through social reenactment, epistemological ages always remain available in the present. They remain enclaves of meaning within the ensemble of multiple realities which makes up social reality as a whole.

Next, I have presented ethnographic evidence on the informal classification of epistemological ages in use among the Malays of Kuala Lumpur from 1970 to 1972. In the context of biography four *masa* periods were recognized; in the contexts of folk religion and Malay culture history four *zaman* periods were named. The *masas* reflected recent political changes; the *zamans* represented a sequence of changing religious and philosophic views. This classification shows that, even within the space of a lifetime, a certain degree of coherence and a sense of permanence must be attributed to the constituted order of society before a given period of history can be recognized as an epistemological age. Times of transition from one such ordered state to another are more or less spliced into the chronology of epistemological ages as each new age is allowed to grow up alongside its predecessor. In the case of the *masa,* which is the minimal epistemological age, pivotal events, such as open racial conflict or national independence, may serve as the metonym for an age, but for the *zaman,* which is already a system of knowledge and therefore transcends political events, temporal concepts, such as "ancient" or "modern" and the names of established religions, are used to name the era. The entire system has two levels, or cycles, one which allows ways of knowing to be lifted out from the course of events, the other which allows events to be placed in the larger framework of world view.

Finally, I have tried to say something new about the sequence of religious change in Southeast Asia. Here we have looked at the interactions between systems of knowledge which have taken form at different times and under differing social conditions, yet which have been linked over the long course of history. In a brief sketch of the process of Hinduization and of the later shift to Islam and Theravada Buddhism, I have shown that the unique features of any given set of symbols used for the legitimation of power can, in part, be traced to the dialogue which obtains between that set of symbols and others which have existed prior to

322

the social condition being legitimized. This dialogue with past forms of knowledge is not only a matter of the survival of previous beliefs, it is a basic commentary on how social change alters the plausibility of previously established meanings. Put crudely, divine kings and cosmic centers become important when there have been no previous kings, whereas pious kings and separate ecclesiastic orders become important once there have already been so many kings that it is assumed that all kings are tyrants.

Basically, I both assume and conclude that the constraints of meaning placed upon the historical process of ideological legitimation are such as preclude the possibility of a direct synchronic justification of some particular social interest. Ideologies are not merely the product of different social classes or status groups duping and being duped by each other's propaganda. They rest more on the efficacy of symbols than on the character flaw of false consciousness. They are the text of society as a whole unconsciously in discourse with itself about the contradictions spreading through its fabric. If the analysis here were to be extended, I am convinced it could account for other changes in Southeast Asian cosmologies besides the two sketched out. More could be said about shifts even among the tribal religions. Also a look at modern mass culture phenomena would show that the contemporary outpouring of short stories and novels is aimed largely at commenting on the gap between contemporary occupational and political life and what are presumed to be traditional and religiously orthodox views of life. The *zaman modan* enters as an attempt to say what is missing in older meanings, while at the same time trying to identify what is right or wrong in new experiences. Modern authors deride the fatalism and narrow moralities of the past and in the same breath condemn the fetishism of rational purpose and the nonmorality that imprison the present. There is an agony in the new ideology which should put any simple notions of rationalization to rest. Alton Becker (this volume) has used the very apt expression ''clashing epistemologies'' in discussing drama and narrative, the problem I have addressed requires the concept of ''clashing social plausibility structures.'' In assessing their confrontations through time I have found it necessary to ask more than the usual Weberian question: ''How does religion function to legitimate modes of power and ways of acting?'' For I believe that one must also ask the Durkheimian question: ''What is it about activities and about the general contours of social life that makes some beliefs plausible and other implausible?''

## ACKNOWLEDGMENTS

I would like to thank Ronald Provencher, Geoffrey Benjamin, Kirk Endicott, Vinson Sutlive, and Alton Becker for their useful suggestions and ideas regarding many of the issues covered in this chapter. Since each of these individuals has contributed a chapter of his own to the present volume, it is certain that my debts in this regard will be all too obvious. I would also like to express my appreciation to Charles Morrison and John Hinnant for reading and commenting on portions of this manuscript. Finally, both apologies and thanks are owed to Aram Yengoyan for enabling the completed version of this essay to be included in the present volume in spite of its late submission to the editors. The analysis presented here is my own and none of the individuals just mentioned should be blamed in the least for the weaknesses to be found within it.

## REFERENCES

Berger, P. L. *The sacred canopy: Elements of a sociological theory of religion.* Garden City: Doubleday & Company, Inc., 1967.

Boon, James. *The anthropological romance of Bali, 1572–1972: Dynamic perspectives in marriage & caste, politics & religion.* Cambridge: Cambridge University Press, 1977.

Coedes, G. *The making of Southeast Asia* (H. M. Wright, trans.). Berkeley: University of California Press, 1967.

Clutterbuck, Richard. *The long war: The emergency in Malaya 1948–1960.* London: Cassell & Company, Ltd., 1966.

Geertz, Clifford. *Person, time, and conduct in Bali: An essay in cultural analysis.* Cultural Report Series No. 14, Southeast Asia Studies, Yale University. Detroit: The Cellar Book Shop, 1966. Reprinted in *The Interpretation of Cultures: Selected Essays by Clifford Geertz.* New York: Basic Books, Inc., 1973.

Geertz, Clifford. On the nature of anthropological understanding. *American Scientist, 63,* 47–53, 1975.

Heine-Geldern, Robert. Conceptions of state and kingship in Southeast Asia. *Far Eastern Quarterly, 2,* 15–30, 1942.

Mills, C. W. *The sociological imagination.* London: Oxford University Press, 1959.

Needham, Rodney. Blood, thunder, and mockery of animals. *Sociologus, New Series, 14,* 136–149, 1964.

O'Ballance, Edgar. *Malaya: The communist insurgent war, 1948–1960.* Hamden, Connecticut: Archon Books, 1966.

Purcell, Victor. *Malaya: Communist or free.* London: Gollancz, 1954.

van Leur, J. C. *Indonesian trade and society: Essays in Asian social and economic history.* The Hague: W. van Hoeve Ltd., 1955.

van Vorys, Karl. *Democracy without consensus: Communalism and political stability in Malaysia.* Princeton: Princeton University Press, 1975.

Wheatley, Paul. Satyanṛta in Suvarṇadvipa from reciprocity to redistribution in ancient Southeast Asia. In *Ancient Civilization and Trade.* Jeremy A. Sabloff and C. C. Lamberg-Karlovsky (Eds.). Albuquerque: University of New Mexico Press, 1975.

# afterword

# Cultural Forms and a Theory of Constraints

Aram A. Yengoyan

University of Michigan

Each essay in this volume revolves around a common general theme: symbolic constructs are not vague conceptualizations with little or no reference to reality, but instead are critical parts of the formation of that everyday reality. As forms of communication, symbols maintain cultural identity by fostering differences while, at the same time, communicating across cultural diversity. As Alton Becker notes in his introductory essay, symbolic constructs are critical metaphors both in confirming and reifying what we know and believe, and also in providing mechanisms for further access to greater knowledge of that world. Conceptual symbols contextualize reality and affirm its meanings; they also serve to facilitate encounter with new realities, new ideas, syntheses of old and new.

We must recognize that the learning process through which symbolic forms are extended to new horizons is not confined to the intellectual process *within* the cultures we study; what anthropologists and linguists call *fieldwork* is equally such a learning process. In this fuller meaning of symbolic process, the field experience must not be limited to the testing of hypotheses, the falsification of theoretical propositions, the sorting of data into etic categories for presentation to scholarly peers. In the name of such a positive scientism, anthropologists have too often brought forth cultural accounts which have no faces and within which people are conceived as "algebraic electronic computers ticking away with no problems to solve" (Leach 1962:133). Real images of living humans sometimes never emerge nor, for that matter, enter into such discourse. Yet field experience is the primary context within which members of a culture unfold and develop their thoughts for a foreigner, be he or she trader, tourist, or anthropologist. In doing so, the members of a culture set forth the basic assumptions critical to what

**325**

they do and what they consider of importance. Thought and its symbols are interdependent, yet the symbol is the primary means to our understanding and our understanding of that very thought. As Ricoeur notes (1967:347), "the symbol gives rise to thought." Assumptions pertaining to the nature of humanity, reality, and thought itself are expressed through symbols, their conceptions of person and self, and through the manipulation of reality in the process of everyday sustenance and survival. In attempting to understand the sociocultural emergence of creative and unique modes of thought, we must recognize culture as an unending learning process.

The authors in this volume have tried to convey this idea of culture as a learning process. In some instances, the learning experience centers around the production of coherence and uniformity. In other cases, it reveals basic contradictions within which oppositions are resolved through a conscious manipulation of symbolic forms. Yet in all examples, be they of Iban, Balinese, Ranau Dusun, or Temiar, individuals conceive of their universe not through vacuous abstractions, but through concrete realities pertinent to life, crises, and change.

In analyzing cultural integration, one can surmise that two relatively distinct types of constraints operate within cultures and, within each culture, according to different forms and emphases. One set of constraints may be termed *organic;* these involve the material limits and confines of environment and economy. The second set of constraints are *logical,* namely, those mental processes, symbolic concepts, and ideological sets which are manifest in aesthetics, ritual, myth, and cosmology. This distinction facilitates description of what Geertz has called *integrative mechanisms,* some of which are logically constructed; others, organically constructed. Within any cultural system these two integrative mechanisms are not isomorphic, and there can be no *a priori* assumption that one mechanism unilineally determines the other (Geertz, 1973: 143–144). The latter point must be continually stressed, since the interaction, determination, and overdetermination of these two sets of constraints are matters of specific cultural determination.

Logical constraints involve actors' expectations and their recognition of consistency, adequacy, and meaningfulness. Organic constraints emerge from material and economic parameters. Thus "beauty," for example, is determined by aesthetic parameters which are culturally specific and thus internalized by individual actors within a culture. Yet as manifest in specific forms of art, beauty is constrained by the technologies and material products utilized in its creation. At some level, artistic creation in the plastic arts confronts certain limiting factors which may condition the association of artistic motifs with one set of material-technical parameters, whereas other forms of artistic creation may be associated with other such constraints. All social and artistic process is conducted within varying organic and logical constraints. The organic base relates a "reality" but individual demands and desires are imperative as "a criterion and selector of reality itself" (Coletti, 1972:30).

The cultural analysis of these constraints must initially recognize their relativism from culture to culture. Not only are the interactional qualities of organic and logical relationships highly variable from culture to culture, but each culture tends to stress different spheres, one of which may provide a pervasive "blanket" over other spheres of cultural life. This dominant sphere may express itself in either the realm of the logic or the organic, but in no case can one assume that any one set of constraints is but a "reflection" of the other. In line with recent Marxist thought, the interaction of ideology and reality is not a simple reflection or mirror image *of* one on the other, but a reflection upon one another (Coletti, 1972; Hirschfeld, 1977).

In Aboriginal Australian culture, myth pervades virtually all aspects of social interaction. From personal conduct to group behavior and the ritualization of society, myth as moral form dominates all aspects of personal and group conduct. The distinction between behavior and its moral basis—a distinction pervasive in the West and, in particular, in American culture—is totally absent in Australian culture. Since all behavior is morally based and thought to emerge from the initial "dreaming," myth is the most critical foundation of Aboriginal life. The centrality of myth becomes all the clearer when one recognizes that myth is commonly verbalized in the imperfect tense and thus is not relegated to the past. All myth is living and takes place in present reality, and the use of the imperfect attests to Aboriginal discussion of myth as if it just occurred. Yet, at the same time that myth provides behavior with its meaning, it constrains and may counteract certain types of thought and activity. For example, individual creativity and individuation are traditionally manifest in songs, which are normally sung in the present tense. Most songs, like those of the Walbiri, tend to break with convention and in many cases deliberately change and invert whole segments of the lexicon, thus promoting individuation and creativity. The creative and constraining aspects of Aboriginal myth represent a dialectic which is resolved either through the complete extension of myth into all spheres of culture, in which the logical thus dominates the organic (the most common pattern), or through the creation of new forms of behavior and thought (the less common pattern).

Although myth is pivotal to an understanding of Aboriginal Australians, religion and cosmology are critical to Balinese life. The dominance of personal titles and social markers, so pervasive in Balinese life, runs throughout the religious stucture of Balinese Hinduism. Hildred and Clifford Geertz (1975) and James Boon (in this volume) have elaborately set forth the structural and symbolic underpinning of religious organization as the dialectical basis of cultural and behavioral forms.

In other areas of Southeast Asia, understanding the dialectics of human activity similarly requires an examination of the structure of interpersonal relationships. Lowland Philippine societies, such as the Tagalog and Ilongo, and Javanese society, in Indonesia, are all characterized by a marked concern with the presentation of self within the social arena. In Tagalog society, the social construction of *pakikisama, hiya,* and *utang na loob* all relate to structural and symbolic expressions of self. *Pakikisama,* as a stated virtue, most literally can be translated as smoothness in interpersonal relations. Individuals, it is thought, should suppress personal convictions so as to maintain a social interaction characterized by solidarity, congeniality, and harmony. The idea of self or person as individual is viewed as secondary to the harmonious maintenance of a social world free of disruptive personal disputes. As a consequence, individuals seldom expose their selves and deepest convictions to others. Shaming *(hiya)* of an individual would thus not usually occur, although on occasion participants may be "hurt" through the loss of self-esteem.

Each of these concepts is central to the perception of social activity and its maintenance through the partial denial of self. The "generation of self" must be understood as part of this context. At the same time, the situation leads to conflicts among individuals who must relate to the social arena and structured series of events [see Lynch and de Guzman (1970) for further elaboration on the conception of self in lowland Philippine society].

The centrality of this question of self and social constraints is specific from culture to culture; thus its expression must be examined in relativistic terms. But this type of relativistic analysis may itself provide the basis for further comparison with the aim of delineating cross-cultural imperatives which require a set of cultural parameters to promote and restrict action. Thus Geertz (1975) has utilized the concept of self or person in three cultural cases with the aim of evaluating how self is constructed as an interplay between the individual, his social milieu, and the cultural symbols which provide the basis for meaningful action. Through comparing the structure of such constraints, we can approach an understanding of the interplay of cultural forms and symbolic structures within which the concept of self is generated.

A dialectric theory of constraints assumes that each culture emphasizes specific cultural spheres which may derive from either organic or logical integrative mechanisms. In this dialectical analysis, we are concerned with the determination of dominance in the sociocultural fabric, as, for example, with the role of myth in Aboriginal Australian cultures. In some cases, one cultural form may override other structures, but in most cases it appears that constraints stem from varied spheres of culture and constrict and curtail the evolution of specific practices. At the same time, the interplay of constraints within the social realm may determine creative cultural responses, specific in form to the culture.

In developing cultural theory beyond the confines of a specific culture, we seek to demarcate the conditions within which particular sociocultural forms may occur. Most anthropological theory deals with the question of rule and behavior, or the interrelationship between pattern and activity. Here the problem is the determination of culture as cosmological structure, and events as the behavioral attributes of a society. The relation of structure to event is again a specifically cultural question; in analyzing their interaction, however, we must approach them as dialectically related. In some societies, such as Bali and Aboriginal Australia, structures or rules, as expressions of cosmologies usually determine or dictate the form of behavior. In Australia, rules which govern ritual activity, marriage arrangements, and interpersonal relationships are expressions of mythological structures which are also the basis of religious life. In such cases behavior is the playing out of rules, and when behavior does not follow established rules, behavior is altered to conform to structural imperatives. Structure, as expression of myth, is paramount; thus changes in behavior are always reworked to support the structure. Structure and rule in this case are not temporary expressions of behavior. Dominance of the rule is established through moral imperatives which provide a "moral canopy" from which rules and conduct emanate.

In many non-Western societies one finds a close fit between morality, cosmological structure, and the rules which govern and generate behavior. Consequently, the domain of structure dominates behavior; behavior change and social fluctuations have a minimal effect on the presence of the rule. Again, Aboriginal Australia is an extreme instance of this, in that rules, reflecting a deeper moral existence, determine the structure of the social arena. Within the cultures discussed in this volume, one notes a close relationship between cosmology and rules of conduct as emergent in action. With the breakdown of cosmological homogeneity and the fracturing of systems of knowledge, the specific interconnection between structure and event takes another course. When moral imperatives and cosmological worlds are modified or collapse, structures commonly become expressions of events. Structure thereby is reduced to being the summation of individual acts and behaviors. This condition not only characterizes most of the industrialized nation-states of the modern world, but also represents a concept of social order common within Western social science.

All societies must regulate the interconnections between structure and event, and the linkages between the two are understandable as a set of constraints linked in dialectical operation. In this context we can understand how certain symbols are amenable to manipulation, whereas other symbolic codes cannot be altered or manipulated in the interest of individual actors. As the various essays in this volume indicate, individual conscious control of symbols in the legitimization of social orders is a situation variable from culture to culture. But in all cultures certain symbols are less amenable to social barter, to manipulation within the arena of social commerce.

In summary, the symbolic structures discussed in these essays are critical elements in the articulation of different forms of meaning. In some cases, symbolic constructs are related directly to organic constraints, but even in these cases the symbolic systems operate to provide meaning for human action. Whatever the origins or determinants of symbols, thought itself emanates from symbol and thus, at some level, thought must resolve the contradiction between organic and logical constraints. Understanding these meaning systems involves a learning process through which a culture communicates itself to an outsider, and outsiders themselves communicate across its borders. Our ability to learn these systems requires an analysis from the "inside out," and it is through this process that we can perceive the actual constraint exercised by these systems upon human beings involved in the rigors of everyday life. In capturing the "inside-out" portrait, we can avoid the overdetermination of human subjects as objects, an unfortunate attitude too frequently characteristic of Western social science.

## ACKNOWLEDGMENTS

I wish to thank Alton Becker, Robert Hefner, Larry Hirschfeld, Michael Lambek, Nancy Lutz, and Paul Rabinow for their patience and understanding in hearing and discussing my thoughts on this subject. Needless to say, they are not responsible for the final outcome.

## REFERENCES

Coletti, Lucio. *From Rousseau to Lenin: Studies in ideology and society.* New York: Monthly Review Press, 1972.

Geertz, Clifford. *The interpretation of cultures.* New York: Basic Books, 1973.

Geertz, Clifford. On the nature of anthropological understanding. *American Scientist,* 1975, *63,* 47–53.

Geertz, Hildred, and Geertz, Clifford. *Kinship in Bali.* Chicago: University of Chicago Press, 1975.

Hirschfeld, L. A. Art in Cunaland: Ideology and cultural adaptation, *Man,* 1977 (new series), 104–123.

Leach, E. On certain unconsidered aspects of double descent systems. *Man,* 1962, *62,* 130–134.

Lynch, Frank, and de Guzman, Alfonso II (Eds.). *Four readings on Philippine values.* IPC Papers Number 2. Quezon City, Philippines: Ateneo de Manila University Press, 1970.

Ricoeur, Paul. *The symbolism of evil.* Boston: Beacon Press, 1967.

# author index

Page numbers in *italics* indicate where complete references are listed.

# subject index